D1524366

NO GUTS, NO GLORY

The Glory Days of International Aircraft Delivery

Robert Moriarty

Also by Robert Moriarty
What Became of the Crow?
Basic Investing in Resource Stocks
Nobody Knows Anything
The Art of Peace
The Money Revelation
Common Sense 2.0
Crap Shoot
Exposed!
Entrapped!

No Guts, No Glory © 2022 by Robert Moriarty. All rights reserved. No part of this book may be used or reproduced in any manner whatsoever without written permission, except in the case of brief quotations embodied in critical articles or reviews.

Typesetting and layout by Jeremy Irwin.

Library of Congress Cataloging-in-Publication Data has been applied for.

ISBN: 979-8-421-71086-8

DEDICATION

For a short period of time a small group of feckless and often fearless pilots took underpowered aircraft over oceans around the world. Many died doing so. Navigation was through dead reckoning, using nothing more than a wet compass, an outdated weather forecast, and a watch. It was called "dead" for a reason.

The best ferry pilot I ever knew was Donn Kerby. He wasn't the greatest pilot but he was all round the best and most talented ferry pilot. He approached the job as a profession. I miss him a lot.

But two of the top pilots I knew and flew with were Paul Briggs, now also gone and missed, and Lisa Kilbourn, later Lisa Briggs. I only flew with a few female ferry pilots but across the board they were better pilots than the males. And a lot more sober.

TABLE OF CONTENTS

APPENDICES

INTRODUCTION

AN AVIATION MILESTONE passed by in the summer of 2018, unseen and unremarked upon by those involved in flying. The airport at Pago Pago in American Samoa stated that it would no longer supply aviation gasoline (avgas).

There is a distance of 2,100 nautical miles between Hilo, Hawaii and American Samoa. With avgas unavailable in Pago Pago, there is no practical way to fly light piston-engine aircraft from the U.S. to the major aircraft importing countries, such as New Zealand and Australia.

That doesn't mean they will no longer buy light airplanes; it means that those airplanes can no longer be flown to their destinations. Instead, Cessna, Piper, and Beechcraft will manufacture them, but then take them apart and ship them in containers. The ferrying of small aircraft to customers in Europe, South America and Africa will continue, but not to Australia or New Zealand.

In 1939, with World War II on the horizon, the U.S. and Canada began work on the establishment of a series of airfields to aid the delivery of aircraft from the U.S. to Europe. There would be a major airstrip in Gander, Newfoundland, another in Goose Bay, Labrador, and one in Frobisher Bay in Nunavut, on Baffin Island. Those jumping-off fields would be only seven hundred miles from a new strip in Greenland, at Bluie West One. From there an aircraft could be flown on to Reykjavik in Iceland and down to Shannon, Ireland or bases in Scotland.

In his 1961 memoir, *Fate is the Hunter*, Ernest K. Gann writes about flying into Bluie West One in weather with low ceilings. You knew you were heading up the correct fjord if you saw the partially sunken ship that lay a few miles short of the airfield. If you didn't see it, you were headed up the wrong fjord and would probably hit a mountain once you were flying over land.

During the ten years or so that I ferried planes I flew into all of the former WW II airfields, some (such as Gander and Shannon) many times. Those fields saw thousands of military aircraft being flown to Europe during the war, hopping in small legs across the Atlantic during even the worst of winter conditions. There were few direct flights from Canada to Ireland during the war because it was considered far too dangerous.

The business of ferrying former military aircraft began during the 1950s. The pilots making such trips were inevitably ex-military, moving the aircraft from sellers to new owners.

One private pilot named Max Conrad really began the whole concept of international delivery flights of small planes. He began flying record-breaking distances for Piper Aircraft in the 1950s, including many record long-distance flights that have never been broken. That sold a lot of aircraft for Piper, and they continued a productive relationship with Max for many years. He logged over 52,000 hours in the air over his career, and completed over five hundred deliveries of small aircraft. The world is laid out in such a way that some places are easy to get to, if you are delivering small aircraft to a new owner.

Until recently the U.S. was the supplier of general aviation aircraft to the world. In 1979 the general aviation industry in the U.S. sold about 19,000 aircraft, including airliners, of course. General aviation constituted about ten percent of all U.S. exports. However, in 1979 Cessna lost a liability lawsuit that cost them over $115 million. Literally overnight, insurance premiums shot higher, and the cost of small planes doubled in short order. In 1980 about 1,800 small planes were built and the light aircraft industry began a long, painful death spiral.

The glory days of the ferry business were from probably 1965 until about 1980, after Cessna lost that lawsuit. There was a bizarre financial incentive that only a few inside the aviation community knew about. The dollar was literally as good as gold from the signing of the Bretton Woods Agreement in 1944 until Nixon took the U.S. off the gold standard on August 15th of 1971, whereupon it began a long decline. But those who bought airplanes from 1965 until about 1980 could pay the full retail price, operate it for ten to fifteen years, and sell it for more than they paid for it. Aircraft weren't an expense; they had become an investment.

The golden years of ferrying small piston-engine aircraft all over the world were from about 1970 to about 1980. There were a number of full-time ferry companies on the east coast, and in Wichita, and in Oakland, California. Because of their success with all the flights made by Max Conrad, Piper led the way into large-scale ferrying all over the world.

Max sold his business to Walt Moody in the late 1960s. Phil Waldman, who I write about in this book, bought it from Walt in about 1974. Piper was moving as much of its production as possible to the better weather of Lakeland, Florida and Vero Beach, Florida from the much less convenient

Lock Haven, Pennsylvania. Phil went on a hiring binge but he wanted only pilots who would relocate to Lakeland, where the new, improved Globe Aero would reside.

With the decline in the dollar, international sales of Cessnas, Pipers, and Beech aircraft soared. All of a sudden there was a demand for every single plane the big three could produce. Cessna and Beech were latecomers to the ferry business but soon realized they had to fly planes to overseas destinations or lose business to the leader, Piper.

Ferry flying of small aircraft was always one of the world's smallest occupations. At its peak in 1978–80, Globe Aero employed about fifty people. Worldwide, there couldn't have been more than about seventy-five full-time ferry pilots. It was the world's least populous occupation, and easily the most deadly. Through missed weather forecasts, aircraft failures, and lots of poor planning and bad judgment, about ten percent of ferry pilots died every year. As I write in 2022, some four decades after my ferrying days, ten percent are still dying each year.

FROM A CONVERSATION repeated many times over the years, in many bars, all over the world. . .

The weather-guessers guessed wrong on the winds for George Martin. It was the dead of winter, with winter winds howling. He ran into an unforecast headwind on the way to Reykjavik, from Gander. Then his wings iced up, slowing him even more. Running on fumes, he was within sight of the shore when his engine faltered and then quit. With no power, he put it in the water safely. Fearing the aircraft would quickly sink, he hopped into a life raft.

That's what killed him.

It was colder outside than a well-digger's butt. His would-be rescuers reached him in their boat within minutes. Too late — he had frozen to death. The airplane was still floating three days later. With the door wide open. With no fuel on board it floated just fine. If he'd stayed in the plane he probably would have made it.

Stupidity on the part of Piper Aircraft management killed Joe Wolfe, the most experienced ferry pilot flying at the time. He took a two-seat Tomahawk trainer to Florida from Lock Haven. Some bean counter had probably saved ten dollars by calling for dual magnetos on a single shaft instead of having two different magnetos. (Magnetos provide the spark for gasoline-powered aircraft engines.) Why the hell would you put two magnetos on a single shaft? The whole purpose of dual mags is redundancy.

The shaft failed. It was a known problem.

Cessna had just released its two-seat version of a basic trainer named the Skipper. Cost was a factor and every dollar might count. But students crash all the time and it's easy to point the finger at a student or an inexperienced instructor. Who's going to miss a few students? I don't know how many people were killed before Joe died, but his accident couldn't be blamed on inexperience. Cessna finally grounded the plane. By then it didn't make any difference to Joe.

Did you ever meet Jeff Tyler? Yeah, nice guy.

He put one down. In Angola, in the midst of a revolution after the Portuguese left. He swears that his boost pump wouldn't shut off, but that's bullshit. If it had been the boost pump he could have shut off his electrical system. With no electricity he wouldn't be able to pick up any radio beacons, but that's better than a red hot stick in the left eyeball or taking a year's vacation in Luanda. He always carried two passports. Funny thing, but the locals in Angola thought he might be a spook working undercover for the CIA. They kept him locked up for twenty-two months. He was, of course.

Tom Willett busted his ass practicing touch-and-go landings in a spray plane. Any idiot knows you don't do touch-and-go landings with your hopper full of fuel. And get away with it. He was an accident waiting to happen for a long time. He had to land in Angola too, a couple of years before.

Some new kid was bringing a bird from the Cessna factory in Wichita to Lakeland, Florida to be tanked prior to its delivery flight. He glazed the cylinders. Small aircraft engines are based around technology from the 1940s. You have to use high power settings to wear in the piston rings to the cylinder walls for the first twenty-five hours or so. If you don't, you build up a thin layer of cooked oil that literally glazes the cylinder walls. You lose engine power and your oil consumption goes through the roof.

He didn't have money for fuel, and brought it from Wichita at about thirty percent power. You know what that does to the engine? He was quite proud of the fact that he hadn't spent a dime for fuel.

But I was talking about Tom Willett. He was burning a quart of oil an hour, and knew it. When he flew a five-hour leg, he used five quarts of oil. A two-hour leg? Two quarts. The engine capacity was twelve quarts. Everything was just fine until that twelve-hour leg. He literally ran the engine dry of oil on his first twelve-hour flight.

He couldn't have picked a worse place to land in Africa than Angola. So they put him in what passes for the Luanda Hilton for the next six months. He acted a little strange when he got back. But then, he acted a little strange before he left. He was one of those guys who pulled a comb out of his pocket and pulled it through his hair every time he saw a mirror. He was a good-looking guy without a lick of sense or judgment.

Bob Iba was pushing sixty and thought he could get away with smuggling drugs. He almost made it. Bob's pushing up daisies in Colombia now.

What was the name of that young Jewish kid that bought the farm over in St. Pete? That's right, Stan Finegold. After cheating death so many times over the ocean, he thought he could forget about basic airmanship. He augered in while taking a bird to St. Pete to get signed off by the Feds. Seems he wrapped it a little tight on final. He crashed doing a turn at an airport. How do you survive flying single-engine airplanes over the ocean but spin in at the ninety-degree mark?

Roger Dowst needed to make a few extra bucks between trips so he was doing some instructing. They landed a little short and a lot hard. It wasn't really the broken back that killed him. He was doing great. Maybe even walk again. But a little blood clot got loose. One minute he was fine. The next he was deader than a doornail. Wasn't really ferrying that got him.

Ferrying got Don Walsh, though. He was on a flight over the coast of Honduras with two other guys. Everybody's flying Tomahawks. They come up on a layer of clouds. The others wanted to go over the clouds. He wanted to go under. They did. He did. They made it. He didn't. The other two guys pressed on. They landed in Colombia and got tossed in the slammer for two or three days. Somebody finally got them out. But for three days nobody even knew Walsh was down.

Raf DeBergiet up in Maryland. He was flying a Mooney. That sucker threw a rod right through the side of the case. He was near an airport but the engine caught fire. Then his ferry fuel tank system went up. Turned him into a crispy critter. Took him two weeks to die. Not a nice way to go at all. It's not fair to blame ferrying. It could've happened to anybody.

Remember Crandall? Yea. He was the guy that used to spend two hours fixing his hair every morning. Wouldn't de-tank an airplane himself because he might mess up his clothes. He had a mid-air with a giraffe down in

Botswana. No shit! I wouldn't kid you. He was on his way to Jo'burg in a 181 and he got bored. Went flat-hatting. Wanted to take a few pictures. Well, he finds this herd of giraffe and goes a tad low. Hits this fucking giraffe right between the running lights. Kills it deader than a doornail.

Crandall wakes up in the airplane. Inverted. Fuel dripping all over him. He's in the middle of the Kalahari Desert, a million miles from anywhere. Spends two days out there before the South African Defence Force comes out and picks him up. The Botswana Army, or whatever the hell passes for the army there, goes out to pick up the remains of the plane. They also find giraffe parts. Seems it's bad form to have mid-airs with giraffes in Botswana. There's still a warrant out for his arrest, for hunting without a license and illegal photography. Can you believe it?

I can't remember the name of that guy on the west coast who went down in the Beech 18. The door came open on him a couple of times on the way to the west coast. How was he to know that it would happen to him on the way to Honolulu? He did a really great job of keeping it airborne for so long. Until the engines burned up. Usually you can survive ditching in the Pacific. Unless you never manage to get out of the airplane. He didn't. He's feeding the fishes now.

But how about Goldstern? He had an honest-to-God engine failure. Right in the middle of the Atlantic. In the fucking wintertime. Damned airplane just said, "Screw you, buddy, my number one engine is out of oil and I ain't flying no more." And he only had one engine with him. Didn't bring a spare. Of course it sank immediately. But he got out of it with that silly survival suit he always carried. And had an emergency locator transmitter with him. That's all. Can't tell you how many times I laughed at the idea of him carrying that suit with him everywhere he went. Before the accident, of course.

A Russian ship picked him up. But they had just come on station and he had to stay on that stupid communications ship for three months until they went back in. The harbormaster in Genoa wanted ten grand just to take him off the ship and land him on the docks. The Russians weren't allowed to land. He told the harbormaster he'd send a check as soon as he got back. I'll bet that stupid bastard is still waiting for his money. But it serves him right; he really tried to put the screws to Goldstern.

It was funny as hell when he went to the U.S. embassy. They wouldn't believe he was a U.S. citizen because of his New Zealand accent. Picture this.

He goes in. Still carrying his suit, and his ELT. Tells these goofballs that he's been on this damn Russian ship for the last three months, after his plane goes down mid-ocean. He didn't have any identification or anything. That was really great, because when he went to the New Zealand embassy, they didn't believe him either. Because of his American accent. I think the Swiss finally helped him get back to the States. At least he made it. I think he's peddling those stupid suits now. I hope he sells a bunch. I bought one, just in case.

Miss, can we have another round of drinks? My glass seems to have a hole in it.

THE WORLD'S FIRST FERRY FLIGHT lifted off from Roosevelt Field on Long Island at 7:52 am on May 20, 1927. Flying with equipment little more sophisticated than that of the ancient Phoenicians, the lone pilot reached Le Bourget airport, on the edge of Paris, 33½ hours later. The wind forecast wasn't reliable. He ran into unforecast weather and icing. Often he was mere feet above the ocean. Undaunted, he pressed on, cold, tired, and hungry. He landed safely at 10:21 pm local time on May 21. Others had been killed attempting similar flights. That pilot, Charles A. Lindbergh, was hailed as a hero by millions of people the world over.

For completing the first non-stop Atlantic crossing, Lindbergh captured the Orteig Prize of $25,000. The U.S. government, in its published inflation figures, admits that to be equivalent to about $500,000 in 2022. Ferry pilots were better paid then, and the glory greater. Not much else has changed. It remains just as dangerous and unforgiving of even tiny errors of judgment.

Airliners cross oceans today as if they didn't exist. Carrying at least two pilots and a flight engineer, they rely on multiple navigation systems capable of navigational accuracy to within a few feet. If any one of the systems is inoperative, no problem: replace it, or don't go. If the flight distance is such that flight duty time will exceed allowable limits, no problem — bring along a spare crew. Lest the crew be brought down with incapacitating stomach problems caused by bad food, the captain and co-pilot will not eat the same type of meal.

You can now find a GPS device capable of navigation within meters in a box of Cheerios. The manufacturers do that because it displaces the more expensive cereal. Everyone has GPS now.

Flying far below the airliners, a few pilots are still navigating with a compass and a watch. No spare crew. No limit on duty time, no lovely stewardess to bring steaming meals. Rotten pay, but some great flying.

At any given time, somewhere in the world, day or night, holiday or weekend, a ferry pilot is landing or taking off, or listening to the rumbling and belching of his engine, wishing time would pass faster. A delivery flight may take a new aircraft fresh from the factory to a dealer, for ultimate delivery to an eager purchaser. Or a tired, worn, used aircraft is being ferried from seller to buyer. It may be flown from Wichita to Sydney, or Brussels to Johannesburg, or Vero Beach to Kassel, or from anywhere there is an aircraft for sale to anywhere a purchaser is located.

For the most part, the aircraft being ferried when I flew were small general aviation aircraft, ranging in size from a Piper Tomahawk to a Cessna 421. Light jets and larger aircraft were generally ferried by the owners' flight crews. During the glory years of the business, the number of single-engine aircraft delivered was about equal to the number of twins.

An aircraft may have been destined for a missionary group in Angola, or a training school in Nigeria. Perhaps it would carry passengers from Dar es Salaam to Diego-Suarez, or move cocaine from isolated jungle strips in Bolivia to a distributor on the coast of Colombia. The new owner might be a rancher in Australia or a crop duster in the Sudan. The ferry pilot didn't care where it was going or what it would be used for upon delivery. He (and I use "he" deliberately) was paid to deliver the big object from one place to another.

This pilot had no regular schedule. Holidays and weekends were foreign concepts. His contract might call for him to fly any type of aircraft, anywhere, anytime. Which route to fly, or how much fuel to carry or when to go, was up to him. Indeed, the decision of whether to go or not to go was also his and his alone. The pilot was paid for delivering the aircraft. How he delivered it was his problem.

Ferry flying was perhaps the world's most honest business — the pilot paid for all his mistakes. One mistake at the wrong time, and he ended up in the drink. The skies have been described as being even more unforgiving than the sea. Add the double threat of flying a light aircraft over the sea, and danger became your constant companion. Most accidents were caused by pilot error. Aviation is terribly unforgiving of carelessness, incapacity, or neglect, and ferry flying even more so.

Considering the skill requirements and danger involved, the pay was terrible. It bordered on slave labor. But the flying was immensely satisfying — like being the piano player in a whorehouse.

PREFLIGHT

THE TOWER TRANSMITS TO ME, "Cessna two-zero-zero-one-zero is cleared for the option."

I respond, "Roger, Danbury tower. Cessna two-zero-zero-one-zero is cleared for the option."

I wonder what the hell "the option" is. I haven't been in the air in the five years since I left the Marine Corps. We didn't have many options back in Vietnam.

I'm working for a flight instructor's rating so that I can get back into flying. My instructor has put me through a meat grinder for the last hour and a half. My shirt is stuck to my back from the heat. All I want is to get back on the ground at Danbury airport and have a cigarette and a nice cold Pepsi. We've played student pilot and instructor long enough for me. If all students are as dumb as my instructor is pretending to be, perhaps I should consider another occupation. The only problem is that I'm too lazy to work and too nervous to steal.

I bank the aircraft onto final and pull the power back. Carburetor heat is on. Fuel pump on. Flaps down. Gear down and welded. We're ready to land.

Just as we are about to land, my instructor says: "OK, now I want you to execute the option."

Back to that damned option again. I haven't a clue as to what he's talking about, so I land. Not a bad landing, if I do say so myself, but then I've always made nice landings. We turn off the runway. I call ground control and request an inbound taxi to Danbury Air Service. As part of the post-flight checklist I turn off the fuel pump, raise the flaps, and push in the carb heat. We turn into the fuel pit.

I can see steam coming out of my instructor's ears. "Didn't you hear me tell you to execute the option when we were on short final?" he snaps.

"Sure," I reply. "I'm not deaf. Which option did you want me to execute? I'm against nuking because it's so messy. Besides, it'll make us look bad in the eyes of the rest of the world. I don't think an invasion will work. We just don't have the troops. After all, we had over five hundred thousand troops in the country in 1968 and '69. All we did was piss the gooners off. I think Tricky Dick did the right thing in declaring victory and bringing them home. If the North Vietnamese want the place that bad, let them have it."

After six years in the Marine Corps and nearly two years in Vietnam, I still tend to think in military terms.

"You dummy! 'Executing the option' means I wanted you to execute a missed approach. You sat there, fat, dumb and happy, and landed. When I request the option from the tower it means I want the option of either landing or executing a missed approach. There might have been another aircraft on the runway."

There was no other airplane on the runway, but that didn't bother my instructor. After all, we were playing a game of Let's Pretend. Do adults really do these dumb things?

This is part of earning my spurs. It's necessary for every fledgling flight instructor to go through the same chickenshit so they can be as mediocre as all the other flight instructors. After all, if you don't play these games with your students they might get to enjoy flying. God forbid. Every flight instructor I ever met thought the only purpose of flight instruction was to make the students dislike flying. If your student has over two thousand hours in twenty different military aircraft, treat him like a student with twenty hours in a Cessna 150.

"If you wanted me to wave off, why didn't you tell me to wave off or take it around? Some day you might get a student who doesn't know what you mean when you say, 'Execute the option.'"

Like me.

I was tired, even before all this. Now I'm tired, bored, and slightly miffed. In the military I'd gotten used to more precise terminology. We've spent weeks boring holes in the sky. I'm not much closer now to understanding how to instruct the civilian way than I was when I started. It gets worse when I have another instructor. It seems that every instructor has his own theory as to what student pilots should be taught. Thank God the VA is picking up ninety percent of the tab for this. I can't imagine paying good money for what I'm getting.

As I crawl out of the Cessna 172, I see a Cherokee Six taxi up to one of the other pits. The pilot climbs over what looks like a giant silver metal box in the passenger's seat. I ask my instructor about it.

"That's not a box, that's a ferry tank. That's Dave Talleur; he's a ferry pilot. If you look in the back of the airplane you will see a couple of fifty-five-gallon drums for more fuel."

"What does a ferry pilot do?"

"He's probably taking that plane to Europe or Africa. He's delivering it to a distributor."

"Can he get there from here?"

"I'm sure he hopes so. He lives here in Danbury and ferries airplanes for some outfit in Lock Haven. When he has an airplane going eastbound he stops here until the winds and weather are right. If you're interested in meeting him, I'll introduce you."

No empieces, Moriarty. Don't start. I know now that if I had just kept my mouth shut, I would never have gotten locked up in the Sudan. Perhaps would not have had my license shredded into a million bits by the FAA for the Eiffel Tower flight. I might have stayed married. But then, I wouldn't have had the chance to fly under the Eiffel Tower. Or break Lindbergh's speed record from New York to Paris, or fly in the first air race from Paris to New York and back. I wouldn't have fallen in heat in Sydney or Paris or Honolulu or Pago Pago. No guts, no glory.

I was using the GI bill to pay for an instructor's permit. I had finished college the year before, in 1973, just in time to get laid off from my job as a systems programmer in computing in the recession of 1974. But I'd had enough of sitting in an office and writing assembler language code for IBM 360s. This working for a living wasn't nearly as much fun as it was cracked up to be. I'd far rather be in the air, flying an aircraft somewhere interesting. Even somewhere boring would be better than being stuck in an office.

"Dave, this is Bob Moriarty. He's interested in what you're doing ferrying this airplane."

That conversation would seal my fate. For the next ten years I flew airplanes to all reaches of the world. The fame was fleeting, the glory little. But it was fun. And it gave me something to put in this book.

"Nice meeting you, Dave. What's this ferrying all about?"

"This is a new Piper PA-32 just out of the factory. I'm taking it to the distributor in Kassel, Germany. The winds across the North Atlantic are pretty good right now. About a thirty-knot push. So I'll leave tomorrow morning. I'll spend tomorrow night in Gander, Newfoundland, and cross the next night. I don't have the range to make it to Germany so I'll stop in Shannon, in Ireland, spend the night and deliver the next day. If I can get into Kassel early enough, I'll de-tank the airplane, get the train to Frankfurt and try to get back the same day. I live here in Danbury, so I'll come back here and wait for another trip. I work for a ferry company called Globe Aero. It has a lot of birds for delivery right now so I'll be out on another trip right away. Since I live here I try to stay away from the Pacific trips but we've a lot of birds going westbound, too."

"How much do you make for a trip like this?" I ask.

"A single-engine aircraft to Europe pays about $750, a twin about $500 to $600. If you take a single to South Africa you can make $1,500, or $1,000 for a twin. Some of the guys won't fly anything except twins, but I'll fly anything that comes up. You make less money if you fly like a white man, but I figure it's worthwhile spending the night in a decent hotel and having white man's meals. If I figure I need some extra bucks, I'll just fly an extra trip or two."

I'm hooked. The idea of flying to places like that and getting paid for it makes me drool. After all, people pay good money to go to those places. Travel the world and get paid for it!

"How many trips can you make in a month?"

Dave tells me that he's been flying hard for the last two months. He's made eight trips. He could have done more but didn't want to go westbound. I do some mental arithmetic. He makes between $2,000 and $5,000 a month. Beats the hell out of a red hot poker in the left eyeball.

I ask Dave what the qualifications are to become a ferry pilot. He tells me that there really aren't any. His boss is named Phil Waldman and he owns Globe Aero in Lock Haven, Pennsylvania. Phil wants pilots to have a commercial license with multi-engine and instrument ratings. He prefers two thousand hours of flying time, but it depends on the quality of that flight time. I've got 2,200 hours of military time in almost every type of airplane. I should have a good shot at a job.

In the meantime, Danbury Air Service wanted me to pick up a new Cessna 172 in Wichita. I grabbed my wife, Kathie, and headed for Kansas. We signed for the 172 and pointed it east. I called Phil Waldman and told him I was interested in a job as a ferry pilot if he had any openings. He asked me how much time I had, and in what airplanes. He expressed quite an interest in my F-4 time as he wanted to get into ferrying military aircraft. I didn't tell him that he hadn't a chance in hell of the military handing over a $5 million F-4 to a civilian for ferrying anywhere. Better to let him find that out.

We stopped in Lock Haven to talk to Phil and his wife Donna. Phil went over my logbooks. He liked the fact that I'd flown so many different types of aircraft. I had heavy jet fighter time but also piston single, piston twin, and tail dragger time.

Then he asked me, "How much of this was pencil time?"

For about five seconds I pondered making him eat my logbooks. Phil had quite a way with words. I didn't know then that it usually took him between three and five minutes to insult anyone he met. For example, a year or so later, upon meeting a Kentucky Fried Chicken sales manager who lived across the street from us in Lakeland, Phil asked him what he did for "Kentucky Fried Rat."

My logbooks meant a lot to me. Every minute in them was a minute earned. I told him, through gritted teeth, "All my time is legitimate." Not for a second did he suspect I was pissed. No one had ever before asked me if I falsified my logbooks. What I didn't realize at the time was that in civil flying, pencils get used a lot. It's far cheaper than actually paying for flight time.

But I soon learned to ignore what Phil said. He was just one of those guys who manage to insult everyone. He didn't mean any harm.

Phil had flown for Globe Aero for five years when Walt Moody owned it. He had bought Walt out some six months before our meeting. He wanted to move Globe to Lakeland, Florida, and expand the business. Not all the pilots wanted to relocate, so he needed some new pilots.

Phil told me that he started pilots by having them go to the factories to pick up new aircraft and bring them to Lock Haven, at which point the ferry tanks were installed. This gave him a chance to evaluate a new guy before releasing him with an airplane over an ocean. The established ferry pilots then picked up the planes in Lock Haven and took them to their destination.

I couldn't see what Phil might learn about a pilot by having him collect an aircraft from a factory and deliver it to Lock Haven. It seemed to me that the only outcomes were either to make it or not to make it. Without being in the cockpit or flying alongside, you can't learn much about a pilot from a flight he made from Vero Beach (home of Piper Aircraft) or from Wichita (the Cessna factory) to Lock Haven. Perhaps this was just a cheap way to get airplanes to Lock Haven. I shouldn't have thought such thoughts so early in my career, but later I did find out that that's all it was: cheap labor.

Pilots have always been prostitutes but ferry pilots were the worst.

Phil told me that after I had made a few deliveries from factories to Lock Haven, he would try to put together two similar aircraft headed over the Pacific and send me on my first real ferry trip. I'm hired. I'm pleased.

Kathie and I talked about ferry flying on our way back to Connecticut. She knew how much I hated my work as a computer systems programmer.

She had no objections to my getting back to flying, my first love. Not then. She encouraged me to give ferry flying a try. If I didn't like it or it didn't work out, I could always go back to computers, after all. Or working for a living.

We owned a condominium in Stamford but could sell it at a profit. From what Phil told us, the cost of living in Florida was much lower than in Pennsylvania. Surely it must be cheaper than Stamford.

Fifteen domestic trips to pick up aircraft from the factory and four months later, Phil had a couple of birds headed westbound. No one ever made any money from bringing new airplanes from the factory to Globe Aero. Phil was just getting cheap pilots.

I started a new phase in my life. Little did I suspect where ferry flying would take me.

FIRST TRIP: LOCK HAVEN, PA to SINGAPORE

1976	from	to	nautical miles	knots	time (hours)			
					flight	day	night	inst.
Jan 28	Lock Haven	Bowling Green	489	92	5.3	4.0	1.3	
	Bowling Green	Memphis	207	74	2.8	2.8		
Jan 29	Memphis	Oakland	1,527	108	14.2	10.7	3.5	1.5
Feb 1	Oakland	San Francisco	17	9	0.5	0.5		
	San Francisco	Oakland	18	9	0.5	0.5		
Feb 2	Oakland	Honolulu	2,091	124	16.8	3.3	13.5	3.0
Feb 10	Honolulu	Wake Island	2,003	126	15.9	3.9	12.0	2.5
Feb 11	Wake Island	Saipan	1,210	133	9.1	9.1		2.5
Feb 12	Saipan	Manila *						
	Manila *	Guam	118	26	4.5	4.5		2.8
Feb 15	Guam	Singapore	2,539	141	18.0	7.5	10.5	1.5
TOTALS		18 days	10,218	117	87.6	46.8	40.8	13.8

* no landing

IN MID-JANUARY OF 1976 Phil Waldman called to ask, "Are you ready for an over-water ferry trip?"

Ready? After four months of domestic trips I was champing at the bit.

Phil's policy was for a new ferry pilot to make his first trip over the Pacific, and to make his first three or four trips escorted by an experienced ferry pilot in another aircraft of similar speed.

The winds aloft from San Francisco to Honolulu are normally strong westerlies from the first of December into February. At that time Globe Aero had an unofficial policy not to fly into more than a ten-knot headwind between the west coast and Hawaii. The headwinds had ranged from fifteen to twenty knots (overall wind component) for weeks. Finally it appeared that they were decreasing sufficiently to permit a crossing.

Phil had three Pipers to deliver: a Seneca and a Cherokee Six destined for Singapore, and an Arrow bound for Manila. Donn Kerby would be my escort pilot, flying the Cherokee Six. I would fly with him in formation in the Arrow. A third Globe Aero pilot, Paul Briggs, would fly the Seneca.

Donn's Cherokee Six had a cruising speed of 125 knots. My Arrow could cruise at 130, but by throttling back a little it would be easy for me to stay with him. In formation flying, the faster aircraft or the aircraft with more potential power should be wingman.

Paul could do 140 knots in the Seneca. There was no particular reason for him to fly in formation with us, and it would be more work for everyone. Paul would take off thirty minutes after us and land thirty minutes before us.

When flying the Pacific we typically took off with the aircraft at 130 percent of gross weight, with dispensation from the FAA, of course. We flew under a special ferry permit. Depending on the aircraft, we could usually gross 20–30 percent over normal maximum gross weight. The FAA never granted dispensation for the out of center of gravity (CG) limits imposed by the aircraft manufacturer, though it was not uncommon for us to fly slightly out of CG.

It seems strange to most people that the distance from the Bay area to Hawaii is less than the distance from Los Angeles to Hawaii, but it's true. Los Angeles lies considerably further east than either San Francisco or Oakland. Indeed, Los Angeles is farther east than Reno. Look at a map.

The leg from California to Hawaii is the longest commonly-flown air route in the world. No islands lie *en route* for refueling or navigation fixes. Flying to anywhere else in the world, you'll find alternative routes. But from the U.S. to the Pacific, there are no practical shorter routes than California–Hawaii.

Donn, Paul and I met in Lock Haven when Globe Aero had finished tanking the three aircraft and the installation had been approved by the FAA. With a new pilot, Phil would spend an hour or two briefing the flight route, the aircraft, the customer, and general ferry flying hints. I soon learned that whenever ferry pilots meet, all they talk about is ferry flying. The bull sessions held in bars the world over would soon give me the knowledge necessary to become a professional ferry pilot.

Phil checked that each of us carried the necessary charts and survival gear. Each pilot then went over the paperwork for his aircraft. We had a checklist to ensure all the paperwork was together and in the airplane. We used the delivery checklist from the factory to be certain that everything ordered for the airplane was indeed in the airplane. Nothing would be more embarrassing than to arrive in Manila or wherever and find that the log books had been left in Lock Haven.

When everything was set up and ready, Phil wrote each of us a check for estimated expenses and a healthy Jesus factor. It may seem strange, in this age of plastic money, but once past Hawaii our plastic money and checkbooks were dead weight. We hurried down to his local bank and cashed them. To fly to Singapore in a single night might require $2,000.

I learned to make a list for the bank of the bills I wanted. In the hinterlands they didn't take plastic money, and they wanted the exact amount charged. If your landing fee in Pago Pago was $6 and the smallest bill you had was a $50, you just paid $50 to land. We carried lots of $1 and $5 bills.

With the briefing, paperwork, and check-cashing completed, we taxied the aircraft to Piper for refueling. Fuel from Piper was at least ten cents a gallon cheaper than anywhere else *en route*, so we tended to load up. Whatever the aircraft lost in speed we more than made up in fuel savings.

Depending on who fueled you, sometimes you could save even more. One old boy working at Piper sold oranges and grapefruit in Lock Haven. He maintained a standing request that any pilot picking up an airplane in Vero Beach, Florida fill the bird with fruit. He would buy it when you arrived in Lock Haven. When this fellow was fueling aircraft, being one of his buddies meant you were good for at least ten or fifteen gallons extra. Free. Ferry pilots never looked down their noses at free fuel.

We put at least five gallons of fuel in each ferry tank. Depending on how far we intended to fly the first day, it might be more. With fueling complete, we taxied out to the run-up area to check the ferry system. With the engine running, we first ran on the aircraft's main tanks, then switched in turn to each ferry tank to ensure proper fuel flow. If those checked out OK, we turned the fuel off completely to be certain the system was operating properly.

Once the ferry system was checked, we tested our radios. At that time, virtually all Piper aircraft going to the Pacific came from the factory with no radios. Radios and accessories carry a much higher profit margin for the aircraft distributor, so planes came from the factory bare of avionics. The distributor would install the radio package after delivery. We flew them from the factory to Lock Haven in daylight VFR conditions with no radios.

Included in its ferry fee, Globe Aero installed temporary radios. We carried one VHF communication radio, one VHF navigation radio (VOR), one automatic direction finding (ADF) radio, a transponder, and a high-frequency (HF) radio for long-range communication. This arrangement was makeshift at best, and was a pain in the ass to carry back after delivery.

When I was going for a flight instructor rating, the instructor wouldn't take any plane that didn't have two communication radios and two navigation radios in perfect working order. Now it seemed that I was to take an airplane halfway around the world with only one communication radio and one VOR.

Kerby told me, "Don't worry about it. There aren't any VORs in the middle of the ocean and you can only talk on one radio at a time. What you don't take with you, you don't have to bring back." Come to think of it, he had a point and a sense of humor. That really helps in ferry flying.

My aircraft had power leads, antenna wires, and headset and mike leads going every which way. Once out of Lock Haven, radio maintenance would be expensive and time-consuming. My VHF comm radio seemed weak to me. Back at the Globe Aero hangar I mentioned it to John Probst, the mechanic. Sure enough, one of my antenna couplings wasn't making good contact. If I had left Lock Haven with the radio in that condition, I would have had a VHF comm range of perhaps thirty miles. The coupling was soon repaired and the aircraft was ready to go. I made an entry in the log attesting to my checkout of the ferry system. The aircraft was ready.

My instructor for this first trip, Donn Kerby, had completed thirty ferry trips. Short, balding, and with a slight pot belly, he was not terribly attractive at first sight. At thirty-six, he had never married, and evidently intended to stay single. Looks can be deceiving, however. Donn was always cheerful and had a good word for everyone. I have never met anyone who made friends quite as easily. Everywhere we went, there was someone he needed to look up. Donn looked upon the whole world as part of his family. Anyone traveling with him was warmly greeted everywhere. I never heard Donn say a bad word about anyone.

Before becoming a ferry pilot, Paul Briggs had flown as a captain for a small commuter airline in upper New York. After he became involved in union activities, the management of the airline politely but firmly asked him to leave. Of all the pilots with Globe Aero at the time, Paul had the most honest-to-God flight time. He also flew as a crop duster, and had flown the mail at night for a while. He was on his fifth trip.

Briggs was in his late thirties, tall and handsome. He knew it. Globe had two great-looking pilots at that time, and Paul was one. Had he been looking to fall in love, even if only for the evening, there were plenty of women willing to oblige him. Paul was single but didn't take advantage of his opportunities. He had a very dry sense of humor and the quickest wit of anyone I have ever met. Whenever we would check into a motel, he would make a quick comment to the gal checking us in. She would have a hard time trying to decide if he was putting her on (he was), but after a glance or two at him, would decide it was OK with her.

Donn received an extra $200 for escorting me on this trip. That money came out of my paycheck. The theory was that the escort pilot incurred extra expenses as a result of going with an FNG (ferry new guy). On this and every other FNG escort, it seemed to me that the instructor farted around a lot. FNG trips were always run at a dead slow pace. A trip that should have taken a week to ten days would end up taking three weeks. Since all expenses incurred came out of the pilot's pocket, the new pilot was hit with a double whammy. He didn't make what he should have because the trip took so long and expenses were consequently high. Then he had to pay an extra $200 for the privilege of being escorted.

I made a mental note that when I became an escort pilot I wouldn't accept the fee. I would fly the trips like a ferry pilot so the new guys could make some money.

Donn rechecked my charts and survival gear to make sure I was carrying what I should. The winds to Hawaii were still marginal, so he decided we should each make our own way to California in a leisurely fashion and meet in Oakland. Oakland airport was preferable to San Francisco because it had less traffic and a longer runway. There was a flight service station and over the water weather-guessers right on the field. It was a good jumping-off point for ferry pilots. We could look at the wind and weather charts, and gain a better idea of what we'd run into than we could have over the phone.

Since this was my first flight in this particular plane, I fueled it in Lock Haven with a minimum amount. I wanted to be certain I was comfortable with the aircraft, and that all systems were working, before I loaded it to an over gross condition. The fear of flying an aircraft in such a condition had been passed on to me by my flight instructors.

Every student pilot is given the idea that one hundred percent of gross weight is the most any airplane can carry without crashing. One ounce over gross and it's "So long, Charlie." You're going to stall, spin, crash, burn, and die. I was soon to discover that if you didn't know that the airplane you were sitting in was ten or twenty percent over gross, you wouldn't notice the difference. The takeoff roll is longer. The aircraft doesn't climb quite as well. The cruise speed is lower. But an overweight condition just is not dangerous. The fear of being overweight has caused more accidents than actually being overweight.

Donn, Paul and I had a few beers in the bar of the motel where I was staying. We spent a couple of hours talking about ferry flying and conditions over the Pacific. I got a good night's sleep and was ready to go. I finished my preparation, left Lock Haven and headed west.

The winds aloft were fairly typical of what you can expect in that area in winter. Light to moderate, from the west and southwest, at about 15–20 knots.

When traveling westbound from Lock Haven, it's possible to take just about any route. In a non-turbocharged aircraft, the effective maximum cruising altitude is 13,000 to 14,000 feet. I was non-turbo and carried no oxygen, so I was pretty much committed to taking the southern route to California. Due to high terrain, when going to California it's necessary to travel via Blythe and Yuma. Winter was still casting its chill over the northern states. At 135 pounds in those days I was not carrying much insulation, so I decided to head south before heading west.

I picked up a heading of about 220 degrees and went straight for Bowling Green, Kentucky. I arrived there about 6:30 pm and refueled. I was comfortable with the airplane by then so I filled it to slightly over gross. I would be making my first-ever over gross takeoff. As I started my takeoff roll, I still remember wondering if I would survive. Sure enough, just as Donn and Paul had said, it was no sweat. I rolled out on a heading of 260 degrees and continued westbound.

While in the Marine Corps, I had made several cross-country flights in the Douglas C-117 (Super DC-3). We sometimes flew ten to twelve hours a day when away from Cherry Point, North Carolina, especially when headed for a good liberty port. In Vietnam, when flying Cessna O-1 Bird Dogs, I often flew eight or nine hours a day. In the C-117 I always had another pilot with me and we would share the flying. When not flying, we would go back in the cabin and lie down to rest.

While flying the Bird Dog, so much was happening that there was no time to get tired. But flying over six or eight hours in a light general aviation aircraft soon becomes tiring. With a ferry tank occupying the co-pilot's seat, there wasn't much room to stretch out and relax my muscles. I was the smallest pilot Globe Aero had, standing five feet and eight inches. To this day

I don't know how the big guys could endure being so cramped. Hell's bells! There wasn't room enough for me in the cockpit with all the ferry tanks. For the first time in my life I was glad to be short and skinny. But I was to find that fifteen hours wasn't much more tiring than eight.

The biggest problem was overcoming the boredom. Sitting in the Arrow watching the instruments soon got old. The weather was clear to the moon. I was not on an instrument flight plan so I had no one to talk to. Luckily I had brought several books along with me, intending to read them on the ground.

I once read a book written by another ferry pilot. It was a "how to" book, telling pilots what they could expect in various locations, and how to get there from here. The author made a specific point that there was never enough time during a ferry flight to read because there was always something to do. I found this to be pure bullshit. On a flight of ten hours or more, you make one takeoff, level off once, set your power once, make a few position reports, switch your ferry tanks a few times, and preferably make only one landing. (The number of landings should always be equal to and should never exceed the number of takeoffs during a particular flight. I learned that as a cadet back in 1965.)

In any case, long-distance flying *should* be boring. There just isn't that much to do. So I read. I found that there was tons of time available to read, even when flying formation. Conversely, on the ground there was always something going on, so even on a three-week trip there was no time to read. This ferry flying was getting to be great fun. I love to read. Now, not only was I being paid to fly to exotic lands, I was being paid to read all I wanted, and the books were tax deductible, too.

By about 11 pm I began to feel the effects of the day's journey. I had wanted to make Dallas and to spend the night there, but I'd left Lock Haven later than planned and my fanny was beginning to drag. So I landed at Memphis. I taxied in, parked my beast, and headed for the nearest motel for a night of well-earned rest. I had finished my first day as a real ferry pilot.

The next day I rose early, had a good breakfast and went to the airport. The forecast called for good weather until I reached California. The winds were still westerly, at ten to fifteen knots. I filled the aircraft with fuel. I was still very uncomfortable with the idea of flying thirty percent over gross, and wanted to be over land during daylight after my first-ever heavy takeoff. Donn had told me to expect to leave Oakland in the evening, in which event we would immediately be over water.

I called for takeoff, being sure to inform the control tower that I was over gross and wanted vectors around populated areas.

"Over gross?" the tower asked. "How much over gross?"

"Piper 7949C is thirty percent over gross," I calmly replied. As if I did this every day.

To say my request put the tower in a panic would be an understatement. In sixty years of operation, Memphis tower had never had anyone admit to being over gross weight. Everyone knows that you can't fly over gross safely or legally. At least, Memphis tower knew that. Memphis tower wasn't about to let me take off overweight.

"Piper 7949C, this is Memphis tower. Please return to base and give us a call on the land line. We would like to talk to you."

"Tower, this is Piper 7949C. Wilco. Requesting back taxi."

The special ferry permit under which we operated was explicit. Each aircraft was inspected by the FAA and approved for over gross operation. The permit required us to notify the tower before takeoff that we were overweight. My problem was that in years and years of ferrying aircraft, no pilot before me had ever bothered to do that. They had all expected it to send the tower into a panic.

I called the tower as requested and explained matters. I was completely legal and had FAA approval for over gross operation. I taxied out again and requested takeoff.

"Piper 7949C is cleared for takeoff. Maintain runway heading."

I could hear the trepidation in the voice of the tower controller. Now we were both in a panic. I knew that the tower knew that I was going to stall, spin, crash, burn, and die. All over his beautiful runway. There would be so many forms to fill out.

I held the brakes, advanced the power. Once the RPM and manifold pressure stabilized, I released the brakes and started my takeoff roll. At eighty knots I eased the nose up. When safely airborne, I raised the gear. The airplane flew just like a real airplane was supposed to. Like Kerby told me, "No sweat."

Fourteen hours and ten minutes later, I landed in Oakland. Never again would I inform any tower that I was over gross weight.

During my previous flights across the U.S., in C-117s and in F-4s, I must have been busy doing something because I had never taken the time to appreciate the scenic beauty of our country. On this trip, in only two days, I had crossed the entire country. The more trips I would complete, the more I would be amazed by the variety of terrain of the USA. We have rolling green hills, deserts, plains, soaring mountains, lakes, rivers, bays, and oceans. Never would I travel to any country with so much diversity. Not for the last time, I sat in appreciation of the U.S.

Neither Donn nor Paul had arrived. I checked into the hotel where we were to meet. Phil issued all new pilots an ID card identifying the bearer as an official Globe Aero Captain. The cards probably cost him two bucks but were stamped with the official Globe Aero corporate seal. Whenever checking into a hotel or renting a car, we always asked for the airline discount.

I never understood the logic of airline discounts. I mean, airline captains drawing good salaries need hotel discounts like they need bigger egos. Conversely, if you walk into a hotel and tell the clerk that you are Joe Schmo, computer programmer, earning a subsistence wage and badly in need of a discount, your chances of getting one are slim to none.

I suppose I should give the airline types a break. After all, sometimes they have to fly seventy-five hours in a single month. They need that discount so they can buy more toys.

"What airline are you with?" the clerk asks.

"Globe Aero," I reply. "We're a non-sched." To be a professional ferry pilot, it's necessary to carry around a good supply of buzzwords.

"I don't have you on our list. What are you flying today?"

"Ah, well. I'm, ah, flying a twenty-eight to Manila. The rest of my crew is checking in later." As in PA-28R, Piper Cherokee Arrow, single-engine LBF (as in little bitty fucker). Also as in, "Let's cut the crap, give me the discount."

Airline types refer to a Boeing 747 as a "forty-seven." Only a wimp would call his airplane a 747. And I'm all the crew that's going to check in. As a matter of fact I'm all the crew.

"Our normal rate is forty-eight dollars but for you it's twenty-four. How many nights will you be with us, sir?"

If you can't dazzle them with brilliance, baffle them with bullshit.

Donn and Paul arrived the next day. The winds were still marginal, so Donn wanted to wait a day or so to watch the trend. The winds were acceptable but would put us in Honolulu with only two hours' reserve fuel. For a new pilot, Donn preferred three hours or more of reserve.

We rented a car and went into San Francisco, to a map store. Donn wanted some VFR charts of the Philippines and Singapore but the store didn't have the charts he wanted. We made a note to try to get them in Honolulu. Kerby was taking his assignment as escort pilot seriously. While in the map store he showed me the navigation instruments he used. I bought whatever he suggested.

Donn's hints about what gear to carry saved me a lot of time and made ferry flying much easier. Maybe the fee was worth paying. I found out later that most of the escort pilots didn't give the FNGs many hints, and that it took much longer under their instruction to become a smooth ferry pilot.

We returned to the hotel. Donn wanted me to work up flight logs for each leg of the trip, using VFR charts. These charts have a much smaller scale than the IFR maps, so the charts are larger. Donn's theory was that if you could work up an accurate flight plan using VFR charts, then it would be much easier using the IFR maps.

"If you need help, ask." He went out to the pool. Forty-five minutes later I'd finished all the flight logs. I showed them to him and received his approval.

During Navy flight training I was given a lot of dead reckoning training. I was a bit rusty but hadn't forgotten the basics. Donn was surprised at the accuracy of the logs, but more so by the fact that I'd finished four legs so quickly.

Virtually none of the other Globe Aero pilots had trained in the military, and they lacked a firm grasp of dead reckoning when they started ferry flying. Donn then took my flight logs, of which I was so proud, and threw them away. I was shocked. I had put a lot of work into them, and now he nonchalantly drops them in the trash.

He explained his rationale. "The absolute accuracy of a flight plan is not that important. But when two or more pilots are flying together, they should use the same flight log. They are given the same winds by the weather-guessers. Each pilot then works up a flight plan independently. By comparing those flight plans, any error becomes obvious. If each pilot uses a different flight log, errors of time and distance are not so obvious."

It was a good tip, and whenever I flew with other ferry pilots after that we all used the same flight log. It was very important for a ferry pilot to have a firm grasp of dead reckoning, but most of the time it would be used in flight, to assess alternatives whenever a problem arose.

Donn had about thirty canned flight plans written down in his little black book, and he let me copy them all.

One ferry pilot, who shall remain unnamed, thought this idea of using canned flight plans unprofessional. He went out and bought the most expensive Texas Instruments flight calculator. He always insisted on working up his flight logs from scratch, for each leg. But he didn't really understand how to use his calculator. He would spend three hours trying to figure the distance and headings for a flight from Oakland to Honolulu. When he finally got it worked out, his log was accurate to a gnat's ass, but any of the other pilots could come up with a SWAG (stupid wild-ass guess) flight plan in under five minutes.

The National Weather Service issued lower level wind forecasts from the west coast to Hawaii every twelve hours. We checked each forecast to determine the trend. The forecasts were given for the 850 and 700 millibar levels (five thousand and ten thousand feet, roughly). The headwind was a ten-knot component when we left Lock Haven but had now dropped to an overall minus five-knot component. Donn was happy with that, and made the decision to launch the next afternoon.

Hawaii lies three time zones earlier than the west coast. We would have about a seventeen-hour flight, so would land fourteen hours after we left, local time. This gets us into an area of argument, whenever two or more ferry pilots were trying to get to the same place at about the same time. Ferry pilots are usually great pilots. But they can't add or subtract worth a tinker's damn.

Pilots fly on Greenwich Mean Time, or GMT. All flight plans are based on GMT. All position reports are given in GMT and we set our watches to GMT. Pilots either add to or subtract from GMT to obtain the local time.

Since we weren't on a tight schedule, we didn't really care what the local time was. But when trying to arrive at a destination at a particular time, we had to convert GMT to local time, first at our departure point and then at our destination, determine flight time, and finally reconvert to GMT so we knew when to take off.

The Pacific was bad enough; you may make a position report at two o'clock in the afternoon by saying the time is 0200 GMT. When the sun is up, it just doesn't seem like 0200. Even 0200 GMT. Since our watches had twelve-hour faces, often at the end of a trip it was damned difficult to determine just what time it was, due to fatigue. I have been so ragged that I would look at my watch and couldn't, for the life of me, read it.

The Atlantic had its problems too. Gander, the prime jumping-off spot for Europe, was three-and-a-half hours west of GMT. I could never figure out what time, local, I should leave Gander in order to land at an airport in Europe at a particular local time.

We wanted to be "zero fuel" (*nada* fuel) during daylight. In other words, if we managed to lose Hawaii, and then ran out of fuel looking for it and had to ditch, we wanted to ditch during daylight hours, and sufficiently early in the day that rescue aircraft could find us before the sun went down.

My preference was always to reach my destination at night, because the ADF received a much more accurate and stronger signal at night. But Donn was leading this trip, so we did it his way.

If we left Oakland at 8 pm, we should arrive in Honolulu about 10 am the next morning. Zero fuel would be at about 1 pm. Donn's happy with this, so that's the plan. Paul will take off thirty minutes after us, cross our position halfway to Honolulu, and land thirty minutes before us.

The big day arrives. We try to sleep in as late as possible, so we won't be tired during the latter part of the flight. I have a few books with me, and a few candy bars. Paul and Donn announce that we're going to a grocery store to do some shopping. Once in the store, I am amazed at how much food Donn is putting in the cart. It's enough to feed an army. There is no way he can eat that much during a seventeen-hour leg.

But he tells me, "Make a policy of buying too much. You might waste five or ten bucks on food that you later throw away, but you never can tell when you might get a craving for a chocolate chip cookie or a banana. You'll tend to get dehydrated, so carry lots of liquids. Don't drink tea or coffee — they make you more dehydrated. Take some Coke with you. The caffeine will keep you awake, and drinking one thirty minutes before you land will give you a boost. Treat yourself. You're going to be living in that cockpit for the next few days. There aren't any stores halfway across."

I'm skeptical as hell, but this guy has been through it before and so far has given me a world of good advice. This turns out to be one of the most valuable bits of advice he ever gave me. Nothing beats ice-cold lemonade or an orange when a flight starts to wear you down.

We carry our baggage and food to our three aircraft, and load them. Cockpits never seemed big enough to carry everything that had to be carried, but somehow we manage to cram it all in. We'd checked out of the hotel. Donn returns the rental car as Paul and I fuel our craft.

My Arrow has a twenty-gallon tank in the co-pilot's seat and two fifty-five-gallon drums in the back. I'm legal for fifty gallons in the forward drum and forty in the aft. Donn had told me it was impossible to get all the fuel out of the barrels, so I should fill them to the brim. I am now a veteran of two over gross takeoffs so I'm not worried about the weight.

Donn makes another good point. "Just because you're over gross doesn't mean you're going in the drink. But if you run out of fuel, I guarantee you'll get your feet wet. There ain't any Feds out here inspecting aircraft, so fill 'er up."

In retrospect, now more than ever, I can appreciate his wisdom. I logged thousands of hours of flight over gross. Most of it was legal. Having that extra hour or two of fuel handy saved me from grief more than once.

Donn returned and fueled his plane, and we taxied out to the compass rose. He shut his aircraft down and climbed out to steer me to the cardinal headings so I could reset my magnetic compass. The compass and my watch would be my primary navigation aids for the next seventeen hours, so an accurate compass is mandatory. The compasses were swung at the factory, but we have so much metal in the cockpit that it's necessary to reset them. My life will depend on the accuracy of the compass, so I spend fifteen minutes swinging it. When I'm complete, I steer Donn. Then we taxi back.

Paul has completed fueling and has already finished his compass swing. He's waiting for us in the weather office. The forecast calls for headwinds: eight knots at ten thousand feet, and five knots at five thousand. We have no fronts or major systems to go through. We'll have cloud on and off throughout the flight, but that's standard for the Pacific. Donn's pleased with the forecast. We each take a copy and sit down at a table to work out our flight plans.

I finish mine first. When Donn completes his, we compare. We used the same flight logs, winds, and air speed, but I show a total time of sixteen hours and Donn has seventeen. One of us has made a mistake. Paul finishes his flight plan and he also shows a sixteen-hour flight. Since his aircraft is faster than Donn's and mine, it is evident that I have made the error.

I recheck my addition and find I have dropped an hour. But I tell Donn that we should use my flight plan as we will arrive in Honolulu earlier. He laughingly tells me, "If we do, we only have to fly sixteen hours but it will take us three weeks to swim that last hundred and forty miles." I see his point right away and correct my plan.

The FAA does not allow formation flight plans, so each of us files a separate plan. Donn will handle communications for his aircraft as well as mine. He files for eight thousand feet and I file for six thousand. Actually, after he takes off, he'll hold the power back until I can catch him. We'll then climb to eight thousand feet together and fly formation. The book says we can't fly formation together under IFR. But then, the book doesn't deliver aircraft.

We are filed, fueled, and fed, and the aircraft are checked. We still have half an hour to kill so we sit down to brief. Donn tells me to request takeoff after he has reported that he is through two thousand feet. Oakland would not let a second aircraft take off until the first had passed two thousand feet on its climb, so ferry pilots reported doing so as soon as their wheels left the ground. That made it much easier for the second aircraft to catch up.

Once I'm in formation on Donn and they switch us to Departure Control, Donn wants me to switch my comm radio to 122.95. He will handle the radio communication with Departure Control and Center, and come up on 122.95 every once in a while to check on me. I am to stay in loose formation on him. If we enter cloud I am to hold my heading and altitude until we come out the other side. Seventeen hours later we will land in Honolulu.

I'm stunned. In Vietnam we would spend an hour and a half briefing a half-hour bombing mission. I'm about to take off on a 2,400-mile flight across water in a single-engine aircraft and my briefing consists of: "Fly on me. I'll do all the talking. Then we'll land in Honolulu."

All the ferry pilots I had met by that time were nonchalant about flying over water, but this was too much. Or too little. First of all, I didn't like being on an instrument flight plan and being unable to talk to or hear the controllers. What if I had a problem? Am I supposed to cope with it until Donn comes up on my frequency? And what's this about punching through clouds with the two of us at the same altitude? I didn't like that at all. Mid-air collisions can kill. Sure, we'll come out of the cloud in the same relative position, but what if that mother is five hundred miles thick? They are, sometimes. No way am I going to stay at the same altitude as someone else. I don't care if that cloud is one mile across or five hundred.

Donn and I had gotten along quite well until this moment. But flying across an ocean was no joke. His brief was no brief. I had been a little apprehensive before, but now I was in a panic. Ferry flying may be easy, I thought, but it can't possibly be this easy. I bit my tongue and kept quiet but I didn't like what was happening. I was going across a lot of unfriendly water and I didn't know what to expect. In the military, the captain is wholly responsible for the safe operation of his aircraft. Here I'm being told, "Follow me, and I'll talk to you once in a while." Ferry flying was great up until just a few minutes ago.

Donn and I went to our aircraft, started our engines, and called Clearance Delivery for our oceanic clearance. We were cleared to Honolulu as filed. I was never anything less than thrilled to call for clearance to a point thousands of miles away. Oakland was used to receiving such flight plans but it was a thrill for me.

Donn called, "Ground Control, requesting taxi for a flight of two from Flight Service to runway two-nine for takeoff." Runway 29 was the long runway right on the bay; the one the airlines used. Ferry pilots always, always wanted as much runway in front of them as possible.

It took ten minutes to taxi out to that runway. I became more nervous by the minute. Eleven years before, in a moment of bravado, I made the mistake of putting my John Hancock on the dotted line for a Marine Corps recruiter. Until my dying day I will remember my first night in boot camp, thinking, "Oh Lordy, what have I done? Please let this be a bad dream. Please let me wake up and all this terror be gone."

I had the same feeling now. "Please God, let this be a joke. People don't really fly single-engine aircraft across the ocean. This is all a joke. Phil and Donn and Paul have been putting me on. They just want to see if I'll break. I want to go home and snuggle up in my nice warm bed next to my nice warm wife. Please, God! Let this be a bad dream."

It wasn't. Donn was cleared for takeoff. He started his roll and I watched as his navigation lights disappeared on the horizon. Finally his nose came up and he was airborne. Moments later he called through two thousand feet.

"Piper 7949C, this is Oakland tower. You are cleared for takeoff."

In movies this is known as the moment of truth. I had forgotten whatever it was that had interested me about ferry flying. I did not want to go. I was scared and I don't mind admitting it. I was about to take a single-engine airplane across a vast stretch of water with nothing but a temporary radio package and a flight brief that was, at best, inadequate. I didn't really have a clue as to what I was doing, and if I went in the water my chances of being picked up were slim. I was about to venture out into the great unknown. Only a few guys had ever done this before me, and a lot of them were dead. But as they say: No guts, no glory.

I released the brakes and started my roll. The aircraft seemed to take forever to accelerate but I lifted off after about six thousand feet of runway. To the west was a gaping black void. I could barely see Donn's running lights but I turned west over the water to catch up with him. My life was now in his hands. We would not see land for another 2,400 miles.

It took me about five minutes to catch up. Donn had his power throttled back, as he had briefed, but he also had a hundred horses more than me. His airplane didn't go as fast as mine in cruise, but in the climb he was much faster. He finally adjusted his power so I could climb with him.

The tower gave us a frequency for Departure Control and told us to switch. Donn told me, "Switch to 122.95. I'll be with you in a few minutes." I switched over.

To the north, south, and east of us were the lights of the Bay area. To the west there was nothing. No clouds, no stars, no moon. I looked over towards Donn's airplane and my worst fears came true. I had lost him already! He was over there somewhere but I couldn't see him against the lights of Oakland. He was on a different frequency and I had no way of contacting him.

Had we been on the same frequency, or had two radios, I could have called him. Since I was probably higher than him, it would have been easy for him to look out to see me. But I had no spare radio and we weren't on the same frequency. Soon, possibly very soon, we would have two aircraft trying to occupy the same space at the same time. My first ferry flight was about to turn into a mid-air, and Donn would have earned his extra $200.

The last frequency I had written down was that of Bay Departure Control. I switched over to them.

I joined the Marine Corps a week after my eighteenth birthday. During boot camp, the drill instructors came and asked if any of us recruits were interested in applying for flight training. Since I was making $75 a month as an E-1 and second lieutenants made $398, and since I could add and subtract, I applied and was accepted. Vietnam was just heating up as I went through flight training in 1965 and 1966. I was the youngest pilot doing so. Our ages ranged from eighteen through twenty-four or so.

We were all young, invincible, full of piss and vinegar. We couldn't be killed and we knew it. I remember vividly a favorite phrase used often during flight training: "It's better to be dead than to look bad."

Since death was impossible, the expression didn't mean anything. But subsequently I had watched several pilots die because they didn't want to look bad. They stayed in aircraft that they could have gotten out of. At the time, I thought dying rather than looking bad was particularly dumb. I still do. Far better to look bad and survive.

I called Departure Control and explained, "I have lost visual contact with my flight lead." Even though we were not supposed to be flying in formation, Departure Control knew what was going on, as every ferry flight that went through did the same thing.

Donn had been switched to yet another frequency, so I still had no communication with him. Departure Control gave me a discrete transponder code to squawk on my transponder, and identified me almost immediately. Donn was at my two o'clock position, at two miles distance. They gave me radar vectors to his position. When I had regained visual contact with him they had me switch over to the frequency he was on.

This was the first time Air Traffic Control went out of their way to help me as a ferry pilot, but not the last. Perhaps the air traffic controllers felt a comradeship with ferry pilots, or maybe they just felt sorry for us. Especially in the U.S., the authorities always went out of their way to give us a break. We regularly did things that were contrary to the Air Regulations, and they knew it. But ATC, without exception, gave us assistance above and beyond the call of duty.

The air traffic controllers' strike of 1981 was yet to come. That caused a lot of hard feelings between pilots and controllers. Any pilots who think ATC is not on their side should try flying in other parts of the world. I learned much that night that I would never forget.

If a pilot thinks he has a problem, he has a problem. All that is necessary to receive the utmost assistance from ATC is to mention the word "help". Should that not get their attention, the word "Mayday" really will, particularly when delivered in a high-pitched scream. Repeat it for added effect.

Donn ordered me to switch to 122.95. He told Center that we would be off their frequency for a few minutes. Center told him to report when back up on their frequency. We switched.

"I thought I told you I wanted you to stay up company frequency."

"You did, Donn. But I lost sight of you and couldn't reach you. So I went back to Departure Control and got vectors from them. I want to be on the working frequency from now on."

"Bullshit. You stay on this frequency and I'll tell you what's going on. Try to keep sight of me from now on. I'm going back to Center."

"Donn, this is *my* airplane. I'm responsible for flying it, not you. We're on an instrument flight plan and I want to know just what the hell is happening. *I'm* flying this bird and *I'm* going to listen to Center. If you need me, tell me to come up company frequency and I'll switch over."

"OK. I'm going back to Center."

Great! Just fucking great. We're less than fifteen minutes into the flight and I've lost sight of my leader, almost had a mid-air, and now he's annoyed because I want to listen to Center. I hope this flight doesn't go downhill from here. It's a long way to Honolulu.

It takes us forty minutes to stagger to eight thousand feet. For the last thousand feet we climb at a hundred feet a minute. At lower altitudes we have more power and the Arrow performs fine. But up here it feels as if it is running out of power. I pick up a loose formation on Donn, staying at his nine o'clock, at a distance of between half a mile and a mile. If I lose sight of him again he should be able to see me.

We return to a cruise power setting and adjust the mixture controls. If I were by myself I'd use best power: fifty degrees on the rich side of maximum exhaust gas temperature (EGT). Since I have to slow down for Donn I use best range (maximum EGT). This gives me the longest range possible.

We are now a hundred miles west of San Francisco and are nearing the limit of the range of Center's radar. Center gives us the last position they had us on radar and clears us to our *en route* frequency.

Donn tells me to switch to ARINC frequency. ARINC handled all the HF communication with aircraft over water, once they passed out of UHF or VHF range. We switch. Donn reports our position, altitude, and next estimated position. He requests our HF assignment. ARINC gives him the HF frequencies we are to use, but includes one frequency that we don't have. Back and forth the conversation goes, until Donn and ARINC agree on the frequencies we will use for the crossing.

The subject of HF radios was always a heated one whenever ferry pilots met. We lugged around those heavy radios that never had the frequencies we needed, and rarely worked. Phil Waldman was too cheap to buy more crystals. He never had enough radios for all the pilots. The pilots knew that the probability of getting the same radio on the next trip was slim, so the radios took a lot of abuse. As a result they never worked properly.

ATC was often bent slightly out of shape by ferry pilots, because no one ever made all their position reports. The pilots were always pissed off because

ATC was on our backs about not making reports, and because we were not allowed to ship the radios home as baggage but had to hand-carry twenty pounds of dead weight. After two or three changes of aircraft on the way home, those radios got pretty heavy. Being slightly built helped when sitting in a confined cockpit hour after hour, but carrying sixty pounds of radios through airport terminals was a real bitch.

The HF communication problem could have been solved if Phil had bought extra radios, installed the proper crystals, and permanently assigned one radio to each pilot. But he was never interested in hearing about that.

Donn had us switch back to our company frequency. He then asked me to get into closer formation with him so we could carry out a compass check. I slid over. He told me his exact magnetic heading, and I gave him mine. It turned out that we were three degrees apart. We split the difference and would use the new magnetic heading for the rest of the crossing.

This was the only benefit of formation flying I ever found while ferrying. Each pilot would swing his compass in a slightly different manner. Also, it's impossible to read a compass with exact accuracy. Two pilots sitting in one plane could read the same compass and come up with slightly different headings. We would compare our compasses while in close formation and come up with a more accurate heading than either of us could independently. I moved back out to a wide beam formation.

We soon began to run into the tops of clouds. We'd go into cloud for a minute or two. I didn't want to lose sight of Donn so I moved into a closer formation. I was the only Globe Aero pilot who had ever been trained in formation flying. I had lots of time flying formation in instrument conditions while flying the F-4. But this was very different. The F-4 was a much smoother flying platform than these light singles. The air was less turbulent at higher altitudes and we had a lot more power available.

I had thought that flying formation in light aircraft would be easy, but this was damned hard work. I wasn't looking forward to another sixteen hours of this. I was working myself to death. I could see Donn's airplane now and then, but we were less than a hundred yards apart and I kept losing sight of him in the clouds.

"Bob, hold your heading and altitude and we'll be in the same relative position when we come out of the cloud on the other side."

The clouds got thicker and thicker. Now we were IFR for two or three minutes without sight of each other. The more I did this, the less I liked it. It seemed to me that the probability of a mid-air collision outweighed any benefit of staying in close formation. I finally told Donn that I would maintain the same heading, but if we went IFR again I would climb five hundred feet and maintain that separation.

"Negative. I told you how we do it at Globe Aero. Maintain the same altitude as me. When we get VFR, I want to be able to see you. This is how we do it and how we have always done it."

The one statement guaranteed to raise my hackles is, "This is the way we have always done it." To me it indicates someone unwilling to think about what the hell he's doing. As stupid behavior cannot be justified on any logical grounds, you're told to behave stupidly because that's the way it has always been done.

"Donn, it's my bird and my ass. I'm going to maintain five hundred feet separation. Out."

We were off to a great start. I didn't like his flight briefs. I didn't like the way he flew or communicated. He didn't like this smartass new guy telling him how he, the new guy, was going to fly his trip.

To be completely fair to Donn, he was running this trip the way he had been taught at Globe Aero. There has always been, and probably always will be, a running battle between military-trained and civilian-trained pilots. A military pilot with a thousand hours of flying time is highly-trained and highly-qualified, while a thousand hours for a civilian may be nothing. If it's Cessna 172 time, there is no difference between two hundred hours and a thousand.

Civilian pilots view military pilots as prima donnas who won't fly without three comm radios, five nav radios, a spare navigator, autopilot, and dual static wicks. Military pilots believe that all civilian pilots obtained their licenses from Cracker Jack boxes, and that they don't really know how to fly but are adept with logbooks and pencils.

To a limited extent, each is right. But I had gone through my baptism of hell during twenty-two months of combat flying in Vietnam. The first thing we did was to throw the flight manual out the window, and fly in a way that made sense. If it didn't make sense, we didn't do it. The pilots who flew "the way we've always done it" died.

Donn was fabulous on the ground. He got along with everyone. He was a rich source of good tips for ferrying; far more so than any other pilot. But no one was going to fly my airplane for me. I didn't allow it in the military and I wasn't going to allow it now.

To the great black void, he and I now added silence.

Until Briggs came up. He took off thirty minutes after us, as planned. It took him another forty-five minutes to clear Center and get his HF assignments. Finally we heard him.

"Donn — you guys up on 122.95?"

"Yeah, Paul, we're up. Where are you?"

"I'm about 110 DME west of San Francisco. How about you guys?"

"We are coming up on one thirty west in ten minutes."

"What altitude are you and what kind of weather are you getting?"

"Bob's at eight thousand, five hundred and I'm at eight thousand. We have been in and out of the clag for the last thirty minutes but you should be in the clear at ten thousand."

Wild as it may seem to anyone who is not a ferry pilot, the altitudes at which we flew had nothing to do with the altitudes for which we filed. The FAA required us to file for separate altitudes. Those altitudes on a westbound instrument flight plan had to be in even thousands of feet. Donn filed for eight thousand feet because he took off first. I filed for six thousand so I wouldn't pass through Donn's altitude. Paul has to file for ten thousand feet because he's faster than we are and will pass us somewhere *en route*.

But just because we filed for an altitude doesn't mean we intended to fly at that altitude. On this leg we would have slightly better winds at a lower altitude but would lose airspeed due to the turbulence. At higher altitudes we gain true airspeed and have slightly lower fuel consumption. There were no other aircraft around below thirty thousand feet. Ferry pilots were of the opinion that the altitude rules applying to the LA basin or the New York–Boston air corridor made less sense over the ocean. We preferred to maintain our own separation.

I remember one departure from Gander, in Newfoundland. The weather had been bad for weeks and there must have been twenty ferry pilots and planes sitting on the ramp. We all left about the same time. In order to legally file, we had single-engine aircraft filed at twenty-five thousand feet. I hope the Canadians didn't really believe we were up there.

I always found it handy to write down my filed altitude on my flight log, so I could refer to it when giving position reports.

Imagine: "Center, this is N7949C. I am 130 west, 35 north at time 0200. Altitude is, er, ah . . . well, you can check my flight plan to see what altitude I'm at." That would be an interesting conversation, indeed.

We settled into the routine we would maintain for the next sixteen hours. Donn had just come back from Honolulu the week before, and kept talking about a woman he'd met and was interested in. He and Paul had made one previous trip together, and had much in common to talk about. I was the new guy, unfamiliar with ferrying. Apart from asking a few questions, I tried to keep my mouth shut. I had enough to do, trying to keep sight of Donn.

He was trying to get a commitment from Paul to go out with his girlfriend's roommate, but Paul wasn't having any part of it. Paul finally asked Donn how old the roommate was. Donn wasn't sure, but said his girlfriend was about sixty and the roommate was older. That killed the issue as far as Paul was concerned. Donn then asked if I was interested. I told him I'd pass.

The first two hours and the last two hours of any ferry flight seemed to drag. It took a while to settle down and become a part of the airplane. To climb and level out takes thirty minutes to an hour. The special ferry permit dictated no use of the ferry tanks until the aircraft is in level flight, but a mandatory rule of ferry flying is to *use your most inaccessible fuel first.* That way, if the aircraft suffers a pump failure or electrical failure, you have more time to deal with it. So as soon as we were established in the climb, on went the ferry system. If a system wanted to fail, we wanted it to fail as close to an airport as possible. We also needed an accurate fuel consumption figure so we knew the aircraft's range exactly.

It was always a source of amazement to me how much difference there was between two supposedly identical aircraft. One airplane might burn nine gallons of fuel to go 130 knots; another, identical model with the same weight, flying in the same conditions, might do five knots more. Each aircraft seemed to have a personality of its own.

Whenever I instructed, both in the military and out, I always told the student pilots to treat the aircraft as if it were a woman. "Be gentle and loving and the bird will be nice to you. Be harsh and ham-fisted and she will give you hell." I was always gentle with airplanes, and for the most part they got me where I was going with a minimum of problems. I wasn't all that good with women, however.

Every five degrees of longitude, we were required to make a position report to Air Traffic Control. The distance between position reports was 140 miles or so. Donn would crank up his HF radio and try to transmit his reports. For the first part of the flight he had good luck. Later on he couldn't make contact and wanted me to try. I reeled out my trailing wire antenna just the way he instructed and tried to make contact, without success. Paul couldn't make contact either, so we switched over to 123.45.

Airlines were required to maintain a listening watch on Guard frequency 121.5 when over the ocean. Whenever we had two radios, we did the same. But airline pilots suffered from boredom over the ocean, just as ferry pilots did, and often talked among themselves on 123.45. Donn called on that frequency to see if anyone was monitoring. Sure enough, an airline came back and was willing to relay our position. Due to the poor quality of the HF radios we carried, we made far more position reports through airlines than we ever did on our own radios.

Afterwards, the airline types always wanted to talk to us.

"This is United 605. Where are you guys headed?"

"United 605, this is N7046C. We have two airplanes going to Singapore and one to Manila. We took off on this leg from Oakland, and estimate Honolulu twelve hours from now. We have a Cherokee Six and Arrow in company and have a Seneca right behind us."

"46C, this is 605. Gee whiz! It's a long way from Oakland to Honolulu. Can you make it non-stop?"

I've been asked that question a hundred times, and each time someone asks it I'm still surprised.

"605, this is 46C. Golly, I sure hope so, considering the alternatives."

"46C, this is 605. I guess I see your point. But guys, I have a big surprise for you."

What he's going to do now is call up one of the stews from the back, get her into the cockpit, hand the mike to her and let her talk. She really isn't used to talking on the mike over the air. She feels a little dumb, because what can you really say to three sex-starved ferry pilots? (We left Oakland all of five hours ago.) She's a little confused when the captain tells her to talk to the ferry pilots because she doesn't know if she is talking to us or to some fag from TWA.

"Hi, boys. How are you doing tonight down there?" she says in a sultry voice. Big surprise. The airline pilots think it great that they're doing their part for the "boys." As if we just came back from two years in Thule, Greenland.

After a while we get tired of talking, and they get tired of talking. We go back to watching our instruments. We have long since left behind the lights of the coast. The stars are out in all their splendor. Perhaps it was my imagination, but the stars looked much brighter than over land. No moon tonight. All I can see is the stars above and Donn's running lights in and out of the clouds. I fixate on a particularly bright star and watch it pass slowly westward and finally set. Then I pick another. It sets also.

I really appreciate Donn's advice about food now. I have a cooler on top of the ferry tank next to me, loaded with food. I break out the cheese and crackers. Then I take a deep drink of ice-cold lemonade. It does hit the spot and makes the trip much easier.

We are halfway across. Paul should be near us but we don't see him. Wait — there he is, to the north of us.

"Paul, this is Donn. Hit your landing light for a minute. I think I have you in sight at my three o'clock. Yeah, that's you. Take a look at your nine o'clock. Maybe twenty miles. I'll put my landing light on for you."

"Gee, Donn. You guys are really off course to the south."

No, Paul. You're off course to the north. Why don't you fly about five degrees left for a few hundred miles. You're going to miss Hawaii completely."

Actually, the Hawaiian Islands chain is a hundred and fifty miles wide and lay perpendicular to our course. It would be difficult to miss completely, but it had been known to happen. Honolulu is dead in the center of the chain. It was difficult to be so far off course as to be unable to pick up any navigation signal from one of the islands. It sometimes happened, though.

For some reason, when aircraft are off course they're always to the north of where they should be. Either Paul is off course or Donn and I are, but we won't find out which until we pick up our first navigation signals from the Islands. Ferry pilots never waste an opportunity to bust each other's chops. "I'm always right and you're always wrong."

The moon finally comes up, but it's a quarter moon and doesn't give us much light. The stars are more beautiful before it rises. If the flying wasn't such hard work it would be a beautiful scene.

Donn continues to transmit our position reports on 123.45 to airlines. Each is cheerful and wants to talk to us. Early in the evening everyone has plenty to say and the conversations last for hours. Later, the conversations become shorter. The spirit gets just as tired as the body.

Finally we begin to see the faint pastel colors of the approaching dawn behind us. Since we're flying with the sun, we have an hour and a half before it will finally peek over the horizon. Donn and I have watched Paul's lights disappear ahead.

Donn told me in one of our barroom briefs that there would be a dramatic change in the type of clouds once we reached the halfway mark at 140 degrees west. Sure enough, the change in clouds is like the difference at the border between California and Arizona. There, it's green on one side and desert on the other. Here, the Hawaiian side has scattered white puffy clouds with tops not above six thousand feet. Donn and I have fought our way through the tops of towering angry gray clouds for the last seven hours. But west of 140 degrees west, the air is much smoother. I don't have to fight to stay in visual contact with Donn.

As the sun rises, I must now confront my fear of heights. Acrophobia isn't at all unusual among pilots. The sensation of height is not perceived over land, due to the visual signals. However, over water, without land masses or well-defined horizons, the fear of heights becomes much more acute. We took off at night, so I have not yet had any sensation of flying over water. My mind is able to pretend I am still over land. But I know that when the sun comes over the horizon, and when I look around, all I will see is water. I dread this inevitable moment.

Donn solves the problem with his usual country humor. "Bob," he says in his soft drawl, "the difference between being involved and being committed is like the difference between ham and eggs."

I think about this for a little while but he's gone right over my head.

"OK, Donn, I'll bite. Go ahead, shoot."

"The chicken, you see, is involved, but the pig is committed."

I'm still not real sure I fully catch his meaning.

"We're out here about halfway between the west coast and Honolulu. You may be scared shitless but you've got just as far to go back as you do to continue on. You're not involved any more, you're committed. Just like the pig."

I understood his point immediately. As if by magic, the irrational fear of heights departed forever, never to reappear. However, I did still get a little nervous whenever the airplane I was in had a door next to me. You never know. That sucker might just open, and in a turn I might fall out.

We continued on. Donn became easier to keep in sight as it grew lighter. Once in a while I would peer into my goodie cooler and nibble on whatever I liked the look of. I had the autopilot set and was well into a good book. Every few minutes I would check on Donn's position and readjust my heading as necessary. We were now within range of commercial broadcast stations on the islands, and were listening to one of them on the ADF. It was nice to have a little mood music to set the tone as we approached America's version of paradise.

Perhaps because I am rarely up early enough to see the sun rise, I've lost my appreciation of the sheer beauty of the dawn. Over the water you are enveloped by the changing colors. The black clouds behind us began to turn gray, then white, then pastel, as the sun started a new day. The sky is at its most beautiful just before and just after the sunrise. Then the pastels begin to lighten and the sun begins to beat its way through the plexiglass canopy.

An hour after sunrise, the sun had become an enemy. The top half of me was too hot and the bottom half too cool. There was no way to adjust the temperature, but on average I was comfortable. I came to learn that this is just a part of the price that ferry pilots pay. The airplane is always a little too warm or cool, no matter where you are in the world.

Donn told me several times, "Think of ferry flying as living in whatever airplane you're in."

The Cokes and lemonade were refreshing last night but are now pressing on my bladder. We have several hours before touchdown in Honolulu and I can't wait that long. Before leaving Lock Haven, Donn insisted that I take along an empty three-pound coffee can "in case of emergency." I begin to understand the nature of the emergency he was referring to. I dig through survival gear and clothing. I find the can, and in a splash, my problem is over.

Briggs is in front of us by thirty minutes but we're still within radio range. He begins to pick up a VOR signal from Molokai and determines he's fifteen minutes ahead of schedule. He's also right on track, which means that we're slightly south of our course. We make a slight correction to the north. His news is good because it means we should arrive early.

When preparing flight plans we tried always to be pessimistic. Running through clouds will cost us five knots. Flying without an autopilot will cost us five knots. Flying in formation will cost us five knots. All these considerations must be taken into account. To arrive early is always a pleasant surprise, but to be even one minute late is painful. If you're an hour or more late, the authorities start to panic. For some reason they suppose that if you are early, it's due to superior airmanship. If you're late, you did it deliberately, just to spite them.

We pick up the VOR signal from Molokai, and then another from Koko Head. Our correction has brought us back on course. We've left the world of ocean flying and have returned to standard instrument procedures. Since I have filed for six thousand feet and am theoretically lower than Donn, Honolulu approach has me start my letdown first.

This is the first time I've ever seen the islands from the air. The view is breathtaking. The standard light cumulus clouds are gently covering the mountains, but all of the island in sight is green and lush. I'm vectored over the water south of Honolulu once past Koko Head. I've lowered my landing gear and have gone through my landing checklist. When I have the field in sight, the tower clears me to land.

Touchdown. One takeoff, one landing. I have cheated death once again. I turn off the runway as instructed by the tower, and taxi to the fixed base operator (FBO) that Globe Aero uses as home base when in Honolulu. Paul is already there, fueling his Seneca. As I join him, he tells me to fill my tanks only to their legal capacity. An FAA inspector has been nosing around, and is checking that all ferry pilots put in only the amount of fuel for which their aircraft have approval. We'll finish fueling later, when he has gone.

A car drives up with the airport authority representative. It seems that some ferry pilots passing through have neglected to pay the landing fee. The ritual is for the representative to come around and collect the fee when pilots come in from the mainland. But since he has other things to do, sometimes he doesn't come around for an hour or two after they land.

This guy cannot imagine that a pilot might prefer to find a bed and get some sleep than to sit around and wait for him to come and collect his $3. I listen to his harangue about how unpatriotic ferry pilots are. Imagine someone actually skipping a legitimate fee.

These damned bureaucrats are just like a junkyard dog. Give 'em a rule they can sink their teeth into and they'll gnaw away forever. It probably cost Honolulu International airport $10 to collect every $3 fee.

Kerby taxied in just after me. While I'm fueling he's inside visiting his friends. Just like everywhere else we go, all the secretaries are after him and want to party. He manages to dodge them, for some reason I can't imagine. Paul has arranged a rental car for us. When we've finished our work, we load the car with our baggage and head into town.

The islands are warm and beautiful, but like every other nice place to go in the world, too many people go there. Honolulu has the same air of sickly sweetness as Disneyland, overrun with tourists. It would be a great place to visit, if fewer other tourists had the same idea at the same time.

We check into a hotel on the beach after pulling our airline discount routine. Paul plays his part perfectly and has the clerk begging him to accept rooms at half-price, even though every place in town is fully booked. The only thing that would have made Paul look even more authentic would have been a stewardess on each arm. We go up to our rooms and pass out for a while.

After being vibrated by an airplane all that time, it took me an hour or two to return to normal. The buzz in my ears soon subsided but I remained keyed up. As soon as I became relaxed, I fell asleep. Later I heard Donn taking a shower next door and awoke, fully refreshed. I looked at the clock and realized with surprise that three hours' sleep had brought me back to the land of the living. I had imagined that after a journey of such a distance, the body would require much more sleep to catch up.

After all the talk during the trip about his sixty-year-old girlfriend, I expected Donn to have plans for a big night. But he made no mention of calling her or going out on a date. I began to suspect that he was much talk and little action.

We were still feeling some effects from the flight and no one was in the mood for a late evening. We went to one of Donn's favorite restaurants and had dinner. He had done a lot of ferrying, and maintaining a list of fine restaurants was at the top of his to-do list. As usual with Donn, we were not disappointed by his choice.

The next leg of the trip would take us to Wake Island, for fuel and an overnight stop. Since Wake was a military base, we had to verify the availability of fuel and obtain landing permission. The Air Force officer with the authority to grant landing rights was based at Hickham Air Force Base, just to the west of Honolulu International airport. Permission had to be granted twenty-four hours before our takeoff, so we made Hickham Field our first stop the next day. Luckily, the colonel was available. We met with him and presented our insurance papers.

Another strange quirk about landing on military fields was the demand for proof of liability insurance. I had no argument with the military's policy of requiring insurance. But to land on a Navy field required one amount of insurance, and to land on an Air Force field required a different amount. A military field is a military field. What's good for one ought to be good for the other, but such was not the case.

The Air Force colonel gave us permission to land. He assured us that he would notify Wake of our expected arrival. His minion ushered us out of his office and then made a mistake; he asked Donn if we needed any charts. If so, we could have any that we wanted from Hickham's master chart room.

That was like asking a sixteen-year-old who has wandered into a whorehouse if he sees anything he likes. Donn's eyes and Paul's eyes started to glaze over. They were drooling. Little pools of spittle were forming around their shoes. I could see their toes curling. The NCO hadn't realized what had happened.

Donn and Paul were obviously in no condition to speak. So I replied, in a voice two octaves higher than usual, "Charts? Sure, we could always use a spare chart or two."

The NCO led us into a room only slightly larger than a small theater, filled with charts. Now to understand what we were going through, it's necessary to realize that the three most important things in a ferry pilot's life are his watch, his compass, and his charts. Sex, drugs and booze are way down the list. This turkey had just handed the key to the chicken coop to the band of foxes.

Donn just wandered around the room for the first few minutes, looking at maps as if he was examining fine wines.

"Look at this, Paul. Here's a 1974 South Africa. Mo, look here, a '72 Greenland. A '71 northern India. This is the 1975 Singapore I've searched for all over the U.S."

Paul wasn't listening. While Donn was examining the southern European vintages, Briggs was grabbing maps and stuffing them under his shirt. This was getting out of hand in a hurry.

I took control. "Come on, guys, they're just charts. For Christ's sake, we can get charts anywhere."

"Just charts?" cried Briggs and Kerby in unison. "These aren't just charts. Ye of little class. These vintage maps of strange and wonderful places couldn't be referred to as *just* charts. These charts are wonderful. These are *free* charts."

I caught their drift right away and started grabbing maps, too. We wandered out of the building burdened with hundreds of them. We made our first over gross takeoff from Honolulu in a little green 1975 Datsun loaded to the gunnels with maps.

The map room looked as if it had been hit by a bomb. Never again was a ferry pilot to be allowed within sniffing range of Hickham's storehouse. We traded charts back and forth for the rest of our trip.

We still had at least a day to kill before we could leave for Wake. We went over to the airport to check the weather and winds. Normally the winds would be light easterlies, but a weather system was on hold to the west of Honolulu. It looked as if it might be several days before we could depart.

We decided to play tourist for a few days until the winds improved. We drove around the island. We collected shells. We went dancing that night. Still Donn made no mention of his girlfriend. I was convinced now that he had been blowing smoke. I was getting pretty lonely by this time. I'd been away from home for a week. On a previous trip Donn had met a younger woman who was very interested in flying. He offered to call her and try to set me up for a date. He did, and I made my plans.

By now we had been at the hotel for four days. Every day we told the desk we'd be checking out; every day we stayed. They finally told us that our rooms had been reserved for weeks and we had to find another refuge. We tried every place on the beach and couldn't find a thing. Honolulu was booked to the gills. Paul went into his act of a 747 captain with a planeload of supplies for East Wobegon and we still couldn't get a room on the beach.

Finally we swallowed our pride and checked into the Holiday Inn near the airport. It had all the class of a Turkish outhouse and we were crammed into a single room with two cots. But it beat sleeping in the airplanes.

We went shopping for clean clothes at the Ala Moana Center. We were walking along, looking in the shop windows, minding our business, when we heard a loud squeal. A lady gorilla weighing two hundred pounds and dressed in a small and tacky colored tent had pounced on Donn. Paul and I tried to drag her off but she wasn't having any part of it. This was the sixty-year-old Canadian girlfriend. She knew what she wanted and was prepared to take it on the spot, in front of God and everybody.

I began to understand why Donn had forgotten her phone number. She didn't let him out of the bear hug she had him locked in until she knew where he was staying and had choked a promise out of him for a date that night.

Donn was in a panic. There were no rooms to be found in Honolulu. He tried to talk Paul into running interference with the roommate, but Paul was far more interested in watching the Winter Olympics than participating in the Honolulu Sex Olympics with a senior citizen. Luckily for me, I was committed to the date that Donn had set up for me.

Donn was rather fatalistic about going out with the gorilla, as if he knew what she had in mind. He left with a small brown paper bag. I asked him what was in it, out of idle curiosity. It was his sex kit. He had bubble bath, baby powder, and baby oil. Talk about a man accepting of his fate.

At sunup, I heard the door open. It was Donn, somewhat sheep-faced. I noticed some stains on his pants, just below his knees.

"How did it go, Donn?"

"So-so. How about you?"

"So-so. Say, Donn. I've been meaning to ask you something."

"Shoot."

"What the heck are those stains on the knees of your pants?"

"Grass."

"Oh," I replied. "I've been meaning to ask you something else."

"Shoot."

"How did you get grass stains on your pants?"

"I was in Fort DeRussy," he said, as if everyone got grass stains on their pants merely by being in Fort DeRussy park.

"Oh," I replied. "Donn, just one more question?"

"Shoot."

"Just what the hell were you doing in Fort DeRussy park?"

"Before or after the MPs caught us?"

"Either." This was getting more interesting by the minute.

"Well, I couldn't get anyone to go out with my girlfriend's roomie so we couldn't go back to her place. Hell's bells, there wasn't near enough room in the Datsun to do anything with her. So she dragged me under this bush and we started doing it."

"Where did the MPs come from?"

"Well, I didn't know it, but we were on the grounds of Fort DeRussy. All of a sudden I heard some noises and these two big, mean-looking MPs were looking over my shoulder. Naturally, I stopped doing what I was doing. They informed us that the curfew was on. We weren't supposed to be on the grounds. Then the stupid bastards asked me what I was doing."

"And?"

"I asked them if they meant before they so rudely interrupted me, or after. Anyhow, that's where the grass stains came from."

It was a most interesting evening, for each of us.

Donn told his girlfriend that we were leaving the next evening and he wouldn't be able to see her. We didn't leave for four more days but he never called her again. His sex life wasn't much other than being really interesting.

The weather system finally passed and we prepared to leave for Wake Island. As was common on escort trips, we were having such a great time in Honolulu that we had started to forget that our real purpose was delivering airplanes.

We made plans to leave that evening. We filed our flight plans, notified Hickham that we were finally on our way to Wake Island, and cleared customs outbound. We went back over to the south side of the field where our planes were parked. There was no sign of the FAA inspector so we finished filling our tanks, to the brim.

Donn and I had spent a lot of our time in Honolulu talking about flying. By now, I had a much better idea of what he expected from me. We fired up our birds and taxied out. Ground control gave us our clearance and we were ready for takeoff.

After having such a memorable time in Honolulu, I really didn't feel like leaving. It was only a greener, warmer version of Tinseltown, but the stop had been pleasant, and it was so much better than anywhere else we would be going that leaving was difficult.

One of the cardinal rules of ferry flying is that you don't ever *have* to leave. But none of us was making any money on the ground.

Donn called for takeoff clearance. When he reported airborne, the tower cleared me for takeoff. With a sigh I advanced the power and released the brakes.

A powerful northeast gale was blowing over the mountains of eastern Oahu. We knew we could expect strong turbulence, but we got more than we expected. As soon as I was airborne I was hit with a strong gust. The stall warning horn came on. It was all I could do to maintain flying speed. Donn, with his horsepower advantage, was climbing like a small bird with a big hungry bird behind him. We took off to the northeast and were supposed to turn as soon as possible.

I could barely keep the plane straight and level. I was working like a one-armed paper hanger. The stall warning horn was blaring like mood music in a disco. I could either climb or turn. If I continued ahead, I would make a big hit on Waikiki beach. If I turned, I would augur in. All I could think of was the FAA finding out that I had been thirty gallons over legal.

I finally wrestled the Arrow around to the southeast. As I passed four thousand feet I came out of the turbulence. I looked at my clock. While an eternity had passed in the cockpit, only twelve minutes had gone by in the real world. I won't say that the takeoff put me in a panic, but I did have nervous moments.

I caught up to Donn and resumed my now familiar position at his nine o'clock. We leveled at eight thousand feet.

The flight was mostly a repeat of the flight from Oakland. At any hour, there is always airline traffic between the west coast and Hawaii. But westbound from Honolulu, it decreases markedly. We could not count on convenient airliners to relay our position reports. With this in mind, Donn had taken our HF radios into the radio shop at the airport and had them checked over and tweaked. Both worked perfectly for the rest of the trip.

Paul was in radio contact with us soon after his takeoff. We chatted for a while. Once again, as the evening passed, conversation dwindled. I had the formation flying down pat by now. With the exception of a small correction now and then, to maintain position on Donn, I did little flying. I sat back and enjoyed my book.

We had made another grocery run before leaving Honolulu. I saw fresh pineapple for sale. I love pineapple, and picked one up for the trip. Bad idea. Carrying a fresh pineapple in the confines of a small, single-engine airplane cockpit over the Pacific is like a monkey fucking a football. It's great fun to watch but very messy. By the time I finally had a few pieces large enough to eat, pineapple juice was all over the cockpit. My hands stuck to everything in the airplane for the next five days.

On this leg we had a full moon. Ferry flying in formation is hard work, but flying at night with nothing but the lights of your wingman and a full moon overhead gives you a totally different perspective on life, love, and flying. This flying was so enjoyable it seemed a damn shame to be getting paid for it. But who was I to object?

We planned to be in Wake by ten o'clock the next morning. Sometime during the night, someone moved the island seventy miles to the west. Finally, it peeked over the horizon. Although we had been pessimistic in our flight planning, we still arrived thirty minutes late.

Donn taught me another important lesson on that leg. I kept seeing islands that turned into clouds as we got closer. We were still not receiving any radio signals from Wake, but every cloud looked like land to me.

"Forget it, Mo. Clouds can look like land, but land never looks like a cloud. If you think it might be a cloud, it is a cloud. Land always looks like land."

Wake Island had been a major staging and refueling station during the Vietnam war. As the war wound down and ended, Wake became a minor military field, as it had been for so long beforehand. The Air Force pulled its units out and turned the base over to Pan American Airlines for maintenance. There was an Air Force commander on the base, a handful of Americans on contract to Pan American, dozens of Filipinos and two white women. It was a great spot.

The high point of the day for these guys was to wander down to the shore and watch the tide come in. Having three airplanes arrive at once was a big deal. As I taxied in, I felt like Lindbergh landing in Paris. Everybody was there. Paul finished fueling and now it was my turn.

I had three guys on each side of the airplane, each with a fire bottle. I was wondering just what they knew that I didn't when the biggest damned fuel truck I had ever seen pulled in front of my airplane. Now I understood what the boys with the bottles were doing. If that mother of a fuel truck caught fire, it would burn for three weeks and be visible from San Francisco. It could have fueled two KC-135 tankers and still had enough juice for my little toy. When they hauled out the hose it looked like an eighty-foot python, or a thousand-pound gorilla in heat. I stuck the nozzle in my tanks and was fueled in a shake.

I always enjoyed the efficiency of the military. From start to finish, it took about three minutes to fuel my airplane.

Now we got to the paperwork, which is where the military really shines. It took two hours for them to figure out how much Paul owed for his 320 gallons of fuel, and then another twenty minutes to make change for him. But things got better. It took only an hour and a half to bill me, and Donn was finished in thirty minutes. To fill out one piece of paper required the perusal of twelve manuals.

While they were farting about, Donn and I wandered around the island. There wasn't anything much to see or do. It was no warmer than Honolulu but the sun was far harsher. By the time we got back to the terminal we were both sunburned. It was a part of the price you paid to be a ferry pilot. It was a tough job, but somebody had to do it.

We placed an order for box lunches to take with us the next day, set up a weather brief, and then went to the BOQ for lunch and some sleep. There were so few people on the island that there was no flexibility whatsoever in the meal schedule. If you showed up while lunch was being served, great. You got lunch. If you showed up late, you didn't eat. There weren't any McDonald's handy. We showed up late; we didn't eat.

Luckily for us, the bar was open. In the military the bar is damn near always open, and cheap. We went in and went on the drinking man's diet. One side benefit of being a ferry pilot was that after a sixteen-hour flight my tolerance for booze was greatly diminished. I could get ripped for less than half the usual price. We did so on about four beers.

We went to get some sleep, and were ready to go again a few hours later. Being a ferry pilot required an exceptional ability to recuperate.

We arrived at the chow hall in time for supper. It was just as tasteless as the military food had been in Camp Pendleton or Da Nang, years before. We got ripped again. There wasn't much else to do on Wake Island.

After a dreadful military version of breakfast, complete with Kool-Aid, we staggered to our airplanes the next morning, bound for the island of Saipan. The weather between Wake and Saipan was typical of the tropics, with a light following breeze to speed us on our way. We had a short hop by ferry standards; only nine hours. We would do this leg entirely in daylight.

Donn took off, with me in close trail. As soon as he became airborne he switched on his autopilot. Which was just dandy for me, as wingman.

The VOR at Wake was three miles to the west of the runway. As an airplane comes close to a VOR, the autopilot starts to seek the station and the bird wanders all over the sky. In climb configuration, my Arrow is barely flying. I'm supposed to be flying wing on Donn as he performs a series of loops and barrel rolls. A flight leader is not supposed to see how hard he can work his wingman. My opinion of his basic flying abilities and his flight sense was deteriorating. Finally, after ten minutes of chasing the VOR radial, his autopilot settled down.

For some reason, when flying at night the time seems to pass faster. The lead aircraft is easier to see because its lights stand out against the dark, so the wingman doesn't have to work as hard to keep proper formation. The cockpit temperature is better balanced. I suppose the sense of time differs because the night is somehow supposed to end, while the day seems to go on forever. In any case, this nine-hour leg seemed to take as long as the far lengthier hops we had behind us, which we flew at night.

We didn't talk much. There wasn't much to say about Wake Island, for or against. We had no girlfriends to look forward to seeing on Saipan. I've heard people say that all pilots talk about in the air is sex, and all they talk about on the ground is flying. That's not far off track. It seemed that most of our airborne conversation was about women. All our talk on the ground was related to flying.

We landed on Saipan in mid-afternoon. On the periphery of the field, old World War II bunkers could still be seen, covered with vines. Construction of a new terminal was under way but there was no mistaking the airport for anything but a tired, ex-military airfield.

Paul was parked on the ramp in front of the tower. In front of his Seneca was a battered, salt-eaten red Toyota pickup with two fifty-five-gallon drums of avgas in the back. One of the fuelers held the spigot in Paul's wing tank as the other turned the hand crank to pump the fuel. Three forward turns, then three back. Three forward turns, three back. At that rate, it would take the three of us several hours to fill up.

Donn and I went inside to clear customs and to pay our landing fees. We came back out twenty minutes later. Three forward turns, three back. We sat under the wing of Paul's airplane as they fueled him. Three forward turns, three back.

When they finally finished his aircraft, they started on mine. Three forward turns, three back. I remembered with wistfulness the monster fuel truck on Wake Island. Three forward turns, three back.

Every forty-five minutes or so they would use up the two drums of fuel. They would disappear for a further few minutes, only to reappear with two fresh drums. Never three drums, or one.

Paul paid his bill and came over to me. They had put 230 gallons of fuel in his plane but had billed him for 275 gallons, which was five drums. He asked me if they had started fueling me from a fresh drum or if they used the remainder of the drum he had started. They had started me on a new drum. We went over to the fellow in charge of the operation.

In the tropics, when the natives are going to screw you their command of the King's English goes to hell. When this guy came up to Paul to start fueling him, he spoke great English. He had now lost that ability. Through pidgin and sign language, Paul inquired as to the whereabouts of the forty-five gallons of avgas he had been charged for, but which were not in his fuel tanks.

Apparently, once a barrel was opened, the pilot was charged for all the fuel it contained, even if he didn't take all of it. We knew this and understood the logic. But with two more airplanes to fuel, we could use Paul's surplus in the other airplanes. We were already paying thirty cents a gallon more for it than we paid anywhere else *en route* — I suppose for the privilege of all the workmanship by hand. They were adding insult to injury.

"No can do. Fruel hab been take back fruel deepo."

"Screw you, buddy. You bring *fruel* back to *aeroplaneo* and *putto fruelo* into other *aeroplaneo.*"

I never realized Paul spoke so many languages.

The missing gallons of *fruel* were brought to my airplane. Paul and I settled the bill between ourselves.

Everybody seemed to have his own scam going, all over the world. This excess fuel in an opened drum wasn't good enough for another airplane, but it worked just fine in the Datsuns and Toyotas of the oil company employees.

Saipan island lies some 110 miles to the north of Guam, in the Mariana Islands chain. It was the scene of some of the bloodiest battles of World War II, between Japanese and U.S. forces. Recently it had been invaded again by the Japanese — the Japanese tourist.

Just as the British consider Miami Beach to be the epitome of a tropical heaven, so the Japanese swarm to Saipan. Just like the British, they drop their bags in the hotel room and rush to the beach to get a head start on a sunburn. It was possible to measure the length of their stay by their color. The first day, they were pasty white. Red the second day; fire engine red on the third. By the fourth day they glowed in the dark.

Like skiers wearing their plaster badges of courage wrapped around their legs, the Japanese marched onto the planes taking them home looking like someone had almost missed them with napalm, smiling as if they enjoyed the pain. The ultimate status symbol in Japan must have been to return from Saipan looking like a crispy critter.

The variation in accommodations between one island and another never ceased to amaze me. In Wake we stayed in a flea-ridden barracks and ate warmed-over mush. On Saipan we stayed in a world-class hotel with continental cuisine, served while overlooking a white beach stretching for miles in each direction.

Ferry flying had its good and bad moments. The good was great; the bad, terrible.

Since Donn and Paul were going to Singapore and I was bound for Manila, we came at last to the parting of the ways. They would leave at night. My leg was much shorter, so I would leave early the next morning. I left them in the hotel and went to the airport. I completed my formalities and departed.

Flying wing on another pilot had been hard work. After ten days, I was tired of Kerby and Briggs. Now I was on my own and happy to be so. I could do things at my own pace. I leveled at ten thousand feet and read my book, unhampered by the need to keep watch on someone else. This was the life.

Approaching the Philippines control area, I established communication with the authorities on HF. They wanted to know my landing permission control number. I wondered what a landing permission control number was. I informed them that landing permission had been applied for two weeks before. I was on a ferry flight, delivering an airplane to the Piper dealer in Manila. That was just great with them, but they wanted to know the number.

I told them to call the Piper dealer for the details. They wouldn't. I must have a landing permission control number or I wouldn't be allowed to land. I took a SWAG at the number of digits, in the hopes of giving them a likely number. I guessed wrong. They told me that what I gave them wasn't a landing permission control number. I told them I must have given them the one for Saipan. If only they would give me the number of digits in the landing permission control number, I might be able to come up with something better. They wouldn't. No sense of humor.

I ended the discussion by letting them know that I was on a legitimate flight. I was filed for Manila and had every intention of landing there. They could sort the problem out on the ground. At least, I thought that would end the discussion.

It seems the Filipinos had a small war going on, and if you lacked permission to land, that meant you weren't going to land. At least, not in one piece. The controller informed me that if I penetrated their airspace he would send fighter aircraft after me.

That *was* the end of the discussion. I had completed my turn back to Saipan before he had formed the second syllable of "fighters."

I was in a quandary. I couldn't go on to Manila. We'd tried to call Phil Waldman from Saipan but the telephone system was abysmal and we never got through. I knew that Guam had more of the accoutrements of civilization. I changed my destination to Guam, hoping that the phones worked there.

Guam made a big point of telling me that the airport was used jointly by the U.S. Navy and civilian aircraft. I had no problem with the Navy using the field. Let them worry about their own airplanes. I had my bird to worry about. I was happy to share the airport with them. They didn't bother me and I had no intention of bothering them.

Just before landing, the tower asked if I was sure I wanted to land. Dumb question. Sure I was sure. They told me, "You might have to pay a fine for landing." I had never heard of such a thing. I landed anyway, fine or no fine. Any time you take off, you have to land.

The commander of the Navy base, a captain, had me standing tall moments later, in front of his desk. Landing was restricted to aircraft having landing rights and sufficient liability insurance for the Navy. I told him about being refused permission to enter Philippine airspace and my need to call Globe Aero for instructions. Didn't do me a bit of good. He nailed me with a $100 fine on the spot.

Never one to let the first failure deter me, I tried to get him to rescind the fine. I finally hit him with my big guns. I let him know that I too was a naval aviator. Besides, the $100 was coming out of my pocket, not Globe Aero's. Nice try, but no cigar. I paid the fine.

Guam was overrun with ugly Americans. Saipan was a tropical paradise. Guam was a western version of the slums of Los Angeles, complete with tacky discos, traffic lights, and the world's biggest McDonald's. The hotel in Saipan was first-class; my hotel in Guam, a dump. Nevertheless, it was a dump with a functioning phone system.

I called Phil and told him about being chased out of the Philippines. He told me to sit tight. He would get in touch with the dealer in Manila for instructions. Each time we had a conversation, a whole day passed. Due to the time difference between Guam and Florida, for me to talk to him during his working hours, I had to call in the middle of the night on Guam. Phil had to call Manila in the middle of the night, Florida time.

He finally told me that the dealer in Manila had screwed up the paperwork for landing permission. I could wait in Guam for two weeks, or fly to Singapore and let the dealer figure out how to get the airplane to Manila. I'd had enough of Guam. I decided to leave the airplane in Singapore.

I left the next evening. Nobody else was doing any flying, so the fellow on Departure Control talked with me for an hour. He had just come back from Singapore on leave, and told me where all the hot spots were. He had the highest praise for the Marco Polo Hotel. He said they had a restaurant in the lobby that was great. While in Singapore, I must go out of my way to eat there. I half-listened to him. I was bored. It was nice to have someone to talk to on the radio, but I had found out long before that most enlisted men's ideas of a great place were usually dives that I wouldn't be caught dead in.

Flying where I wanted and when I wanted was great. With Donn, we were forever worrying about winds. We had to have just so much reserve fuel. With the wind forecast I had from Guam I should be able to make Singapore non-stop, but there were several alternatives available *en route* if they blew the forecast. I filed and left.

The forecast was accurate. I found Singapore early the next afternoon, right where it was supposed to be.

I had a heck of a time understanding the controller as he vectored me for landing. English is the international language of aviation. In theory it's possible to land at any international airport in the world, speaking only English. The controller understood my American English perfectly but he couldn't speak it. He spoke only Australian and that was impossible to understand. Finally I realized there was an airport in front of me. I was probably supposed to land. I did.

I taxied to the Piper dealer. Phil had called him and told him to expect me. My propeller was still turning as the dealer's crew attacked my airplane and pulled the ferry system free.

As I opened the cockpit door, a large cold Singapore beer was thrust into my hand. One mechanic seemed to be in charge of getting me plastered. Every time I came close to finishing a bottle, he handed me another.

Grins spread from ear to ear as the mechanics found my supply of girlie magazines. Donn told me always to carry some skin mags to hand out. Greenbacks are the universal lubricant but handing them out is sometimes considered bad form. Skin magazines are always appreciated.

One hour later the ferry tanks and portable radios were out of the plane and my bags were packed. With great pleasure I filled out the log book and handed the dealer the keys to the airplane. They had my ticket and reservations back to the States ready.

It was my first visit to Singapore and I wanted to play tourist for a couple of days. They got me a room in town and pushed me into a taxi with another fresh beer in my hand.

Then I started the most perilous journey I have ever made.

The eighteen-hour leg to Singapore had half knocked me out, and four powerful Singapore beers finished the job. I nodded off in the taxi. I awoke moments later, just as the driver rolled out of a 6g turn. I was wrecked, but not so wrecked that I didn't realize this suicidal idiot was driving on the wrong side of the road.

The turns had me rattled, but his driving on the left had me petrified. I was about to grab the wheel and return the vehicle to the correct side when I saw that everyone was driving on the wrong side — even the oncoming traffic. I finally realized these guys were following the British rules of the road. Mentally, I knew my driver thought he was on the right side, but I knew damn well he was on the left. I hoped no one else would realize it at the same time.

We drove the twenty miles into town in not more than fifteen minutes. I sat on the edge of the seat the whole time. The driver grinned as if this was a great adventure. It was, for him. I had just completed a trip of ten thousand miles across endless stretches of water. Now I was going to die in a taxi.

I closed my eyes and started whispering the Lord's Prayer. Finally, with a screech of brakes, the cab fishtailed to a halt. I cautiously opened one eye. We were in front of a small hotel. I opened the other eye and looked at my driver. He was still smiling at the thought of having set a new land speed record.

I threw some money at him and dashed into the hotel.

Lying at the crossroads of Asia, Singapore has a mild climate considering it lies only a few miles from the equator. Fourth in size among the world's shipping ports, it was bustling and thriving with commerce. I was eager to do some shopping and wanted to take a tour of the harbor defenses. But first, I wanted sleep. Perhaps my heart rate would slow down.

During my two years in Vietnam, I managed to shoot about five rolls of camera film. I swore to myself that if I were to continue ferrying I would buy a decent camera and take lots of pictures. For years I had my heart set on buying a Rollei 35 miniature camera. Now I had my chance. The lenses were ground in Germany but the camera was assembled in Singapore and should be a good buy here.

After taking a nap, I set out to buy a camera. I visited several camera stores, and the prices for the Rollei were all within a span of a few dollars. Finally I settled on one store and set out to bargain for the best price. After forty-five minutes, and with tears in his eyes, the owner of the shop parted with a new Rollei 35. I parted with one hundred and twenty-eight U.S. dollars.

Two weeks later, while in New York City applying for a South Africa visa, I saw an identical camera for sale at $98. I'd have sworn that the tears in the eyes of the salesman in Singapore were real.

The next day I took a junk cruise of the harbor. We watched as small boats called lighters moved cargo from the freighters to the docks. Even though Singapore was a major shipping port, the docks were too shallow for large ships. Everything moved from the big boats to the little boats to the docks, and back.

Our junk cruised to where the British had mounted the sixteen-inch guns used in the defense of the harbor. Or at least, intended to be used. The British military swore that Singapore would never be successfully attacked from the sea. It wasn't.

The Japanese, lacking the education granted every Englishman, didn't read the books pointing out that they were supposed to attack from the sea and be blown to smithereens by the big guns. When it came time for them to go to Singapore for the season, they walked down the Thai peninsula and captured Singapore from the rear, without a shot ever being fired from the sixteen-inch guns. They had not read the books that would have shown them the impossibility of attacking via the Thai peninsula.

As we motored our way back to the docks, a lovely Australian girl came up to me. "Pardon me, I hope you don't think I'm forward, but are you by yourself?" she said with an impish smile.

"As a matter of fact, I am," I replied.

"I've been in Singapore for a week now, on holiday, and haven't met anyone. I'm off for Kuala Lumpur tonight. I'm lonely. You have a friendly face and I would like to have dinner with you. Of course, only if you don't mind."

Mind? Hell no, I didn't mind. This lovely apparition of sweetness just told me I had a friendly face. It wasn't as if I was desperate to return to my room by myself and order room service, again. This gal had just made my whole day, maybe even my whole trip. That's how I met Deslee I—, from Sydney, Australia. We were to be good friends for years.

Des had checked out of her hotel and dropped her bags at the train station. She had nothing else to do until her train left. We spent the rest of the day wandering the streets of Singapore. I can't enjoy something or someplace nice unless I can share the pleasure with someone else. Donn and Paul were long since gone, and Des had better legs anyway. We were like kids in a candy store.

Mind? No, Des, not for a moment did I ever mind spending time with you.

Around five, our feet started dragging and we went back to my hotel for a rest. We got up at seven.

I enjoy nice restaurants and great food, but when I'm by myself I will not go into a good restaurant. Half of the enjoyment of a meal is sharing it in the company of good friends. I had passed the Marco Polo and was impressed, but wouldn't go in by myself. Now was my chance to enjoy a good meal with a beautiful companion.

We had our first spat. She didn't want to go. Being on a budget, she couldn't afford it. Since she had invited me, she should pay for the meal, or at least her share. That's the Australian way.

I told her, "Fine. In Australia you can pay for the meal, or at least your half, but we're in Singapore."

I was a ferry pilot who had cheated death just coming over to meet her. Ferry pilots were all filthy rich and threw away anything smaller than a $50 bill. I wanted to go to the Marco Polo for dinner. She could buy me dinner, my next time in Sydney.

The controller in Guam should have received an award as a master of understatement. The Marco Polo was magnificent.

We started with cocktails in the lobby. We moved into a cozy private corner of the restaurant. The waiter hovered over us. No sooner had I pulled out a cigarette, he was there with a light. He brought a cart with slabs of fresh prime beef for our selection. All we had to do was indicate the size of the cut we desired. It was custom cut and cooked for us in minutes. It was perfection.

We had wine. We had dessert. Finally, the waiter came out with a small dark ball on a plate that smoked. It was a ball of vanilla ice cream, dipped in chocolate, served over dry ice. The perfect finish to a perfect meal.

The bill came.

Bear in mind, I wasn't a real ferry pilot; not yet. I had flown only one trip. I didn't really throw away everything smaller than a $50. Only everything smaller than a $10.

The Marco Polo didn't mention prices on the menu. Presumably, if you needed to know the price, you couldn't afford it.

The waiter — casually, as if he did this every day — slipped the bill down next to me. I glanced at it.

In an instant my face paled. My heart slid to a stop. I took a deep drink of wine and tried to light a cigarette at the same time. I ignited the wine and gulped the cigarette.

Deslee asked, "Is everything all right?" I told her, "Sure, everything's just fine." Especially the cigarette I just ate.

I asked the waiter, "Would you be so kind as to double-check the bill?" For any errors. When he had finished putting out the wine, he looked it over. He smiled grimly and said, "I'm sure it is correct, sir."

I dumped a stack of bills onto the tray with the check. The waiter returned with my change. He wished us a good evening and we left.

Cocktails, dinner, wine, dessert and brandy came to twenty-eight U.S. dollars. For the two of us. For the classiest meal I had ever eaten.

I've never let Deslee know how much it cost. If I had set out to impress her with my taste and class, I couldn't have chosen a finer spot anywhere in the world. Twenty-eight dollars, for the two of us. For a moment it almost made the cigarette I had eaten taste good.

Deslee was soft and warm and comfortable. It was a damn shame she was leaving for Kuala Lumpur. But we had had a memorable day and a great meal, and I would see her again soon. I put her on the train and went back to my hotel. That night I went to sleep with a big grin on my face.

The next day I caught a flight to Copenhagen. We made a brief stop in Bangkok, and twelve hours later arrived in Copenhagen. I spent the night there and left for New York the next day.

Three weeks after departing on my first trip, I was home again.

One down. And, although I didn't know it at the time, two hundred and forty to go.

SECOND TRIP: LOCK HAVEN, PA to SYDNEY, AUSTRALIA

1976	from	to	nautical miles	knots	time (hours)			
					flight	day	night	inst.
Mar 6	Lock Haven	Lock Haven	0		3.0	3.0		
	Lock Haven	Wichita	945	123	7.7	4.0	3.7	
Mar 7	Wichita	Oakland	1,181	121	9.8	9.8		3.5
Mar 9	Oakland	Hilo	2,025	153	13.2	10.2	3.0	0.6
Mar 10	Hilo	Hilo	0		1.3	1.3		
Mar 15	Hilo	Pago Pago	2,235	151	14.8	5.8	9.0	3.0
Mar 16	Pago Pago	Faleolo	123	177	0.7		0.7	
	Faleolo	Nandi	637	108	5.9	5.9		3.0
	Nandi	Sydney *	1,709	132	12.9	3.9	9.0	5.0
Mar 17	Sydney *	Bankstown	15	75	0.2		0.2	
TOTALS		11 days	8,870	128	69.5	43.9	25.6	15.1

* Mascot airport

It took a long time to get Ernie Kuney fired up. We spent days staring at the walls of our hotel in Hilo, Hawaii. The kindest thing that could be said about the place was that it didn't have rats. No self-respecting rat would have been caught dead in such a dump. But we were saving five bucks a day.

Once Kuney was fired up, nothing could stop him. Not lack of fuel, not common sense, not exhaustion.

ONE OF THE BEST THINGS about ferrying airplanes was the ability to tune out the rest of the world. When you are a thousand miles from the nearest land, you tend to concentrate on real problems. Will I have enough fuel? Can I find a little speck of land? What will I do if the engine quits? Whether or not the American Express bill has been paid just doesn't mean very much. When you finally arrive at your destination and turn off the engine, the trip is finished. You had enough fuel, after all. You managed to find Singapore or Sydney, and the engine kept turning.

But, just like the cartoon, the job isn't finished until the paperwork's done. I got back to the U.S. after the Singapore trip and went to Lock Haven to finish the paperwork. The money Phil had advanced me had run out long before, because we were gone so long.

Phil called me into his office and shut the door. That should have been my first clue. We talked about the trip and what I thought about ferrying over the water. He made a special point of asking me what I thought of Donn Kerby. My answer was noncommittal. Then he dropped his bombshell.

Upon his return, Donn had had nothing good to say about me. I was too damned independent and wanted to do everything my way. Here I was, on my very first trip, making suggestions to and even demands of a pilot who had flown thirty ferry trips. I had even had the audacity to suggest that paying money to have someone escort me was outrageous. I was going to be a rotten ferry pilot because I was too damned independent, and Phil could have saved himself a lot of grief by firing me as soon as I walked through the door.

Now that Phil had opened this particular subject, I let Kerby have it. He couldn't fly his way out of a wet paper bag. His planning on the ground was great but he was hopeless in the air. He had no clue how to brief someone for a long ocean crossing, and he was a flying menace. That he had survived thirty trips was amazing. He flat couldn't fly a plane.

But someone who has flown thirty trips is a known quantity. Someone who has completed one single trip is an unknown. Phil didn't fire me, but my instructor on my next trip would be Ernie Kuney, his best pilot. If Kuney turned his thumbs down on me, I was through as a ferry pilot.

We settled the financial details of the Singapore trip. After paying Kerby, I made about $300. I had now devoted several months of my life to the ferry business and made a total of $300. Such a deal.

Kerby and I hissed and spit at each other for the next six months. Then we each figured out, independently, that the other person might, just might, have something going for him. We made up and became the best of friends. Donn died in 2021 and the world lost the best ferry pilot ever. I miss him.

Phil called me a couple of weeks later. "I've got a trip for you. Would you like to take a Piper Lance to Sydney, Australia?"

I was all for it but I had to ask, "How many engines does a Lance have?"

He thought I was kidding, but I wasn't. All of my experience was with military equipment. I knew that Cessna 172s had one engine and Cessna 310s had two, but that was about the sum total of my knowledge of civilian aircraft.

Ernie would be flying a Piper Navajo. A fellow named Andy Knox would go with us in a Piper Aztec. Just like the last trip, I would have to do the whole trip in formation on someone else. The Aztec was the slowest of the three, so Andy would take off first and land last. I went to Lock Haven to pick up the plane. There I met them both.

Ernie was short and squat. If he had been six inches taller he would have been perfectly proportioned. He was bald and mean-looking. A movie production agency casting for an undersized Marine drill instructor would have thought him perfect for the part. I had developed no love for DIs while in the service, and wasn't sure how I was going to get along with Ernie.

Andy was on his first ferry trip for Globe Aero. He'd made a couple of trips over the Atlantic for another ferry company but Phil wanted to break him in on a Pacific trip. Andy was about fifty-five, tall and gray. He grumbled a lot. What a crew.

Ernie laid the law down in a hurry. He was the boss. As long as I did what he said, when he said it, we would get along just fine. If I stepped one inch over the line, he was going to cream me.

He made it clear that he was the only ferry pilot in the business who knew his fanny from first base. There wasn't another pilot around who knew anything about ferrying. Only Ernie. The only reason the other pilots weren't dead was because God hadn't bothered to kill them yet. If I flew just exactly like him, maybe God wouldn't kill me yet.

I can't say he was prejudiced against other pilots. He hated all of them. He held no special prejudice against any racial or religious group. He hated them all equally, and believed that God admired him for doing so.

We cashed our checks and checked over our planes. Ernie insisted we do a test flight. I thought it was dumb, but out of the goodness of my heart, did it anyway. Besides, if I hadn't, Ernie would have "creamed" me. If the fuel system worked on the ground, it was going to work in the air. You couldn't check your radios properly on a short flight because you couldn't gauge the quality of the signal you should be getting. To test fly an airplane properly, you have to put some time on it, not a ten-minute flight.

Everything seemed OK. We made plans to leave the next day.

Ernie was the exact opposite of Donn Kerby in many ways. As far as Donn was concerned, the ferry flight began on the west coast. He said, "Go to the west coast and meet me." But Kuney wanted his little bunnies in tow all the way from Lock Haven.

The differences between Donn's style and Ernie's would continue to manifest themselves throughout the entire trip.

We adjourned to the hotel for dinner and drinks. Ferry pilots all drink. Some are hard drinkers. Kuney, Knox and I all managed to put away more than a few that night. On my first trip, Paul, Donn and I had talked about ferry flying, and ways to do it easier. On this night, Ernie talked about the other ferry pilots and how lucky they were to be alive. There was only one way to fly – his. He had no tips to offer on how to have fun on a trip. I could tell right away it was going to be in a different category.

When Kuney wasn't talking about how very dumb every other ferry pilot was, he told us stories of his many and varied exploits in Vietnam. Not only was he the world's only pilot, he was the only genuine war hero to survive Vietnam. I nodded my head whenever he told me to, which was often.

We left early the next morning. He had a friend he wanted to meet with in Wichita. I would fly in formation on him all the way to Australia. I needed more close formation experience. I didn't get enough as a fighter pilot.

We launched. I was to fly on Kuney's left wing. He was doing the navigation, but I followed our route on my charts.

My VOR navigation radio was OK at best when we left. An hour out of Lock Haven, it gave up. I told Kuney that it had quit on me and that I couldn't pick up any stations. He reacted as if I had broken it on purpose, just to inconvenience him. But since we were so near Lock Haven, I could return and have it fixed or replaced. When fixed, I should catch up with them in Wichita. I turned back.

Back in Lock Haven, John Probst played with the radio for a few minutes. It turned out that one of the antenna leads was faulty. He replaced it and I was on my way. I took off and headed west.

Given the choice of flying to the west coast and meeting up there, or doing the whole trip as a group, Donn Kerby had the right idea. There was nothing to be gained by traveling as a mob. But Kuney was the boss.

Flying by myself was a lot more fun and not nearly so much work.

I got to Wichita that evening and went to the motel to meet Kuney and Knox. Andy was there but Kuney was visiting his friend. It turned out that Kuney's idea of a ferry trip was to have his troops sit in the barracks while he went on liberty. This became a pattern that would be repeated many times.

I don't want to knock Ernie's selection of a motel, but the name may give it away: El Dumpo. It was. Nothing was too cheap for the troops.

We got our marching orders for the next day when Kuney returned to the motel. We would leave for Oakland at the crack of dawn — since Wichita was so close to the ocean, I supposed. Ernie wanted us to slow down to Andy's speed. The three of us would fly formation all the way to Oakland.

Any time Kuney was in the air, he was instructing. He was a certified flight instructor and it showed. He went over everything. This is the only way to taxi. This is the only way to take off. This is the only way to lean the mixture. It was valuable information for me. I used to think there were several ways to do each of those things. Turned out there was only one — his way. But I needed the job. Ernie wanted things done his way, so that's the way I flew.

As soon as we were airborne, he started instructing. On this day he covered the importance of a thorough weather brief. As we droned over western Kansas and into Oklahoma, he described all the bad things that could happen to pilots who neglected to get a proper brief. They could run into lower and lower ceilings until they were just above treetop level, too low to contact Center to file an instrument flight plan.

As we flew, the clouds got lower and lower. We were just above treetop level, too low to contact Center.

I looked over to see Andy Knox shaking his head. I couldn't remember us getting a weather brief before we took off. It seemed to me that we were running into the exact conditions Ernie was warning us about. I wondered if it was some kind of initiative test, to see what we would do. But as much as I needed the job, I valued my skin. I asked Ernie if we should split up the flight and climb to an altitude where we could file a flight plan and get under Center control. He wanted to continue, in the hope of finding better weather.

This was only the first instance of Kuney warning us about something dangerous and then doing what he had told us never to do.

As the clouds got lower and the ground got higher, I became more nervous. I'm willing to take chances, but only when there is something to be gained. For the life of me, I couldn't figure out why we needed to stay in formation.

Andy broke first. I saw him pull up into the clouds. I waited long enough to gain separation and then I followed him into the murk. He climbed to ten thousand feet so I climbed to eight thousand.

At this point, we were illegal. We were both flying under instrument conditions without a clearance. I found a Center frequency on my chart and called for a clearance. I had followed our progress on my chart so I knew exactly where I was. Andy spent a few minutes determining his position. Minutes later, we heard Kuney come up the frequency, also requesting an instrument clearance.

Center was slightly discombobulated by three aircraft showing up all of a sudden and at about the same position, each requesting IFR clearance, but gave us no problems. We continued westward, now under positive control.

During my years of ferrying aircraft, I would continue to see flight leaders get into dangerous situations just like this, again and again. There was nothing to be gained by our flying together, but Ernie insisted on it. He gave us a radio lecture on the importance of getting a proper weather brief, just after taking off without a weather brief. Then he led us lower and lower, until a junior pilot had to make the decision to pull away and continue under instrument control. Ernie gave some great advice, but he didn't fly the way he talked.

We arrived in Oakland safely. The ceiling there was down to three hundred feet. Even if we had been able to stay above the clouds getting there, we would have had to shoot separate instrument approaches. Nobody could be so dumb as to insist on a formation instrument approach down to such a low ceiling. Or so I thought.

Donn Kerby took the view that the easiest way to conduct formation flying was to leave late in the afternoon and do most of the flying at night. Naturally, Ernie insisted that the only way to fly formation was during the day. So we would leave early in the morning. Most of our flying would be during the day, so it would be easier to see each other.

I had now made one and a quarter trips with Globe Aero, and had learned something valuable. Formation flying is easier during the day, and easier at night. Both statements couldn't be right. But I would soon learn that no one agreed on the easiest or safest way to do anything. The only thing I had really learned was that all these guys worked a lot harder than they had to. Some of the practices they advocated were not only dumb, they were dangerous.

Every motel Ernie picked on this trip was $2 to $5 a night cheaper than the places Donn picked. Every place was so far off the beaten path that the extra cab fare canceled the savings. Every one of his selections was a dump.

Ernie didn't have a whole lot of class. I didn't think much of Donn's flying, but he was a classy guy to be around.

In the bar that night, Andy and I heard stories of how dumb all of the other ferry pilots were, and what a hero Ernie had been in Vietnam. We nodded our heads a lot. Ernie didn't say anything about having to go IFR without a clearance. Perhaps he had forgotten about it.

We fueled our airplanes the next morning, and spent thirty minutes on the compass rose adjusting our wet compasses. Ernie advocated one pilot getting out of his airplane and pointing the exact magnetic headings for the pilot adjusting his compass. I must say that all the Globe Aero pilots, without exception, knew how to swing a compass. (I would learn later that most west coast ferry pilots didn't even realize that a compass could be adjusted.)

The winds and weather looked fine for the crossing to Hawaii. After filing our flight plans, we made a trip to the food store and then adjourned to the hotel to get some sleep. We went to bed early. We had to get up at 3 am to make our takeoff time.

Andy took off at 4:30 am. Ernie and I followed at 5 am.

Runway 29, the long runway at Oakland, was about three miles from the general aviation parking. The long taxi gives the fledgling ferry pilot lots of time to think about the trip ahead.

There is a hell of a lot of water between the west coast and Australia. We'd fly about nine thousand miles in total, and often the nearest land would be more than a thousand miles away. Was this really such a great idea, in a single-engine aircraft? Or in a twin, for that matter? Was the money really worth the risk? I would fly dozens of trips from this same airport. The same questions went through my head every time.

I always came to the same conclusion. I was getting used to having food on the table and it was so nice to have money in the bank. The taxi reminded me of the epitaph W.C. Fields proposed for himself in 1925, as a joke; all the same, I would rather have been in Philadelphia.

Generally we were limited to 130 percent of gross weight for a ferry permit. The airplane was quite willing to fly at that sort of weight but needed a lot of time to think about it on the takeoff roll. At normal gross you might need 1,200 feet to take off, with no wind. At 130 percent you might need 5,000 feet. Eventually it would agree to fly; it just took some time.

Ernie got his takeoff clearance and started his roll. As soon as his wheels were in the wheel well, he reported he was through two thousand feet. The tower gave me clearance for takeoff. I started my roll. A few minutes later I was tucked in close to Ernie. I still had sleep in my eyes. Maybe it was easier to keep each other in sight during the day, but I sure would have liked a good breakfast under my belt. At this early hour, nowhere had been open.

We cruised at 160 knots. The Arrow I had flown on my first trip would do only 130. The difference may not sound like much, but the trip sure did seem to go faster.

I had gotten some great sex tips from Donn and Paul during the first flight. All Ernie ever wanted to talk about in the air was flying. How boring. We had all that time on the ground to talk about flying. I thought Andy might have some interesting sexual positions to discuss, but all he ever wanted to talk about was his wife and her alcohol problem. I rather wondered about that, because Andy drank about as hard as anyone I ever met.

Finally, Ernie grew tired of instructing. He badmouthed all the other pilots again and then tired of that, too. Andy didn't have much to say at all. Silence reigned.

I was content not to say anything. I could tell right away I wasn't going to learn any new sexual tricks. These guys never seemed to mention my favorite subject. Maybe they didn't do it.

As usual, my HF radio didn't work. Ernie had no luck with his, either, so Andy was given the dubious pleasure of having to make all our position reports. Occasionally, not having a working HF radio was a blessing.

I never really decided whether night formation was easier than day formation. I knew they were both hard work. There was no question in my mind, though, that flying at night was more peaceful. I made a mental note that I would do most of my flying at night. If you can't see the ocean, you can ignore it. The airplane doesn't know it's over water, anyway, even if the pilot does.

We droned on. Our flight plan called for us to make Hilo at about 5 pm. Unlike on the previous leg, the weather was beautiful all the way. We had the ever-present sea clouds, but nothing at our altitude. Every hour or so Andy would go out on the HF to relay our position. The flying was uneventful, just as it should be.

As we approached Hilo, Ernie asked about my instrument formation experience. I assured him that I was quite good at formation flying.

Surely he wasn't contemplating an actual instrument formation approach? He told me that any ferry pilot should learn to fly on someone else during an actual approach. If the second aircraft had lost its navigation radios, it might save his life. I agreed, but doing that was a lot like practicing dead engine landings. When you have to do it, you had better be able to, but practicing them was plumb dangerous. I kept my mouth shut, though. If he wanted me to shoot the approach inverted, I would have tried to accommodate him. I needed the income.

Hilo was reporting a ceiling at four hundred feet. We entered the clouds some forty-five minutes from Hilo. My ass was dragging, but if Ernie wanted me to fly formation on him, I was game. It seemed a particularly dumb stunt. If he did it with every new ferry pilot, he would kill someone sooner or later.

Being a particularly ornery cuss, I have always made a habit of keeping track of where I am during actual instrument conditions, even when flying close formation. It is so easy to become separated from the flight lead. When around granitic cumulus, the direction in which you *don't* want to turn becomes even more important than the direction in which you *do*.

I had to mention to Ernie that we were well past the point at which we should have started our turn back to the airport for landing. We were at about nine hundred feet and rapidly closing on some good-sized chunks of mountain. He started his turn back. A few seconds later I looked with horror at my artificial horizon. Ernie had us wrapped up in a seventy-degree bank. I wouldn't consider doing a bank that steep, even if it was clear to the moon. He was doing it in solid IFR with a wingman in tow.

I was growing less impressed with Ernie by the minute. He may have talked a safe flight, but he sure didn't fly the way he talked.

I maintained my position until we had the runway in sight. When we had the runway committed, I broke off from Ernie and made S-turns until he was safely on the ground. I landed and followed him in for parking.

He was pushing his aircraft back as I pulled up. I shut the airplane down and stretched before crawling out. Thirteen hours of formation flying followed by a formation approach down to instrument minimums wasn't my idea of fun.

"Good formation work, Bob. But why didn't you land with me? You didn't have to do those S-turns. The tower cleared us to land. It really looks good to the tower to have us land together."

"Ernie, we were never allowed to do formation landings in the service. We considered them much too dangerous. I've never done one before."

"Well, get used to it. I think they look great."

That's all I need. Now we're going to do formation landings, to impress someone on the ground who we don't even know.

A little later, Andy blew a tire on landing but didn't hurt the Aztec. The line crew towed in the plane. Ernie was convinced that Andy had made a bad landing, which caused the blown tire. He was probably right. That's exactly why the military doesn't allow formation landings. The wingman doesn't have flying speed, and has no place to go if the leader loses directional control.

We went to Ernie's favorite hotel and checked in. Naturally it was the pits. I had to give him credit: here we were in paradise and he had managed to find another dump for us. Naturally, it saved us $3 a night.

We went to the bar to discuss the flight. All Ernie wanted to talk about was Andy's landing. Maybe Andy did screw it up, but an hour of discussion didn't change anything. Ernie did say that I did a nice job of staying with him.

I told him, "Since I showed you that I can do a formation approach down to minimums, I'd really rather not do any more without some compelling reason. By the way, that seventy-degree bank so near the ground was a little much."

Ernie acted as if I hadn't spoken. He never admitted making a mistake. He was the only pilot in the ferry business who knew how to fly. All the rest were dangerous. I continued to nod my head whenever indicated.

The winds to Pago Pago (pronounced *pango pango*), on American Samoa, were nothing to write home about. We had an unseasonable fifteen-knot headwind. Ernie and I had plenty of range, but Andy would have only two hours' reserve at Pago Pago. Ernie thought that insufficient for a first trip, so we would wait for the winds to improve. We would be delayed by a mere day or two.

Hilo had the advantage of being seventy-five miles closer to Pago Pago than Honolulu is, but it lacked the advantage of an oceanic weather office. We trotted down to the flight service station twice a day to get the winds from Honolulu. Unfortunately we couldn't look at the charts, so we couldn't see the progress of the pressure systems.

We went down to the airport the next day to get Andy's tire changed. Ernie then suggested a test flight. Andy and I were already bored with Hilo so we decided to go up together. The Aztec was one of the few planes that we ferried that didn't have a tank installed in the co-pilot's seat, so I went with him. We spent an hour or so flat-hatting the countryside. We didn't do any test flying. How can you test a tire? But we had some fun.

Andy didn't think any more highly of Ernie's flying stunts than I did, but we figured we should keep our mouths shut. The important thing was that Ernie sure was impressed with Ernie's flying prowess. After all, we were both paying him $200 to pass on his skills.

We settled into a routine. We would sit around the hotel all day, have a few drinks at night and hit the sack. We checked the winds twice a day but they never seemed to change. Andy and I were getting twitchier by the day. A little of Ernie Kuney went a long, long way. We finally convinced him that we were getting cabin fever. We rented a car and took a tour of the island.

The city of Hilo lies on the east coast of the big island of Hawaii. Tourists may land at Hilo, but they take one look and split for the other side of the island. We drove around the entire island. It's beautiful. But once you've seen one sugar cane field, believe me, you've seen them all.

After five days of murderous monotony, we made our ritual daily run down to flight service. Andy and I looked over the winds. No change. To our surprise, Ernie grunted once or twice and said they were great. We'd leave that night.

Andy gave me a questioning look. If anything, the winds were not quite as good as they has been when we arrived. But Ernie was the boss.

We worked up our flight plans. Sure enough, Andy would now have only ninety minutes' reserve fuel at Pago Pago. Five days before, a two-hour reserve had been judged insufficient. Now, an hour and a half was enough. We filed and prepared to leave. I noticed that this time, Ernie got a thorough weather brief.

We left about midnight. Again, Andy took off before Ernie and me. Once airborne, I tucked into my now customary position. Ernie commenced his evening lecture. Tonight, it was on the merits of a thorough flight brief. The ferry pilot must not only get a complete picture of the weather, but should also check Notams and any other pertinent information on his destination.

I didn't remember seeing him check the Notices to Airmen, or Notams. Maybe he'd check them in Pago Pago.

Andy then said something that got Ernie started, spouting off about guns and hunting. There were just a whole lot of things that Ernie hated, but he loved his guns. He had dozens of them. He just had to tell us about his most recent display of manliness.

It seemed that the squirrels in Pennsylvania had just made their annual reappearance after the winter. Naturally, Ernie had to greet them with a bang. He had an elephant gun, a .458 caliber rifle. It fired a bullet just short of half an inch in diameter, weighing about 1½ ounces. When such a bullet hits an elephant of average size, it knocks the elephant into the next county. There being a shortage of elephants in Pennsylvania that year, Kuney picked on the nearest equivalent: squirrels.

The mere thought of using a rifle of that size on such a small target made me sick to my stomach. That was like getting rid of fleas on your dog by using napalm. I listened to his story with growing horror.

"What you do, see, is crawl up to about fifty yards from the tree you see 'em in," Ernie drawled. "You have to settle down and be real quiet. Then they poke their little noses out to see where you are. Blam! You blow them away. Then you wait for a few more minutes. The second one is still trying to figure out where the first one went, 'cause there ain't anything left of that first one, after that .458 blows him to squirrel heaven. So the second one pokes his little furry head out. Blam! He's in squirrel heaven too. There ain't nothing left but hair, teeth, and eyeballs."

I grabbed the nearest plastic bag and puked. The macho part of hunting had always left me cold, but this was ridiculous. Just *dropping* one of those shells on a squirrel would have been enough to kill. Atomizing them from a distance wasn't my idea of sport. Ernie probably would have voted Attila the Hun as "Sportsman of the Year."

He continued on in this vein for hours. He enjoyed talking about killing squirrels even more than he enjoyed badmouthing the rest of the world.

I wished Andy had never mentioned whatever it was that had got Ernie started. He ended his squirrel reminiscences by announcing he was glad to be flying the Pacific rather than the Atlantic, "Because I can carry my gun."

"Ernie," I said, "you're not really carrying a .458 rifle with you on a ferry trip?"

"Moriarty! What the hell do you think I am? Some kind of a gun nut? Of course I'm not carrying a rifle with me. I'd never be able to get it through customs. All I'm carrying is my fifteen-shot nine millimeter automatic pistol. You can sneak that in anywhere."

Did I think he was some kind of a nut? What kind of a question was that? Of course I did. But you don't tell a gun freak that you think he's a nut. Especially when he has a gun and you don't.

If Ernie had to put his plane in the ocean, his approach would differ from mine. I had already spent a lot of time thinking about sharks. All ferry pilots do.

I have an understanding with sharks. I don't mess with them and they don't mess with me. I can't imagine doing anything that might irritate them.

"Nice sharky. Wouldn't you like to be eating a big fat tuna right now? I thought you might. I saw a whole bunch of them right back there, about a hundred miles. That's right. Just keep heading that way and you can't miss them. Maybe a hundred and ten miles. Nice sharky. *Bon appetit!*"

Ernie, on the other hand . . .

"All right you mothers, it's either you or me. If you've got the guts, come and get it." Blam-blam-blam-blam-blam-blam-blam-blam-blam-blam-blam-blam-blam-blam-blam! Click.

Chomp, chomp, chomp.

We approached Pago Pago around noon. We were finally getting to the South Pacific of *Tales of the South Pacific* fame. So I thought.

Ernie wanted to do a formation landing again. How do you argue with a man with a gun? Until now, my biggest fear had been his creaming me with his plane, or getting me fired. Now I realized I might get shot if I didn't obey fast enough. If Ernie wanted to do a formation approach and landing, my only question was, "How close do you want me?" We would make the Blue Angels look like rank beginners. Anything for the man with the gun.

As we drew close to the island, Ernie briefed me on the fuel situation at Pago Pago. It was actually out of the way when destined for Australia, but you could save $100 or so on fuel. That money went into your pocket.

It seemed that the gauge on the fuel pump there had been malfunctioning for years. The slower a ferry pilot pumped fuel into his tanks, the less registered on the gauge. We were getting fuel for almost nothing. The price of avgas was already low; about sixty cents a gallon. But if you pumped real, real slow, you could fill a fifty-five-gallon drum and only twenty or thirty gallons would register on the meter. It was a license to steal.

Ferry pilots had made a game of it, competing to see how little would show on the register after filling their plane. But you were caught in a quandary. If you took two hours to put three hundred gallons in your plane, you might pay for only a hundred gallons. But all the while, the idea of a cold beer or a nice warm bed sure was tempting.

Ernie would fuel first, so he could go sit in the coffee shop and have breakfast while I fueled my plane. But the best laid plans of mice and men often go awry.

"We no hab fruel."

"What the hell do you mean, you *no hab fruel?*" yelled Ernie at the top of his lungs.

"We run out fruel two weeks ago. No hab fruel maybe one month more."

"Why the heck didn't you put out a Notam, and tell pilots who might be coming here that you don't have any avgas?" Hadn't Ernie just spent hours telling us to make sure we checked the Notams?

"We do it. Meebee ten day ago."

Mentally I chalked up one more little boo-boo to Ernie. I wasn't about to mention that he hadn't bothered to check the Notams while in Hilo. A fellow could get himself shot.

Andy landed and taxied in as we were talking. We went in to have breakfast and discuss the situation.

American Samoa had been under the administration of the U.S. government since the end of World War I. Although part of the same island chain, Western Samoa (as it was called at that time) had been given its independence ten years before. If there was no fuel in Western Samoa either, we had just earned ourselves a month's rest in Pago Pago.

Faleolo, the main airport of Western Samoa, lay about seventy miles northwest of Pago Pago. Ernie and I were all right on fuel, but Andy wouldn't have a whole lot left.

After breakfast we went over to the flight service station to see if there was any fuel in Faleolo. Luckily for us, there was. We made plans to fly there the next day.

American Samoa suffered from the same malaise of every welfare community. The people were lazy and not good for much. They had learned over a period of seventy years that the federal government would take care of their needs, forever. Here they were, in paradise. All you had to do was walk to the nearest tree and knock down a coconut to feed yourself. They wanted to depend on government handouts.

And they drank. They drank a lot, and the small Samoans weighed in at just under three hundred pounds.

There were dozens of tuna boats in the harbor, filled with fishermen from Japan and Korea, but you couldn't buy fresh fish there. The Samoans imported all their meat in cans from New Zealand and the U.S. They had gotten to the point where they were too lazy to drop a fishing line over the side of a boat. This was not *Tales of the South Pacific*.

We rose early the next day and flew to Western Samoa. Ernie wanted to do a three-plane landing this time. Having learned about the gun, Andy didn't comment. He just slid into a tight formation position on Ernie's right wing. I'll bet the troops on the ground were real impressed. All two or three of them.

After Ernie finished fueling his airplane, he came over to Andy and me. It seemed that he wanted a friend of his to take a look at his HF radio. The best way to pay him for his work was with fresh skin magazines from the U.S. He confiscated ours. Who were we to complain? We fueled. Unfortunately this fuel gauge worked properly and we had to pay for the entire load.

Andy and I walked into the bare-bones terminal and sat down to wait for Ernie. And wait. We got there mid-morning; he didn't reappear until 4 pm, with his HF under his arm. I was ready to split for the hotel and get some rest. We hadn't done much flying, but I was dragging from waiting for him.

Ernie had a better idea. He had filed us for Nandi, in Fiji, a mere nine hundred miles away. Since it was so close, we could slow down to Andy's speed, so he would have the pleasure of flying six hours of formation. I think I heard Andy mumble, "Oh, goody."

We did our now customary formation takeoff and headed to the southwest. We got to Nandi about eight o'clock at night in a blowing gale. Ernie wanted to do a formation instrument approach. Gun or no gun, Andy and I begged off.

It was time for some well-deserved rest. Kerby had told me what a jumping spot Nandi was, filled with little fucklings from New Zealand and Australia. I was eager to play tourist after nearly a week of staring at the walls of our hotel in Hilo.

Ernie had a better idea. "I'll go file flight plans for us. We might as well go on to Sydney tonight. We wasted all that time in Hilo. Might as well try to make up for it."

Andy and I murmured "Oh, goody" in unison, but not loud enough for Ernie to hear. We had just worked a twelve-hour day to fly seven hours. Flying another thirteen hours with no sleep or rest was just what the doctor ordered.

We left for Sydney and got beaten and battered by weather all the way. Ernie was in and out of the clouds the entire trip. I can't really say that I had an especially hard time keeping him in sight. Hell, I had an especially hard time just staying awake. Somehow, we made it.

When we contacted Sydney approach, Ernie requested a formation approach and landing. That took the cake. It had taken a crowbar to pry him out of Hilo. Now, after twenty hours of flying, this yoyo wants to impress the troops. I was in no shape to do any more tight formation. I looked around the cockpit for something to drop on his airplane, to cripple him.

Sydney approach told him that formation flying in Australia was restricted to the military. We would be allowed in their control area only as separate aircraft. I breathed easier and put down my bag of tools. We landed and cleared customs at Mascot, the main airport in Sydney.

Once we had cleared customs we were allowed to fly to the general aviation airport, Bankstown, a few miles away. We heard Andy coming in to Sydney as we landed at Bankstown.

I wanted to shed my airplane and get some sleep. Donn had also told me that Sydney was a dynamite town, and that I should plan on staying a couple of days. I was looking forward to seeing Deslee and going out to dinner.

After we shut down our planes, Ernie came over and told me that after taking the tanks and radios out of my airplane, I should help the Piper mechanics de-tank his airplane. He would be inside, talking to the customer.

Andy arrived. Two hours later we had finished de-tanking the three airplanes. Andy and I were weary. Ernie looked as fresh as a daisy as he came out to check our progress. I made a mental note: if I still had a job, I would not take any more ferry trips with Kuney any time soon, or maybe ever.

By the time we had all our bags packed and ready, the Piper dealer had a taxi waiting for us. Naturally, Ernie expected Andy and me to carry his bags to the taxi. Naturally, we complied. We sank into the seat and went to sleep.

I awoke expecting to see our hotel. Funny, but it looked just like an airport. Matter of fact, it looked just like the main airport in Sydney.

Ernie announced that we had just enough time to make the afternoon flight on Qantas back to the U.S. Oh, goody.

I hoped airport security would catch Ernie's gun and lock him up for a well-deserved thirty-year rest, but it was not to be. He must have stashed it somewhere in his baggage. We stumbled to the gate and crawled onto the airplane. I didn't know if it was day or night, and by then I didn't really care.

The 747 took off for San Francisco with the three of us on board. I had completed my second ferry trip. Andy fell asleep during the main course. His nose ended up in the peas as he snored. I was too tired to wake him.

THIRD TRIP: LOCK HAVEN, PA to TIRSTRUP, DENMARK

1976	from	to	nautical miles	knots	time (hours)			
					flight	day	night	inst.
Mar 25	Lock Haven	Bridgeport	192	106	1.8		1.8	
Mar 26	Bridgeport	Bangor	292	108	2.7	2.7		
	Bangor	Moncton	186	143	1.3	1.3		0.3
	Moncton	Gander	449	140	3.2	2.5	0.7	0.5
Mar 29	Gander	Shannon	1,727	127	13.6	8.6	5.0	6.5
Mar 30	Shannon	Tirstrup	692	130	5.3	3.0	2.3	1.5
TOTALS		5 days	3,538	126	27.9	18.1	9.8	8.8

I continued to be annoyed that new ferry pilots had to pay for escorts across the ocean. I had paid two experienced pilots $200 each to lead me across the Pacific. Now I had to pay another pilot $100 to lead me across the Atlantic.

In my view, I had not received the value I paid for from the first two guys. Should I have expected any more from the third?

When Ernie Kuney returned from the Sydney trip, he had nothing but kind words to say about my flying skills. Not only that, I had learned to keep my mouth shut and so didn't spill the beans on him. I would keep my hard-earned job as a ferry pilot.

After paying Ernie, I had now earned a total of $600 for several months' work. This was called "earning your spurs." Alternatively you could call it slave labor.

A WEEK LATER, Phil Waldman called to ask, "Do you want to take a Rockwell Commander 112A to Denmark?"

My flight leader would be Dave Grey. He'd be flying a much faster airplane so we couldn't fly in formation. My heart was broken but I quickly overcame my sorrow.

"Come on down to Lock Haven to pick up the airplane and get briefed by Dave," Phil said.

I showed up in Lock Haven and checked out the airplane. I had previously picked up a few Rockwell single-engine planes in Oklahoma City, back in my "domestic trips only" days. Admittedly it was slow, but it made up for it by being noisy. Rockwell just started making them and they were selling like hotcakes. Phil had a policy of slicing ferry prices to the bone in an effort to gain market share. He had picked up all of the new Rockwell dealers.

The left wing was still attached, and the right one too. The engine was out front, where it belonged. The ferry system worked fine and the plane had a full set of radios and an autopilot. I signed for it.

By this time I was on the verge of starvation. The first two trips hadn't earned me much money. I had exhausted my savings. If I was going to start making some money, it had best be soon.

When flying over the Atlantic, the ferry pilot didn't have to worry about the weather a week ahead and halfway around the world. The winds across the Atlantic were either acceptable or they weren't. I could stay at home in Stamford until they were good enough for me to go.

Dave signed for his airplane and sat down with me to brief me on flying across the Atlantic. Since the distance was so much shorter, I had to pay him only $100 for his services.

"Get a life raft and an extra ADF radio from Phil," Dave began. "He has a list of questions that the examiner will ask you in Moncton. Get them from him. Clear customs in Bangor. Get your single-engine waiver in Moncton and meet me in Gander."

Some brief. It sure was brief. Perhaps he planned to give me a more complete training session in Gander.

The Canadians had a funny system. Single-engine aircraft were forbidden to fly across Canada in conjunction with an Atlantic crossing, except with a waiver that permitted flying across Canada in conjunction with an Atlantic crossing. This document was called a single-engine waiver.

A Canadian DOT examiner (equivalent to our FAA) inspected the airplane to check that all the required paperwork had been completed and was legal. He made sure the pilot had all the required survival equipment, including fish hooks and paddle, and sufficient fuel to make his intended destination with a reasonable reserve.

The pilot was then given a tough test consisting of the following three questions.

1. When can you fly VFR in Canada over an overcast?
2. What is the lowest VFR altitude you can fly going over water eastbound?
3. On what frequency do you contact the ocean station vessels?

The answers were: Never; 5,500 feet; and 121.3.

However, there had been no ocean station vessel between Canada and Shannon since 1972. It takes the Canadians a while to change their tests. They were still asking that last question in 1984. I expect they have gotten around to updating it by now.

After cashing my check, I took off from Lock Haven and flew to Bridgeport, Connecticut. Kathie picked me up and we went home. I left for Gander early the next morning, via Bangor and Monckton. After clearing customs in Bangor, I flew on to Moncton. The single-engine waiver examination was a piece of cake. I flew on to Gander to wait for Dave Grey.

This was my first whiff of Canadian weather. Their regulations require a flight plan when coming into Canada, so I filed instruments. It was just as well. The weather tends to be soggy. I had to make my approach into Moncton to a fairly low ceiling, and then again into Gander. I was glad of my experience in the Marine Corps, because instrument flying in Canada is much tougher than in the U.S. since low ceilings are common. Canada was no place to learn to fly under instrument conditions.

It seemed that every ferry pilot had his preferred places to stay at every fuel stop. Dave Grey liked the Sinbad Motel, so that's where I stayed. He showed up two days later with Ernie Whelen, another Globe Aero ferry pilot. Ernie was going to Germany and had decided to tag along.

We met in the bar for drinks and dinner. I was still waiting for my flight brief. After all, I was paying Dave $100 for it.

Ernie said flying the Atlantic was a piece of cake. "Go up to Gander and take a right. The first island you hit is Ireland. If what you hit isn't an island, you either went too far north or too far south and you're in Europe. No sweat. You can't possibly get lost."

The wintertime winds across the Atlantic tend to be from the west. If the pilot has lived an especially clean life, sometimes the Trim God makes them strong westerlies. Such was the case. We had a fifty-knot wind, right on the tail. The crossing would be relatively swift.

Dave and Ernie had fast twins and so would cross in less than ten hours. I would make Shannon in about eleven hours.

Ernie handed me a flight plan for the 1,700-mile trip to Shannon. I noticed with some surprise that it called for us to fly over Ocean Station Charlie. No ocean vessel had been at point Charlie for almost four years. We would be flying thirty miles out of our way to pass over a bit of water where there *used* to be a vessel. I pointed this out.

"Oh, yeah. I haven't gotten around to figuring out a new flight plan yet," Dave replied.

Four years, and he hadn't taken ten minutes to prepare a new flight plan that would save him thirty miles of exposure to a hostile ocean. The more I saw of experienced ferry pilots, the more I wondered.

The last thing we did before leaving Gander was to swing our compasses. The unused runway, 09–27, might have been made for the purpose. It was perfect. It never took more than ten minutes to swing a compass there. I picked up my clearance and left. Ernie and Dave left soon after me.

FNGs tended to be viewed with suspicion by the older, more experienced pilots. Dave and Ernie had flown together for years. Each knew the other's habits, and they were comfortable with one another. I was the new guy. They weren't interested even in talking to me, much less helping me. If I made it, fine. If not, then I'd be one of the ten percent killed each year. It was clear to me that either option was OK with them. New ferry pilots were a dime a dozen.

Of our three HF radios, mine was the only one that worked, so I had the duty of making all the position reports. But halfway across, my radio crapped out too. We transmitted our positions to commercial aircraft flying far above us. The North Atlantic was always a veritable freeway for commercial aircraft. Someone was always willing to relay our position to either Gander or Shannon, depending on our location.

Ernie and Dave were much faster than my 125 knots, but we were flying the same track. They should have passed me about four hundred miles out of Gander.

As we flew closer to Shannon their radio transmissions became weaker and weaker. The strength of a radio signal is a clue to the receiver's distance from a transmitter. If the signal is strong, you're close to a station. The further you are from a station, the weaker the signal becomes.

At eleven thousand feet I should have been able to hear them clearly, out to at least a hundred and fifty miles. At this point they should have been no more than a hundred miles in front of me, but I had lost them completely.

Somebody was off track. Since they presumably knew what they were doing, I was probably the one who was lost.

Like the old airline captain said, "I've got some good news and some bad news for you, folks. The bad news is, we seem to be hopelessly lost. But the good news is that we're making fabulous ground speed." I was off track but making great ground speed.

In a gratuitous moment, Dave had mentioned that Shannon had a strong ADF station on a frequency of 252. I dialed that into my ADF. Sure enough, the needle pointed about ten degrees to the left of my nose. I turned left and pointed to the station. Somehow I had managed to fly south of the track.

Or had I?

As I got closer to the transmitter, I turned up the volume to identify the station. I wrote down the Morse code and then checked it in my flight manual to confirm I had the right station. The Morse letters were not those of the station I was tracking.

I searched the chart to find the station I had identified. Oh, God! I was homing on 253, which was a station in northern Norway. I was off track to the north instead of the south. By turning left I had compounded my error.

I started dialing in VOR frequencies to get a cross-bearing. By the time I had pinpointed my location, I was two hundred and fifty miles north of Ireland.

Now I was in a quandary. Should I press on to Denmark or fly to Shannon as planned? Dave was expecting me in Shannon. But if I turned south to Shannon it would cost me several hours of fuel, and at my expense.

I turned south. It really wouldn't be fair to let Dave think he lost me.

By the time I arrived, all the restaurants were closed. I found Dave and Ernie in the bar of the Shannon airport hotel. All there was to eat was a warmed-up ham and cheese sandwich. I sat down to eat the first of the dozens of ham and cheese sandwiches I would eat at that hotel.

"Where have you been? We've been waiting for hours."

"I somehow ended up two hundred and fifty miles north of track. I was homing on a station in Norway."

"You dumb shit!" said Ernie. "Fly your flight plan. If you start homing on a station halfway across the ocean, you're going to get lost every time. The signal strength is just too weak, that far out."

"I *was* flying my flight plan, until I figured I was about two hundred miles out. I was off track right from the beginning. I can't figure out how."

Dave asked, "Where was the stick when you swung your compass?"

"Right there, stuck in the panel. Where it always is." What kind of question was that? I wasn't about to put the yoke on the back seat until I finished the trip.

"No. What I mean is, did you pull the yoke back into the position it's in when you're flying?" Dave continued, "The compass on the Rockwell is super-sensitive. If the yoke isn't in exactly the same position as when you're flying, your compass will be ten or fifteen degrees off. Didn't you know that? I thought everyone knew that."

My nostrils flared as I replied, "Gee whiz, Dave. Thanks for telling me. This is the first Rockwell I've ever swung the compass on. I've never heard of a compass so sensitive that the yoke position affects it. Sure glad you happened to mention it. How about telling me in advance next time?"

I was fuming. What the hell was I spending $100 on?

"Ernie and I figured you were going off track. We just wanted to see when you would figure it out."

The pricks. I couldn't help but wonder what they would have done, had we been over the Pacific.

Dave said the best procedure was to leave Shannon early in the morning. We could deliver to the customer in time to remove the tanks and catch a return flight to the U.S. the same day. There was no sense in wasting money on an extra day in Europe unless I felt like playing tourist.

That was the only thing Dave taught me on the entire trip that made any sense. A hundred bucks didn't buy much, even then.

I got up early and flew to Denmark. Since I had no portable radios, the de-tanking took but a few minutes. The customer shoved me on a flight to Copenhagen and I was home that evening.

This trip had taken only six days. Even after paying Dave Grey, I cleared over $500. There was money to be made in the ferry business after all.

Thinking about my three flight leaders, I realized that I had learned something valuable from each of them. It takes a strong ego and big *cojones* to fly across the ocean in a general aviation aircraft.

Clearly, of the three, Donn Kerby did the best job of showing a new pilot what to expect from ocean flying. His brief and flight plans were superb. He was by far the best at planning.

Ernie Kuney did the best job of training, even if he didn't follow his own advice very well.

Dave Grey taught me that if I used my head, I could make mistakes and still survive.

I wasn't impressed with the overall job that any of them were doing. But maybe I could devise a style of my own that would get me across the ocean safely, allow me to have some fun on the ground, and make money at the same time.

After I finished this third trip Phil Waldman told me, "Now you're fully qualified for both Pacific and Atlantic crossings. You're on your own, tiger."

No longer would I be tied to the vagaries of another pilot. I was a ferry pilot.

Now it was time to show what I could do.

SIXTH TRIP: LAKELAND, FLORIDA to SINGAPORE

1976	from	to	nautical miles	knots	time (hours)			
					flight	day	night	inst.
Apr 20	Lakeland	Dallas	818	120	6.8	6.8		
	Dallas	Yuma	906	121	7.5	5.0	2.5	
Apr 21	Yuma	Oakland	477	106	4.5	4.5		
Apr 22	Oakland	Honolulu	2,091	133	15.7	11.7	4.0	2.0
Apr 24	Honolulu	Wake Island	2,002	140	14.3	8.9	5.4	2.5
Apr 25	Wake Island	Saipan	1,210	138	8.8	5.8	3.0	1.5
Apr 27	Saipan	Bandar Seri Begawan	1,931	131	14.7	2.7	12.0	3.5
	Bandar Seri Begawan	Singapore	703	121	5.8	5.8		
TOTALS		7 days	10,138	130	78.1	51.2	26.9	9.5

Figuring out time zones and using the date line to determine which day it is on either side is easy, once you learn the trick. Unfortunately it takes about twenty years to learn the trick. I've seen ferry pilots who were math majors in college go crazy trying to figure out time zones.

"Let's see, if it's 4 pm in Lakeland, and England is five hours difference, then it must be nineteen hundred Zulu in London. Or is it oh-nine hundred? Hello, I need London information. What time it is right now?"

PHIL WALDMAN HAD BOUGHT Globe Aero in 1975. He started to change it immediately from a one-man band into a more professionally run business. He was picking up new customers left and right by charging far less than any other ferry company.

But those were the glory years, and every ferry company had all the business it could handle. The dollar was falling to new lows every day. The price of avgas had doubled, but was a long way away from choking the sales of new airplanes. Cessna, Piper, and Beech were selling every airplane they could make. It seemed like it would last forever.

Without exception, every ferry pilot I ever met wanted to fly heavy iron. If Phil offered a choice between a Piper Warrior (single engine) and a Piper Navajo (twin), every pilot would immediately jump in the twin.

But I was flying Phantom jet fighters when I was twenty years old. Pure speed didn't mean squat to me. After you've done Mach 2, what's a few knots between friends?

A Piper Navajo to Australia might pay $800. A Piper Lance at the same speed, but with one engine less, would pay $1,200. For exactly the same flight time. You didn't have quite as many gauges to worry about, either. Phil always had pilots salivating over the twins, but a pilot willing to take the less desirable airplanes could make more per trip, and could make more trips.

As I mentioned, one of the reasons Phil was in the market for new ferry pilots was his planned move to Lakeland, Florida. When he bought the business from Walt Moody, Walt was operating out of a hangar in Lock Haven little larger than a garage.

Piper had opened a major facility in Lakeland. Phil visited Lakeland and liked it immediately. It had a major airport sitting virtually empty, in the center of Florida. It was near Tampa and Orlando, so getting to and from it was easy. He negotiated a very favorable lease and proceeded to build a Globe Aero facility. But most of Globe's pilots were from Pennsylvania, and some weren't interested in making the move south.

While I was gone on one of my trips, I sent Kathie down on a scouting expedition. She picked out a house that we fell in love with. We loaded our secondhand VW and furnishings and three cats into a U-Haul truck and made the move south. We were settled in comfortably before Phil had his first airplane tanked.

I wasn't in the business to pick up twin time and I wasn't worried about whether a plane had an autopilot. I had as many trips available to me as I could handle. Once Phil set me free to fly on my own, I really started to make some money. He started to learn that he could always count on me to fly the trips no one else wanted.

When I returned from Denmark, Phil had planes lined up on the ramp, ready to go. I made two quick three-day trips to Europe in singles and then spent a few days resting at home. In a matter of three weeks, I made over $2,000. Not bad for a new guy.

Then the phone rang. It was Phil, asking me to take a Cherokee Six to Singapore. I hadn't been to the Pacific for a month, so I agreed.

The airplane was bound for Manila. By now, we'd figured out that the dealer in Manila wasn't doing anything about getting us clearances to enter Philippine airspace. I'd take the plane to Singapore. They could sort out how to get it to Manila. The plane had a full set of radios but no autopilot. This was no big deal for an experienced ferry pilot of five trips.

Being in Lakeland was so much easier than flying out of Stamford. In Stamford we had a small, comfortable condo purchased three years before. We were ready to move up to a larger house, but a decent size house in Connecticut would cost $60,000 or more.

Imagine, $60,000 for a house.

But in central Florida we had a large, brand new, four-bedroom house for $41,000. Kathie found work as a secretary to the director of engineering at Piper. She was happy as a bug in a rug. As for me, rather than spending $100 and the best part of a day to get to Lock Haven, my trip to the airport in Lakeland was a ten-minute drive.

I looked the airplane over. The Cherokee Six had fixed landing gear, but a powerful 300-horsepower engine. At crossing weight, it was just as fast as the Rockwell singles we were taking to Europe. I fueled it, tested the ferry system, and prepared to leave early the next day.

One advantage of flying westbound was that you always chased the sun. Instead of having ten or twelve hours of daylight, you might have fifteen.

I left Lakeland at 8 am, intending to visit an old friend in Dallas. Arriving at Dallas, I learned from his wife that he was on a flight and wouldn't return until the next day. No problem; I could visit him on the next trip. I jumped back into my winged chariot and continued westward.

As I continued toward the Pacific, my mind turned to the important questions of life. I had hours to kill and could consider questions worthy of philosophers, such as what I'd like to eat, and where. If I were to continue on to Oakland, it would be midnight before I arrived. But I could stop somewhere *en route*, such as Yuma. I remembered the great Mexican food we used to eat there when on weapons training.

So I landed in Yuma. Mighty Phantoms took off on one side of the airport; little Cessnas practiced touch-and-go landings on the other. It was evening. I went into the airport bar to have a beer and watch the planes take off. The military runway must have been a half-mile away, but I could feel the walls tremble when the afterburners of the twin J-79 engines of an F-4 were turned on. Was I really flying that monster when I was a kid?

This was really the life. All my bills were paid. I had money in the bank. I owned a beautiful home and had a wonderful loving wife. The previous week I'd been freezing my buns off in Geneva. A week from now I might be getting a suntan in Saipan or shopping in Singapore. If I felt like having Mexican food I could hop into my chariot and fly to Yuma. It was enough to make me wonder what the peasants were up to.

I finished my beer and went out to eat. It was just as good as I remembered. The only thing that could have made it better would have been to share it with a good loving woman. This was how the upper crust were supposed to live.

I left the next morning for Oakland. I had about a ten-knot tailwind to Honolulu. That was fine with me, so at zero dark early I left. I arrived in Honolulu, refueled the plane and headed for downtown.

Donn Kerby had the right idea. Ferrying is hard enough work. When you get to a nice spot, enjoy it. I still had to obtain permission from the Air Force to land on Wake Island so I had a couple of days to kill in Hawaii. I lived it up. This wasn't such a bad way to earn a living.

Once I had received the Papal dispensation to land at Wake, I was on my way. I made great time on this trip, and the expenses that I avoided went directly into my pocket. I left that evening and felt the sadness I would feel every time I flew out of Honolulu. The place had tourists running around like a dog with fleas, but I never had an unpleasant stay.

I arrived on Wake Island the next morning. Since it was on the other side of the date line, it was either the same day I departed Honolulu or two days later. I never could figure out which.

The line chief came out and asked if I wanted to fuel now, or three days from now. I told him that I didn't want to do either. I wanted to get a good night's sleep and leave the next day. It seemed I couldn't do that. I had landed on a Sunday after taking off from Honolulu on a Friday. Wake was closed on Monday and Tuesday. It was a choice of fuel and leave today, or wait for three days to leave.

Wake Island was the pits. There were only two white women there, both married and ugly. After a three-night stay the sheep would be looking good. And there weren't any sheep. The island's only socially redeeming quality was the dirt cheap booze. You could stay ripped for three days for a few dollars. I wasn't sure my liver was up to the job.

I made my first mistake right then.

"Fuel me right now. I'm leaving as soon as I can file my flight plan."

Saipan was only 1,500 miles west of Wake Island. Nothing, for a real ferry pilot. The winds were easterly, at twenty knots, so I had a tail wind all the way.

But my plane had no autopilot. I had flown fourteen hours to Wake and my bod was already dragging. What would another nine hours do to me?

But I had a secret solution to the problem. This was my second (but not final) mistake.

I filed my flight plan. By the time that was done, they had my plane fueled. It took only a few minutes to pay for it, and my landing fees. I was in the air less than two hours after my arrival. At this rate I would be in Saipan by 9 pm.

One of my fellow Globe Aero ferry pilots lived on the west coast. Like everyone else on the west coast seemed to be, he was a purveyor of fine chemical substances. I have never used dope in any form and had no intention of starting. But he convinced me that it wasn't a bad idea to carry a few bennies. If I ever grew really, really tired on a ferry trip, not only would the pill make me feel great, the amphetamine would wake me right up.

I was exhausted. It was all I could do to keep my eyes open. I had made a mistake in deciding to leave Wake without a rest. I was in no condition to fly. Three days there would have been a bore, but wouldn't have killed me. If I fell asleep in the airplane, I would become another Amelia Earhart mystery.

I wonder what really happened to Bob Moriarty? He was such a great pilot, but he disappeared on a trip to Saipan.

Who?

I popped one of the bennies.

Nothing happened immediately. Matter of fact, nothing seemed to happen at all. But I soon started feeling much better about the trip. Nothing could kill me. I was invincible.

But I noticed something strange. Right about the time I started feeling better, my watch slowed down. Way, way down. My supplier of chemical substances had told me about the sensation of well-being but had not mentioned that time slows down. My watch showed a flight time to Saipan of almost nine hours but the trip seemed to take three weeks.

As I neared the island, every bone in my body was aching. I felt like I had toothpicks keeping my eyelids open. But at least Saipan always had good weather. I wouldn't have to shoot an instrument approach.

Well, Saipan *almost* always had good weather. This time I could see a thunderbumper towering to fifty thousand feet and beyond. Right in the heart of that cumulonimbus was the airport.

I tightened my seat belt as tight as it would go and went to fight the fierce dragon. I was so tired that by this time I was seeing double. I couldn't focus on the instruments. But it didn't matter; they were bouncing up and down at an incredible rate.

I fought my way through the clouds and saw the runway. Or, I should say, I saw all four runways. I landed on one and managed to find a turnoff. I finally shut down the engine after flying over twenty-three hours, with one fuel stop and no rest. It took time to gather enough strength to fall out of the cockpit. I almost drowned as I crawled into flight operations. Death would only have made me feel better at that point.

I never took another bennie.

My flight from Saipan to Bandar Seri Begawan in Brunei was boring. So was the last leg into Singapore, just the way a good ferry flight should be.

12th TRIP: LAKELAND, FL to ABIDJAN, IVORY COAST

1976	from	to	nautical distance	knots	time (hours)			
					flight	day	night	inst.
Jun 4	Lakeland	Bridgeport	903	103	8.8	8.8		
Jun 5	Bridgeport	Boston	119	100	1.2	1.2		
	Boston	Gander	798	109	7.3	4.3	3.0	
Jun 6	Gander	St John's	114	114	1.0	1.0		
	St John's	Tenerife	2,034	136	15.0	7.0	8.0	3.0
Jun 7	Tenerife	Abidjan	1,810	121	15.0	5.0	10.0	2.5
TOTALS		3 days	5,778	120	48.3	27.3	21.0	5.5

Now that Phil Waldman was letting me go out on my own, I was setting the world on fire. I flew four and five trips a month. I was on the way to setting a new record for the total number of ferry trips flown in one year. I flew anything, anywhere, any time. I made so much money and made ferrying look so easy that other pilots were becoming a bit jealous.

Phil knew he could count on me to take the airplanes that none of the other pilots would fly. He was counting pennies a little too closely and thought he could take advantage of me. He could, but I would be pushed only so far.

GLOBE AERO GREW TO BE the largest ferry company in the world. It was also the cheapest. That had a lot to do with it being the largest. But while pilots working for competitors were making twice the money per trip, they were making only one-third as many trips. At Globe Aero a pilot could make as much or as little money as he wished. Some pilots wanted to ferry only twins, and were content with ten trips a year. I would fly anything and was well on my way to delivering forty-two planes in my first year.

We had another big advantage over all other ferry companies. Phil's customers spanned the globe. Expressed as dollars earned per day, a trip to Europe paid the most. But due to the decline of the dollar, Europe was expensive. You couldn't play tourist and make money. But we had lots of trips over the Pacific as well, to Australia and New Zealand and Singapore. If you wanted a break from the rigors of Atlantic flying, you could take a nice comfortable Pacific trip and improve your tan.

The west coast ferry companies flew the Pacific. Period. The east coast ferry companies flew the Atlantic. Period. Globe Aero went everywhere.

I was down at the hangar one day. Phil asked, "Want to take a Cherokee 181 to Africa?"

It was the smallest and slowest airplane Globe delivered. None of the other pilots would fly it at any price. I said, "Sure, but how much is the contract?"

It was going to Abidjan, in the Ivory Coast. He would pay $1,500 for the trip. I was game. Why not? Delivery of much faster singles paid $1,500 to go to South Africa. I'd fly about the same number of hours. It was a good deal, if not a great deal.

I had traveled to most of Europe by now and had completed four Pacific trips. I was keen to see Africa. Our resident travel guide, Donn Kerby, had said that Abidjan was a great stop. I cashed my check and made my preparations.

By now I was used to the long legs and foul weather we ran into on every trip. I cleared customs in Boston and flew to Gander to spend the night.

One factor that made it possible to fly so many trips in such a short time was that I was more adaptable than the other ferry pilots. A pilot would get into the habit of clearing customs in Bangor, for example. If the weather in Bangor was particularly soggy, then rather than consider alternatives, he would sit and wait for Bangor to open up. I didn't give a damn about the weather. If Bangor was closed, I went to Boston. There was always a way to get a plane through.

Gander was our customary jumping-off spot for Europe. The weather office had the best facilities in the world and the hotels weren't bad. But St. John's in Newfoundland was a hundred miles closer to Africa than Gander was. I could have left from Gander but instead flew on to St John's. I refueled there, and flew on to Tenerife in the Canary Islands. The winds were about a zero overall so I didn't get any help. But I didn't get hurt, either.

That was my first visit to the Canary Islands. Fuel was a little pricier than I was used to, but food and lodging were dirt cheap. I slept during the day and left for Abidjan in the evening.

Given the choice, any ferry pilot would rather fly over land than over water. No matter where in the world you are, you can walk to your destination faster than you can swim to it. And navigation was far easier over land.

But this was my first trip over Africa. I flew an established air route, but none of the beacons seemed to work. I passed over a thousand miles of land and didn't have the slightest clue as to where I was.

Although used to some pretty primitive weather forecasts in the Pacific, I was unprepared for the weather brief in Tenerife. The weather office had a grand total of one wind map on the wall, and it was for thirty-five thousand feet. It wasn't much use to me, at ten thousand. I figured out a by-guess-and-by-golly flight plan. I threw in a ten-knot headwind, and went.

Abidjan is right on the coast of the Ivory Coast, so all I had to do was find the ocean. Abidjan would then be either to the right or to the left.

For the entire night, I had no cloud. But three hours after dawn I came up on a solid overcast. I wasn't about to fly under it. There were mountains around. But if I couldn't see the ocean, I sure wouldn't be able to tell where it was. I believed I was within a hundred miles of Abidjan, but wasn't receiving a thing on any of my radios.

I spotted a landing strip. I figured there must be someone around down there who could tell me where I was. I landed. A native came up to the airplane and peered inside. Evidently he had never seen a light plane with so many fuel tanks in it before.

I pulled out my chart and asked him where I was. He didn't speak any English and I didn't speak any of whatever he was speaking. Evidently, he had never seen a map before. I could see that he thought it was pretty. Matter of fact, he wanted to take it, I suppose to show his wife or wives. But it was the only one I was carrying, and I wasn't letting go of it.

Finally I managed to learn from him that this was indeed the Côte d'Ivoire. I kept saying "Abidjan" and finally he pointed to the south. I couldn't establish how far it was. But if I was in the Ivory Coast and Abidjan was to the south, I wasn't far off track. I took off again and headed south.

When I say that a ferry pilot lives in his plane, I mean that emphatically. Everything I would do during the day or night, I did it in the airplane. Except make love or play poker. There wasn't enough room for either. Or anyone to play with.

I had eaten in Tenerife. I felt a bodily need coming on. My piss jug was built to unsuitable design criteria. I needed to do a "number two," as a child in the second grade might say. Or take a dump, as one of the more couth ferry pilots might describe it.

I had no special container for the purpose, but did have a two-quart insulated jug. I had bought it for this trip, to keep lemonade cold, thinking that if necessary it could double as a toilet. Normally, at the end of the trip I'd have given the jug away. They cost about $5 and weren't worth carrying back to Florida.

I did my job. Everything came out just fine. I made a mental note to be sure to dispose of the jug in a responsible manner once I reached Abidjan.

If I could ever find the place.

I flew on. About an hour later I started picking up a VOR signal from Abidjan, and a while after that I landed. The customer met me at the airplane and turned his mechanics loose, to pull out the tanks and temporary radios. I found the nearest trash barrel and stowed the jug under some trash.

Evidently I had been observed. While packing my gear into my flight bags, I saw a native sneaking over to the trash. I could tell by the way he was looking at me that he intended to retrieve that jug. I walked back over and retrieved it myself. When I thought he wasn't looking, I pushed it much deeper into the trash.

One hour after my arrival, I was packed and ready to go. I had reservations back to the U.S. on Pan Am the next day. I took a taxi into town and checked into the beautiful Intercontinental Hotel. As we drove past the trash barrel, I saw my now familiar native pulling out the juice jug yet again. I'll bet he was surprised when he opened it.

I got into Abidjan early enough to get some rest and still have time for a look around. By the time I boarded the Pan Am flight I was carrying three masks, a spear, and a few bracelets. Kathie never showed any appreciation, but I always brought her something from everywhere I flew.

I was pleased with the trip. I had left Lakeland four days before and had flown almost fifty hours. I was able to pace myself on my trips and still fly ten to twelve hours a day. I was back in Lakeland five days after I left.

I went into Phil's office to settle up. It had cost more than he had planned, so he would have to come up with some extra money if I was going to clear the promised $1,500.

Phil went into a song and dance about how he had not quoted the customer enough for the trip. If he paid me $1,500, he wasn't going to make any money. I told him that I ran the trip faster and cheaper than any other

Globe pilot could have done. If he had underpriced it, that was really his problem and not mine.

He persisted and I finally settled for $1,200. It left a sour taste in my mouth that took years to go away. It wasn't right to renegotiate the price of a trip after a pilot has put his life on the line. I was being taken advantage of and I didn't like it.

13th TRIP: LAKELAND, FL to NEUCHÂTEL, SWITZERLAND

1976	from	to	nautical miles	knots	time (hours)			
					flight	day	night	inst.
Jun 11	Lakeland	Bridgeport	903	120	7.5	2.0	5.5	1.8
Jun 14	Bridgeport	Boston	119	99	1.2	1.2		
	Boston	Portland	87	87	1.0	1.0		
Jun 15	Portland	Portland	0	0	1.2	1.2		
Jun 16	Portland	Gander	724	151	4.8	3.8	1.0	2.5
Jun 17	Gander	Jersey	2,021	156	13.0	5.0	8.0	3.0
Jun 18	Jersey	Neuchâtel	385	128	3.0	1.0	2.0	0.5
TOTALS		7 days	4,239	134	31.7	15.2	16.5	7.8

Every ferry pilot I knew drank. Some of them might be said, uncharitably but accurately, to have drunk to excess. But I had never seen any pilot anywhere take a drink, leap into a plane, and then pull out a bottle for some more. Right after pulling up the landing gear. But then, I hadn't flown with any European pilots before.

I had thought that merely flying across the ocean was an adventure. But nothing could match the adventure of flying from Neuchâtel to Geneva with a drunken pilot.

AS SOON AS I RETURNED from the Abidjan trip, Phil had another Rockwell for me: a 112TC to be delivered to Switzerland. I signed for it and got my check from him.

We ferry pilots flew on a contract basis. I seem to remember that the contract for a Rockwell was about $1,400. Fuel for a single to Europe was about $150; for a twin, about $300. We could count on spending $300 for airfare home and maybe $250 on all other expenses. A well-run trip to Europe would net the pilot $700 to $800 for a single, maybe $600 for a twin. A fast trip would take three days. Rarely would any trip to Europe take more than a week.

I left Lakeland and flew to Bridgeport, Connecticut. The winds to Ireland went sour for a few days, so I sat until they improved. Once they became acceptable, I flew to Boston and cleared customs. The Department of Commerce keeps track of all exports from the U.S., so we had to stop at customs and provide export documents on every trip.

As I left Boston, my engine-driven fuel pump quit. I turned on my electric fuel pump and diverted to Portland, Maine for maintenance. The nearest Rockwell dealer was there.

We had a recurring problem with fuel pumps on Rockwells that took six months to fix. For some reason, the ferry system got air bubbles in the fuel lines. Instead of delivering a steady stream of fuel to the pump, air got in the lines. The mechanically-driven diaphragm pump was designed to pump liquid, not air. Often it would fail due to the shock of air in the lines.

At first we tried replacing the pumps with overhauled pumps, but they would fail after only a few minutes of use. It had to be a brand new pump, and they often took days to arrive. Pilots know that airplanes break sometimes, but we had so many delays due to broken fuel pumps that Phil almost had a revolution on his hands. We told him, "Fix it, or we ain't flying 'em." Any expenses due to delays caused by mechanical failures came right out of the ferry pilot's pocket.

This time it took only a day to get a new pump installed. The winds to Europe were great, and after a night in Gander I was on my way. I had a forty-knot push all the way.

Phil believed that the image of ferry pilots needed improving. He wanted us to stop overnight somewhere close to our final destination, get a good night's rest, and then deliver the airplane wearing a suit or a sports coat and tie. After a long day in a cockpit, any pilot started to smell a little gamey. I crawled out of a plane in Sydney once, and a goat munching grass downwind of me keeled over and died.

Maybe Phil had a point. But one of my reasons for taking the job had been that I hated wearing suits or ties (and still do). I'd get out of the plane wearing a coat and tie, but they would come off two minutes later.

I had been into Shannon half a dozen times by now. I was bored with Ireland. The weather forecast was always the same: drizzle and low clouds. I wanted to find an overnight spot with a little more action. Donn Kerby had favorable things to say about the island of Jersey, just off the French coast, so I made it my destination.

Everything Donn said about Jersey was true. Shannon had seen so many ferry pilots come and go that we were commonplace. But in Jersey we were a novelty. Someone would always come up and want to talk to you about the trip. Even though we were ferrying every day, it was always fun to talk about it. The fuel was cheap there, and there was a neat little hotel about a quarter of a mile from the airport.

The English had some strange drinking laws. Everything was regulated, from opening times to closing times to the amount of beer in a glass. Even at the end of my ferrying days, years later, I still didn't know all the rules.

The bar in that little hotel also had some unwritten rules. The women had to outnumber the men by four to one. They had to be fine-looking and horny. Phil's policy of getting a good night's rest before delivering went right down the tubes. "My dear," said I, "wouldn't you like to come up to my room and see my tattoos?" Or something.

Early the next morning I stumbled out to my airplane and launched for Geneva. Maybe the controllers wouldn't bug me too much and I could get some rest in the plane.

I arrived in Neuchâtel about 9 am. If I could get to Geneva by noon, I could catch an early flight back to New York. The dealer met me and took me over to the airport café while his mechanics pulled out my tanks and HF radio. He had a friend flying to Geneva who would wait until I was ready.

The Europeans had a far more civilized approach to general aviation than we had in the U.S. Aviation there was still a sport. Every airport had a little café where you could sit in the sun, sip coffee, and watch the planes come and go. I ordered coffee and a roll and sat down to enjoy the scenery.

There was another fellow there who seemed to be drinking his breakfast. I've known a lot of problem drinkers but drinking your breakfast was a little much. He strolled over and sat down to talk to me about ferry flying. I had just finished my thirteenth trip, so I was an expert.

The dealer came over and announced, "My engineers have finished de-tanking the plane. Are you ready to leave?"

I finished my coffee. I looked around for the friend who would take me to Geneva. There wasn't anyone else in the café but the drunk.

He lurched over to a nearby twin Bonanza. I threw my bags in the back and buckled up in the co-pilot's seat. He fired up the engines and taxied onto the runway. The time from starting up the first engine to the point he advanced the power for takeoff couldn't have been sixty seconds. No warmup, no magneto checks, no nothing. Fire it up and go. His treatment of the airplane was criminal.

The runway at Neuchâtel was fairly short; about two thousand feet. He advanced the throttles, released the brakes, and off we went. The end of the runway got closer and closer. At the very last second he yanked back on the yoke and we were airborne.

Sweat poured off me. I hadn't flown across the Atlantic in a single-engine airplane in order to die on a little hop to Geneva. Had I?

As soon as we were in the air, he simultaneously raised the landing gear and flaps and rolled the airplane into an eighty-degree turn towards Geneva. I tasted my breakfast again. I turned an interesting shade of green. He rolled the plane out on the heading for Geneva and set the autopilot. The autopilot would fly the rest of the trip, all the way to touchdown at Geneva. I hoped it was more sober than the pilot.

He turned to me and smiled. "Some plane, eh?"

I tried to smile back. For the life of me, though, I just couldn't force it.

He reached around behind his seat and pulled out a bottle of Scotch. "How about a little bracer? We still have twenty-five minutes before we get to Geneva."

"Thanks, but I'll pass. I think I can wait until we get there."

During that brief flight my entire life flashed before my eyes. The autopilot found Geneva and somehow made the landing. When I got out of the airplane there were teeth marks on my seat cushion.

The flight back to the U.S. was boring. Thank God.

32nd TRIP: BROMMA, SWEDEN to SUMBURGH, SCOTLAND

1976	from	to	nautical miles	knots	time (hours)			
					flight	day	night	inst.
Nov 24	Bromma	Sumburgh	588	75	7.8	7.8		2.5
TOTALS		1 day	588	75	7.8	7.8		2.5

The wisest ferry pilot I ever met once told me that there were only two kinds of pilots: those who had crashed, and those who were going to. He believed that the pilots who had crashed were better off — provided they survived — because they knew which category they were in. All the others had to wonder when they would crash. He hadn't crashed yet but knew he was going to.

Two weeks after that conversation he had his first crash. He walked away from it.

Once I had walked away from my crash, my attitude towards crashing a plane changed dramatically. As part of the check ride for a commercial ticket, the student pilot should be given an old wreck and told to go out and do a crash landing.

Everyone would benefit. The mechanics would have more work. The manufacturers would sell more planes. Pilots would learn that crashing an airplane isn't that big a deal. The fear of crashing has killed far more pilots than the actual crashes.

NONE OF THE GLOBE AERO PILOTS wanted to fly Piper Cherokee 181s. They were the slowest airplane we flew. They weren't sexy. But I wasn't flying to pick up more flight time; I flew to pick up the flight pay. By being willing to fly the slow airplanes, I could have a trip any time I wanted.

Phil had a Cherokee 181 going to Sweden. I picked it up and was in Stockholm three days later after the delivery to Nyköping. I can't remember anything about the trip, so it must have gone smoothly.

Before I left Lakeland, Phil had told me, "There might be an airplane to pick up in Stockholm. Be sure to call the office once you have delivered the Cherokee."

Any money my fellow pilots and I could save on a trip went straight into our pockets. On the rare occasions when we could ferry a plane back to the U.S., we saved the price of an airline ticket, which was our biggest expense. The Cessna dealer in Stockholm had sold a used 402 twin to a dealer in Washington, D.C. One engine had just been overhauled and the other was "midtime", meaning it was not yet due for an overhaul.

Ferry pilots are as superstitious as people in any other occupation. None of the other pilots cared to fly singles. They took them when they had to, but wouldn't go out of their way to fly one. I would lie, cheat, and steal to fly the little airplanes.

I would look into the cockpits of some of the heavy iron that the other pilots fought to fly. To me, more engines and more systems just meant more possible failures. At the weight we flew, a single turned into a submarine about ten minutes after the engine quit. A twin turned into a submarine about twenty-five minutes after *either* engine quit. The twin had at least twice the probability of losing an engine. The other pilots thought I was crazy, and I knew they were, so everybody was happy.

When I first started to ferry, I was nervous about flying brand new equipment. I soon learned that, with the exception of Cessna, the factories did a great job of testing the plane and engine and delivering it to a customer or a ferry pilot.

The kindest thing I can say about Cessna's quality control is that it sucked. At least half of the planes I picked up from Cessna had to be returned to fix some minor or major problem. Had I owned Cessna, I would have fired every single person in the aircraft delivery section. They just didn't give a damn about the customer.

If something was going to fail on a new airplane, usually it would fail during the first 5–10 hours of flying. By our being located in Florida, every plane we took across an ocean had 10–20 hours' flying before it ever saw any water. Our failure rate over the water of engines and critical systems was extremely low. Ferry flying may seem dangerous, considering the possibility of mechanical problems, but it really wasn't.

Used airplanes were another matter. They are like used cars. Nobody sells one unless there is something wrong with it. The owner is unlikely to be entirely candid with the prospective buyer, or the ferry pilot. Remarks like "You'll probably make it," were common. I wasn't interested in "probably" making it. I wanted to make it *definitely*.

In short, new airplanes were a known entity and used airplanes were an unknown entity. Anything might happen with a used plane.

The Piper dealer in Sweden was located in Nyköping, about sixty miles north of Stockholm. Once I had finished de-tanking the Cherokee and handed over the log books and papers to the customer, I got a ride into town and caught the first train for Stockholm.

One habit I got into as soon as I started ferrying was to try to pick up a few words in the language of whatever country I was delivering to. Just by knowing the words for "please" and "thank you" and "yes" and "no" and "How much does that purple and black scarf cost?" you can hold a short conversation with just about anyone. I never counted the times someone would jabber away for an hour, while at what I judged to be suitable intervals, I murmured "Oui, oui" or the local equivalent.

As the Piper dealer loaded my baggage into the trunk of the car, I said "Tak," meaning "Thank you." He beamed at me. "Oh, you speak Swedish?"

Not exactly. That was almost the full extent of my vocabulary. But the word served its purpose. All the way to the train station, he talked to me in Swedish. At suitable intervals I said, "Ja, ja." We got along great.

Back in Stockholm, I took another taxi out to Bromma, the city's domestic airport. I went over to the Cessna dealer. The 402 was just about finished. I should check into a hotel for the night. It would be ready for me to leave "first thing in the morning."

Used airplane dealers are a lot like used car salesmen. Not every word out of their mouths is true. The fourth-biggest lie in the world is, "Your airplane will be ready first thing in the morning." This means, "It isn't ready yet, but check back. It will be ready someday."

I showed up at nine o'clock, bright-eyed and bushy-tailed, ready to take the plane on its first leg, to Iceland. It wasn't ready. "Check back in an hour."

I checked back in an hour.

"Check back in another hour."

The airplane wasn't ready until that evening. I hadn't done one minute of flying all day and I was already bushed. But I didn't want to spend another night in Stockholm. The place might be decent but it was expensive. I took off for Iceland.

We were well into wintertime conditions over the North Atlantic. There was a fierce gale blowing in the North Sea. I would be fighting a fifty-knot headwind all the way.

The weather was rotten in Iceland, with low visibility and a ceiling at two hundred feet. But if I couldn't get into Reykjavik, the military base in Keflavik was only about thirty miles to the west. I knew they could talk me down through anything.

About halfway between Norway and Iceland I lost the alternator on the left engine. This wasn't a major concern to me because the alternator on the right engine could carry the whole electrical load.

Until a few minutes later.

I noticed smoke and flames coming from the right engine. That got my attention right away. I shut it down. Now I had one engine without an alternator, and about forty-five minutes of charge left in my batteries. I swore at twin-engine aircraft in general and cursed used twin-engine aircraft in particular. For a few moments I tried to remember if the right engine was the overhauled engine or the midtime engine. Then I realized it simply didn't make any difference.

If I pressed on to Iceland, I might find myself above an overcast with dead batteries and thus no navigation radios. My ground speed heading westbound was down to about fifty knots. There was no way I could continue.

I turned off every radio that I didn't desperately need. I switched to the emergency frequency, 121.5, and started screaming "Mayday! Mayday!"

I was within range of stations in northern Great Britain. They asked what my intentions were. Hell, I didn't know. I was in serious trouble — of that I was certain. Norway was completely socked in. Britain was completely socked in. My options were running out in a hurry.

They launched an air-sea rescue plane from England. It came out to my position but the pilot couldn't find me. He was talking about my landing on the water, and rescuing me once I went down. I knew, and he knew, and I knew he knew, he wasn't about to land in twenty-foot seas. If I went down, nothing would follow but sad music, slow walking, and soft talking.

I had to land, and damn quick, or become shark bait. I realized the only real option I had was to let the winds carry me east until the sun came up and I could find a place to land.

I could imagine the conversation. "Phil, I've got good news and bad news. The airplane is just fine, but I landed in Siberia. The Russians think I'm a CIA spy and want to lock me up for thirty years."

"You idiot!" he would roar. "I told you to take it to Dulles. I never mentioned Siberia. Give me a call when they let you out. If they let you out."

We went through the entire list of possible landing strips. It seemed everything was flatter than a pancake, with the ceiling right on the deck. Except Sumburgh in the Shetland Islands, to the north of Britain. They reported a ceiling at six hundred feet. Maybe I could get in there.

I didn't have an approach plate for Sumburgh so I asked the pilot of the air-sea rescue plane to read me the details. The airport was surrounded by hills. It had a very short runway. The visibility was down to zip, and the ceiling I already knew about. Once I began my landing approach, I was committed. With one engine, the airplane would be unable to climb back up.

I had only one chance to land safely. If I blew it, I was dead. Sounded just great to me.

My batteries still had some juice in them. I wanted to land quickly. Soon they would crap out completely. Then I would have major problems.

The controller vectored me over the airport. He wanted me to shoot the published approach. I wasn't about to. When I was headed westbound, I had a ground speed of forty knots. Eastbound, my ground speed was 180 knots. The difference was so great that I couldn't possibly keep track of where I was with my watch. I came over the field, turned to the west and started my descent. If there was a runway under me when I broke out of the soup, I would live.

As I passed through four hundred feet I picked up the runway lights. The wind on the ground was in excess of eighty knots, but it was coming right down the runway. I dropped the gear and landed. It was a beautiful landing. But then, I always made nice landings.

My knees were shaking as I shut the plane down. It must have been because of the cold.

There was a hotel right at the airport. I told the tower operator and controller to call all of their friends, and to come over and have a drink.

I walked into the bar and pulled out a couple of $100 bills. "The cash register is now officially closed," I announced. "Nobody in this room pays for another drink until I run out of money, and I've got more. Drink up."

I got very drunk that night; very drunk indeed. But then, I deserved it.

I stumbled out to the airplane the next day to check the damage. The mechanics already had the cowling off the right engine. The entire problem was caused by the right alternator.

Rather than being belt-driven, like in most other airplane engines, the alternator on the Cessna 402 ran off a shaft. The alternator was putting out too high a voltage, which took the left alternator off line. Then the alternator seized, which caused the parts to fly off.

Everything could be fixed by replacing the right alternator. I located one in England but the dealer was not prepared to send it to me without having the cash in his hands. I took a taxi into town and went to the main bank. Everyone on the island had heard of my escape from death. The chief cashier cashed a check for me and assured me that he would contact the parts dealer to let him know his money was on the way.

Three days later the alternator was installed and I was ready to leave for Iceland.

I got up bright and early, ready to depart. The right engine was fine now. But I was more than a little scared of this plane. It had done its best to kill me just a few days before. I hopped in, with trepidation. I turned on the battery master switch. Nothing. The batteries were dead.

The mechanics took them out of the plane and started charging them. "No problem, we can have them fully charged in four or five hours."

Oh, great. I wanted to fly to Iceland during daylight, in late November, and now my plans were wrecked. I sat around the hangar for five hours and thought about all my sins.

Finally the plane was buttoned up and ready to go. I filed another flight plan for Reykjavik. I started the plane and taxied out. The wind was blowing fifty knots at forty-five degrees to the runway. The takeoff would be an adventure in itself.

I went through the engine checks but my mind was on other things. Such as, why wasn't I flying a safe new single-engine plane out of Pago Pago?

I had learned to fly piston-engine twins on Beech 18s and DC-3s. The recommended procedure in such a strong crosswind was to advance the throttle of the into-the-wind wing. I did that, and soon had takeoff speed. Soon after that, I had a lot more than takeoff speed. The airplane seemed glued to the runway, though.

I put my hand on the elevator trim wheel and rolled in some nose up trim. Pilots use trim in all three dimensions to take the pressure off the controls. It is possible to literally fly the aircraft using just trim.

Nothing.

I rolled in a lot of nose up trim.

Still nothing.

I seemed to be glued to the runway. The end of the runway came near.

I pulled back on the stick as hard as I could.

Still nothing.

The damned airplane was acting as if the control lock was still in place, locking the controls. Matter of fact, the control lock *was* still in place.

And I had rolled in so much nose up trim that if I pulled it out, I would execute a loop and probably not come out of it.

Goddamned used planes.

I grabbed every throttle and control I could put in both hands and yanked back, as hard as I could. I would run out of runway in a few moments. It was time to shut her down and run her off the runway, or try to figure out how to swim to Iceland.

I ran the plane off the right side of the runway. It had been raining cats and dogs for days and the ground was soft. I prayed it would slow me down before I went over the cliff at the end of the runway. The plane came to a stop twenty feet from the edge.

I calmly shut down the engines. I turned off the fuel. I turned off the mags and the master switch. I opened the cockpit door and walked to a safe distance. When the plane blew up I didn't want to be standing too close.

The total elapsed time, from making the decision to run it off the side of the runway to standing two hundred yards away from it, was about 3.5 seconds.

The plane was a write-off. Both main landing gear were broken. The props were wrapped into pretzels. One wing hung down.

I had committed the cardinal sin. I had crashed an airplane. I had no one to blame but myself. If someone had handed me a gun right then, I would have shot myself. Real pilots don't crash airplanes, ever.

I had left the control lock in place. I had neglected to go through my checklist. I hadn't even checked to see that the controls were free. Pilot error, pure and simple. I could talk all I wanted about how good a pilot I thought I was, but the truth was rolled up in a little ball right next to the runway.

I called Phil to tell him. The first words out of his mouth were, "But are you all right? We can always fix the plane." Although Phil and I fought over every contract, when it counted he always did the right thing.

I was all right. But there wasn't going to be any fixing the plane. It was history.

I called our customer in Sweden. He didn't sound the least bit bothered that I had just turned his $75,000 plane into scrap metal. He said he wanted me to stay in Sumburgh until he could come over with his insurance man to inspect the wreckage.

"Do you think the airplane's a write-off?" he asked.

"You bet," I responded. He actually seemed happier that it was completely wrecked.

They flew over to Sumburgh on a commercial flight two days later. I put myself through seven kinds of hell as I waited for them to land. I was guilty of crashing a plane. I expected two somber-looking individuals to get off the plane. But I couldn't identify them. Maybe they had missed their flight.

Only two guys got off the plane, and they were as drunk as skunks and laughing. Surely they couldn't be my customer and his insurer? But they were. I felt like a five-year-old telling his father he just broke the neighbor's window. But they weren't in the least upset. They were truly concerned about whether I was OK, which I was.

We went to look at what used to be a slightly whacked Cessna 402.

"You're right," the insurance man said. "It's a write-off. Let's go have a drink and celebrate."

The Swedish dealer had sold the airplane to a dealer in the U.S. for $75,000 but had insured it for $150,000. As soon as I called him and told him that I wrecked the plane, he got on the phone to the dealer in Washington to tell him the deal was off. The guy in Washington was pissed because he too had the plane insured for $150,000.

I had just put $75,000 in the Swede's pocket. He was as pleased as Punch. He had saved himself the price of a ferry fee, to boot.

I caught the first plane I could get back to the U.S. All I wanted to do was to forget that Cessna 402.

A week later we had a pilots' meeting at Globe Aero. I was the star attraction at that one. All the other pilots agreed, in unison, that they would never do anything quite so dumb as to leave the control lock in place, freezing control movement. Each was a super aviator and never made mistakes, ever.

Bob Campbell stood up and said, "Lay off Moriarty, guys. There are only two kinds of pilots . . ."

36th TRIP: LAKELAND, FLORIDA to ZARIA, NIGERIA

1977	from	to	nautical miles	knots	time (hours)			
					flight	day	night	inst.
Feb 1	Lakeland	Boston	1,014	143	7.1	7.1		
	Boston	Gander	798	153	5.2	1.0	4.2	2.2
Feb 2	Gander	St John's	114	114	1.0		1.0	
	St John's	Tenerife	2,034	151	13.5	5.5	8.0	8.5
Feb 3	Tenerife	Kano	1,708	125	13.7	5.2	8.5	2.5
Feb 4	Kano	Zaria	92	153	0.6	0.6		
TOTALS		3 days	5,760	140	41.1	19.4	21.7	13.2

After my first ferry trip I made up my mind that I didn't want to fly with other ferry pilots if I could avoid it. The combined IQ of ferry pilots falls by twenty per cent as each plane is added to the gaggle. Every time I participated in a group flight, I saw pilots do dumb things that they wouldn't do if they were responsible for their own decisions.

Or would they?

IN PHIL WALDMAN'S VIEW, a primary cause of my accident on the Shetland Islands was that I'd been flying too much. When I returned, he told me that he was going to nail my feet to the floor and not let me fly so much. I flew only three trips in the next two months.

I couldn't stand spending so much time on the ground. I kept bugging him about it. He finally consented to let me fly more trips. But I'd have to make one trip in company with his chief pilot, Tony Vallone.

Tony was chief pilot solely because he had flown for Phil longer than any other pilot. Ferry flying doesn't lend itself to the concept of a position of chief pilot. We all flew the way we wanted. But if I had to go through the drill of passing a check ride, I was game. I would have done anything to get off the ground again.

Phil had three Piper Aztecs going to a training school in Nigeria.

Pilots all have their own preferences about planes. As I've mentioned, some Globe Aero pilots — most, actually — wanted only twins. Some wanted only to fly with other pilots. I wanted singles and had to be dragged by a team of wild horses to join a formation flight.

But I had to fly a check flight, and so I consented to taking one of the twin-engine Aztecs. Tony had another. Tim Peltz would be in the third.

Every ferry pilot is an FNG when he starts. What he doesn't know then is that he will be a new guy forever. Tony and Tim had each completed over a hundred trips and I had only thirty-five behind me, so I was a new guy. But to them I was still an FNG when I'd made over two hundred trips. They started first, so I was a new guy. Only the old hands knew how to fly.

We signed for our airplanes and departed Lakeland early one morning. Tony was from Boston, so that's where we went to clear customs. Tony liked Boston. It was the only place he ever went to clear customs.

This was another case of habit defying logic. Boston could fit one general aviation plane into the pattern with all the commercial traffic, but it took over an hour for all three of us to get on the ground. There was another delay while we all refueled in turn, and another hour to clear customs.

I could have gone to Bangor by myself and been in and out in half an hour. But Tony was chief pilot and we were going to do it his way. We were off to a great start.

Tony liked launching from Gander, even though St. John's was closer to Africa. So we went to Gander. We checked into his favorite hotel there, to spend the night. He liked to wait until after dark to leave Gander. So we sat around the next day, killing time until dark. Finally he was ready to go.

Most single-engine aircraft used heat from the exhaust to heat the cabin. Most twin-engine aircraft had a separate heater that burned gasoline to produce cabin heat.

Back then, Piper had been having problems with the cabin heater on the Aztec and the Navajo. It had a temperature-sensing circuit breaker attached to it. This circuit breaker was designed to measure the difference between the outside air temperature and the temperature of the heater. If the heater became too hot, the circuit breaker popped and shut off the heater.

It was designed to prevent heater fires. What it actually did was to shut off the heater in the most bitterly cold weather.

The heater in the Aztec was in the rear of the plane, and couldn't be reached in flight. If the circuit breaker popped, you were without heat for the duration of the trip. Experienced ferry pilots would take a piece of wire and cross the circuit breaker's terminals. Naturally, no one bothered to tell me about the heater problem beforehand.

The weather in Gander was cold and nasty. We sat around there all day. I was half-frozen before I ever got in the plane.

Gander ground control had to read the complete clearance for each airplane, even though they were exactly the same. We each had to read the entire clearance back. No wonder I liked flying by myself.

Finally we got takeoff clearance. No sooner was I airborne than I turned on the heater. It worked for a few seconds and died. The temperature-sensing circuit breaker took a measure of the night air at minus fifteen degrees Celsius and said, "No, thanks. Too cold for me."

It was pretty cold for me, too.

I was in a pickle. I wasn't wearing long johns or my cold weather woollies. We would fly most of this leg to Tenerife at night and it would be many hours before the sun came up. But we were going southeast, into a warmer climate. I thought I would press on to see how cold it would get.

I had my answer in a hurry. We were flying at eleven thousand feet. The temperature outside was minus twenty-five degrees Celsius. The good news was that it was far too cold to pick up ice on the wings. The bad news was that I would freeze to death long before we arrived in the Canaries.

I called Tony to tell him, "I'm going to stop in St. John's. I gotta get my heater fixed."

"Didn't you jury-rig the goddamned circuit breaker?"

"What? Nobody told me about a heater problem."

He responded, "All the experienced ferry pilots know how to rig the heater."

"I said, "Thanks for the information."

You prick.

By the time I landed in St. John's I had lost all sensation in my legs. I couldn't feel the brakes. I taxied in using differential power. After I shut down the airplane I couldn't walk. Two linemen carried me into the terminal.

At least I had picked the best place in Canada to freeze. St. John's had a sauna fired up in the terminal building. In I went. It took only a matter of minutes to thaw out.

I crosswired the heater and was on my way. Tim and Tony were now about an hour ahead of me. By the time I reached Tenerife, they had refueled their planes and were fast asleep in the airport hotel.

Ferry pilots would do anything to save a dollar, so we were all in the same room. That was a serious mistake. Tony snored more than anyone I had ever met. He made a buzzsaw seem quiet.

Two hours after my head hit the pillow, he was shaking me. "Wake up, Bob. We have to leave."

"Are you out of your mind? I just got to sleep."

"But tomorrow's Friday. I just realized Phil told me that we have to deliver by Friday."

I blinked my eyes and tried to think.

"Tony, are you really figuring that out right now? I just about froze in Canada and my bod is weary. I'm in no shape to fly another fifteen hours."

"That doesn't matter. We have to leave now."

"How about planning the trip a little better next time? We did nothing but fart around for three days, and now it's all a big rush."

We left for Kano. If I'd been flying by myself, I would have spent some of the flying time asleep. But you can't fly formation and sleep. Tony was in the lead. He, however, flipped on his autopilot and went to sleep. I muttered curses at all chief pilots under my breath.

This was my second trip to Africa. I had seen nothing of Africa on my first trip because all of my flying was done at night. I'd been looking forward to seeing something of it this time. But now we were in a big rush to deliver and were again flying at night.

To this day, I don't know what Africa looks like. I have never seen it during the day.

By the time the sun came up, the ground was covered by a dust storm. We were above the muck at eleven thousand feet. We shot individual approaches into Kano. At least Tony, unlike Ernie Kuney, wasn't going to go through a formation approach routine.

I was the last to land. I taxied over and parked next to Tony and Tim. Our airplanes were surrounded by a dozen soldiers, all carrying AK-47 submachine guns. None of them looked as if he knew which end was which. I didn't like that one bit. I had been at the wrong end of too many AK-47s to like them.

We went inside to clear customs and immigration. The Nigerian officials gave each of us a form to fill out, declaring how much currency we were carrying. I'd done just enough traveling to know that when a country demands to know how much money you've got on you, their money is no good. I always made it a policy to under-declare how much I had. What they don't know about, they can't steal.

The dealer's representative showed up a few minutes later. He had been taken off guard by our unexpected arrival. It seems he had told Phil that he didn't want the airplanes until the next week. We had *banzaied* across the Atlantic for nothing. If looks could kill, Tony would have been lion bait.

We were supposed to take the planes to a training field at Zaria. The dealer put a student pilot into each of our planes and off we went. Visibility was less than a mile but the students didn't seem to notice. The dust storms last for six months in that part of Nigeria. They've learned to live with it.

The conditions were below VFR minimums for flying in the U.S. but the students were quite unperturbed. We caught a glance of the ground about every five minutes, but they knew right where we were.

My guide told me to drop the landing gear and start my descent. I didn't even see the runway until we were right up to the threshold but he knew where we were. We landed and taxied to our parking position.

Every delivery was different. On this one, we caused an enormous stir when we brought in the three Aztecs. All they had at this school was single-engine Cessnas. Everyone on the field wanted to see the new twin-engine trainers.

But nobody was interested in helping us remove our radios and tanks. We had flown twenty-eight hours with only two hours' rest. Sure would have been nice to have their mechanics do the messy job of de-tanking. But we were soon finished. They crammed us and our gear into two Cessna 172s and we headed back to Kano.

Our plan was to fly to Lagos, catch a flight to London, then home. The dealer shook his head and said, "Only a fool would want to go to Lagos, my friends. There are no rooms anywhere in Lagos."

Nigeria was in the middle of its oil boom. We should stay in Kano and catch the Air Nigeria flight direct to London, departing in two days' time.

We checked into a hotel in Kano. I use the word "hotel" loosely. The place had been a British army barracks, back in the days when the sun never set on the British empire. I think the last time anyone cleaned it was some time before World War II. It was grim.

But at least it was expensive. The three of us shared a room at a cost of $175 a day. When we checked in, they wanted a deposit of $500. We were to stay for only two days and couldn't possibly charge that much. Tony wanted to pay cash but I told him to put his greenbacks away. I put the deposit on my American Express card. I wasn't real interested in having a pile of "funny money" that couldn't be changed back into U.S. dollars.

My suspicions about the real value of the Nigerian naira proved true. The official rate was $1.50 per naira, but the taxi driver was quite happy to give me two naira to the dollar. Everybody in town was quite happy to get rid of naira at a fraction of the official rate.

Tony wouldn't deal in the black market money exchange. He pointed out, "It's illegal. Besides, we have to declare our money on the way out."

I shrugged. I hadn't declared all my money on the way in, so I wasn't in the slightest worried about how much I took out.

We returned to the hotel just in time to miss lunch, and dinner didn't start until 7 pm. We were out of luck. Kano was the second most civilized city in Nigeria, but that still wasn't saying much. And Colonel Sanders hadn't gotten around to setting up any Kentucky Fried Chicken stands.

But the bar was open, so we did the second best thing we could do. If we were too late to eat lunch, we'd just have to drink it.

Doctors haven't even named all the diseases you can catch from drinking Nigerian water or adding ice cubes to your drink. We stuck to beer. It doesn't matter where in the world you go, you're usually safe sticking to beer. This beer was cold and strong. I can't remember how many we drank. But with the lack of sleep, it didn't take too many of them to knock us on our fannies. I can't even remember crawling back to our room. I was badly wasted.

I woke up sometime during the middle of the night.

Or maybe I could more accurately state that I sobered up sometime in the middle of the night. I was standing in the center of the road, two blocks from the hotel. I was attired in my Rolex watch, a gold chain around my neck, and a pair of skivvies. I wasn't real sure why I was there or what I was doing. My head sure hurt. I wandered back to the hotel.

One common denominator among most civilizations is the general attitude toward crazy people. Only a crazy person would want to take a moonlight walk in Kano, Nigeria, wearing a gold Rolex and skivvies.

When I first showed up in the hotel lobby, on my way out, the guards understood that I was some crazy white guy, so they let me walk out. But when I returned, I had sobered up and wasn't crazy, and they didn't want to let me in. These two guards had a light machine gun set up in the lobby, presumably as an aid to turning away unwelcome visitors, like me.

Finally I convinced one of them to escort me to Globe Aero's temporary quarters. I knocked. Tony came to the door. He looked at me as if I went walking in the moonlight every night of the week. He let me in and went back to bed.

In the morning I asked him what happened. He told me, "You woke me up and said you had to go for a walk. I warned you. I said, 'Someone is going to rob you, Mo, or rape you, or something horrible's gonna happen.' But you said you'd be OK."

I was. Maybe I wasn't so crazy.

I had got into the habit of buying local touristy goodies wherever I went. Nigeria had lots of goodies to buy. I filled up two large bags with my souvenirs. I was there once, and once would last me a long time.

As we left the country our bags were searched. While I had been smart enough to under-declare my cash upon entry, there was a technical detail I hadn't considered. My currency form showed I had brought $500 into Nigeria, and that I was now taking $500 out. But if I hadn't spent any money, how could I have filled two bags with artifacts? As we filed through our customs inspection, I began to panic.

Tony saved the day, inadvertently. He had changed some money the legal and proper way. Now he wanted to sell his remaining Nigerian money and buy U.S. dollars. It was illegal to take Nigerian money out of Nigeria, but no one would change it for him. Why should they change money at the official rate when the street rate was three times better?

Tony started making comments about their "goddamned funny money." These remarks made him the center of attention. The Nigerians knew their money wasn't worth the paper it was printed on, but after all, it was their country and their paper money.

I remember a line from one of the old spaghetti Westerns with Clint Eastwood: "The man with the gun makes the rules." I have never forgotten the line. Good movie, great line.

Here was Vallone. He had played the currency game and followed the rules. But he forgot that it was these guys that wrote the rules. They were stealing from him, and he knew it.

Nigeria might have had "funny money" but it was *their* funny money. They didn't want some foreigner reminding them about it while they were stealing. My two bags of goods went through unnoticed as they pondered what to do with Tony.

The head guard flipped a coin. Heads, they'd take Tony out and stand him up against the nearest wall and shoot him. Tails, they'd take all three of us out.

The guy inspecting my bags looked up at me. "Are you with him?"

"Who, me? I've never seen him before in my life. Damned Americans think they own the whole world." I picked up an English accent in a hurry.

They confiscated all of the naira Tony had bought and then let us on the Nigerian 747 going to London. There were only about ten passengers. I sat as far away from Tony as I could and still be in the plane.

The baggage handlers stole one of my bags. I never said a thing. I also never went back to Nigeria.

The trip paid $600. I know of a lot of easier ways to earn money than flying to Africa.

37th TRIP: ALBANY, GA to BARQUISIMETO, VENEZUELA

1977	from	to	nautical miles	knots	time (hours)			
					flight	day	night	inst.
Feb 11	Albany	Lakeland	250	93	2.7	2.7		
Feb 12	Lakeland	Ft. Lauderdale	151	66	2.3	2.3		
	Ft. Lauderdale	Gt. Inagua	484	88	5.5	5.5		
Feb 13	Gt. Inagua	Barquisimeto	684	91	7.5	7.5		
TOTALS		2 days	1,569	87	18.0	18.0		

Globe Aero maintained a remarkable record in safety and speed of aircraft delivery. In a field of aviation where the pilots prided themselves on their eccentricity, it managed to maintain a highly professional group of pilots. For fifteen years, Globe not only delivered more aircraft than any other ferry service; those aircraft were also delivered safely. The pilots could fly any aircraft anywhere and at any time, by themselves.

But, as with most group ventures, the mass gaggles tended to turn into Chinese fire drills. Whenever three or four seemingly safe, experienced, mature airplane drivers flew in a formation, it was almost incredible how stupid the group could be.

PHIL WAS DOING EVERYTHING in his power to pick up new customers. Price was the primary tool. He charged less than any other ferry outfit. Once established, a customer just couldn't afford to switch to another company.

As with most initial quotes given to any customer in any area of enterprise, Waldman tended towards the use of a little "bait and switch" routine. The first jobs for any new customer almost always cost him money. After a few months and a few trips, he increased the price. Once in a long while, the tactic backfired.

Everyone in any job goes through a process of earning his spurs. I mentioned that Phil used what we called "domestic" ferry trips as a means of breaking in fledgling ferry pilots.

Pilots knocked on his door daily. He needed some process to separate the eagles from the turkeys. So the new guys would find themselves on their way to Wichita or Oklahoma City to pick up the newly-assembled aluminum butterflies.

I had my share of domestic trips in my early days at Globe. They paid peanuts, and were about as exciting as counting grains of sand on a beach. But somebody had to do it, I guess. Certainly, any time Phil wanted to clear out the ready room, all he had to do was ask for a volunteer for a domestic trip. A quarter-second later, a dozen beer cans stood suspended in mid-air. I used to see people move at similar speed when the Viet Cong started dropping 122 mm rockets on our squadron BOQ in Da Nang.

Many of Phil's new customers were based in Central and South America. Flying an aircraft there required no special skills, but the distances were much greater than on the domestic trips.

The new guys loved these trips because they were to foreign destinations. The old hands hated them because of the rotten pay. A three-day or four-day trip to South America paid $200 or $300. We made $600 to $800 for a European trip of similar duration.

Someone called Globe one day and asked for a quote on an agricultural plane. How much to pick it up in Albany, Georgia and deliver it to Barquisimeto, Venezuela? Phil quoted a lowball figure.

The fellow came right back: "Fine. I have four planes ready to go. Please have them taken to Venezuela by the end of the week."

Phil didn't have enough "domestic" pilots available to deliver all four planes at the same time. He called some of the international pilots. No one wanted to take one of the paltry $200 contracts. Phil was in a bit of a bind.

When Phil was in a crunch, we were all in a crunch.

A smile of steely determination came over his face. "There will be no further international trips until these four birds arrive in Venezuela."

I "volunteered" to take a plane. The pay didn't appeal, but I hadn't been to Venezuela. We could make a busman's holiday of it. Again, Tony Vallone would lead the flight. Andy Knox took one. Tim Peltz flew the fourth.

The four of us hired a plane in Lakeland to take us to Albany, Georgia. On the flight north, we discussed the planes and how to fly them. They had round engines. I was the only one of us with any experience of radial engines, but I'd never flown an ag plane before, and hadn't flown a round-engine plane in ten years.

Agricultural planes or spray planes are designed with only one function: to deliver chemicals on crops. A spray plane is a chemical tank with wings on the side, an engine up front, and a pilot in back more or less directing matters.

Ag planes don't fly fast, or high, or very far. The pilot's attention is concentrated outside the cockpit, since most missions are flown at an altitude of a few feet above the ground. A very well equipped ag plane might have one comm radio, one nav radio, and no instruments. The planes we were to fly were about as well equipped as ag planes ever are.

The hoppers do make great ferry fuel containers, though. The factory had rigged each of them such that we could use fuel from the hoppers on the long legs. When all four of them were ready we jumped in and flew south to Lakeland for the night.

The next day we fueled the planes and left for South America. We stopped in Fort Lauderdale to clear customs. The wind on the ground was gusting to twenty-five knots. As we taxied out to the active runway, Tim Peltz managed to catch a gust of wind just as he was turning. He quickly reacted by jamming the throttle. That only made him spin around faster. Those planes were taildraggers (they had a wheel supporting the tail, rather than a wheel under the aircraft's nose), and were easy to ground loop.

Tim swears he made only three complete turns. I thought I counted four. Neither he nor the plane was in any danger. Big taildraggers tend to humble even good pilots unfamiliar with their ways.

The tower missed the whole thing.

We filed a VFR flight plan for a formation flight to Port-au-Prince, Haiti. I forget what the reason was, but we left Lakeland later than planned. We were now awful tight on time to reach Haiti before night fell. Those planes had no gauges for either night flying or instrument flying.

Night falls like a hatchet in the tropics. We passed the island of Great Inagua in the Bahamas as the sun dove into the western sea. We discussed landing there but Vallone wouldn't hear of it. We had filed for Haiti, and by golly, that's where we were going.

Individual pilots with plenty of experience can be very intelligent and very sensible. But for some strange reason, when flying in a group those same pilots can become stupid. If I'd been on my own I'd have landed at Great Inagua without a second thought. Airplanes don't care where they spend the night; good ferry pilots feel the same way. As long as it's not in the ocean.

At our latitude, twilight might last five minutes or fifteen. Long before we reached Port-au-Prince, it would be dead black. We pressed on.

It got darker and darker. We had no moon, and little visual reference with the ocean. I began to think of the fate of Flight 19 back in 1945. I was scared, but absurdly, I didn't want to be the first to turn back to Great Inagua.

The night looked like a black hole. Maybe it really was. If light couldn't escape due to the incredible gravity, what chance would we have, in our 110-knot ag planes? In my mind I saw ancient maps marked, "Beware. Great dragons here lie."

I wasn't certain what the other three were going through, but my knees started knocking. We were begging for a mid-air collision, or worse.

Andy came up on the radio. He intended to return to and land at Great Inagua. Tim and I peeled off the formation at the same instant. From afar it must have looked like one of those fancy Blue Angels maneuvers. We didn't need to discuss it.

Tony was irate and pressed on for another five minutes. Then he too decided that $200 wasn't worth dying for.

We landed in Great Inagua just as night came down. One by one we taxied in and shut down. I felt intense exhilaration; the glory of being alive after going to the very edge. How stupid we had been. Had we not been in a formation flight, I'm sure each of us would have calmly made the simple decision to land at the last safe airport. As a group, we fell into groupthink.

The Morton Salt company had an enormous salt facility on Great Inagua. They let seawater into a pond, then blocked it off. When the sun had dried the salt, they bulldozed it into a great pile and started all over again. It was real exciting to watch.

Morton maintained a guest house for company officials and the rare visitor to the island. It was in Matthew Town, the only settlement on the island. We hopped into the only taxi and headed for the guest house.

I don't remember what it cost to stay the night; a few dollars. A maid came in to fix our dinner. She even left each of us a bag lunch for the next day. We had no liquor, no entertainment, no women.

It was still a wonderful stop. It was wonderful just to be alive.

It bugged Vallone that we hadn't continued on to Port-au-Prince. He didn't understand what was so funny about landing in Great Inagua. Every time he walked out of the room, we started talking about him and laughing. We smiled a lot.

We wouldn't have gained anything by pressing on to Haiti, and we could have lost everything. Each of us had allowed our ordinary good sense to be overridden by prior plans. Each of us felt the angel of death perching on the wingtip.

It was good just to be alive.

If Tony felt we were undermining his authority as chief pilot, that was very funny. Seniority among ferry pilots was a lot like virginity among whores. Survival counted for far more.

We left early the next morning for Venezuela.

That flight, and our return to the U.S., were uneventful.

53rd TRIP: LAKELAND, FL to DAR ES SALAAM, TANZANIA

1977	from	to	nautical miles	knots	time (hours)			
					flight	day	night	inst.
Jul 23	Lakeland	Augusta	250	109	2.3	2.3		
	Augusta	Boston	900	155	5.8	5.8		
Jul 24	Boston	Gander	797	150	5.3	5.3		
Jul 25	Gander	Shannon	1,727	201	8.6	2.6	6.0	3.0
	Shannon	Bern	708	147	4.8	2.8	2.0	1.0
	Bern	Malta	739	139	5.3	5.3		1.0
Jul 26	Malta	Khartoum	1,555	145	10.7	6.2	4.5	2.0
Jul 27	Khartoum	Dar es Salaam	1,405	149	9.4	0.9	8.5	1.4
TOTALS		4 days	8,081	155	52.2	31.2	21.0	8.4

Some folks just can't take a joke. After completing this trip, I learned that Sudan had a warrant out for my arrest. For all I know, it may still be outstanding.

No one can become a real ferry pilot until he has spent a night or two in jail. This was the first time I was locked up, but it wouldn't be the last. I have not returned to the Sudan and have no plans to do so.

AFRICA IS ALWAYS IN TURMOIL. Uganda, Kenya, and Tanzania once formed what was known as British East Africa. After the Mau Mau rebellion in the 1950s, the colony was broken into more manageable pieces. As each country gained independence, it assumed a new name and formed a new government.

At first the ties between the countries were strong due to their common colonial past, but as time went on, each took on a new identity. Idi Amin took control of Uganda and went on to slaughter as many of his countrymen as possible. Communication and cooperation between Kenya and Tanzania became strained, and then came the day that Tanzania abruptly closed its border with Kenya.

The liberalism of the *New York Times* notwithstanding, tribal bonds and hatreds have far more to do with politics and revolution in Africa than any boundaries on a map, whether they were drawn in 1870 or 1954.

The area now known as Kenya has, and always has had, far greater natural wealth than Tanzania. The government of Tanzania, under Julius Kambarage Nyerere, was one of the few truly non-aligned nations in Africa (or the world), but the country has always been dirt poor. Business and industry tends to concentrate in Kenya.

When the border with Kenya slammed shut, dozens of Kenyan aircraft were impounded in Tanzania. Very few Tanzanian aircraft were impounded in Kenya because there weren't many Tanzanian general aviation aircraft.

Many people in the U.S. and Europe would like to believe that light aircraft are rich men's toys, serving no useful purpose. But aircraft are like cars. It would be silly to suggest that cars serve no useful purpose, or that the only reasonable form of transportation is a bus. It's more efficient to fly people around in a Boeing 747, but sometimes you don't have enough people who can afford to fly. When Tanzania closed its border and impounded Kenyan aircraft, it disrupted an important part of the Kenyan transportation system.

Much of the natural wealth that Tanzania did have came from the offshore spice island of Zanzibar. With most general aviation aircraft now unavailable due to the conflict between the governments of Tanzania and Kenya, there was, all of a sudden, no way to get to Zanzibar except by slow boat. The need for swift, reasonably-priced transportation between Zanzibar and the capital, Dar es Salaam, soon became apparent to everyone, even the government. Somebody's brother-in-law was swiftly given the right to fly the route, and three Piper Navajos were placed on order for the fledgling airline.

Phil called and asked, "Interested in a trip to Tanzania?"

I'm always interested in going to someplace I've never been, so I quickly agreed, even though I don't like flying twin-engine aircraft, as I may have mentioned. Bob Campbell had taken another of them, and had left about five days before the second aircraft (mine) was released. I forget who took the third. The folks in Dar es Salaam were extremely interested in getting their hands on their air force as early as possible. Phil picked me because he knew I could be counted on to make a swift delivery.

But adjusting to the vagaries of African politics would sometimes prevent swift trips, if you let them stop you. Which I didn't.

Phil started sending telexes out to get the clearances I'd need to overfly the countries *en route*. I had to stop in Switzerland to pick up a visa for Tanzania. My route would then be: Switzerland to Malta, with a night in Malta; overfly Libya and Egypt, and spend that night in Khartoum, in the Sudan. The last leg would be from Khartoum to Dar es Salaam.

I would have used Nairobi in Kenya as an alternative, but with the political problems, we were anxious that the Kenyans may have been as eager to impound Tanzanian aircraft as the Tanzanians were to impound theirs.

Qaddafi hadn't completely lost his mind back then. It was still possible for U.S.-registered aircraft to overfly Libya. Egypt was easy to get overflight permission from. Sometimes we had problems getting landing and overflight permissions from the Sudan. I could overfly Kenya but landing there was out of the question.

Learning such seemingly minor facts was an important part of any ferry pilot's continuing education. We did most of our classwork in the bar.

I spent the first night of my trip in Boston. I arose bright and early the next day and left for Canada. I then had a good tailwind and nice weather all the way across the Atlantic, to Shannon. I arrived in the wee hours of the morning. I'd flown only fourteen hours since leaving Boston. After all the single-engine airplanes I'd flown, that was nothing.

I refueled and flew on to Bern, Switzerland. I had expected to spend the night there, but getting my visa for Tanzania took only a few minutes. I was still in pretty good shape so I made up my mind to fly on to Malta. I could save one night's expenses.

Since ferry pilots were paid on a contract basis, we did everything we could to save money. If we could avoid a day's expenses by pushing on, we did. I took a taxi back to the airport and fired up my chariot.

Now that I'm older and wiser, or at least older, I realize that we did a lot of dumb things in the quest to reduce expenses. I was tired. By anyone's definition I had already put in a full day's work. But the idea of saving $80 or $100 by avoiding a Swiss hotel room appealed to me.

I left Bern about 3 pm. The weather was closer to midwinter than July; chilly and damp. The cloud base started at twelve hundred feet and only God knew what the tops were like. The Alps to the south of Bern climbed to fifteen thousand feet. With the solid cloud, I had to get above them quickly.

I had a panel filled with interesting instruments, a full oxygen bottle, and a matched set of power levers. Fifteen thousand would be a piece of cake. Or would it? I had only 850 miles to travel. With a trip of only four or five hours, I would barely have time for a nap.

Of such complacency, accidents are spawned.

The good Lord above seems to look out for drunks, little children, and ferry pilots. To this day, I'm not sure if that's two categories or three.

The cheaper we ran a trip, the more money ended up in our pockets. The Navajo carried twin Lycoming TSIO 540 engines of 350 horsepower apiece. I was far more used to my LBFs daintily sipping 8–12 gallons of joy juice per hour. This fire-breathing, gas-guzzling bitch gulped 60 gallons per hour during takeoff and climb. Normal cruise consumed a more sedate 36–40 gallons per hour.

As the power levers moved forward, the money was sucked from our pockets and blown out the tailpipe in the form of heat and noise. My aluminum eagle transformed $30 to $80 worth of fuel into smoke each and every hour. My tender 135 pounds of twisted steel and sex appeal might be worth $20 per flight hour, at best. At worst, the airplane got fed but I didn't.

No wonder I didn't like twins. It's somewhat embarrassing when a hunk of metal is worth four times what the pilot is worth, just in fuel.

I had filled my beast with the elixir of flight in Shannon. Duty-free fuel was still pretty cheap there. I had no idea what fuel cost in Switzerland because we never flew through Switzerland.

When I arrived in Bern I tried to fuel the Navajo. As the fuel man arrived at the aircraft, I asked the duty-free price of avgas. Duty-free fuel was about $1.25 a gallon, but duty paid fuel cost nearly $2. The duty-free price compared favorably but the duty paid price was damned high. I told the lineman to go ahead and fill up the plane.

As he inserted the nozzle in my left main tank, he said, "You know that U.S.-registered planes must pay the duty paid price, don't you?"

I gasped. "Whoa! Halt. Stop. Quit. *Finito.*" I managed to spit out every word I knew in every language. Two-dollar fuel in my plane? I'd rather commit adultery. But then, I'd rather commit adultery than just about anything.

"I'm on an international flight. I left Ireland this morning. From here, I'm going directly to Malta. How do you figure I pay the duty paid price?" I asked the lineman.

"All aircraft with United States registration must pay duty on fuel, regardless of origin or destination. Switzerland doesn't have a treaty with the

United States for duty-free fuel," he said nonchalantly. As if it meant nothing to him that full tanks would cost me an extra $100 or so.

Almost every country in the world had two prices for fuel, duty-free and duty paid, except the U.S. We charged no duty on gas or any petroleum products. Or, if you like, we charged a zero percent duty, so the duty-free and duty paid prices were the same.

Most other countries had concluded an agreement with Switzerland. On international flights they wouldn't charge duty to the Swiss if the Swiss wouldn't charge them.

Fair enough, I suppose. But the Swiss didn't need a treaty with the U.S. to get the duty-free price — all our fuel was duty-free. But we needed a treaty with them to buy fuel free of international duty. No treaty, no duty-free fuel.

I told the lineman to wrap up his hose. I wasn't interested in carrying a lot of extra fuel around. Especially seeing as how the cost was coming right out of my pocket. I would have only an hour's reserve by the time I landed at Malta, but their weather was clear to the moon.

That duty charge, and my objection to it, may have saved my life.

I filed my instrument flight plan, cleared the immigration paperwork, and left. A minute or so after the wheels hit the wells I entered solid cloud. I made a gentle turn to the south and continued climbing.

Non-pilots, and even many pilots, associate ice and icing conditions only with winter. This is an error. Icing is strictly a function of temperature and moisture. Airframe icing normally occurs at temperatures between zero and minus fifteen degrees Celsius. When the surface temperature falls to 8–10 °C, as it did that day in Bern, airframe icing can start at 4,000–5,000 feet above the surface.

As I passed through 8,000 mean sea level (MSL), I started picking up ice on the wings. At first there wasn't much, but I was a little concerned. I was flying through solid cumulus with lots of moisture. The temperature was optimum for ice formation and I had some pretty tall rocks to cross. I had not purchased fuel in Bern. My airplane was well below even normal gross weight and climbed like a small bird being chased by a big bird.

I continued to pick up ice at a pretty good clip. When I had first entered the clouds, the plane was leaping through two thousand feet of altitude per minute. By the time I passed through twelve thousand feet, I had collected enough ice for a good-sized cocktail party. I was picking up more by the moment.

Personally, I'm a lot like the captain of the *Titanic*; warm martinis or not, I don't like stopping for ice. Ice belongs in tea and lemonade. With aluminum butterflies and Irish whisky, it sucks.

Ice adds unwanted weight. Even worse, it messes up the aerodynamic grace of the wing. Butterflies float through the air. Bricks only plop. My graceful butterfly was rapidly assuming the aerodynamic characteristics of a brick.

My twin Lycs had turbocharging. I could pull the full 350 horses all the way up to eighteen thousand feet. But by the time I passed fifteen thousand, the plane was reduced to a rate of climb of five hundred feet per minute. Einstein's theory of relativity needs one minor modification: time *really* slows down as your aircraft loads up with ice.

When filing my flight plan, I had asked for seventeen thousand feet. But the ice was still forming on my wings as I approached that altitude. It sort of looked as if the Trim God was fixing to punch my ticket.

I called Air Traffic Control and requested and then demanded nineteen thousand feet. I was still in heavy icing conditions. I not only had to clear the peaks, I had to get above the icing conditions in the clouds, or sooner or later my magnificent bird would tire of the load and fall from the sky.

At least, being over the Alps, there wasn't far to fall. The ground was but a few thousand feet below.

At nineteen thousand feet I still wasn't free of cloud. I wasn't requesting anything from ATC any longer. I demanded twenty-one thousand. Poor ATC were more than a bit flustered. European controllers aren't used to pilots telling them what to do. If I didn't get out of the clag in a hurry, I would go spinning down to earth.

Good pilots make a habit of glancing at their engine instruments regularly. Ferry pilots don't like to, because all they can tell you is bad news. No news is good news, unless it's a call from the governor.

By now, my plane was inching upward at 200–300 feet per minute. The plane climbed on its props and the pure guts of the Lycomings. But the strain showed. I had insufficient forward speed to pass enough cooling air over the engines. All my temperatures and pressures were in the red, and climbing. If one of those darling engines decided to shed a piston, I would have my hands full in a hurry.

The engines kept groaning and we kept inching higher. The cockpit was cold but sweat was pouring down my back.

I passed twenty-one thousand feet. Still I wasn't free of the clouds. I received clearance to twenty-three thousand. By this time, all the basic rules of aerodynamics had passed by the wayside. Through sheer guts, my plane still flew. All of the gauges were now against the stops, but we still flew.

At twenty-two thousand feet I started flying in and out of the tops of the clouds. Five hundred feet higher I cleared them completely. At twenty-three thousand I was just high enough above them that I still had a sensation of rapid flight.

I set the autopilot. The airspeed increased. My temperatures and pressures slowly, ever so slowly, returned to normal. After a long while, my heartbeat returned to a somewhat normal pace. Eventually the friction of the air passing over the wing wore away the ice through sublimation.

Flying has been described as hours of boredom, broken by moments of stark terror. Due to its peculiar nature, with long legs and vast distances between stops, ferry flying consisted of timeless periods of boredom broken by hours of stark terror. As pilots, if we opted for perfectly safe flying, we delivered no aircraft and made no money. Taking a diversion of a few hours around potentially bad weather might make the difference between a profitable trip and some free flight time. None of us went looking for bad weather but we managed to find a whole heap of it. Ferry pilots flew a lot closer to the edge of the flying envelope than any other kind of pilots I knew.

Our envelope was not only much larger than that of most pilots; we might be called upon at any time to go right to the edge. Then fly there for hours. Mistakes could easily result in death. The trick lay in knowing exactly what you could and couldn't get away with.

I landed in Malta just before sunset, and acted as if flights like this happened to me every day. I checked into the hotel, ate dinner, had a few drinks, and then hit the sack. I slept the sleep of the innocent.

My ability to knock out one trip after another was predicated on running things at my own pace. I could fly twelve hours daily, day after day, if I was left to do it *my* way. I was useless as teats on a boar hog before 10 am. If I had to get up at dawn, say, I'd be lucky to find my plane, much less fly it.

My body finally signaled its willingness to stir the next morning. My heart started pumping. My blood warmed and began moving to my extremities. After a leisurely breakfast, I sauntered out to the airport and left Malta.

Much ferry flying consisted literally of "winging it." I might just have enough fuel to go all the way to Dar es Salaam. Or I could refuel in Luxor in

Egypt, but my fuel bill would look like two weeks of the GNP of Saudi Arabia. Fuel in Khartoum in the Sudan was cheap but I hadn't quite gotten permission to land there. Nairobi, Kenya was the best stop, but I had "Tanzanian Air Services" painted down the sides of the plane. As it seemed that Tanzania and Kenya had a bit of a war going on, landing in Nairobi might be the flying equivalent of waving a red rag in front of a very angry bull.

I made my decision by carefully weighing all the facts and potential problems. Then I flipped a coin. It came up Khartoum, with Nairobi as an alternative.

If you choose to wave a red flag in front of an irate bull, at least do it in the dead of night. Momma Moriarty didn't raise any dummies.

I set out on what I hoped would be another long and boring trip. As I passed over Luxor some guy radioed me from the ground. I responded. He had spent ten days sitting in Luxor waiting for landing permission in Khartoum. He wanted me to contact Khartoum to request approval for his flight over the Sudan, and landing rights in Khartoum.

Regulations required me to be equipped with an HF radio. As usual, I didn't have one, so I couldn't make long-range contact with the authorities in Khartoum. I told him that I'd do the best I could for him, but couldn't make any promises. He may still be there, waiting to hear from me.

But his problem started me thinking. Globe Aero had requested permission to overfly the Sudan, with landing rights at Khartoum, but hadn't received an answer. I didn't have permission, but they hadn't said no, either.

So I pressed on. I've always sorta figured it's a whole lot easier to be forgiven than to get permission. Just to be sure, when I got to the border between Egypt and Sudan, I turned off all my communication radios.

As I neared Khartoum I pulled out my whiz wheel and did some calculations. I didn't have the range to make it to Dar es Salaam but could easily fly to Nairobi. I'd land at about 4 am. I could refuel, file and depart before anyone realized I was the enemy. I wrote down my new flight plan.

When I flew in Vietnam, I always kept in mind that anything could happen at any time. Flying over Africa tends to generate the same kind of feelings. Not that our political leadership is a whole lot higher quality, but in Africa, acre for acre, mile for mile, they had more political nuts than a good-sized pecan grove. It made good sense not to tell the controllers precisely what your position was. They love sending up fighters after little bitty airplanes. Can't fight back and all that.

I passed Khartoum. Once safely south of the city, I turned on my radios and called to change my flight plan.

"Khartoum control, this is N27227. Over."

"N27227. Theese iss Khartoum. Go ahead weeth your position."

"Khartoum control, N27227. I would like to cancel my landing at Khartoum and proceed to Nairobi for landing. Are you ready to copy my flight plan? Over."

"N27227. Khartoum, roger. What iss your position?"

I wasn't real happy about all those questions about my position.

"Khartoum, 227 presently estimating my position thirty miles north of Khartoum." This wasn't entirely a lie. My DME showed my position to be some thirty-five miles south of Khartoum. But thirty miles north was as close as I was willing to admit.

"N27227. Theese is Khartoum. You are instructing to return to Khartoum for landing. We show you souse of the city of Khartoum by nearly forty miles."

Damnation. They had primary radar that worked. This was a first for me in Africa. How come they never have it when the weather is two hundred feet in overcast with a quarter-mile visibility in blowing sand the size of golf balls?

"Khartoum, this is 227 requesting clearance to Nairobi for landing. Unable to land Khartoum due to landing weight."

Even at the time, I realized this was pretty feeble, but I figured every airplane had to have a landing weight. If mine was malfunctioning, maybe it would confuse them as much as it did me. I knew I had a landing weight, but wasn't too sure where it was packed.

Every minute I could dazzle them with this nonsense, I was three miles closer to Nairobi.

"N27227, Khartoum. We will scramble fighters to shoot you down if you do not return and land at Khartoum. Immediately."

That "immediately" got to me. After all, there was a limit to what these guys would put up with. I banked the airplane to the north and landed a little later. I gathered all the official-looking paperwork I could find. Official-looking papers went a long way in Africa.

Flanked by two armed guards, I marched upstairs to ATC. It was one o'clock in the morning, with nothing going on. An officious-looking and very fat functionary started to question me. Or, more accurately, he started to harangue me.

It seemed the Sudan hadn't issued any overflight permissions to anyone in the past six weeks. Since they hadn't given anyone permission to overfly, I couldn't possibly have the right to overfly or to land. He did have a point.

I tried my "drown them in official-looking papers" routine. But either he couldn't read or he had no sense of humor. I sighed. Especially since I had a spare *Playboy* and a *Penthouse* in the plane. I offered to get them. I figured even he could understand those. He didn't think I was very funny. I thought it was hilarious.

When he finished yelling at me, he stuck me in a room about the size of a closet, with two chairs and two guards. Guess who stood up all night?

For hours, one of the guards just stared at me and flicked the selector on his AK-47 from full auto to single shot, then back to full auto. I tried to figure out what went on in his head. Really, I did. He never said a word, just flicked that damned selector back and forth.

I went to sleep, more or less, leaning up against the wall. All ferry pilots place a high value on their beauty sleep. I counted the clicks from the gun's selector like some people count sheep.

Someone brought the guards coffee early next morning. Maybe they were short of cups, since nobody offered me any. I woke fully refreshed. Or at least, as refreshed as you can be after sleeping standing up, next to a guard who can't decide if he wants to kill you with one shot or a whole bunch.

Later I was brought out of my cell. Someone motioned to me to pick up a telephone. It seemed that the Director of Civil Aviation of the Sudan wanted a word with me.

"Am I speaking to the pilot of N27227?"

"This is Captain Moriarty. I am the pilot of N27227. What can I do for you?"

"I am Mister Q. I am the Director of Civil Aviation for the Sudan. You are charged with violating the territorial integrity of my country. Under international law we could have shot your aircraft down. You did not have permission to land in Khartoum or to overfly my country."

"First of all, Mister Q, my company [notice that "my company"] has been delivering general aviation aircraft all over the world for fifteen years. We filed our request for overflight at least a week ago, in accordance with international regulations [note the "international regulations"]. We received no response from your office. I have a copy of our request, if you would like to see it. Naturally, since we maintain good relations with your country, it never

132

occurred to me that there might be a delay in obtaining your approval. Second, I did not want to land at Khartoum. I was forced down. And third, now I'm here, what would you like to do with me?"

"You damned Americans act as if you can fly anywhere you want, at any time you want. I'm putting you under house arrest. You are to report to me once each day. I'm going to make an example of you."

He did have a point. Most places in the world allow convenient access through their airspace. Americans are unused to petty despots closing off the airspace of an entire country to foreign aircraft on a whim. But this was Africa.

My beauty sleep hadn't done all that much for me. I was already as beautiful as I was ever likely to be. My fanny was dragging along behind. I took my bags from the plane, took the first taxi I could find, and headed for the first decent hotel I could find. The Director of Civil Aviation had recommended one. It probably belonged to his brother-in-law.

After checking in, I ate lunch and pondered my fate. One thought kept occurring to me.

One of the most difficult things to explain about ferrying aircraft was that it was actually quite a lonely business. Sure, on a week-long trip, a pilot would encounter various people, but all in a superficial way. I got to tell a lot of people to "Fill 'er up, please" and ask "What's the weather like?" but that was about it.

The trip started when the ferry pilot picked up the keys to the plane. It didn't end until the keys were handed to the customer at the other end. My thoughts were never very far away from my plane, the weather, how much fuel I needed for the next leg, or any of a myriad of other potential problems.

Lunch in Khartoum may sound positively romantic. But for the duration of the trip, no matter how long or how short, the airplane was my mistress. The food barely qualified as palatable and the prices didn't help. My lover and I were under house arrest for an undetermined period.

But ferry pilots are hired to solve problems first, and to ferry planes second. I did the only logical thing I could think of. I went upstairs and slept. There's no such thing as being too rich or too beautiful.

I awoke that evening and lay in bed on my back for a while. One thing that had occurred to me earlier in the day was that after all, this was Africa. Here, nothing works in quite the way it is supposed to. At the best of times, communications were abysmal. This was neither the best nor the worst of times; just average. On average in Africa, no one tells anyone else anything.

I started thinking. The personnel on duty in ATC on the midnight to eight shift knew of my arrest. The guys on duty from 8 am to 4 pm probably knew about it. But I was willing to bet that the shift working now, this evening, had no clue. I decided to test this theory.

I checked out of the hotel and took a cab to the airport. My airplane stood proud and unfettered. I stowed my bags inside and called for the fuel truck. Once I had filled the tanks and paid for the fuel, I went into ATC to file my flight plan and check the weather. I kept thinking, "This is too easy."

Air Traffic Control took my flight plan, signed it, and returned my copy to me. I smiled. On my way out, the senior controller wished me a safe flight. I smiled even more. As I climbed into my iron eagle I said to myself, very quietly, "I can't believe I'm getting away with this!"

Takeoff, climb, and cruise were normal in all respects. This leg had reverted to being just another boring, normal leg of a ferry trip. Exiting Sudanese airspace was a pleasant moment, however.

I landed in Dar es Salaam a little past sun-up the next morning.

It took the Director of Civil Aviation for the Sudan nearly a week to notice that I wasn't doing all that great a job of reporting to him daily. It took him another week to learn that I was long gone, right out from under his very long nose.

A friend of mine went through Khartoum a few weeks later. He reported that the Director of Civil Aviation for the Sudan was still madder than a wet hen. Prominently posted in ATC was an arrest warrant describing my various transgressions.

I haven't been back since. They aren't very friendly there.

After turning my plane over to its new owners, I learned that it wasn't much easier to get out of Tanzania than it had been to get there. The political strife with Kenya had resulted in several airlines bypassing Dar. Rumor had it that weeks might pass before a seat out became available.

However, what I lacked in size, I more than made up for in tenacity. I figured I'd wait at the airport until the first flight out, late that night, and try to talk to the flight crew. A few days in Dar and I'd be out of money and have to go on welfare. Welfare in Dar es Salaam consists of walking up to the nearest coconut tree and giving it a kick. I didn't much care for coconuts in the first place. I never quite mastered the knack of peeling them.

My hosts made reservations for me at a hotel right on the beach. I didn't plan on using it, but it was reassuring to know that at least I had a place to lay my head. Time passed ever so slowly as I waited for the flight to arrive. By 10 pm, a large crowd had formed to greet it. At least, that's what I thought.

The commercial flight finally arrived after midnight. The crew that I had planned to speak to didn't even get off the plane. As a matter of fact, only a few of the passengers did.

Sure was a heck of a crowd to greet so few arrivals. I forced my way to the ticket counter to ascertain my chances of getting a seat. The service agent was curt, at best.

"Sir, all these people want seats out. If I put you on the list, you will be number two hundred and thirty-nine. We have ten seats available."

I know when I'm beat. I hopped into a taxi and gave him the name of the hotel. I arrived at my sojourn palace after a rough journey. By now, I'd been awake for about twenty-eight hours. I'd had, at the most, six hours' sleep in the last fifty or sixty. I dragged myself and my bags up to the check-in counter.

The hotel comprised a number of stone-and-mortar huts with thatched roofs. The reception area, bar, and restaurant were located in a large open area, also with a thatched roof.

I gave my name to the clerk and started to fill out the registration card. He had that look on his face that you make when you step in something nasty. He looked at me and lifted one eyebrow.

"I'm sorry, sir, but all our rooms are booked."

"No problem," I responded. "I'm Captain Moriarty. Tanzanian Air Services made a reservation for me."

He squirmed a little before replying. "Sorry, captain, but we thought you caught the flight out. We canceled your reservation."

"Better uncancel it. I'm here. The flight had about two hundred people trying to get on it in front of me. I'll be here at least two days."

"Very sorry, captain, but all our rooms are booked. We have no room."

"Really?" My clock was ticking slower than normal. Information took time to sink in. "How about calling a taxi for me and arranging a room somewhere else?"

"Sorry, captain. The telephones do not work after midnight."

"Really?" I could barely glimpse the faint glow from the tail lights of my departing taxi as it disappeared into the African darkness. "How far is town?"

"Very far, Captain. We are perhaps twenty miles from town."

"Really?" I could just see myself trying to carry my luggage and the radios all that way. It wouldn't take more than a week. With a hell of a tailwind.

"Does your roof leak?"

"Of course not, captain. How can you suggest such a thing?"

"Good. Tell you what. How 'bout finding me a blanket and a pillow? I'm a bit bushed. I'll make up a bedroll and sleep over there in the corner. I'll need some hot tea and toast first thing in the morning. I'm a real bear until I get a bite to eat."

"Really?"

The clerk wandered off in a daze. He said something under his breath about finding the manager. In the darkness, his eyes looked like a pair of burning coals. Mine just felt like burning coals.

The hotel manager rushed up a few minutes later. He listened to my tale of woe with great patience.

"We can't have you sleeping in the lobby. How about . . . I have two English girls staying in my cottage. We have two bedrooms, so I'm sure we can arrange something comfortable."

I looked at him closely. He didn't look gay. This was getting more interesting. Any fool can divide four by two and come up with something comfortable. Even a slightly ragged ferry pilot. Or perhaps, especially a slightly ragged ferry pilot.

The less fine-looking half of the pair of English girls looked damn fine. The fine-looking half looked stunning.

Let me see now. Four divided by two goes . . .

At his cottage, my host brought each of us a beer. He had me repeat the story of my trip. The women were wearing short, see-through nighties. All kinds of possibilities were going through my head. As I finished my story, I started to nod off. My chosen honey quickly took my arm. I sighed.

"You must be absolutely knackered. We must get you to bed."

Did I hear the word "we"? As in the royal "we"?

Everyone not already undressed rapidly became undressed. Everyone walked around half-naked, quite unconcerned. I went into my room, waiting patiently for everyone else to sort out the sleeping arrangements. All three of them went into the other bedroom and closed the door.

I heard my preferred honey through the door.

"Do you think he'd mind if I slept with him?"

I know mental telepathy doesn't work. I'm dead sure of it. That night I tested my ability to send messages. None of them got through.

My idea of two into four is not three, remainder one. I slept alone.

It took me a lot longer than normal to get to sleep that night. You see, I've always had this fantasy. It involves two lovely ladies and me. Right on the other side of the door were two lovely ladies in one bed. And my host. Rats.

It took me three days to get a seat on an outbound flight. The pair of English lovelies left the day after my arrival. The thought of them in bed with my host has stayed with me, all down the long years.

As I mentioned, Bob Campbell had left Lakeland for Dar es Salaam in the sister ship to mine, a few days before me. He arrived in Tanzania two weeks after I left. He was arrested in Saudi Arabia on his way down from Malta. He spent almost two weeks in jail.

Three months after I delivered the Navajo to Dar es Salaam, a former East African Airways pilot neglected to lower the undercarriage lever as he came into the pattern. He landed with the plane gear up and came to a rather sudden, rather embarrassing, rather noisy stop. No one was hurt except the pilot, who was bruised and battered. Or rather, his ego was bruised and battered. I know how he felt.

That aluminum butterfly was given a permanent resting place next to the runway. She had a good heart and came to a sad end.

58th TRIP: VAN NUYS, CA to MELBOURNE, AUSTRALIA

1977	from	to	nautical miles	knots	time (hours)			
					flight	day	night	inst.
Oct 6	Van Nuys	Van Nuys	0	0	1.3	1.3		
	Van Nuys	El Paso	621	135	4.6	4.6		1.0
Oct 7	El Paso	Lakeland	1,293	287	4.5	4.5		
Oct 19	Lakeland	El Paso	1,293	144	9.0	9.0		
Oct 20	El Paso	Van Nuys	621	155	4.0	4.0		
Oct 22	Van Nuys	Van Nuys	0	0	1.1	1.1		
Oct 23	Van Nuys	Oakland	293	147	2.0	2.0		
Oct 24	Oakland	Honolulu	2,091	149	14.0	14.0		2.0
Oct 25	Honolulu	Pago Pago	2,268	164	13.8	1.8	12.9	1.0 *
Oct 26	Pago Pago	Nandi	714	134	5.3	5.3		
	Nandi	Nandi	0	0	0.4	0.4		
Oct 29	Nandi	La Tontouta	689	153	4.5	4.5		
Oct 30	La Tontouta	Melbourne	1,443	144	10.0	10.0		1.5
TOTALS		24 days	11,326	152	74.5	62.5	12.9	5.5

* check time

Some pilots are born to fly, and some aren't. Some aircraft almost fly off the design table, and some fall off.

The Rockwell 685 airframe sported almost everything an aircraft needed to make it a best-seller. It was fast, comfortable, easy to fly, safe and sleek. It was also big, for a general aviation aircraft. That meant it was heavy, which in turn meant it needed big engines. There was the rub. The airframe design was fabulous. The engines sucked.

The 685 carried a pair of massive Continental GTSIO-520K power units, each capable of pumping up 435 horses at takeoff. When they worked, they worked great. But lots of horses generate lots of heat. Engines like heat about as much as Frosty the Snowman does. The geared 520K engine broke down all too often.

But a good engineer likes to design things to serve more than one function. The 520K doubled as a great fishing weight. That is, any time you have a desire to put a whale on your fish hook. If you were hunting a really record-sized whale, you could buy an entire 685 for little more than the price of a pair of engines.

With even more powerful turboprop jet engines, the 685 evolved into the Rockwell 690. The 690 flew and sold well.

PHIL WALDMAN liked to maximize revenues by having his pilots do double duty. Often, we would arrive at a destination to find instructions waiting for us to fly commercial to another location for another aircraft pickup.

In early October of 1977 I completed an uneventful delivery of a Beech Bonanza to Sydney, Australia. When I stopped in Honolulu on the return trip, I called Phil to see if he had any new instructions for me. Sure enough, he wanted me to divert to Los Angeles and go to Van Nuys airport to conduct a checkout of a Rockwell 685. I was then to sign for the aircraft and fly it to Lakeland for tanking.

In the good old days, before Oil Shocker II, we wouldn't bat an eyelash at flying a plane from the west coast to the east coast just to have it tanked. In the shadow of Oil Shocker II, it became far cheaper to move Phil's whole operation out to the west coast, rather than pay the price of a thousand gallons of avgas.

In 1977 I was young and impressionable. I still believed the nonsense regularly handed out by my elders. If the powers that be required a checkout of a particular aircraft, there must be a valid reason.

As the hours in my logbook mounted up, I learned that all airplanes fly about the same. Generally, if I could figure out how to start its engine or engines, I could fly any airplane. Whenever someone suggested that a pilot needed a checkout in a plane, it was a heavy hint that the plane barked. Usually, they were trying cover their ass in case of an accident.

With a solid night's rest behind me, bright and early the next morning I wandered out to the Rockwell dealership to find that my aircraft wasn't ready. This often happened in the ferry business; an airplane was promised to be ready, but wasn't. But it would be ready "soon". I sat for hours, chewing the fat with everyone who walked in the door.

As with every person, every airplane has its own unique story to tell.

Wayne Newton, the Las Vegas singing star, maintained a home a one-hour flight north of Los Angeles. When his wife came down with a slight skin problem, she required treatment in LA once a week. God knows, he had some spare cash. He purchased N57095 to spare his wife a weekly eight-hour drive. That's what airplanes are for. I suppose that's also what money is for.

Once her skin condition cleared up, Newton put the airplane on the market. Due to the potential engine problem, and the cost of replacing both of them, used Rockwell 685s were dirt cheap. Put another way, you couldn't give the damned things away.

This particular plane, its pedigree notwithstanding, sat for a year or two waiting for a new owner. Finally, a fellow from Australia decided to buy it. He contracted with Globe Aero to tank the airplane and fly it to Melbourne.

Lang Hancock, the buyer, was a story in himself. He had prospected the Australian outback in the 1950s. Hancock didn't find a gusher or discover the motherlode. He just prospected.

Hancock's story was that he was flying over a valley in November of 1952, with his wife, in a small plane. A thunderstorm hit the area and he flew down a river valley. He noticed that the walls of the valley were bright red, due to iron staining. While iron deposits in the Pilbara were known as far back as about 1890, it took Lang Hancock and his financial partner to drag Australia kicking and screaming into becoming the biggest and richest source of iron in the world. Alas, the Australian Bureau of Meteorology has reported that no rain fell there on any day of November 1952. It is vital that a good pilot never lets irritating facts interfere with a great story.

But no picnic is complete without a few ants. Under Australian law, Hancock could stake his claim, mine his iron, and sell it to anyone in Australia who wanted to smelt it. His only problem was that there wasn't a single iron foundry in the entire country, and he couldn't export raw ore. That tended to reduce the value of his mountain of iron. Matter of fact, the world's richest iron mountain might more accurately be described as the world's biggest white elephant.

Quietly, Lang staked his claims and waited. And gnashed his teeth, a lot.

Australia woke up to the wonders of international economics in the early 1960s. Lang Hancock stuffed his claims into a scruffy old briefcase and took a flight to meet with Rio Tinto. He shook a few hands, talked a little business, signed papers, and returned to Australia with a deal.

He had turned his claims over to Rio Tinto. In return, he would receive 3½ percent of the value of every single chunk of iron ore taken from his mine until his great big mountain turned into a little bitty molehill. Or forever, whichever came first. For doing absolutely nothing.

The first year, Lang picked up a check for $10,000,000. And the next. And the next. Within just a few years, he could even afford to keep engines on a Rockwell 685.

Hancock was a prospector, but he made up for it by being a rich one. He wanted to flit around Australia and demanded a high-wing twin in which to flit. For more serious travels, he already had a spare Lear jet or two.

I do kid once in a great while, but the following is the straight scoop. Hancock chose the 685 because he wanted to be able to look out while he flew. This was so that if perchance he flew over another mountain of iron, or even copper, he could stake another claim, notwithstanding the fact that he needed more money in the same way Custer needed more Indians.

As was usual in the aircraft business, work on my 685 was finished five minutes before closing time. After spending six hours sitting on my duff, I figured the time was right to start earning my keep. I went out for an hour-long check flight with the dealer's chief pilot.

The Rockwell 685 was similar to every other plane I've ever flown: pull the yoke back to go up, push forward to go down, power levers all the way forward for takeoff, all the way back for landing. No sweat. Thank God flying is so simple.

I left California early the next morning. With a fair following breeze, I made it to Lakeland in time for dinner.

Phil Waldman had one habit that flat rubbed me the wrong way. He wanted pilots to fly the planes they had checked out. I could have briefed any of our pilots on the foibles of the Rockwell 685 in five minutes or less. But Phil's view was that since I had conducted the formal checkout of this particular beast, I should remain with her until the customer did us part.

I never understood why, but most overseas aircraft deliveries were required between March and November. Globe was just entering its slow season and I was stuck with the 685. It wasn't much of a plane, but it was mine for the duration.

By this time I had completed over fifty international flights in brand new planes, with no major malfunctions. I had finished perhaps half a dozen trips over water in secondhand beasts, with problems on every trip. I began to realize that used airplanes were never a good deal for the ferry pilot. Often they were very bad deals, and not infrequently they were plumb dangerous.

Whenever we brought a plane in from a factory to Lakeland for tanking, we always filled out a squawk sheet on it. Globe could tank an aircraft for a ferry flight in a few days. My list of gripes about this plane wasn't serious for a flight across the U.S., since all planes give a pilot something to complain about. It wasn't a bright idea, however, to go tripping across oceans unless all the systems worked properly.

I waited patiently for the plane to be fixed. She and I may have been married, but I would earn nothing until we started moving westbound. I waited and waited.

One day I was out at the hangar. Slowly but surely, I was going out of my tiny mind. The 685 had tied me up for nearly two weeks at that point, and in Lakeland I was 2,500 miles further from Melbourne than when I had started. I had yet to make one red cent.

I told Phil that it would be faster and cheaper to get the plane fixed in Van Nuys. The Rockwell dealer knew the plane and had better access to parts than we did. Phil agreed. I should go ahead and fly it to the west coast for the work it needed. Also, he said, my passenger on the west coast had completed his business and was ready to leave.

"Passenger? What passenger?"

Phil smiled that smile of his. "Did I forget to mention it? Hancock's son-in-law is a pilot. He wants to fly back to Australia with you. Of course, I'll reimburse you if you have any extra expenses due to him."

The only thing worse than flying a broken-down, worn-out beast across the ocean is doing so with a passenger on board. And the worst possible passenger is another pilot. They all want to help. Especially when the pilot-passenger is the owner, or even worse, the owner's son-in-law. These guys tended to think that just because their name was on the bill of sale, they owned the cotton-pickin' plane.

When I'm driving and I'm over water, the plane belongs to me.

"You haven't mentioned any passenger, especially a rich passenger. Given the choice between a co-pilot and a wet soggy sandwich, I'll opt for the sandwich in a second. And a pilot — damn! I hate flying with other pilots. They all think they know how to fly. Give this trip to someone else. It's been nothing but a pain in the ass to me. I didn't want it in the first place. What else ya got? How about a nice single-engine going somewhere?"

"Gee whiz, Bob. You've already got two weeks invested in this plane. You're the only pilot I've got qualified in the 685. I might not have another airplane ready for you for a month. Maybe two months." He smiled again.

I caught his drift practically right away.

"I don't like having my arm twisted, Phil. OK, it's my trip. But I'm the boss. If he causes any problems — any problems at all — I'm dropping him off on the nearest speck of land. For all I care, he can swim the rest of the way. I hate passengers. And a rich creep, to boot. You owe me, Phil."

I took the 685 back to Van Nuys. After handing it over to the dealer with my list of gripes, I checked into a local hotel. My passenger, Greg, met me for breakfast the next morning.

Nearly every trip I ever took with another passenger turned into a pain in the neck. Or lower. The trick to ferry flying was to fly at a pace at which I was comfortable, and to make use of every cubic inch in the cockpit (and there usually weren't many) to make myself comfy.

Greg and I had about sixty hours ahead of us, flying together in a highly confined area. If his space tended to encroach into mine, it would be a miserable time. Everything I knew told me that I wasn't going to like this guy. I was pleasantly disappointed.

A very cheerful fellow wandered up to my breakfast table. This was my passenger. Greg was an unpretentious young man, about twenty-five years old. He was bright and easy to get along with. Born and raised in England, he had moved to Australia four years earlier. He freelanced as a photographer.

As young men are apt to do, he met a pretty young miss and fell in love. As young couples are wont to do, they married.

Lang Hancock was considered to be either the second or third richest man in Australia. Greg's new bride, Lang's daughter, his *only* daughter, won the honor, hands down, of richest woman in Australia. But the dowry brought to this marriage didn't change Greg in the slightest. Greg was good ol' plain folks. I realized we'd get along just fine. He impressed me. At least I wouldn't have to put up with some rich kid with his nose in the air.

Maintenance completed, we set off from Van Nuys for Oakland on October 22. The Rockwell had already presented me with more than a few systems failures. Rather than fill my ferry tanks to the brim, I had opted for only half-tanks. The plane was about fifteen percent over gross as we started our takeoff roll. As decisions go, it turned out to be a pretty good choice for the spur of the moment.

We climbed and leveled out at sixteen thousand feet. At that altitude, the really big guys were above us and the little bitty fellows were below. Maybe these pressurized twins weren't all that bad after all.

The Continental 520s powering the 685 delivered more horsepower than any other general aviation opposed engine. Our airplane still suffered from insufficient power, though. I guess it took twenty-five minutes to make our climb. It was nice to have such information. Our cruise wouldn't be hurt badly, but it sure was going to take a long time to get to altitude.

As I leveled out I began adjusting the fuel–air mixture controls, to set the proper blend for our altitude. The right engine gave me no problem. But the mixture control for the left engine didn't work properly. The mixture became leaner and leaner. The temperatures rose well above normal and acceptable levels. Instead of showing a normal consumption of eighteen gallons of fuel per hour, the gauges for the left engine registered only 10–12 gallons. Adjusting the mixture to the "full rich" position made no difference.

The more I fiddled, the lower the fuel flow went. Something wasn't right. I turned back for Van Nuys. If the fuel flow indicator was accurate, I was fixing to blow up the left engine. I shut it down.

Many pilots like twin-engine aircraft because the extra engine gives them a strong sense of redundancy. Few take the time to study the flight manual closely. The 685 had a single-engine ceiling of about eight thousand feet with normal gross weight and tight new engines. We were fifteen percent over gross weight, and the single engine turning was old and tired. With full power on the right engine, we came down at a rate of five hundred feet per minute.

Van Nuys, the nearest airfield, was forty-five miles south of us. We had some hills between us and the field, and were descending like a duck with a ruptured radiator. Our real single-engine ceiling just about matched that of the USS *Nautilus*.

To beat it all, Greg sat next to me acting as if things like this happened to him every day. He never batted an eyelash during the whole ordeal.

I declared an emergency on the distress frequency, 121.5. Not many general aviation planes would have heard me, but I wanted every controller in the area to know I had just purchased every single bit of necessary airspace between me and the field.

With my mayday call completed, I switched back to Center. I now owned a heap of airspace in one of world's busiest traffic areas. I felt like lighting a fat Cuban cigar for each of us. Meanwhile, we kept coming down.

As we descended into denser air, our rate of descent decreased. All the sweat that was pouring off me may have helped. We cleared the hills with a few thousand feet to spare and were home free. I came overhead the field at a safe fifteen hundred feet and made an old lady approach to landing. Center cleared me over to Van Nuys tower for landing.

"Hello, Van Nuys tower. This is N57095. I have an emergency in progress. My left engine is tarred and feathered. Requesting permission to land. Gear down and locked."

"N57095, this is Van Nuys tower. You are number one and cleared to land. We have emergency vehicles standing by on the first taxiway. Say again, 'tarred and feathered'?"

Tower, 095. My left engine got tired, so I feathered it."

"095, tower. Roger."

If you can keep a sense of humor in any emergency, you've got it half-licked. In the history of aviation, I don't remember hearing about anyone cracking up who could still joke.

We landed smoothly, rolled out, and turned left at the first turnoff.

I was puzzled now. My left engine was shut down. The plane was safely on the ground. Normally the crash truck returned to its cave at that point. But a guy had got out of the truck and was pointing to my right engine. He made eye contact and drew a finger across his throat, meaning "Kill your engine."

All I could think was that the dummy couldn't even figure out that it was the other engine that wasn't working, even though its blades were stopped in the feathered position. I motioned that I wanted to taxi the plane in. He persisted with his throat-cutting motion.

To humor him, I did as he asked. I hopped out of the airplane, ready to chew his donkey. We were at least a mile from the hangar.

I didn't chew him out; not even a little. What he had seen, and I had not seen, was the broken exhaust stack swivel on the right engine. All the exhaust from the engine was going into the cowling.

When did it break? Probably when I came back on the power for landing. But we were only moments away from having a fire in the right engine. I thanked him profusely.

The dealer came over to the airplane. He told me that they could fix it and we could leave the next day.

I had now flown nearly twenty-five hours in this airplane, and was just over one mile from the dealer's shop. So far I was working for free. Phil wanted to keep all the pilots as independent contractors because if we worked for him he would have to pay us. My hatred of used airplanes went up another notch.

Greg and I went over to the car rental place and rented the same car we'd turned in only a few hours before. I let him drive us back to the hotel.

I turned to him. "I have to admit, you were really cool and collected out there. You acted as if you went through single-engine over gross landings all the time. I don't know many pilots who wouldn't have gotten just a little nervous. How do you do it?"

"Well, Bob," he began, "I looked over. You looked like you knew what you were doing. If you had it under control, why should I be scared? You really did make a marvelous landing, too."

"Let me tell you a little secret. I am pretty cool during an emergency. But the reason you're driving is that my knees are shaking."

The plane was a piece of crap. But the kid was cool. This might not be a bad trip after all, if we could make it all the way to Australia.

The Rockwell dealer delivered the aircraft as promised, early the next morning. The problems were serious in flight but easy to fix on the ground. Our trip to Oakland proved uneventful.

The buyer had heaps of money. I don't usually carry much in the way of sea survival equipment. But the plane was a tired old lady and it was a long way to Melbourne. Greg and I burned up $1,800 buying extra survival gear.

Looking back, I suppose buying all that extra gear turned the tide. I'd like to think the Trim God looks out for ferry pilots who prepare.

Our first leg over water, from Oakland to Honolulu, proved to be fourteen hours of pure boredom. We flew another fourteen boring hours to Pago Pago, and still another five hours of sheer boredom to Fiji. Times change, however, and all good things seem to come to an end.

When I say "boring" I mean there were no further emergencies. Greg proved to be a first-class travel companion and aircraft gofer. We talked about all sorts of interesting things yet never tired of each other's company. Although we flew a pretty fast trip, we got a hot dinner, a few drinks, and eight hours' sleep every night. I wouldn't have dreamed of admitting it to Phil, but this guy turned what should have been a deadly dull trip into a real kick. Most important of all, he politely kept his junk on his side of the cockpit.

That five-hour leg into Nandi, Fiji seemed so short that after a brief discussion we decided to press on to La Tontouta, on the island of New

Caledonia. The island swarmed with cute little fucklings in the teensiest bathing suits, if you like that sort of stuff. When they wore suits at all.

Greg refueled the plane in Nandi while I paid the landing fees and filed a flight plan. He learned fast and we worked well as a team.

We had spent much of our time together talking about iron ore and how rich the Pilbara was. Greg had the numbers down pat. The Pilbara had enough iron to satisfy all worldwide demand for four hundred years. Not only was it the world's richest deposit in terms of grade; it constituted thirty percent of the entire world's iron reserves. I was getting to the point where, after hearing the same thing again and again, I hoped to myself that he would find something else to gnaw on.

He did. Shortly after takeoff, Greg turned to me and casually asked, "How much of an oil leak does it take to be serious?"

"What kind of question is that? If you can see an oil leak, it's a serious oil leak. Is there any particular reason you asked?"

"We seem to have a serious leak on the right engine."

"Greg, what's this 'we' shit? You got a frog in your pocket? That's your engine. Why don't you take better care of it? Mine's running just fine."

I crawled over and leaned past him to have a better look out of his side window. I had seen less oil coming out of good-sized gushers in Texas. You could say we had a serious leak. I came back on the power to both engines, to reduce the oil pressure. On one engine, this plane had the flight characteristics of a brick. We were thirty percent over gross after taking off from Fiji and we were going to come down quickly.

I called the tower and told them we were returning for landing. The ferry tanks were full for this leg and the airplane was as heavy as I had ever flown it. Nandi was hotter than the hinges of Hades. The plane came in hot and fast. The runway was almost 2½ miles long, and we used almost all of it trying to stop. I guess we didn't use the last ten feet or so, but we barely had room to turn at the far end.

Now you have to picture this in your mind. For the entire trip, Greg had been a quiet, charming, unassuming fellow. But he changed from a tadpole to a toad right there, right then, right in front of my eyes. I couldn't quite believe what I saw. It was like having a front row seat outside Superman's telephone booth.

"Bob, I need to use the radio for just a minute," he said in a perfectly normal voice.

"Sure, go ahead. Who ya calling?" I shrugged. So far on this trip I had done all the radio work.

"I thought I might talk to Qantas." He picked up the mike. "Hello, Qantas Nandi. Hello, Qantas Nandi. This is N57095. Hello Qantas Nandi, N57095. Do you read?"

I couldn't help but wonder just who he knew at Qantas. Maybe someone who could help us out.

"N57095, this is Qantas Nandi. Reading you five by five. Go ahead with your traffic."

"Qantas Nandi, N57095. We are a Rockwell six eighty-five. We have an engine problem. We are taxiing into the fuel area. Would you be good enough to request your station manager greet us at the plane, please?"

"095, Qantas. Our ground crew is on strike. We are unable to provide any maintenance support. You will have to find your own mechanics. We are quite unable to assist you," they crisply responded.

"Qantas Nandi, N57095. I want your station manager to meet us immediately upon arrival. Pass on the message, please." With each transmission, Greg became more forceful.

This guy hadn't just turned into just a toad. He'd metamorphosed into a fire-breathing dragon. While impressed with his manner, it occurred to me that he was pretty much blowing any chance of Qantas Nandi ever being willing to help me again. I planned to fly a lot more trips through Fiji. I couldn't afford to piss them off.

"Greg, what the hell are you pulling? I get on these guys' shit list and I'll never ever get any maintenance in the entire South Pacific."

"I've got it under control, Bob. Follow my lead. Let me do the talking."

I had to admire his *chutzpah*.

The station manager drove up in a station wagon and came to a screaming stop in front of the airplane. If looks could kill, we were shark bait.

"What the hell do you want, captain? My entire staff is on strike. I have four people to run our entire operation, with a 747 arriving in two hours. Just who do you think you are?"

Greg stepped in. I was sure glad I didn't have to think of a response.

"Sir, I'm sure you don't remember me. I came in with Lang Hancock last year, in our Lear. The three of us ate together at the governor's mansion. Sir X—, the chairman of Qantas, assured me, the last time we talked, that if I ever needed assistance from any Qantas base I was to telex him. Would you be so kind as to let him know that we have arrived in Nandi safely? Oh, by the way, we need two mechanics."

I would pay a million dollars for a tape of that conversation. Greg had delivered the best line I'd ever heard. He spoke softly, with great assurance. The best part was that he never cracked a smile. Hell, I knew him and he almost had *me* believing his story. If he ever wanted to drop photography, I thought to myself, he had a heck of a future as a con man. Or even as a ferry pilot. Anybody who could carry that off didn't even have to know how to fly, and he'd still have a job with Phil.

Roughly 12½ minutes later, the station manager reappeared with a telex in his hand. I knew we were sunk, but Greg had given it his best shot. He still deserved an A for effort.

The station manager positively beamed. "Sir, Qantas would be happy to be of service to you. May I offer you both a beer?"

No more than five minutes later, three mechanics started pulling the prop off the right engine. It seemed that the rubber prop seal had deteriorated as the craft sat out in California, waiting for a buyer. When I landed in Nandi the first time, I must have come back on the power a little too fast. Geared engines don't like that at all. It's very easy to blow a prop seal.

I would still give six months' pay for a copy of that telex from the chairman of Qantas.

Once safely encamped in the bar of our hotel, Greg told me the other side of the story.

A few years before, the prime minister of Australia had leased an aircraft from Qantas for a nationwide political tour. He was on a tight schedule when the aircraft suffered a major systems failure in some podunk town in northern Australia. Qantas was in deep, serious trouble.

The chairman of Qantas knew Lang Hancock. In desperation, he called to see if he could help. A few hours later, Hancock's Lear was at the disposal of the prime minister for the duration of his dog and pony show. The chairman of Qantas owed Lang a big favor. He now showed no reluctance at all in repaying that debt.

A new prop seal was flown in from Melbourne on the first available flight. I never learned just how the Nandi station manager came up with three qualified mechanics at a moment's notice, especially in the middle of a strike. Some things are better left unasked.

Greg found a telephone booth and disappeared for a moment. When he reappeared he was once again wearing spectacles, an ordinary suit, and the rest of his Clark Kent disguise. But he didn't fool me for a second.

He and I spent three days at the beach, where he informed me again how rich the Pilbara was in iron ore. Did I know that it was the richest iron deposit in the entire world, and the biggest? I told him that I would be sure to write that down and remember it. Thirty-two years later, knowing that would help me to become part of the biggest gold find in the last hundred years. The same process that dumped all that iron ore on the Pilbara dumped a similar quantity of gold, in an identical way. But I've told that story in another book.

This trip had already taken far longer than either of us had planned. We were anxious to be on our way. Once all the big pieces were reattached to our plane, we departed for La Tontouta.

Other than a few minor problems, like radio failure and burning up both of our batteries, the rest of the trip passed uneventfully. We made a delightful overnight stay in La Tontouta. Unfortunately we bypassed the sunglazed white beaches festooned with bevies of sunglazed bronzed goddesses with little tiny swimsuits. But I had far more trips ahead of me than behind me. The beaches and the beauties would still be there on another trip.

Our ten-hour trip from La Tontouta to Melbourne was acceptably boring.

After we landed and came to a halt in front of the Rockwell dealer's hangar, I turned to Greg. "Any time you want to go on another delivery, give me a call." I handed him the keys, grabbed my luggage, and started walking to the passenger terminal.

For a passenger, he wasn't half bad.

I still wonder what that telex said.

After I settled with Phil, I suppose I put $800 in my pocket, after twenty-four days. All things considered, I wasn't even making minimum wage.

But the stories . . .

68th TRIP: LAKELAND, FLORIDA to PORTLAND, MAINE

1978	from	to	nautical miles	knots	time (hours)			
					flight	day	night	inst.
Feb 8	Lakeland	Augusta	250	125	2.0	2.0		
	Augusta	Gander	1,695	184	9.2	9.2		
Feb 9	Gander	Portland	724	85	8.5	6.5	2.0	2.5
TOTALS		1 day	2,669	135	19.7	17.7	2.0	2.5

Some airplanes are born to fly, just as some pilots are. Some are born to sit. As with booze and flying, the two don't ever mix.

I once believed I could fly any aircraft. Some aircraft, though, were like some women; they would dig their heels in and wouldn't budge for anything or anyone. The best any pilot could ever do was to give it his best shot, and when beaten into the ground, try to limp away. The best of pilots and the best of men can be defeated. There were other airplanes, other ferry companies, and other women. Look at it as advanced training for a better class of vehicle.

FROM 1978 TO 1980, U.S. general aviation sales and international aircraft deliveries both reached their all-time peaks. The dollar was in freefall. With each drop, another plane was sold overseas. In 1978 about eighteen thousand new general aviation planes came off the assembly lines. Over three thousand of them went overseas.

Back in 1975, when I was a mere fledgling, Globe Aero employed ten full-time ferry pilots. As the pace of deliveries increased, Phil hired new pilots almost daily. We had so many, it was possible for a new guy to make five or ten trips before meeting all the other pilots. Rather than assemble a small, elite crew, Phil would hire anyone who walked through the door, then abuse the hell out of us all financially. He knew that the constant stream of new guys would put up with anything he tried to pull.

As my experience increased, I found myself earning less and less per trip. I loved international flying. It was one of the most dangerous occupations in the world. I was willing to take my chances, but not for a peon's wages. Phil was rapidly approaching the limits of my tolerance.

Doing favors for Phil had a nasty habit of turning around and biting you on the butt. I had checked out that Rockwell 685 to help him out. During the absurd three-week duration of my subsequent trip in it, I could have made three or four quickies to Europe in singles. Each would have paid as much as I had made on that seventy-five-hour Australian debacle. And another thing: new singles were a bit slower than used twins, but they were many times safer.

Now another Rockwell 685 was standing on the ramp of Globe's hangar. I wasn't pleased. My name appeared to be plastered all over its sides. Or was that my imagination?

On my westbound trips I tried to make a habit of flying out of Oakland. Oakland airport was uncrowded, the fuel cheap, and the National Weather Service maintained a facility right on the field. I had noticed that two west coast pilots, Bruce Hacke and Earl Covell, had joined forces and formed a new ferry service based there after buying the rights to ferry Cessna's planes to Australia. They called it Transair.

Somehow undercutting the already low prices of Globe Aero, they had picked up the contract to deliver all the new Cessnas going to Australia. Globe Aero delivered all the Pipers, Rockwells, and Beech aircraft that were flown there, but the big juicy plum was the Cessna contract.

For years, the Australian Cessna dealer, Rex Aviation, had been crating and shipping all the single-engine Cessnas bound for Australia. After years of watching Globe Aero safely deliver one single-engine plane after another, they could no longer maintain the fiction that flying single-engine aircraft over the Pacific was dangerous.

A contract to deliver only twin-engine Cessnas to Australia provided just about enough flying to enable two pilots to starve fashionably. Transair had been moving perhaps fifteen or twenty airplanes a year. With the addition of a hundred or more singles, they leapt into the big time overnight. But neither of them could deliver more than one plane a month to Australia by himself.

Bruce Hacke flipped a coin. When it landed on its edge, he decided that he would be president and resident genius of the new venture. As the sole pilot, Earl Covell flipped the coin to decide who should be chief pilot. When it stuck to the ceiling, he awarded the position to himself. Between them, they just about had enough sense to pour piss out of a boot, provided instructions were printed on the heel.

The distance between the east and west coasts of the U.S. measures about 2,500 miles on a map. The gap between west coast ferry pilots and east coast ferry pilots, though not measurable in miles, is far wider.

All the ferry companies had started life as a one-man band. A pilot with some contacts at a major manufacturer would con someone into letting him ferry a plane or two. If he survived, he picked up the customer and the contract. Or he'd undercut the price of the fellow who already had a contract with a dealer, until the dealer allowed him to start flying his planes. The ferry company would build from there, usually by cut-throat competition. Everyone knows that a pilot is a pilot is a pilot. And they are all whores.

Because there was a greater number of individual customers in Europe, most ferry companies started by delivering to Europe. Only a few operations started out by flying Pacific trips, as there were only a few dealers in the entire area. As a result, the pilots flying Pacific trips flew planes built by a single manufacturer to a single destination.

Only Globe Aero flew everywhere. Globe Aero pilots were qualified to fly anywhere and with anything, at any time.

Even then, I had a reputation. I delivered airplanes when most pilots were still telling war stories in the bar. Plus, I wasn't a prima donna, insisting on fast twins only, with a panel full of instruments.

Bruce Hacke tried for months to get me to move to the west coast and fly for him. The flying would soon get boring but the pay was a whole lot better. As far as Phil Waldman was concerned, I was just another warm body. He had twenty-five warm bodies. Losing one now and then was no big deal. Hacke told me that any time I wanted to move, I had a job at Transair. At least I had an ace in the hole.

Sure enough, when I went up to Phil's office, I learned that I was scheduled to take the Rockwell 685 to England. For $500. Once again, a past favor became a millstone. I disliked twins in general and I hated the 685.

We then had a long talk about the wisdom of flying Cherokee 181s to Australia. The Australian Piper dealer had been pressuring Phil for years to fly his 181s there, rather than having them crated and shipped. With the high cost of money and the delay involved in sea freight, it cost him more to import Piper's second-smallest single than it would to fly them there.

Phil said, "I'd pay two thousand dollars per trip, Bob." That was at least fifty percent more than we pilots made on any other trip. "No one else will commit to flying the 181s. Everyone wants twins. Big twins."

Like all groups of people, ferry pilots can fall into groupthink. I gave an example in an earlier chapter.

The little singles carried no status. I had delivered a bunch of them to Europe. With its new high-performance wing, the 181 was now only a few knots slower than the planes we were already delivering to Australia.

Since Phil couldn't get anyone except me to commit to flying the Cherokee, he had declined to take them to Australia. I begged him to reconsider. I could make thirty trips a year to Australia. By delivering nothing but Cherokees to Australia, I could double my income while flying the same number of trips, and be at home more often. But Phil wouldn't buy it. He told the Piper dealer he wouldn't fly them.

Five years later, all of his senior pilots would have killed for a $2,000 trip to Australia. Dragging the plane behind them if they had to.

I completed my preflight planning and paperwork on the Rockwell 685 bound for England. To save a few dollars, Phil hadn't installed as many tanks as he had in the one I flew to Melbourne. If I were to arrive at all, I would have to go to high altitude and have a following breeze.

The more I learned about this airplane, the less I liked it. As with my previous 685, it had sat on the ramp for a couple of years, waiting for a buyer. I was learning. Airplanes and women must be exercised regularly. If they are not, they dry up and fly grumpy. This plane hadn't flown for two years.

I looked over at my chariot. It has hate at first sight.

On February 8, 1978 I departed for Augusta, Georgia. The 685 gulped avgas at a prodigious rate. Somehow, the way ferry pilots do, I had learned that avgas in Augusta was fifteen cents a gallon cheaper than elsewhere. By refueling there, I put another $50 in my pocket. I continued on to Gander.

Every ferry pilot carried a little pocket notepad. We found it convenient to keep records of our trips, and to write a short squawk sheet on each plane. I started to write down the deficiencies I found on N135EX. I soon realized that I would run out of notepad before I had listed all the problems. This was fixing to turn into another shitty trip and another lousy daily rate.

After a leisurely breakfast in Gander, I packed my bags and headed to the airport. My first stop was at the weather office. Strong headwinds precluded flying to Iceland. The distance was three hundred miles less than from Gander to Shannon, but the winds and weather were rotten.

On the previous day, when I arrived in Gander, the winds to Shannon were about eighty knots on the tail and expected to continue. But winds change, especially when you need the help. Closer examination of the weather charts showed that today, I might get a forty-knot push if I could coax this beastie all the way to twenty-four thousand feet. A fresh low pressure system was moving in quickly. With any delay, the winds would deteriorate further.

I frowned. Phil hadn't installed nearly enough ferry tank capacity to provide what I considered the minimum of two hours' fuel reserve when over Shannon. I worked out a flight plan. If everything turned out as well as forecast, I might have a one-hour reserve. I was used to arriving overhead Shannon with ten hours' fuel on board in a single-engine plane. I often flew from Canada directly to Germany or Switzerland, a further thousand miles. Phil's decision to save $40 or $50 in fuel tanks was going to cost me a couple hundred dollars in extra expenses. Or perhaps my life.

With great trepidation, I filed my flight plan and left Gander at about two o'clock. By now, my gripe sheet numbered eighteen varied items. By itself, each should have been a minor problem. Taken as a whole, however, I had on my hands an airplane that barely flew. If I encountered any more problems I might find myself in the dead man's corner of the envelope. Few pilots return from that corner.

Two and a half hours out of Gander, I switched to my internal ferry system. For a few minutes the fuel pumps ran smoothly. Then their smooth purr became a more troubled groan. I put a hand on one pump to see if overheating was the problem. Much to my surprise, the pump was cold.

During my overnight stay in Gander, the temperature had dropped to minus fifteen degrees Celsius. After twelve hours of this bitter cold, the fuel in my tanks had been chilled to the ambient air temperature.

When fuel pumps fail, it's usually caused by overheating due to a lack of fuel flow. My pumps were about to fail due to the flow of cold gasoline. If this were to happen mid-ocean, I would be unable to make landfall anywhere, since I had next to no reserve. At best, I might make it to within three or four hundred miles of Ireland before the engines ran out of fuel, while I tried to figure out what to do with two fifty-five-gallon drums full of unusable, cold avgas. Since Phil didn't pay us to get *almost* across, I had to find an alternative.

I called ATC and advised Gander of my intention to return. I turned back for Canada.

As I flew, I mulled over my options. This waste of a flight had just consumed about $200 worth of fuel. I could expect to spend at least two or three days in Gander, waiting for better weather and winds, all at my expense. Once again, Phil's habit of pinching every penny meant that for him to make an extra $50, I would make several hundred dollars less than I should have. I had just flown unpaid hours in an airplane that required $10,000 worth of work on it to qualify it as a piece of shit. All in the dead of winter.

I needed unpaid flight time like I needed a co-pilot. I changed my mind. Rather than land in Gander, I continued on to Portland, Maine, the home of the nearest Rockwell dealer.

My gripe sheet grew to the size of one of John MacDonald's lengthier novels. I was no longer willing to risk my life for free. But at least I could give whoever flew the 685 to England a fighting chance of flying a safe airplane. I left the plane and all my squawk sheet notes with the Rockwell dealer in Portland.

That trip marked the end of an important chapter in my life.

Phil Waldman gave me a start in ferry flying, at a time when I didn't know the difference between a Piper PA-23 and a PA-32. But he took advantage of me for far too long. Ferry flying is a dangerous job, but the risks can be minimized with proper equipment and qualified pilots. Flying airplanes for free across two thousand miles of water made no sense to me, since Phil often chose to make money at the pilot's expense.

I called him from Boston, on my way to California. I told him that Transair had just hired one slightly worn ferry pilot. As far as I was concerned, Phil could take the 685 and shove it where the sun never shines. For the first time ever, an airplane had beaten me.

The indomitable Donn Kerby flew up to Portland to try to fly N135EX over to England. He couldn't even start the left engine. He left it there in disgust and went home to Lakeland.

Dave Grey tried next. The dealer had managed to fix the engine starting problem. Dave got as far as Gander, but only barely, as he almost crash-landed in blinding fog after suffering total communications radio failure. He too abandoned the plane in disgust.

Six months later, in the summer, the owner from England picked up the airplane himself. It was still sitting in Gander. He flew the little old lady route: Greenland, Iceland, Scotland, England.

That plane was the first that Globe Aero (eventually) had to turn down. For years, Phil had made a point of taking anything — out of pride, I suppose, but money must have played a part, too.

That Rockwell cost Phil the best and most dependable pilot Globe ever had. But he learned that some airplanes weren't fit to be flown across the ocean. After that, whenever one of his pilots told him that a plane shouldn't be flown, he listened. He turned down more than a few planes after that. He prevented more than a few deaths.

69th TRIP: OAKLAND, CA to SYDNEY, AUSTRALIA

1978	from	to	nautical miles	knots	time (hours)			
					flight	day	night	inst.
Mar 23	Oakland	Oakland	0	0	0.5	0.5		
	Oakland	Honolulu	2,091	128	16.4	4.4	12.0	2.0
Mar 27	Honolulu	Tarawa	2,138	144	14.8	5.8	9.0	1.0
Mar 28	Tarawa	La Tontouta	1,282	109	11.8	11.8		2.0
Mar 29	La Tontouta	Sydney *	1,064	118	9.0	9.0		
Mar 30	Sydney *	Bankstown	15	30	0.5	0.5		
TOTALS		7 days	6,590	124	53.0	32.0	21.0	5.0

* Mascot airport

As far as ferry pilots were concerned, there were half a dozen key airports in the world. At one time or another, every ferry pilot had flown through them. We often ran into pilots from other ferry companies there. All that each of us was trying to do was to deliver a plane from one point to another. Our primary concern was survival. We also hoped to make some money.

The management of every ferry company disparaged the management of every other ferry company. But once pilots left on trips, differences were laid aside. We often filed flight plans together. It wasn't unknown for pilots from competing companies to fly a leg together. At least you had someone to talk shop with.

Up to this point I had thought that whichever ferry company you flew for, the flying was done in about the same way. After all, the water below was the same for all of us, and we all got the same weather briefs. I was dead wrong.

I learned a lot about flying from Bruce Hacke and Earl Covell. They were a real pair. Transair was to ferry flying what the Ringling Brothers and Barnum & Bailey were to large, empty lots. All they lacked was the elephants. Left to their own devices, even that wouldn't have surprised me.

Transair had existed as a ferry company for probably five years before I went to work for them. The company had never delivered more than twenty or thirty planes in any year. Bruce and Earl had flown a few trips a year for

Transair's previous owner. When he decided to sell the company, they made him an offer. Then they immediately hit the jackpot, when Rex Aviation decided to ferry all its single-engine planes to Australia.

I never did figure out what either of them did to earn his keep. I suspect they never really figured it out either. They did have one nice asset: acres and acres of shiny new single-engine Cessnas destined for Rex Aviation. Each plane was just waiting for someone to jump in and go make some money.

BY THIS TIME the dollar was so weak that it looked as if America had held a fire sale on all U.S. goods. Every plane made in the U.S. was sold long before it rolled off the assembly line. Quantity, however, neither spells nor means quality.

In the competition for the general aviation dollar, Cessna had been at the top of the heap for so long that it had become fat, lazy, and very sassy. If any buyer were to object to the trash Cessna produced, others stood patiently in line waiting to plunk their money down. I've picked up new airplanes from every manufacturer in the world. None compared to the quality, or rather the lack of quality, built into every single Cessna I signed for.

Most manufacturers gave the distributor a call when his new plane was ready. The distributor then called or telexed the ferry company. The ferry company sent a pilot to the manufacturer. The pilot inspected the plane, signed for it, and took off. November Sierra — no sweat.

When a ferry pilot arrived at Wichita to pick up a new Cessna, however, he underwent the torture of the damned. Cessna should have hung a sign over the door of its delivery center: "Abandon hope, all ye who enter here."

Nothing, but nothing was either easy or convenient. Like with every other aircraft company, you first took a taxi to the factory. Once there, you learned that your plane had to be picked up at another field, usually over in East Woebegon. Cessna provided, at a purely nominal charge, a stagecoach to take you there. It ran every three months, and the previous one left yesterday.

The pilot spent all week getting to the other field. He arrived at 4:04 pm on a Friday. The surly receptionist told him, "We're closed." He must catch the stagecoach back to town, and return on Monday.

But the worst part of picking up a Cessna was not the absence of concern or of good manners on the part of its staff. The worst part was trying to fly the damn planes.

Cessna couldn't even spell quality control. Usually, but not always, the engine was installed. Sometimes the radios worked (Sundays and alternate Thursdays). The Cessnas most favored by visiting ferry pilots featured a fixed undercarriage, a single engine, and no radios. Anything more complex than that was bound to fail in some way.

Anyone who could deliver a new Cessna from the factory in Wichita to the west coast in less than a week was a magician. That, or the Second Coming was around the corner.

Chief pilot Earl Covell had mandated, "All new pilots start by picking up new planes from the factory. No exceptions."

Now, I was dumb, but not as dumb as he thought I looked. In simple yet forceful terms, I expressed my displeasure. I also told him to get stuffed. Transair paid me to ferry planes, not nursemaid or drag them. Let the new fish bite on that particular worm.

While working for Transair, I never picked up a new aircraft from the factory. From our very first conversation, Earl and I just loved each other.

By this time I had completed almost seventy ferry trips. This was far more than Bruce and Earl put together. If I could work at my pace, I could move planes across oceans faster than anyone else. That was the rub — I wanted to do it my way, at my pace. I wanted the freedom to do it the way I knew worked for me.

Lum and Abner didn't see things my way. Collectively, they had agreed that the only way to fly was to stuff as many planes as you could into a gaggle. When I first learned that, I blanched. Group flying is like group sex; it's messy, and nobody's real sure about who's doing what to whom and when. But Lum was president and Abner was chief pilot. I was but a lowly ferry pilot. Hell's bells! I'll try anything, once.

I waited for three or four days for Lum and Abner to try to organize themselves. I could have completed a delivery in that time if I'd been by myself. Anything once, but some things only once.

Another Globe Aero pilot lived in the Bay area. This was Bill Delong, otherwise known as Long Delong. The "Long" didn't refer to any physical attribute, but to the records he set for the duration of ferry trips every time he got his hands on a plane. Without question, I flew the fastest trips in the ferry business. Bill stood at the opposite end of that spectrum.

Bill had provided free entertainment for the crew at Globe Aero for years. He would sign for an airplane destined for Australia, take off, and then disappear for weeks. Then someone would run across him in New Orleans or El Paso or Yuma. I think his record trip took six weeks, with no weather or mechanical delays. I don't mean his slowest trip — six weeks was his fastest.

Bill was slow, but a great guy. He was the only other ex-military pilot flying for Globe Aero. When he went through Navy flight training, I think they were still using biplanes. Phil Waldman lost a lot of sleep trying to figure out how to explain to customers why their planes kept disappearing for long stretches of time.

Phil didn't like pilots who wanted to fly only one ocean. Bill Delong wouldn't ever fly the Atlantic, so he went to work at Transair with me. If he and I could have come up with a mutually acceptable flight schedule, we would have made a great pair.

Hacke and Covell burned the midnight oil for weeks, preparing four Cessnas for the trip to Sydney. I couldn't for the life of me see what the problem was. Globe Aero could do the paperwork for as many as four planes in one day. Tanking took a couple of days but they were quick on the administration and paperwork.

At the last minute, Hacke decided not to fly one of the planes himself. As president of Transair, he had to stay home and fight fires. To this day, I'm convinced that the thought of ferrying planes across water scared the hell out of him. He scheduled himself to fly many times, only to cancel at the last moment. As for his firefighting, all I ever saw him do was set a fire, then put it out. Set another fire, put it out. I guess that's what the president is supposed to do. Interesting guy, but flaky.

Covell called another local pilot, stuck him in Hacke's plane, and off we went. If our start was any indication, this whole crew was way behind the power curve.

But Transair did do a few things the way I thought they should be done. For a start, we agreed that the only time a plane had too much fuel on board was when it was on fire. These planes were tanked from stem to stern. It was possible to fly our longest leg, from Oakland to Honolulu, in anything short of a hurricane and still have lots of reserve. I've landed in Honolulu with ten hours' reserve fuel. That's my idea of a reserve. You can make all kinds of navigation errors and survive.

Transair also installed permanent HF radios. Every HF radio worked, every trip. And the pay was a whole lot better. In exchange for all of this, I could put up with a lot.

Or could I?

We ran our four-plane formation to Honolulu. Trying to keep everyone in sight was a great pain in the neck. But I always had someone to talk to. Great, if you enjoy sixteen hours of chatter.

Earl suffered from a condition not uncommon to the chief pilots of ferry companies. He continually wanted to make decisions. It didn't seem to bother him in the slightest that I had five trips to each of his. He insisted that each of us know just who was boss.

We arrived in Honolulu at noon. Earl told us to follow him to park the planes. Then we sat under the blistering Hawaiian sun while each of us refueled, in sequence, from the single fuel pump this place had.

I pointed out to him that it made no sense to have three of us sitting and watching one guy refuel. I'd taxi over to another FBO, refuel, and return. While they continued to refuel, I could go rent a car for us, take our baggage to a hotel and check in for the group.

He looked at me with a dead stare and said, "Forget it, Mo. We'll each refuel in order." The four of us would then go to rent the car. Then the four of us would check into the hotel. I couldn't believe he wanted to make such hard work of it!

From landing, it took six hours to make it to a hotel room. Thank God the four of us didn't have to sleep together.

It got worse. It seemed that Covell thought everything should be done together. We ate breakfast together, as if it mattered. We ate dinner together. Fortunately I never considered falling in lust on this trip. Covell might have wanted to do that together, too.

One of the most important tricks I learned in ferrying was never to duplicate effort. Formation flying for sixteen hours was tough enough.

Our group should have nominated one fellow to fuel all four planes. The other three should have gone and rented the car, driven off, dropped one guy off to get a preview of the weather on the next leg, and another guy to check all of us into a hotel. The driver would then return to pick up the refueling pilot, who by that time would have finished his chores.

The very few really good ferry pilots all worked this way. Nobody got paid a cent for showing how hard we could work. Working smart, though, was worth a bundle.

We went through an even more incredible procedure the following day. We rose in unison, ate breakfast together, formed an orderly queue at the checkout desk, and drove to the weather office *en masse*. There, in order, each of us received identical weather briefs. The other three pilots spent half an hour studying a high altitude "loop".

This so-called loop showed the progress of the cloud band in the intertropical convergence zone (ITC or ITZ or ITCZ, depending on who is using the term). I yawned a lot. I never could figure out what looking at yesterday's weather had to do with today's weather. After much serious discussion, it was decided that yesterday's weather precluded safe flight through the ITZ today. I yawned again. We went through the same routine for a couple of days. I think that Earl finally got bored with Honolulu, because one morning he announced that the weather looked great to him. I looked at it this time. Damned if it didn't look exactly the same as it had for the previous days. It was time to go fly.

Due to the Coriolis effect on a spinning sphere (the Earth), the prevailing winds flow from the west in the mid-northern and mid-southern latitudes. Due to the effects of friction, the prevailing winds at the equator and in bands on either side of the equator blow from the east. The zones from five degrees to eight degrees of latitude, both north and south of the equator, are where the prevailing westerlies converge with the prevailing easterlies. A lot of weather is associated with this convergence area or zone.

Truly, it would be great to have an accurate forecast of any weather you expect to have to fly through. But yesterday's weather had nothing to do with today's weather, or next year's weather for that matter.

I tended to base my decision on a pilot's competence on whether he bothered to review the loop. I can think of no information more useless to a ferry pilot flying the Pacific. If he made a big deal of it, he usually had no idea what he was doing. There were more than a few ferry pilots like that.

We left Honolulu as a quartet, bound for the atoll of Tarawa, one of the Gilbert islands. We went through a similar drill there. After a day's rest, we left for La Tontouta in New Caledonia. I really didn't believe it possible, but Covell's antics screwed up even La Tontouta as a rest stop. It was such a great place that I thought it impossible not to enjoy it, but he continued to work his ass off to make the trip as tedious as possible. After another rest day we finally pulled into Sydney. The trip had been a long one, made longer by being dull.

Our chief pilot didn't know how or where to clear customs in Sydney's Mascot field. I had to lead him around by the nose to show him every detail. We then flew in unison over to Bankstown airport, our final destination.

I didn't think much of Cessna products then, and still don't. However, the Australian distributor, Rex Aviation, had some first-class people. Of all the customers I ever delivered to, they were the best. Once our planes rolled to a stop, their mechanics literally swarmed over them. Within moments we each had a beer or a mug of tea in our hands. Their crew wouldn't allow a ferry pilot to do a single thing. When they had finished, our radios, fuel pumps, tank straps and other assorted ferry gear were presented to us in a neat, tidy package, ready to turn over to the airline.

As soon as I arrived, I gave Deslee I— a call. I had a standing invitation to stay with her. A week spent putting up with Covell and crew had been nearly too much to bear.

Earl had made plans for us to take a taxi, in unison, to a hotel where we would perform another formation check-in. Just about the time we finished de-tanking, Deslee walked into the hangar. Every eyeball in the place swiveled as she ran up and kissed me. Boy, Australian women were friendly. Since we had such an appreciative audience, we held our liplock for a few extra heartbeats. The Rex mechanics let out a collective sigh as our suction was broken.

I told Earl I'd meet him at the airport for our return flight the next night. As Deslee and I walked out to her car, hand in hand, he stood open-mouthed and dumbfounded.

If you've got the name, you have to act the part.

83rd TRIP: OAKLAND, CA to SYDNEY, AUSTRALIA

1978	from	to	nautical miles	knots	time (hours)			
					flight	day	night	inst.
May 26	Oakland	Honolulu	2,091	172	12.1	12.1		
May 27	Honolulu	Pago Pago	2,268	177	12.8	1.8	11.0	2.5
May 28	Pago Pago	Norfolk Island	1,487	165	9.0	9.0		
May 29	Norfolk Island	Sydney *	911	175	5.2	5.2		
May 30	Sydney *	Bankstown	15	30	0.5	0.5		
TOTALS		4 days	6,772	171	39.6	28.6	11.0	2.5

* Mascot airport

Airplanes are like shoes. Some fit perfectly, the first time you put them on. Others bind and chafe. No matter how much time you spend in them, they never quite wear well.

Spending many hours a day airborne demands maximum performance from a pilot. Without being hedonistic in the slightest, I opted for maximum comfort in what I wore. My flying wardrobe consisted of loose-fitting cotton shirts, wool or cotton pants or shorts, and a pair of well-fitting leather shoes. I wore only natural fibers. When I went out to California to fly for Transair, all I took with me were enough clothes for a two-week trip and one pair of comfortable shoes.

My shoes disappeared. One minute they were there and the next minute they were gone, forever. Later I did see a pair almost like mine, even down to the scuff marks. But I wore size 8½ and these were a size 2 or 3.

BRUCE HACKE AND I sat down for a long heart-to-heart when I got back to Oakland. He had to sneak me in, after the girls in the scanty costumes standing on the backs of the white horses prancing around the circle, and before the clown act.

My forte lay in moving airplanes from one point on the Earth's surface to another. When I first started trading time spent in airplanes crossing oceans for checks with only a few zeroes on them, I learned that one airplane equaled one paycheck. Each time I turned over a keychain with two silver keys on it, I got paid. More keychains meant more paychecks. By now I had all the flight time a man could spend in a lifetime, but oh, that filthy lucre.

Flying the Transair way meant a whole gaggle of planes arriving on Rex's ramp once in a long while, all at great expense, and with much wear and tear on the poor pilots. But I moved planes easily, smoothly, rapidly, and safely. Regularly, too.

By this time my wife and I had moved back to Pennsylvania. She had had several miscarriages and we wanted children. We moved her in with her parents. That left me free to fly for anyone, anywhere, and to make money doing it.

If Bruce and Earl wanted to play the role of bright and bouncy young transportation executives, it was OK with me. But I was a ferry pilot. I moved airplanes — or at least I would, if these bumpkins would get out of my way.

Hacke and I came to an agreement. He could run the company any damned way he wanted, and run trips in any fashion he wished. I would be left alone to deliver Cessnas to Sydney, my way. All Transair had to do was keep polishing those silver keys and handing me a set every time I reappeared.

It was a mutually acceptable solution. Rex got a new airplane each and every week, for fifteen weeks. I flew like a madman. Over a period of three and a half months, I averaged almost eight hours in the air per day. I delivered more airplanes in a shorter period than any other ferry pilot ever did or ever would.

The FAI keeps a record book of aviation matters, in Paris. It deals with such mundane matters as speed, distance, and altitude records. But the aviation community in general, and ferry pilots in particular, keep track of some looser and more informal records. Most ferry pilots liked to believe themselves to be a little better than any of the others in this tiny field of endeavor. I had already raised more than a few eyebrows when I flew a record-setting forty-two deliveries in my first full year of ferrying. Ferry trips are like babies: some are long, some are short, and some are fatter than others, too.

Once a week I departed Oakland in a brand new Cessna. I turned west into that great gaping black void of night over the Pacific. Every week for fifteen weeks I covered the stretch between the west coast and Honolulu, the longest nonstop puddle of water between two points of land anywhere in the world.

Every Pacific controller came to recognize my voice. Every Qantas 747 crew flying between Sydney and San Francisco knew the diminutive Captain Mo. At the end of my short career with Transair, every ferry pilot in the world spoke my name with just a little awe, never quite believing the feat. But I could do anything, if I could just do it my way.

On one such delivery during this period, with each trip running into the next, I took the familiar taxi ride out to Honolulu airport. I finished my preflight planning. My plane had been fueled. My flight plan was complete. I had my little rituals that I was comfortable with. I never rushed anything, but neither did I waste time.

I had arrived from Oakland at 7 am. By 8 pm I'd be back in the cockpit, headed for Pago Pago. My tan wasn't anything to write home about, but I had a good chunk of cash in the bank.

On this particular evening I had slipped off my shoes, packed everything in my plane just where it belonged, hopped in, and called Honolulu clearance delivery to put my clearance on request for my international flight plan. A few minutes later, my radio crackled back as clearance delivery approved my instrument flight plan to Pago Pago. I closed the door of the Cessna, fired up the engine, taxied out, and took off over the water.

It took me three days, sometimes four, to fly from the west coast to Sydney. Qantas took two days to get me back because they flew eastbound, across the international dateline. Then it took a day or so for Lum and Abner to ready another aircraft in which I could go and do it again.

When I flew in an airplane, I lived in it. Each leg took 12–18 hours of flying. I carried a one-gallon jug of ice-cold lemonade, a full ice chest of Pepsi, cold cuts, and various snacks. The very first thing I did after takeoff was to remove my shoes and make myself comfortable.

All of these airplanes carried autopilots. At times, on the odd occasion, they even worked. I would lower the back of my seat and go to sleep. All I had to do was make a heading adjustment and a radio report once every hour or so. When I wasn't resting or picking my navel, I'd read a book. I averaged five or six books on each trip. All this and a paycheck, too. It wasn't all that bad a life.

When I arrived in Pago Pago on this particular morning, after my plane rolled to a stop I shut my engine down. I hopped out and luxuriated in the freedom of being able to stretch in every direction. As the fuel crew drove up, I rummaged through my belongings to find my shoes. I looked and looked, but couldn't find them. I wrinkled my brow trying to remember where I had put them. I'd worn them when climbing into the plane in Honolulu so they had to be in there somewhere, unless I had picked up a couple of packrats along the way, or they had fallen out of the airplane. But I couldn't find those shoes anywhere.

I wasn't worried. It wasn't uncommon for loose articles to slip under the wooden frame supporting the fuel tanks. By this time the fuel folks had finished filling my ferry tanks so I couldn't check underneath. No problem; just no shoes, and no spare pair.

I gathered my bags for the death-defying, hair-raising, knee-knocking taxi ride to the Rainmaker Hotel. The Rainmaker had earned its reputation as easily the finest hotel in American Samoa. It was also the only hotel in American Samoa. Since I couldn't find my shoes, I took off my socks. I didn't want to look the complete fool.

By far the most dangerous legs of the 7,000-mile journey from California to Australia were the taxi rides between the airport and the hotel in Pago Pago. Occasionally the driver was sober. The smallest of them was humungous. All were mean. I never dared to complain about the reckless speed or dangerous driving. A head-on crash at a hundred miles an hour or a tumble over a cliff edge might be survived, but talking back to a Samoan cab driver meant instant death.

Somehow, perhaps because of my guardian angel, I survived yet another voyage into the valley of the shadow of death. I pushed a lump of soggy greenbacks toward the driver. They may have been hundreds for all I knew, or cared.

As I completed the registration form at the Rainmaker, the manager passed through the lobby. He smiled when he saw me and came over to chat.

"Captain Moriarty, welcome back. Did you have a good trip?"

"So-so. I've got a twin this trip. A little faster. Still got my room for me?"

"Of course. Pardon me, but you're not wearing any shoes."

I suppose I did look a little silly, standing there in the middle of the lobby, barefooted. I went through the whole story for his benefit. He nodded sagely but looked at me as if I was transmitting just slightly off frequency.

I ate, squeezed in six hours of sleep, and set out to battle dragons once more. I survived the harrowing trip to the airport. Weakly I made my weekly trip to the flight service station, to file my flight plan to Sydney. The briefer was talking on the phone as I padded in, so I glanced through my weather brief until he finished.

"Hey, Bob. How's it going?"

"OK. Looks like I've got some headwinds. Any weather?"

"None until you get past Lord Howe Island. It ain't much. Twenty percent chance of morning fog in Sydney, but it should burn off by the time you get there. Say, Bob, how come you're not wearing any shoes?"

I ran through my story once again. He began to look at me with a strange glint in his eyes, as if one of us was a little wacky. I hoped it was him.

The fourteen-hour trip from Pago Pago to Sydney passed swiftly. Nothing happened. Everything worked, except me. That's the trick.

Sydney still had a bit of the morning fog remaining. I landed and taxied in to my regular spot, near customs. I shut the engine down and waited for the Customs and Health Service officer. Upon arriving in Australia, the pilot was required to sit in his closed and sealed cockpit until an officer showed up and handed over an aerosol can of insect fogger through a side window. The pilot then sprayed the aircraft thoroughly before alighting. I'm not sure it killed any bugs, but I'm pretty sure we lost a couple of pilots to it.

I unstrapped myself and hopped out of the cockpit.

"Captain, Australian flight regulations require the pilot of an aircraft to wear shoes while flying."

Interesting set of regulations. I couldn't help but wonder what other interesting rules they had thought up.

"I know. But I'm not flying now, am I? My feet got so tired after fourteen hours of confinement during the flight. I always wait until the engine comes to a complete stop before taking them off. It's so relaxing after a long flight to take them off."

He looked at me skeptically. For the spur of the moment, it wasn't a bad story. We walked a half-mile through the terminal. I wore my complete ferry captain uniform, *sans* shoes. I felt like a fool.

After my ferry tanks ran dry the previous night, I unfastened the fittings and lifted the tanks to look for my shoes. They weren't under the tanks, or anywhere else. I couldn't find them.

Formalities completed, I returned to my beast, fired her up and flew the few miles over to Bankstown airport. Ten minutes later I rolled to a stop in front of Rex Aviation.

My favorite mechanic rushed over when he saw me pull up. We shook hands. I told him the story of my shoes. He laughed and told me he'd have them for me in just a few minutes. Five mechanics and twenty minutes later, he came over to where I sat sipping a cup of hot tea.

"Bob, are you sure your shoes were in the airplane?"

"Yeah. I had them on when I left Honolulu. Then the damned things vanished on the way to Pago Pago."

"Sorry to be the bearer of bad tidings, but there are no shoes anywhere in that plane. Are you sure they didn't wind up in your luggage?"

"I've looked there three times. If they aren't in the plane, and they aren't in my luggage, I wonder what the hell happened to them."

He shook his head. "I dunno." He looked at me strangely. Maybe I'd eaten them in a mad feeding frenzy and just wouldn't 'fess up.

I never found those shoes. On the trip back to Mascot airport, I had the taxi driver stop at a shoe store so I could buy a pair to wear home.

Funny thing. We take no notice of shoes until we don't have them any longer. Then everyone notices their absence.

My fifteenth trip to Australia in fifteen weeks was also my fifteenth and last for Transair. It bugged Hacke and Covell no small degree that I made more money than either of them. I'd had my fill of their poor organization, too. They could take the easiest trip in the world and somehow turn it into hard work. Between the two of them, it would have taken a week of effort and thousands of dollars to inflate a balloon and get it into the air.

They disliked having me around because I made it look easy. I disliked being around them because they turned ferry flying into needlessly hard work. So I quit, and never looked back. Transair faded into dust after a few years.

I went on to bigger and better things. I never found out what happened to Lum and Abner. Earl probably flew paper airplanes. Hacke probably went on to bigger and better things, too; a shoe salesman, perhaps.

And then one morning I parked in my usual spot on the ramp in Honolulu, after a trip from Oakland. I stepped out of my airplane and tripped over a pair of shoes. At first they looked like the pair I had lost months before. They were sun-bleached and rain-spattered. They looked very similar to mine, except that they were several sizes smaller. I wondered who had left them there on the ramp.

84th TRIP: SAN ANTONIO, TEXAS to PARIS, FRANCE

1978	from	to	nautical miles	knots	time (hours)			
					flight	day	night	inst.
Jun 14	San Antonio	Nashville	715	275	2.6	2.6		1.0
	Nashville	Williamsport	528	251	2.1	2.1		1.0
	Williamsport	Portland	361	278	1.3		1.3	1.0
	Portland	Gander	734	319	2.3		2.3	1.0
Jun 15	Gander	Narssaq	777	299	2.6	2.6		1.0
	Narssaq	Keflavik	670	319	2.1	2.1		1.0
	Keflavik	Stornoway	584	234	2.5	2.5		1.0
Jun 16	Stornoway	Shannon	351	251	1.4	1.4		1.0
	Shannon	Paris	473	225	2.1	2.1		1.0
TOTALS		3 days	5,193	273	19.0	15.4	3.6	9.0

Solo ferry trips were November Papa: no perspiration. I found flying in the company of others, in formation, an ordeal. But flying with passengers was a fate worse than deflowerment, and flying with the aircraft's owner, agony. Flying with any other pilot, especially if not a ferry pilot, was sheer torture.

Thus, to fly with a passenger who was a pilot and the owner of the aircraft was the absolute depth of despair, and sometimes a disaster. Or almost so, or I wouldn't be here to write about it.

BACK IN 1975, when I began flying little bitty airplanes across great big areas of water, a pilot worked for one ferry company, and only one. From a legal point of view, the ferry pilots served as independent contractors to the ferry companies. We didn't *work* for the ferry company; we *contracted* with them for the duration of the trip. This legal maneuver shifted the entire legal burden of liability onto the pilot's back.

But when over the ocean, the pilot had the plane firmly strapped to his behind. When our iron butterfly fluttered, we fluttered. On the not infrequent occasions when a plane went down, the pilot almost always went along for the ride. The ferry pilot was always the first person on the scene of the accident. Luckily for us, lawsuits and summons to appear were hard to serve at the bottom of the ocean. Besides, we often had more important things to think about. Such as developing a way to suck oxygen out of seawater, or to swim a thousand miles.

Legally speaking, we were contractors. Actually, we were serfs. Ferry pilots received no paid vacations, no paid holidays, no overtime, no benefits, no workers' compensation, and no unemployment insurance. In short, no rights other than to fly one trip after another. And often, we had no trips.

By the late 1970s a few ferry pilots had gained one valuable commodity — experience. But the vocation of ferry flying was highly unusual in one respect: shiny new ferry pilots still crisp from the box got exactly the same pay as the battle-scarred veteran of a hundred trips.

Slowly but surely, the pay per trip went down as expenses, primarily the price of fuel, skyrocketed. Each year I logged a greater number of trips completed. Each year, I made less per trip.

But I did have some great experiences.

While flying for Globe Aero, any suggestion that you might be interested in flying for another company was grounds for instant termination. At Transair, Lum and Abner waxed eloquent on the mutual benefits of an independent contractor relationship. What was left unspoken, but was understood, was that a pilot who demonstrated independence and chose to fly even one little trip for someone else would wait a long, long time for the next phone call from Transair.

Though we were slaves to the companies, a few of us were experienced slaves. I left Transair, made a couple of phone calls, and had a new job lined up. Ferry pilots liked to gossip, and it didn't take me long to find out that Bob Iba had lots of planes going to England, and needed an experienced pilot.

Bob Iba was ferrying planes back when J.C. was in flight school. He flew Navy fighters in the Pacific during World War II. Experienced in all types of aircraft, after the war he operated a company ferrying surplus war birds from one country to another.

At first he was buying and selling those aircraft. He soon learned that delivering them was far more profitable than tying up large chunks of money in them for long periods of time. As civilian aircraft sales boomed during the 1950s and 1960s, he switched to delivery of general aviation aircraft.

Bob was short, portly, and nearly sixty. He was at least as wide as he was high. He had the most interesting habit when he ate dinner. He would always eat his dessert first. In a field of grouchy, snappy pilots, I never heard a single bad comment about Bob Iba. He had personally delivered nearly one thousand planes to Central and South America. He was a certified character. Everyone who ever met Bob loved him.

He knew my reputation well. His only concern was the safe delivery of his airplanes. If I wished to freelance for anyone else, that was fine with him.

Bob's business was planned and organized, to an extent that no other ferry company ever successfully emulated. He knew, weeks in advance, exactly what planes were coming up. If I was willing to commit my services in advance, he could guarantee all the airplanes I wanted to fly.

His first available trip was a Piper Cherokee going to England in two weeks' time. I told him I'd be down to pick it up.

It was the best of all worlds. Transair paid better than Globe Aero. Bob paid better than Transair, and was busy. I would be free to pick up any other business I could find. But in the meantime, a job came along via Globe Aero.

When I flew for Globe, I was the only pilot qualified in pure jets. When a job to deliver a Morane-Saulnier MS.760 Paris jet came up, Phil Waldman asked me to take it. The trip, from Hamburg in Germany (home of the *real* St. Pauli girls) to Chicago, was uneventful.

Now, the same customer wanted a second Paris jet moved. He had called Phil to request my services. Phil told him that I no longer flew for Globe, but considerately gave him my phone number. So, two weeks after my final trip for Transair, I headed to San Antonio, Texas, to pick up my second Paris jet.

The Paris jet was designed as a military trainer, in the 1950s. For a jet it was slow, underpowered, had a very short range, and just loved long, long runways. It was also more fun than just about anything you can do with your clothes on. A fellow named Art Sikking, with a partner, purchased several squadrons of them when they became surplus. They imported them into the U.S. for years. The MS.760 didn't do much, but it sure was fun. At any fuel stop — and it required frequent fuel stops — it was an instant attention-grabber.

I was never keen on carrying passengers, but Art had proved himself a soulmate. He was one of the most interesting people I ever met. In his fifties by this time, he retained the spirit of a teenager. Somehow he managed to maintain a wife and a mistress, and to keep them both happy. To tell the truth, I was fascinated to hear how any man could manage to do that.

Art and I had flown together on the Hamburg–Chicago trip. Now he wanted to take another bird from Texas to a new home in Paris, France. The pay was right, and with Art along, I knew we'd have a good trip.

We met in San Antonio to pick up the airplane. Art's son, a mechanic, finished his work on it just as we arrived at the airport. We counted wings and engines. All the big parts seemed to be reasonably well attached, so we checked into a nearby hotel for a night's rest before departing.

Ferry pilots normally flew long legs, with one leg a day being a normal maximum. In its own contrary fashion, the Paris flew like a bat out of hell compared to any piston-engine aircraft but had legs shorter than a medium-sized grasshopper.

We rumbled and roared our way down many thousands of feet of runway in the San Antonio heat before becoming airborne. It seemed that every time we got comfortable, it was time to start looking for another runway and lowering the landing gear again. We flew four legs that first day, finally settling in Gander for the night. It was crazy; all we did that day was go up and down. I've had sex without that much activity.

On the first leg, Art did all the flying from the left seat while I made our radio calls and navigated from the right. After a while we switched seats so that I too could play captain. He flew the plane a lot better than I did. It had two jet engines, but I'd seen mockingbirds with more thrust.

The trickiest part of each flight was the takeoff roll. The nose had to be rotated to exactly the right attitude. Too much or too little nose attitude made the plane use a lot more runway.

We left Gander the next morning for Narssaq, Greenland. I thought I had the takeoff procedure down pat, but evidently I left the nose a little low, since I used two thousand feet more runway than Art had used in identical conditions.

I was determined to do it exactly right in Greenland. We started our takeoff roll. At seventy knots I set the nose right on the donut. Jets almost always have an angle of attack gauge. We called it a donut.

I turned to Art and smiled. "See, Art? Nothing to it."

Art smiled right back and smartly raised the landing gear. The gear started up while the plane staggered, some twenty knots short of flying speed. I could feel it settle back into ground effect before it wobbled into the air. When any aircraft is very close to the runway it has the effect of compressing the air under the wing, giving you more lift. It's called ground effect.

"Art, I don't mean to be critical, but if you *ever* touch that landing gear handle again without me telling you to, I'll break your arm. Or we'll break your nice plane."

"Sorry, Bob. I thought you were calling for the gear. It won't happen again."

The trip went smoothly. On the northern route, at that time of year, we had nearly twenty-four hours of uninterrupted sunlight. Every time we neared an airport, we landed for fuel. We hit Greenland, Iceland, Scotland and Ireland before finally touching down in Paris.

We had completed nine hops in three days. We still slept in comfortable beds and ate hot meals every night.

Years before, in the military, I developed the habit of making a complete post-flight inspection of any aircraft I flew. When I started ferrying, I continued the habit. I found fewer bullet holes, but oil and hydraulic leaks were not uncommon.

In the hangar at Transair (not the same Transair I had just quit) at Le Bourget, France, I walked around N760Q making my final inspection. I noticed something, but I wasn't real sure what. It took several moments of concentration for me to realize just what was wrong.

When we started the trip, in San Antonio, we had a six-inch blade antenna for our ADF on the belly of the plane. Now it appeared to be missing. I bent down for a closer look. No, the antenna was still in place. But we had ground it down to nothing during our miscommunication at takeoff in Greenland. But for the antenna, we would have ground away the belly of the plane instead.

Of such scrapes, ferry delivery tales are born.

I probably took a dozen of the tiny Grumman Cheetahs to the UK myself. It was a cute little bugger. Grumman AA5A

I managed to fly some interesting aircraft over the ten years I ferried aircraft. The Pilatus Porter had the same engine as the OV-10 so at least I could start it.

The Britten-Norman Trislander was the strangest plane I think I ever flew. It carried eighteen passengers. The company sold a total of seventy-two aircraft.

Paul Vandor of Jonas Aircraft who sold the BN-2 Islanders in North and South America. The factory produced a total of twelve hundred and eighty and sold every one of them at a loss.

I took a Beech Bonanza A-36 on a tour of Europe with the owner to visit his various companies. This is a wonderful aircraft to fly.

All Cessna deliveries to Australia would clear customs in Sydney then hop over to Bankstown airport for Rex Aviation. This is a C-310 in Bankstown.

I delivered a Cessna 185 on Floats to Sweden to the 2nd richest guy in the country. This was for his son. He had a large jet for himself. I didn't get to fly that.

In a race from New York to Paris in 1985 one crew got a little carried away with their paint job. But they still won.

In the late 1970s Rex Aviation in Australia bought hundreds of Cessna singles and twins. I ferried seventeen of them to Sydney in seventeen weeks. Cessna 206.

Ferry gaggle of different Cessnas being taken to Australia for Rex Aviation. This is on Norfolk Island, one of the most beautiful spots on earth.

Ernie Kuney and Andy Knox on my 2nd trip. Ernie was a whole lot more impressed with his own flying ability than anyone else.

On many of the islands we flew through in the Pacific we had to refuel using hand pumps and 55-gallon drums. The locals kept the extra fuel we paid for.

Globeaero sent four of us up to Rockwell in Georgia to pick up four Ag planes for Venezeula. I'm on the left, Tim Peltz on the right and Tony Vallone next to him.

Cessna 310 on the way to Rex Aviation in Sydney. We often used Norfolk island as a resting stop.

March 31st 1984 at 11:15 AM. Some things just need doing.

A used and abused C-404 I picked up in Sweden and dropped off in
Sumburgh about one hundred meters short of a cliff. See the ocean spray in
the background.

Donn Kerby next to a Cessna 182RG he plans on taking from Lakeland to the UK. He was the best of us all.

Donn Kerby in the door of a Piper holding the universal lubricant. Except in South Africa.

These Air Tractors scheduled to go to Egypt but issues with customs delayed the delivery so Tom Danaher and I took them to Sweden to the dealer.

Tom Danaher over Canada on the way to Sweden. Fuel problems came very close to putting him down in the North Atlantic.

The Gander Newfoundland weather guessers were the best in the world at predicting conditions over the most dangerous ocean in the world to fly over.

Art Sikking and I picked up his airplane in San Antonio. The plane was fast but had short legs so we went the northern route through Greenland and Iceland, then Scotland and down to Paris.

Art Sikking and I in Greenland with his Paris Jet destined to go to Paris. It does get cold up there.

For the Air Transat Race from Paris to New York to Paris in June of 1981 we had two meetings in advance in Paris to discuss the rules but they were never really settled.

I picked up Mike Smith's N111MS in Kansas and took it to Texas to pick up Tom Sanders for the positioning leg to Paris.

"Barrel" Fisher once flew with Tom Danaher in an Air Tractor from Texas to Europe sitting next to him in a one-person aircraft. She was a real sport.

Tom Sanders put up part of the money we needed for the race and rode with me to position the aircraft in Paris. The Windecker Eagle was faster than us but I wasn't going to tell anyone that.

Tom Danaher and I won 1st Place for Speed and 2nd Place for Handicap. We set a new record for Paris to NY and cut Lindberg's NY to Paris record in half. June 1981

The only time Jaromir Wagner stood up on the plane was when he was taking off or landing. They strapped him in a cage. While he might freeze, he wasn't going to leave the airplane.

I'm not sure if the Jaromir Wagner flight was the dumbest stunt I ever saw but it was certainly close. He failed to make money because he didn't speak English in interviews.

Richard Fenwic and I flew N111MS in another race in 1984 from Paris to Libreville but had to drop out due to engine problems.

The French pilots took the overwater flights a lot more seriously than I did. But I had done thousands of hours over the water. You either live or you die.

Mike Smith put together a wonderful V-35 for J. Richard Blissit of Tulsa. We flew it in a race from New Jersey to Paris in 1985 and took 2nd place.

I'm in the mining business now and a bit older but not necessarily any wiser.

1978	from	to	nautical miles	knots per hour	time (hours)			
					flight	day	night	inst.
Jul 6	Portland	Gander	734	153	4.8	4.8		0.5
Jul 7	Gander	Santa Maria	1,454	156	9.3	2.0	7.3	4.0
Jul 9	Santa Maria	Las Palmas	734	153	4.8	4.8		2.0
Jul 10	Las Palmas	Abidjan	1,759	160	11.0	4.0	7.0	4.0
	Abidjan	São Tomé	754	130	5.8	5.8		
Jul 11	São Tomé	Windhoek	1,499	136	11.0	5.0	6.0	3.5
Jul 12	Windhoek	Johannesburg	638	128	5.0	5.0		1.0
TOTALS		6 days	7,170	139	51.7	31.4	20.3	15.0

I started flying for Bob Iba after delivering the Paris jet to Paris. Ninety percent of Bob's trips were single-engine planes going to Oxford, England. They paid well but were boring as hell. But with them as my bread and butter, I was able to make contact with other ferry companies. I'd occasionally pick up trips they had, for which they couldn't afford to hire a full-time guy. By helping them out in this way, I set the stage for better trips later.

Compared to any other kind of flying, the most mundane delivery was interesting. When a ferry trip turned interesting, it seemed to go on forever. Before I finished this trip, handing over the set of silver keys, I would run out of fuel through my own error, make a forced landing, get arrested, get thrown out of one country, get jumped by fighter aircraft over another, land at night with no runway lights at an airport in a country at war, and almost get thrown in jail because of Miss Barbi Benton's unclothed form.

It was all in a day's work for a ferry pilot. But did it all have to happen on just one trip?

AS A TRULY INDEPENDENT ferry pilot, I found myself as popular as a hooker on Saturday night. At one time or another, nearly every ferry company had an airplane it needed moved in a hurry, and no available pilot. Each preferred to maintain a regular stable of pilots, but I had flown nearly everything, everywhere. I needed only a check and a five-minute brief to go anywhere. Like other prostitutes, though, temporary ferry pilots were there to be used and then dumped.

While resting at home one day, I got a phone call from one of the smaller ferry companies. This outfit delivered fifteen or twenty planes a year to the Piper dealer in South Africa. That dealer, like a few others, split his delivery work between Globe Aero and one of Globe's competitors. This policy reduced dependency on any one company or person, and kept delivery costs competitive. A pilot bound for Johannesburg in one such delivery plane had flown it as far as Portland, Maine, before catching a cold in his feet.

We agreed on a price. I flew to Portland to pick up the plane and complete the delivery. It was a Piper Arrow.

I wasn't a big stickler for detail, but I did try to plan my trips. Even before leaving Florida, I pretty much knew where and when I planned on stopping. I ran a lot of trips. One of my secrets was always to get a good night's rest. But at times, the gods have other plans for us mere mortals.

My trip from Portland to Gander was uneventful. I checked the weather and scheduled a weather brief for the next afternoon. I preferred to leave Canada in the late afternoon, fly through the night and arrive at my destination early in the morning. Flying at night was more beautiful, the air smoother, and that was restful to the soul. You couldn't see the ocean, either.

I took off from Gander the next afternoon, about two hours before sunset. I gently turned my aircraft toward the southwest, bound for the beautiful resort island of Las Palmas in the Canary Islands. When the plane reached cruising altitude I rechecked my heading, switched to the ferry system, and set the autopilot. I lowered the seat back and prepared myself for a nice boring thirteen-hour trip to Las Palmas.

I remained bored right up to the point when my ferry fuel tanks ran dry, three hours ahead of schedule. I'd planned on having only a two-hour reserve at Las Palmas.

I wasn't bored any more.

I calculated and recalculated my fuel burn rate. The two hundred horsepower engine on the Arrow normally consumed about eight gallons an hour. Somehow, with all my engine instruments indicating normal, I had managed to go through eighteen gallons an hour since leaving Gander. The answer came to me in a flash — a flash of horror.

I had been flying Piper Cherokee 161s and 181s, which carried a Lycoming engine. The Arrow, however, sported a four-cylinder Continental engine. Apart from the Arrow's retractable landing gear and turbocharged engine, the airplanes were identical. But the Continental's fuel injection system returned unused fuel to the tank from whence it originated. Except when ferry tanks were installed.

When I had leveled off, I'd switched to my ferry system without thinking about the vapor return. It took eighteen gallons per hour from the ferry fuel system and ran it to the engine. Only eight gallons were burned, though. The other ten gallons an hour were returned to my right main tank. My *full* right main tank. Then it went right out the fuel vent. I must have left a fuel slick eight hundred miles long. It was a dumb mistake, but not uncommon when pilots switched from the Cherokee to the Arrow.

I had discarded about thirty gallons of fuel over the side. More to the point, I would run out of fuel well short of Las Palmas. I relayed a message through a passing airliner to Las Palmas ATC, to advise them of my plight. I made plans to divert to Santa Maria in the Azores. I also made plans to do some fast talking after I landed.

Regulations required that all flights across the Atlantic carried an HF radio for long-range communication. Ferry pilots, to a man, hated the damned things. They were heavy, bulky, and rarely worked. Installation was slipshod at best. Most of us took the convenient view that ATC couldn't do a cotton-pickin' thing for us if we went down offshore. Any time we thought we could get away with it, we left them at home base.

Some airports wouldn't let us take off without a working HF. When accompanied by another aircraft, it wasn't a big problem. One pilot would carry a working HF. His buddy would run back and forth between the two airplanes, using his radio for VHF contact and the buddy bird's HF.

The best sight was when we had five or six aircraft in company, with only one working HF. Each of the four or five HF-less pilots would stand in line, like at a crowded restroom, waiting to make his mandatory radio check.

I knew that Santa Maria was the stickliest of sticklers: no working HF, no onward flight. Whether or not mine worked was immaterial, as I didn't have one with me. But being an experienced ferry pilot doesn't mean experience only in flying.

I landed safely in Santa Maria at perhaps 4 am. Once I had put my beast to bed, I made a beeline to ATC.

"Hi, guys. I'm the pilot of N3841M. Is your HF working? I mean, has anyone else reported problems getting through to you tonight?"

The shift supervisor looked at me with a gratifying hint of panic in his eyes. "No, señor. It seems to be working perfectly."

"Well, I want it checked out. I've been trying to call you on 8824 and 5638 for hours. I came in short of fuel and you folks wouldn't answer me on the radio. My radios worked perfectly when I left Gander. [Not untrue. The radios I carried did indeed work.] If the problem isn't with my radios, it must be with yours. I want them checked. What kind of service is this, anyway?"

"Si, señor. I'll have it checked most thoroughly."

If you can't dazzle them with brilliance . . . No one asked me for a radio check when I left for Las Palmas the next day. They didn't dare.

I had a trip scheduled for Bob Iba after this one. My unexpected stop put a slight crimp in my schedule. At the time I was still young enough to think that it made sense to try to keep a precise schedule. I later learned that schedules and airplanes mix like oil and water.

My plan had called for an overnight stay in Abidjan, in the Ivory Coast. But on the ground there, I decided to continue to my next overnight stop, São Tomé, on a small group of islands off the coast of Africa. In Abidjan, once I had finished refueling, I filed a flight plan and departed. Nearly six hours later, I rolled to a stop in front of the terminal in São Tomé.

It has been said that the best laid plans of mice and men oft times go awry. Whether we most resembled mice or men, I know not. But the best laid schedules of ferry pilots seemed always to go awry.

My reception committee in São Tomé consisted of about six gorillas dressed as soldiers. Each carried a half-sized, locked and loaded AK-47. At least, the guns looked half-sized. The tourist brochures had not mentioned either the animal life or the red carpet treatment for ferry pilots.

My armed guards marched me into the head gorilla's office, where I was subjected to a two-hour interrogation. I knew that I wasn't a CIA spook on a spying mission, but they didn't. I kept insisting that I was a legitimate pilot flying a legitimate aircraft delivery. Even though I wasn't.

Single-handedly, South Africa produced ninety percent of the gross national product of the entire continent. It could hardly be a surprise that it purchased ninety percent of the aircraft bound for Africa. But South Africa found itself surrounded by black-led countries whose attitudes towards it ranged from lukewarm to hostile.

The government of South Africa in 1978 was no worse than any other in Africa. It was far better than most. But it was white, and as such, all black-led governments could unite in opposition to it. No black-run country allowed free passage to aircraft bound for South Africa, international agreements be damned.

In an effort to avoid the problems associated with delivering to South Africa, we maintained the fiction that these dozens and dozens of new aircraft were all destined for poor, broke, neighboring Botswana. On the last leg we would file for Gabarone, the capital of Botswana, but would fly instead to Windhoek (now in Namibia, but then in South West Africa).

I doubt that anyone in Africa ever really believed it. As stories go, it was neither the best nor the worst I've ever told. But as stories go, it was a story.

My captors in São Tomé continued to insist that my destination was South Africa. As best I could, I kept a straight face and insisted I neither knew nor cared about South Africa, and that the plane was destined for Botswana.

They broke before I did. The head man told me to refuel and leave, post haste. I had done enough flying for the day and I was tired, but who can refuse a request like that? After all, they had the guns.

My fanny dragged on the ground behind me, but the chance to steal a few minutes sleep' in flight seemed a wiser choice than an unknown period of time in some rat-infested African jail. I quickly fueled, filed, and fled.

The next ordeal was to make it safely past Angola.

Every ferry pilot had a favorite destination. But all agreed that Angola won, hands down, the ultimate accolade of *least* favorite place to go in the entire world. Several ferry pilots who made the unfortunate mistake of being caught flying over or near Angola then endured a months-long interlude in the Luanda Hilton, complete with iron bars, dreadful food, and pet bugs.

But we had to fly over or close by Angola to reach Windhoek. My boss for this trip had told me, "No sweat. Wait until you get past Luanda, then turn in over Angola direct for Windhoek." But he wasn't on this trip, and I was.

I did so. Once safely past Luanda, the capital, I slipped into the airspace over hostile Angola. As I passed the coastline, I could feel my sphincter muscles tighten.

Twelve hundred hours of combat flying in Vietnam had taught me to take nothing for granted. I turned off my position lights, dimmed my cockpit lights, and richened my fuel mixture to eliminate the telltale blast of yellow flame from my exhaust. Just to be safe, I turned off my radios. I climbed to a non-standard altitude and tried to scrunch myself into as small a bundle as possible. I thought it best to stay awake until Angola was safely behind me.

My eyes were wandering around the midnight sky over Angola when I spotted a most unwelcome sight. I had an intruder with flashing running lights just above and behind me. My heart stopped. My blood ran cold. Somehow the Angolans had picked me up on radar that they weren't supposed to have. I now had a pair of fighters on my tail.

My heart restarted at twice its normal rate as I pondered my options. I couldn't identify the aircraft, but I knew that every fighter plane built since 1917 could outrun and outfight me. Since they obviously had me on ground-controlled radar, I couldn't hope to outmaneuver them. I resigned myself to my fate, however dismal.

The fighters wove back and forth for thirty minutes. Finally I realized that they couldn't see me well enough to either shoot me down or force me down. I doubt they were any more interested than I was in having a midnight mid-air. They knew I was there. I knew they were there. I was rushing for the border as fast as I could. The best I could hope for was for them to run low on fuel or for me to cross the border before they caught a proper sight of me.

I looked around yet again, and the fighters were gone. I rechecked my heading for Windhoek and went to sleep.

Once in the far safer airspace of South West Africa, I turned my radios on and attempted to make contact with ATC. Much to my surprise, I couldn't reach Windhoek control. I couldn't reach anyone else, either.

For all practical purposes, a state of war existed between Angola and South West Africa. I had been jumped by fighters once already this evening. I wasn't in the slightest bit interested in a tangle with the South West African Air Force as well. But I couldn't reach anyone at all on the radio. I received no response to any of my repeated radio calls.

Finally I was within radio range of Windhoek tower. I couldn't raise them either.

When I arrived overhead the airport in Windhoek, the runway lights were off. The passenger terminal was bathed in light, as were the taxiways, but there were no runway lights. I could figure out where the runway was, but couldn't see either end of it. Those were the conditions in which I made my landing approach: no lights, no radio contact.

To preclude landing short, I touched down at what I guessed was the mid-point of the runway, abeam the passenger terminal. My landing lights then gave me enough light to see by. Unfortunately, though, the Arrow still boomed along at a fair clip. The end of the runway was damn near. I came to a screeching stop at the very end of it.

Windhoek airport had a 12,000-foot runway. I had overflown nearly all of it in the darkness, and landed on the last two thousand feet. I taxied in and shut my chariot down. It had been a hell of a flight.

I remained in the cockpit for some time. The plane was on the ground but I was still coming down from the flight. Sometimes, we need the fear caused by the presence of deadly peril to remind us how valuable life really is. I felt like a thundering herd of wildebeest had stampeded over me. I had spent thirty-two of the past forty hours in the air. My tongue was drier than the Kalahari desert.

As a piston engine cools, you can hear it "ping" as the metal shrinks. I could hear my joints pinging. I felt like I had been "rode hard and put away wet." I managed to exit the airplane and went in search of an official.

The airport seemed completely deserted. I suppose it was about 4 am. I had so many hours of flight behind me, I wasn't even sure what day it was. As far as I could judge, my landing had attracted no attention.

Like a miner sniffing out the motherlode, my nose led me to a wooden cot in what appeared to be a guard's shack. I really only wanted to test it; I had no intention of going to sleep. I fell onto the cot, dragged a flea-laden blanket over my corpse, and passed out.

A week or so later, or perhaps it was only a few hours, I was reincarnated as a weary ferry pilot. If reincarnation really does depend upon past performance, I might have expected to have been reborn as a flying insect, perhaps a butterfly or a wasp. I reappeared as a ferry pilot who smelled like a cross between a goat and a piebald skunk.

The airport had awakened during my suspended animation. I wandered out of my boudoir into the blazing midday sun of Africa.

A few minutes later I stood tall in front of the shift supervisor of Air Traffic Control. He had a list in front of him of the various national and international regulations which I was accused of violating. It was not a short list. One by one, bite by bite, he proceeded to chew me out.

I allowed him to continue for a few minutes before cutting him off.

"That's all very well. But I got jumped over Angola last night, and I'm damn glad to be alive today. And I'm not real interested in your petty regulations at a time like this. Good day, sir."

What could he say? For that matter, what else could I say?

I filed my flight plan for Johannesburg. Once refueling was completed, I took off on the final, five-hour leg of my trip.

Flying right on the edge of the envelope has a tendency to sharpen one's senses as no drug ever could. Far above the Kalahari my vision seemed crisper, my sense of smell keener. It was a good day to be alive. Especially considering the alternatives.

After all I had been through, it was obvious to me that nothing else unusual could happen. Just as obviously, I was dead wrong.

I landed in Jo'burg and taxied the Arrow to the Piper dealer. They were most surprised at the speedy arrival. For that matter, so was I. A couple of mechanics were detailed to remove my ferry system so I could be on my way back to the States.

One universal commodity and medium of exchange I had discovered on my very first ferry trip was the ever-popular art and literary journal, more commonly known as a skin mag by my more uncouth brethren. These publications served a dual purpose. Ferry pilots, being of a higher moral and intellectual order, could appreciate them for their literary excellence. Those few of us able to read, that is. The rest of humanity, mostly male, could slobber over the titillating pictures of nude or semi-nude females.

On this trip I carried the current issue of *Playboy*, which displayed Barbi Benton in all her natural glory. She was alright, I suppose, if you like big boobs and a narrow waist. Some men are attracted to that sort of female.

These magazines were kept only to give away to anyone who did something to help me along the way. But perhaps I should describe my T&A magazines as an *almost* universal commodity.

After my aircraft was de-tanked and my baggage packed, with great ceremony I presented the chief mechanic with a magazine, conveniently opened to the pages featuring the bountiful Miss Benton. He stepped back in horror, as if I had presented him with a lunch tray filled with what comes out of the southern end of a northbound mule. Images of Miss Benton had a strong effect on most men, but this reaction was perhaps unique.

"You can't give that trash to me! That's illegal," he snarled.

"Illegal? What are you talking about?" I was confused.

"You can't bring *Playboy* into South Africa. It's an *immoral* magazine."

I know, deep down inside of me, that it's wrong to sin. I do hate it. But just thinking about it can't do much harm, can it?

A discussion took place among five or six of the mechanics. Two wanted to turn me over to the South African sex police. Two or three wanted to take me to the nearest brick wall and shoot me.

One of the older and wiser fellows came up with a mutually acceptable solution. With a gleam in his eye and a smile on his face, he said, "Turn those over to me. I'll make sure they get into the right hands."

Miss Benton, I hope you rested well. You were in the right hands that night.

95th and 96th TRIPS: ANCHORAGE, AK to HONOLULU, HI

1978	from	to	nautical miles	knots	time (hours)			
					flight	day	night	inst.
Sep 14	Anchorage	Cold Bay	548	137	4.0	4.0		1.2
Sep 15	Cold Bay	Honolulu	2,037	134	15.2	3.0	12.2	6.5
Sep 16	Anchorage	Cold Bay	548	130	4.2	4.2		0.5
Sep 17	Cold Bay	Honolulu	2,037	114	17.8	5.8	12.0	5.8
TOTALS		4 days	5,170	125	41.2	17.0	24.2	14.0

Ferry flying — the art and science of delivering small planes across giant, forbidding bodies of water — was perhaps the world's smallest occupation. At its peak in the late 1970s, there were no more than seventy-five pilots at any one time earning a full-time living ferrying airplanes. Today, there may be half a dozen in the world.

Since there were so few of us, few people, even among our fellow pilots in the general aviation community, really understood the kind of flying we regularly undertook. I can't recall how many times I sat drinking coffee in some fleabag coffee shop in a hangar, listening to a pilot who was not a ferry pilot insist that having over five hours' fuel in a plane was insane, since no pilot could possibly survive the rigors of such a long trip.

When appropriate, I would nod my head sagely in keen appreciation of such deep wisdom. Then I'd saunter out to my aircraft and take off on another of the several hundred trips of over ten hours that I completed.

Everyone, pilots included, thinks within a frame of reference of their own experiences. If an experienced pilot has flown five-hour trips, maximum, obviously no one can fly for longer than that. It sounds all right, I suppose, in a canteen. But every ferry pilot I ever met regularly did things that were far outside the experience of most pilots. To tell the truth, I always got a kick out of hearing the hangar tales. I'd just keep nodding, knowing that the "expert" knew nothing about how we flew. The truth, especially when it's "obviously" the truth, isn't always true.

AFTER I LEFT TRANSAIR, I entered the most interesting period of my ferrying career. Most of the trips I flew for Bob Iba were tiny little single-engine Pipers going to CSE Aviation in Oxford, England. I delivered dozens of them.

After a few deliveries, these trips started blurring one into another. I didn't punch them out like clockwork, as I had with all those Cessnas going to Australia. Some months I might fly two trips, some months three.

But I also had the time and the freedom to branch out. I made some interesting trips, simply because few other ferry pilots who flew as freelancers were qualified for both Pacific and Atlantic crossings.

At home one day, between trips, the phone rang. A friend of mine in Honolulu wanted two Beech 18 aircraft brought down from Alaska. "Give me a quote for delivery of the pair, Bob."

My affair with the Model 18 twin Beechcraft started when I was a bright-eyed, bushy-tailed, brash young Marine officer sporting brown bars on my collar. After a bout with ulcers, I was restricted to flying from the right-hand side of the plane for six months; as co-pilot only, in other words. Since the F-4 Phantom had only one pilot's seat, I couldn't fly it.

For some people, flying becomes a addiction they cannot do without. I was a flying addict. Co-piloting wasn't quite as cool as piloting, but it was still flying. Soon I found myself in the right-hand seat of C-45s and C-117s. The C-45 was the military version of the Beech 18. The C-117 was the Navy's stretched version of the Douglas DC-3. Anyone who could fly that pair could fly anything with wings. Or mostly; now and again there were exceptions.

Before encountering the C-45 I had thought, just thought, that I knew how to fly twin-engine aircraft. The F-4, my primary aircraft at that time, carried twin J-79 engines.

I soon learned better. A C-45 took off and landed like a bucking bronco. Totally docile in the air, it could be more than a handful on the ground, both coming and going. Once a pilot mastered the C-45, every other twin-engine airplane ever built became an absolute piece of cake to fly.

My friend told me that the two aircraft were sitting in Anchorage, tanked and ready for flight. Since eleven years had passed since I had last strapped on a Beech 18, I quizzed the new owner as to the location of the nose wheel. The military version carried the nose wheel on the tail. Some (but not all) of the civilian versions had the nose wheel where it belonged. I always preferred nose wheels to be up front. This pair had them in the right place.

Seemingly, the distance between San Francisco and Honolulu is the longest flying distance, with no alternatives, between any two points of land in the world. Well, that statement is not one hundred percent true. Upon departing San Francisco, and by diverting five thousand miles or so up to Cold Bay, Alaska, in the Aleutian chain, a pilot could cut the distance to Honolulu by almost seventy miles. Needless to say, no ferry pilot in history ever flew that route. Far easier to install an extra seventy miles of range and find a longer runway.

I flew commercial to Anchorage. I'd never been to Alaska before. According to the calendar, it was late summer. According to the weather forecast, winter roared just around the corner.

I didn't merely dislike ferrying used airplanes over water; I hated it. Before these two trips, I had fought my way through about ten major emergencies in used airplanes.

Most used airplanes sit for a long time, waiting for a new owner. Airplanes don't like sitting on the ground for any length of time, any more than real pilots do. But although these Beech 18s were used, real used, I could tell just by looking at them that someone had done a great job of maintaining them. They had only recently been removed from service. I could see that they wanted to make it to Honolulu just as much as I did.

I fired up the Pratt & Whitney R-1340 engines of N99801. Once they were warmed up and my engine checks were completed, I took off on my first leg to Cold Bay. All my systems worked perfectly, even though the plane was older than I was. Back in those days, designers didn't cram in a whole bunch of systems. Systems not installed never fail. My voyage to Cold Bay proved pleasant and beautiful.

It took less than an hour to refuel there. I took off into the gathering darkness. The propensity of the round engines on the twin Beech to suck up oil was awesome. We never used oil replenishment systems on the opposed engines we normally flew with, on the smaller general aviation airplanes, simply because they didn't use much oil. But round engines always used lots of oil. Many times, the endurance of a round-engined plane was limited not by its fuel capacity but by its oil capacity.

So this Model 18 had an oil resupply system rigged up for use in flight. Every three hours or so I hand-pumped two or three gallons into each engine. I felt as if I was on a medical resupply flight for the Chinese, right out of *Terry and the Pirates.* All I lacked was a white scarf.

I touched down in Honolulu, fifteen uneventful hours later. I taxied in and shut down among the sister ships belonging to my customer, a sightseeing company. One cup of coffee later, I was in a taxi headed over to the passenger side of the field for my return trip to Anchorage. Luck was with me, and I caught a flight out on Western Airlines almost straight away. From touchdown to liftoff, I had spent no more than an hour on the ground.

Back then, Western held an interesting contest for its passengers flying from Hawaii. The captain would provide the upper wind forecast and cruise speed of his beast. The passengers were asked to guess the time of passage over the exact halfway point. Western gave away a bottle of booze or a decorative plate commemorating the feat.

One might suppose that ferry pilots would excel at this little competition. I had tried it probably ten times on previous trips. I never even came close — charts, whiz wheels and electronic calculators aside. My new technique was to take a wild stab somewhere near half the total time of the flight. Very scientific.

I was in a middle seat. A very lovely lady sat on my right. Her boyfriend occupied the seat on my left. From the way he talked, I could tell he was a pilot. I tried to strike up a conversation with him, and failed. Once he learned I now lived in Pennsylvania, all I heard was how stupid and inexperienced "lowland" pilots were. If you hadn't survived at least ten years of winter flying in Alaska, you couldn't possibly know how to fly around in ice.

Compared to flying over Greenland and Iceland, Alaska had a veritable myriad of navigation facilities. I had had more than my share of winter flying. I didn't need instruction from this bozo.

I turned my attention to his lovely. Seemed she had figured out that the middle point of a six-hour trip should be about two hours. I did a pretty good job of explaining my by-guess-and-by-golly technique.

The boyfriend cut in and made another smart crack about lowland pilots. If she needed advice about flying matters, she could get it from him. I shut my eyes and mouth and went to sleep.

As we neared Anchorage, the winner of the contest was announced by the stewardess. I let her try to find "Captain Moriarty" for a few minutes. She was on the point of telling the captain that she had lost a passenger somewhere between Honolulu and Anchorage when I came out of my apparent snooze.

"Oh, she must mean me. I rarely use my professional title."

It was so sweet, stepping over the clod to collect my prize. The lovely on my right *oohed* and *aahed* appropriately over my bottle of booze. I presented it to her, for being a good sport. She awarded me a big warm smile in return.

For the remainder of our trip, the cabin smelled of burning rubber. I never discovered the source. I did, however, see a few wisps of smoke coming from the ears of the jerk on my left. There really was a Trim God just for ferry pilots.

I didn't even bother with a night's sleep before setting out with the second Beech 18. She fired right up and we were on our way.

Winter was setting in rapidly. The cloud bases formed at about four thousand feet. Some of those clouds hid mountains of five thousand feet and more. I cruised along at eight thousand. Soon I started picking up ice on my wings. I was hardly in a panic, but I did call Center to find out what the weather was like ahead of me. I reported light ice at eight thousand feet.

Someone cut in on the frequency and suggested that I switch to another frequency for a minute. Being a most curious person, I switched over to see what he had to say. He started off by asking how much experience I had flying in Alaska. Being an especially truthful person, I replied "None."

Sure enough, he too went into the song and dance about lowland pilots. He suggested, but really it was more of an order, that I go underneath the clouds. I responded, "I have no Alaskan experience, but I've done a bit of cold weather flying. I'm not about to go under clouds with ice in them."

It hardly ever makes sense to go down, especially when you don't know what you're going down into. And it never makes sense, when you know that mountain tops are hidden in the clouds. I went up instead.

I made another quick one-hour turnaround in Cold Bay. I had lost some of the tailwinds of two days before, but the picture still looked pretty good. I took off for what I expected to be another dull leg.

It was dull, too — at least, until I was two hundred miles out to sea.

I was cruising at ten thousand feet, which was about as much as I could squeeze from my overloaded metal camel. Then, for no apparent reason, she started descending at about five hundred feet per minute. She kept coming down, no matter what I did to the power setting.

I watched with growing horror. She and I got closer and closer to the dismal green ocean below. I was well out of range of any radio station, so I couldn't even call "Mayday" to let someone know I was going down. Not that anyone could have helped.

Non-turbocharged engines gain power as altitude decreases. But not us; not this day. The altimeter kept ticking down, all the way to three thousand feet. I gripped the yoke with both hands, white knuckles glistening. I kept a firm grip on my seat cushion, too. In a cockpit as cold as a grave, sweat poured from my brow.

The rate of descent slowed, then stopped. Then, all of a sudden, I was out of whatever I had been in. The airplane began to climb, just like a regular plane. I continued on to Honolulu and made a safe landing.

I learned later that I had probably flown into an unusual condition called "wave," caused by strong winds hitting mountain ranges at exactly the right angle. Had I been at six thousand or nine thousand feet, I might have flown right into the water without being able to do anything about it.

Occasionally, ferry pilots earned their pay merely by sitting.

As I taxied in I noticed the owner of the sightseeing company, Doris Tom. I stopped, shut down, and exited the newest addition to her fleet.

She invited me into her office to have some tea and relax. She was anxious to know when she could expect her second plane from Anchorage.

"But that *is* your second plane," I said with pride.

"I know that, but when can I expect N99801?" she asked.

"Two days ago." I still had that big, shit-eating grin on my face.

"Bob, you don't understand. When will I have both airplanes here on the ramp in Honolulu?"

"About twenty minutes ago. That's the second plane. I got in with the other one the other day."

Doris grew more exasperated by the second. I took her into the hangar where the mechanics were at work de-tanking the first plane. She looked at me in disbelief.

"But you can't have delivered two planes in three days all by yourself. It can't be done."

I can. I did. No sweat. Well, maybe just a touch.

97th TRIP: SPARTANBURG, SC to KEFLAVIK, ICELAND

1978	from	to	nautical miles	knots	time (hours)			
					flight	day	night	inst.
Oct 18	Spartanburg	Perkasie	463	122	3.8	3.8		
Oct 19	Perkasie	Bangor	383	128	3.0	3.0		
	Bangor	Gander	560	117	4.8	2.3	2.5	2.0
Oct 20	Gander	Keflavik	1,367	108	12.6	2.2	10.4	8.5
TOTALS		2 days	2,773	115	24.2	11.3	12.9	10.5

Over the years, God and I reached an agreement. If I wouldn't ferry used singles, He wouldn't kill me. Over the years, He gave me many opportunities to learn my lesson. However, I was stubborn. Just to let me know who was boss, on this trip He took an engine from me while I was far to the west of Iceland, over the most unforgiving stretch of water in the world.

And I had only one engine when I started.

It can only have been by the grace of God that the airplane and I made it safely to land. It sure wasn't through the grace of the U.S. Air Force.

I flew three trips for George Jensen. I got screwed or almost killed on every one of them. God didn't have to tell me that this didn't make a whole lot of sense.

GEORGE JENSEN CALLED in early October 1978. He wanted a Helio Courier taken from Spartanburg, South Carolina to London, England. I still hadn't flown every model of airplane ever built. I had never flown a Helio Courier. We set a price. A day or so later, I was in South Carolina.

Messing pilots around was a common failing of all ferry company operators. I had spent five days flying bits and pieces all up and down the east coast for Jensen, for peanuts. So I had a little "man to man" with him. Once he realized I was a ferry pilot, a *paid* ferry pilot, we got along better.

I signed for the airplane and was on my way. The H-295 Helio Courier was designed for short field operations in southeast Asia during the Vietnam era. Of limited utility, it never sold well in the U.S., where runways a half-mile long were considered "short field." Whatever it gained in short field ability was sacrificed in speed and range. It lacked the fuel capacity for a nonstop direct shot to Shannon. While it had long legs for a general aviation aircraft it had short range for a ferry trip. I would have to travel the northern route.

I made my way to Gander in Newfoundland. I did this in three hops, touching down in Perkasie, Pennsylvania and Bangor, Maine.

While I waited in the weather office in Gander for my ocean briefing, my mind went back exactly one year. In Bob Iba's stable, I had replaced a highly experienced and capable pilot named George Martin. George had departed Gander for Iceland one year earlier, to the day. His wind forecast proved inaccurate. His airplane picked up some strong, unforecast headwinds and he ran into heavy icing conditions. The plane loaded up with ice and he ran out of fuel a mile or so short of the shore of Iceland. By the time an Air Force helicopter arrived over his position, he was dead from exposure. Though I was overdressed for the Gander weather office, I couldn't help but shiver involuntarily.

My brief complete, I returned to my aircraft, parked out on the Shell Oil ramp. Preflight and refueling complete, I departed a few minutes later.

Ferry pilots traveling between Gander and Iceland generally preferred a slight dogleg route to the southern tip of Greenland, Cape Farewell, then direct to Iceland. It added thirty miles to the journey but gave the pilot an exact position when about halfway across. To this day, I'm not sure why I chose to fly the direct route. But I did. I saved myself thirty miles' worth of fuel, but the only times when I would know exactly where I was would be when I left Gander and when I found Iceland. If I found Iceland.

My weather brief predicted a slight tailwind. Added to my snail's pace of 120 knots, my ground speed should have been 135 knots or so. From my vantage point at ten thousand feet, I watched below as the whitecaps passed slowly behind. This sure didn't look like 135 knots to me.

The trip should have taken about ten hours. As the ten-hour milestone came and went, none of my navigation radios even flickered. Either Iceland was lost or I was. I switched my communications radio to the emergency frequency monitored by everybody: 121.5. I started screaming "Mayday!" for all I was worth.

George's big mistake had been to delay declaring an emergency. I didn't want to try swimming the last mile in the freezing water two miles below.

A DC-8 on a westbound flight answered my mayday call. I told him that I was lost. I requested that he notify Sea-Air Rescue (SAR) at Keflavik, Iceland of my plight. I also requested that he relay to Greenland, to see if any of the spook stations high on the icecap had me fixed on their radar.

The U.S. government maintains a number of semi-secret radar stations on the Greenland icecap. Previously I had overflown two of them, Sea Bass and Sob Story. Without a little help from someone, I might soon be feeding the sea bass.

If I'd had to make a list of choice duty spots, the top of the Greenland icecap would have been on the last line. It did beat floating in a little yellow life raft just off the coast of Iceland, but not by much.

The Air Force launched a C-130 SAR plane while Air Traffic Control fired off the Icelandic Queen Air, providing identical services. It did seem to me that the C-130 was taking an unusually long time to find my position. Though a far faster plane than the Queen Air, position reports showed their speeds to be almost the same.

Another commercial carrier radioed to me. The spook stations had fixed my position at 250 miles west of Iceland. I not only didn't have a tailwind, I had at least a ten-knot headwind. I still carried three hours' fuel — more than sufficient to reach Iceland, if I was where the spook station thought I was.

As the C-130 with the Queen Air in tow approached my position, I learned why it was flying so slowly. It had gear problems. When they took off from Keflavik, the landing gear neglected to follow orders. So it headed westward with all that drag hanging down. So far, this was a typical rescue effort; all screwed up.

Its landing gear wasn't the C-130's only mechanical problem. Its VHF directional finding gear worked, but the radar didn't. Then I learned that the radar did work on the Queen Air, but not its directional finder. I already had a rough idea of my location from the information the spook stations passed on. It appeared that I was more or less on track, but two hours late.

I was real happy that this hadn't been an emergency. It was fixing to turn into a Chinese fire drill with all the equipment carried but not in service.

After many radio conversations between the C-130 and the Queen Air, they agreed on an exact position for me. They were still about twenty miles from my position. Since we were all in agreement that I didn't really have a problem any longer, the commander of the C-130 asked if I minded continuing the operation as if I did have a continuing emergency.

Clearly, these guys could use the practice. I agreed.

I flew eastbound at about nine thousand feet. Both rescue planes spotted me visually, then slid into position to monitor my progress. The Queen Air maintained position on my right side, at ten thousand feet. The C-130 flew on my left side, at eight thousand.

Just as the C-130 had moved into position, something happened. I didn't know what. All of a sudden, I heard a sound like the hammers of hell. The plane started to shudder. I realized at once that now I *did* have big problems.

I screamed "Mayday! Mayday!" for all I was worth. Both the C-130 and the Queen Air heard my call loud and clear. "This is not a practice. Mayday. Mayday. Mayday. N68861. Mayday. Mayday. Mayday." Then, just for good luck, I picked up the mike and repeated my call over the radio.

I explained to the C-130 commander that it felt as if something broke or had come loose on the airplane. I wasn't sure if it was an engine problem or something loose. But if it got worse, I would be in big trouble.

I looked over the gauges. Everything seemed normal, but my airspeed had dropped by about ten knots. That told me nothing, except that something had slowed me a little.

The C-130 commander kept telling me that I had no problems. He carried para-rescue personnel on board that he could drop to me when I went into the water. What he also knew, but didn't mention, was that he required prior approval from Omaha to do so. Sure, they could give me a hand. As I made a flawless belly flop into the icy water below, they could applaud in unison as they flew past on their way back to Iceland.

I told him — ordered him, really — to get on the horn to Keflavik. If he didn't have a helicopter overhead when I went in, I would become a flash-frozen fish fillet.

We plodded on towards Iceland. I called the C-130 again after about fifteen minutes, a period of time that seemed to stretch from here to eternity.

"Dumbo. Dumbo. What's the status on the chopper?"

He hesitated a moment before responding. "861, this is Dumbo. They should be launching the Jolly Green any time now. Stand by."

"Dumbo, 861. What do you mean, 'should be'? I want to know exactly when he's leaving. If he isn't overhead, I'm going to die."

"861, Dumbo. Well, ah . . . actually we haven't been able to reach Iceland. You see, our UHF doesn't work and we're too far out to reach them on VHF. But we'll keep trying."

Typical, in every rescue I ever saw. Everybody's brain seems to turn to mush. Here we are, two airplanes watching me as I struggle toward Iceland, neither of which will be of the slightest use if I go in the water.

"Hello, Queen Air. This is 861. Do you have a working HF?"

"N861, Queen Air. That is negative."

"Queen Air, 861. Do you have oxygen on board?"

"861. That is affirmative."

"Queen Air, 861. How about climbing until you are high enough to reach Iceland on VHF? Get the message through to them. I must have that Jolly Green overhead if I go in."

I wasn't doing anything else productive. I might as well run the rescue effort.

"861, Queen Air. Wilco. I understand and will comply."

We pressed on towards Iceland. Time seemed to have come to a complete halt. Later, I looked over the written records of both the C-130 pilot and the Queen Air captain. The whole thing took only two hours. For some reason it seemed a whole lot longer to me.

A half-hour later, the helicopter still hadn't launched. I couldn't believe my lying ears. They could have *built* a chopper in less time than it was taking the Jolly Green to launch from Keflavik.

Finally I was within radio range of Keflavik tower myself.

"Hello, Keflavik tower. N68861. What is the status of the Jolly Green?"

"N68861, tower. We're doing our best. The Jolly Green should be leaving at any time. Please stand by."

"Tower, 861. I don't know what you mean by 'doing our best'. If that chopper isn't overhead when I go in the water, I'm gonna die. Launch the fucking chopper."

"861, tower. You have no need to use that kind of language. As soon as we get a hold of the rescue center, we will pass your message."

Huh?

"Tower, 861. Just what do you mean, 'get a hold of them'? Are you or are you not in contact?"

"861, tower. We've been trying to reach them for over an hour. But the phone's been tied up. We haven't actually gotten through to them yet."

Oh, my aching back. The phone was "tied up" so the rescue effort came to a halt. I wondered briefly if I could try walking on water. Somebody did that once.

Now, while all this inaction was going on, it would reflect well on me to imply that I acted the part of the cool, calm, collected ferry pilot. But that wouldn't be true. I was scared silly.

I flew some 830 combat missions in Vietnam. The VC or VNA shot at me on most of those missions. In some, in the O-1 Bird Dog, I could even hear the staccato bursts of fire from the AK-47s. But even in heavy combat, you're under fire for only a few minutes. Of course you're scared. Any human would be. But as the pilot, you can control how close you come to enemy fire, and how often.

Now I was caught in the nightmare of every ferry pilot. I had a serious, albeit unknown problem that I could do nothing about. The C-130 had rescue personnel on board, but the restrictiveness of military regulations meant that those men would be flying back and forth over my crash site for hours after I went in. There was no question in my mind: if a chopper wasn't overhead as I went in, it was all over.

The temperature of the water was about three degrees Celsius. Survival time on the charts showed about ten minutes. I had a wife at home carrying our first child. I gave the captain of the C-130 my home telephone number and asked him to notify my wife. At least she wouldn't have to endure hours or days of rumors.

Time passed slowly. Still the Sea-Air Rescue helicopter hadn't launched.

After a near-endless passage of time, finally I saw the Iceland land mass, far off in the distance. My bargeman for the trip over the River Styx sat on my left shoulder, the angel of death on my right. We three waited patiently to see what would happen.

The land came closer. The Jolly Green still didn't get airborne. I called the tower. I told them to have someone drive over to the rescue center. If the phone didn't work, perhaps they should knock on the door.

Somewhat abashedly, the tower told me that that was an idea. Someone from the tower did drive over to the rescue center. He told them the chopper was needed immediately.

I was close enough to Keflavik air base to watch the CH-53 Jolly Green lift off. He reached me just as I passed the shoreline. Perhaps if I crashed now, they could snap some live action photos of me kicking the plane after it came to a stop.

God only knows how, but the disabled Helio reached the runway. When I reduced power for the landing, the engine stopped. I didn't need it any more, anyway. I shut all my switches off. I made a nice, sweet, normal, no-engine, three-point landing. Amid a deafening silence, the Helio rolled to a stop. But then, I always made nice landings, engine running out or not.

I got out. After delivering a few loving kicks to my beast, I rode to the terminal in a crash truck. As far as I was concerned, the airplane could figure out how to swim to the hangar.

I made my way immediately to the Air Force SAR Center. Amid smiles and handshakes, I made my way to the Jolly Green aircraft commander.

"What took you guys so long to launch? We started trying to reach you two hours ago. If I'd gone down, I'd have frozen."

"You might want to talk to that captain over there. We received no message until twenty minutes ago."

"Captain, I'm Bob Moriarty. The commander of the CH-53 told me to talk to you. Why was the phone tied up for an hour and a half?"

"Well, er, ah . . . I was talking long-distance to a colonel in supply from the Pentagon. He's rather long-winded, but he's a colonel. I didn't want to tell him to get off the phone. He's the guy who writes my efficiency reports."

"Really? Your detachment is knee-deep in the middle of a rescue. You're on the phone with some fucking supply guy? Are you shitting me? You weren't really talking to some dumbass colonel. Tell me it isn't so!"

The Air Force had spent millions of dollars on men and material, to provide Sea-Air Rescue capabilities at the airport in western Iceland. One dumb captain brought the whole kit and caboodle to a screeching halt. All because some Pentagon bozo liked to talk on the phone. But then, all rescues turn out the same.

In vainglorious defeat, my steed was towed to a nearby hangar. A mechanic pulled off bits and pieces. One cylinder had a broken valve stem. The face of the valve had been hammered against the cylinder head for two hours. It had not only sounded like the hammers of hell had been at it, it looked like the cylinder was destroyed. The mechanic took out an entire handful of broken and crushed pieces of cylinder, piston, and valve from the delicate innards of my engine. The engine was a write-off.

I pored over the engine log for any clue to the cause of the malfunction. What I found, I couldn't quite believe. The engine had gone through not one, but two replacements of the same cylinder. The engine wasn't safe for a thirty-mile trip, much less three thousand miles with no chance of rescue. This idiot I was flying for might as well have signed a death warrant for me.

I remained in Iceland, arranging to have the engine removed. If someone else wanted to fly this hunk of crap the rest of the way to London, it was fine with me. I wouldn't fly it another inch.

The mechanic working on the engine informed me that it was a miracle it had run for two hours with such mortal wounds. That's just what it was — a miracle.

That was the last used single-engine plane I ever took across the water.

98th TRIP: WINSTON-SALEM, NC to TEHRAN, IRAN

1978	from	to	nautical miles	knots	time (hours)			
					flight	day	night	inst.
Oct 25	Winston-Salem	Bangor	740	224	3.3	3.3		
	Bangor	Gander	560	200	2.8	2.8		1.0
Oct 26	Gander	Keflavik	1,367	236	5.8	5.8		1.0
	Keflavik	Reykjavik	19	63	0.3	0.3		
Oct 27	Reykjavik	Shannon	813	203	4.0	4.0		1.0
	Shannon	Munich	814	170	4.8	3.3	1.5	1.0
Oct 28	Munich	Istanbul	858	191	4.5	4.0	0.5	1.0
Oct 29	Istanbul	Tehran	1,103	208	5.3	5.3		
TOTALS		5 days	6,274	204	30.8	28.8	2.0	5.0

Once in a career, a ferry pilot might get a chance to fly a real man's airplane.

I've never much worried about being a "real man." But it was fun, of a kind, to pilot a commercial craft on a ferry trip, complete with co-pilot, mechanic, two wives, one kid, a pregnant stewardess, and a rear cabin full of goods to be smuggled into an Iran on the brink of revolution. The only thing missing would be to get booted out of the destination country.

WAY BACK IN 1969, representatives of certain oil-producing countries sat around a big table and bemoaned their fate.

The U.S. dollar, the international pricing unit for oil, was declining as a result of our insane little incursion into Vietnam. Having nothing to do other than count giant stacks of crisp $100 notes which bought less and less, the oil producers decided to start a little club. Its purpose would be to maintain the price of oil at its current level. There was no thought of raising the price — all these guys wanted to do was to keep it where it was. The cost of production and the price of oil had been declining for years, and that had to stop.

After much discussion and dissent, they settled on a name. OPEC was born of the meeting.

The major oil-producing countries, hiding behind the delusion that was OPEC, succeeded for the next four years in their objective of maintaining oil prices. Then, during the Yom Kippur War in October 1973, the major Arab producers tried a new and unproven technique. They turned off the oil spigot. More accurately, they turned the tap back about a quarter-inch. The psychological shock to oil-consuming countries, primarily the U.S., was devastating. The oil price leapt from under $4 per forty-gallon barrel to $12. By late 1978 it had reached nearly $17.

That innocuous meeting in 1969 resulted in the most massive shift of assets in history. The pleasantly surprised oil-producing countries handled their newfound wealth the same way that you or I would — in the old-fashioned way, by throwing it at everything that sparkled, gleamed, or moved.

Luckily for me, airplanes moved.

Major price increases, reported as and popularly believed to be agreements reached as a result of OPEC meetings, were actually determined by two of the largest oil-producing states, Saudi Arabia and Iran. One week, Saudi Arabia would unilaterally raise the price. The next week, Iran would leapfrog that price. Conspiracy theories are always favored over facts. The public was told, untruthfully, that OPEC caused the increase. OPEC never existed, other than as a publicity gesture.

Not unnaturally, Saudi Arabia and Iran cleaned up. Nepotism ran rampant in Saudi Arabia. The newfound largesse was promptly spread among the thousand or so royal princes. The poorest prince in Saudi Arabia became pretty damn rich. In Iran, unbridled nepotism was less common. They kept it in the family, so to speak.

The Shah's twin sister received what might be referred to in some countries as a "goodie." In others still, it might be called a "license to steal." She was granted the absolute right to negotiate all the intra-Iran travel of oilfield workers. Henceforth, oil companies operating within Iran had to pay her to fly their employees back and forth within Iran. Pay they did, right through the nose. It wasn't hard to persuade them, since the only alternative was to have their employees walk very long distances.

By late 1978 her fleet consisted of some twenty-five Fairchild F-27 aircraft with a capacity of forty-four passengers each, fifty Lear jets, and almost a hundred more mundane, eight-passenger Rockwell 690s. This particular Iranian was cleaning up, in the vernacular. The fleet paid for itself every three months, in cash.

By October 1978, not a few individuals were aware that the Shah's days were numbered. One of them called me to ask if I wanted to deliver a newly renovated F-227 from Winston-Salem to Tehran. No idiot, he. The writing was on the wall. This guy had had a great business for a year, just delivering to Iran. He saw the change coming and figured that it was time to share his good deal with some other sucker. Me.

So I set out in the last aircraft to make it to Iran before the Shah was tossed out. Could have been worse, I suppose. It could have been the first plane going in under the Ayatollah Cockamamy.

For years I'd wanted to take my wife Kathie on a trip with me, but it had never been convenient. I could hardly fit myself into the cramped quarters of the singles I preferred, much less add a passenger. I rarely flew twins, and never found one that was suitable when Kathie had time available.

The F-227, call sign EP-AMT, had all kinds of room. Or so I thought.

I flew to Winston-Salem, the maintenance base for Piedmont Airlines. After retiring this aircraft from service, Piedmont had refurbished it. It had then been sold to the Shah's sister's company in Iran. The guy handling the ferrying to Iran kindly provided me with a retired Piedmont captain and an Iranian-born mechanic.

When I arrived in Winston-Salem, I learned that my crew had much the same idea as me. Each planned to bring his wife. The mechanic planned to remain in Iran, so he and his wife took along their little daughter as well. This was going to be one hell of a trip. We had a crew of seven, which was seven times as many as I was accustomed to.

Since we had lots of space remaining, the new Iranian owner had the mechanic pick up a few things. When the plane was fully loaded we had four beds, a TV set, lawn furniture, and even a full-size freezer. When I first saw the loaded aircraft, I felt like Noah just as the first raindrops began to fall.

We set out on our voyage on October 25. I planted the retired captain firmly in the left seat. He knew the plane and its systems intimately. I really didn't need to learn how to fly an F-227. I could read a checklist. I learned cockpit coordination while flying multi-pilot aircraft in the Marine Corps. My partner took charge while the engines ran. I did all the work on the ground. It was a handy arrangement, and it worked.

The first night, we stayed in Gander. I had been telling Kathie stories about Gander for years. Now she had the opportunity to see it. That didn't take long. There isn't much to see there, and even less to do.

We flew a mere six or eight hours or so each day. That was a snail's pace for me. For my retired co-captain, it was a week's worth of flying. The trip, like everything else I tried to do for my wife, proved to be a bad idea. Kathie expected a three-week tour. I was quite incapable of being a tour director. I was also unwilling to manage the schedules of six adults and a child.

Each day we were supposed to be ready to go by 9 am. Each morning we didn't get started until 11 am or so.

We spent one night in Gander. The next night was passed in Reykjavik, the next in Munich. We weren't doing diddlysquat in the way of flying. But trying to coordinate the activities of seven people was exhausting.

The abilities of the retired captain surprised me. He had no difficulty flying the airplane, at least until Air Traffic Control started talking to us. Then he tended to come unglued. He would spend minutes trying to figure out their instructions while the aircraft continued in the wrong direction or went through his assigned altitude. I was quite amazed. Removed from his canned flight plans and frequently traveled routes, he functioned at a minimal level at best. This was my very first flight with an airline type. The pattern was confirmed with each and every airline crew member I ever flew with.

Things reached a climax on our approach into Istanbul, Turkey. The field reported rain, an 800-foot overcast and a twenty-knot crosswind as we came down the pike. I could tell he was worried. He kept throwing "what if" questions at me. I wasn't greatly worried. There were no other aircraft within flying distance. I knew, I just knew, we would land in Istanbul. With just a little luck, and perhaps in one piece.

As we came down the instrument landing system (ILS) glide slope, I saw him fighting and over-controlling the plane. We got farther and farther from the centerline. I still wasn't much worried. When we broke out underneath the clouds we would have lots of time and altitude with which to recover.

His antics became almost frantic. He called "Gear up" and demanded full power for a go-around.

I told him, "Relax. These are not the crowded skies you're used to. We don't have anyone in front or behind. All you have to do is break out underneath this cloud."

If we had to, we could do a 360-degree turn. He was entirely unused to such a relaxed set of rules. Finally we broke out. It took a minor course correction to land safely. As we touched down I heard a collective sigh emitted from six bodies.

Our troubles had hardly begun, though. We had contrived to land in Turkey on the fiftieth anniversary of Turkish independence. Every good hotel in town was fully booked. The seven of us drove around for hours, looking for a place to stay.

Finally we located a fleabag resort right on the beach. For a ferry pilot, it was average or better than average accommodation. My now mutinous crew had a different viewpoint. I thought it wasn't all that bad, if you didn't mind a few cockroaches, sand in the sheets, and cold water only. Kathie hated it. And I had thought she really wanted to see what it was like to be a ferry pilot.

It turned out that we had to schedule our arrival in Tehran very carefully. Up until now, no one had bothered to mention to me that we were supposed to smuggle into Iran all the goodies loaded in the back. Customs had already been paid off, but we had to arrive between 7 pm and 8 pm. I asked our Iranian mechanic what the time difference was between Tehran and GMT. He told me it was five hours. He was off by only two hours.

We pulled into Tehran right smack on schedule, and therefore two hours late. But it didn't seem to matter. I expected to be directed to the customs area for clearance. Instead, we were directed to the ramp area of the company to which the airplane was being delivered.

A crew of Iranians swarmed over the plane like locusts. In a very short period of time, everything not attached to the airframe was removed. These guys even tried to take our belongings. We had to fight them off. After the aircraft was picked clean, we fired up the engines and taxied over to customs. The customs inspector climbed aboard. With an absolutely straight face, he asked if we had anything to declare. I informed him that we did not.

Many people in the U.S. believe that the Iranians hate Americans. This is only partly true. The Iranians suffer from xenophobia. They hate everyone equally.

Regulations required that all visitors to Iran held a visa. Our Iranian-born mechanic and his family were citizens. My co-captain and his wife had visas. I didn't need one, since I was part of the flight crew. That left one slight problem. Actually, it left 1½ problems. Kathie was six months pregnant. She looked as if she was smuggling a basketball.

I solved this technicality in my usual manner. I took Kathie aside and told her that for visa purposes, she had just become a stewardess. As part of the flight crew, she was now exempt from the visa requirement. As was to become habitual in the years ahead, she ignored me.

We were handed immigration cards to fill in. After we did so, the immigration inspector carefully compared them with the data in our passports. Even then they were looking for CIA spies.

We all passed inspection until he came to Kathie's form. Under "Occupation" she had written "Housewife." I looked at her in disbelief. The inspector looked at me with a gleam in his eye. I could feel the bite coming.

"What is this? On your general declaration you listed Mrs. Moriarty as a stewardess. On her immigration form she says she is a housewife. Which is correct?"

"Sir, what we have here is a failure to communicate. Let me have the form for a moment."

I took her entry form, scratched out "Housewife" and wrote in "Stewardess." I handed it back to the inspector with a little smile.

This immigration inspector was not a man given to displays of frivolity. He grabbed Kathie and me. We were hustled into the departure lounge. He told us to catch the next flight out of the country, no matter where it went.

We sat in the lounge trying to figure out where to go. I wondered if I should have tried to bribe him.

We then had a stroke of luck. The owner's agent walked in and spotted us. He came over to ask what the problem was. I explained the slight misunderstanding that had arisen between the immigration inspector and me. He laughed and said he would take care of it. A few moments later, a now smiling inspector escorted us to the taxi stand. He even helped with the bags.

I asked our friend what he had done. He told me that he had bribed the inspector.

See? I thought I should have tried it.

Tehran in those days, immediately pre-post-Shah, wasn't all that friendly. Matter of fact, the natives were downright hostile. We spent two nights there. Each night we could hear distant gunfire. By the time we left, the ground crews of all the airlines had gone on strike. We had to carry our luggage for about a half-mile to our Pan Am flight. Then we went without food or drinks on the eight-hour trip to London.

That was my second ferry trip with my wife and my second trip to Iran. That is to say, in each case it was both my first and my last.

111th TRIP: BIGGIN HILL, ENGLAND to LOCK HAVEN, PA

1979	from	to	nautical miles	knots	time (hours)			
					flight	day	night	inst.
Mar 29	Biggin Hill	Southampton	91	91	1.0		1.0	
Mar 30	Southampton	Shannon	275	98	2.8	2.8		
Apr 1	Shannon	Shannon	0	0	14.5	2.5	12.0	2.0
Apr 3	Shannon	Gander	1,727	115	15.0	12.0	3.0	1.5
Apr 4	Gander	Bangor	560	93	6.0	6.0		
	Bangor	Concord	157	105	1.5		1.5	1.0
Apr 5	Concord	Perkasie	226	75	3.0	3.0		
Apr 6	Perkasie	Lock Haven	103	69	1.5	1.5		
TOTALS		8 days	3,139	70	45.3	27.8	17.5	4.5

Ferry trips normally ran in one direction: from the U.S. to a distributor overseas. I would then jump on the first available commercial carrier home. The very best deal a ferry pilot could get was to run one plane to a destination, and then run a second plane back. Then we made our normal fee twice, and saved the price of two homeward-bound airplane tickets.

It looked like a good deal, unless one of the planes was stolen. But that was still OK, if you were stealing it from the guy who stole it before you.

IT'S UNFORTUNATE BUT TRUE. Bums often have better stories to tell than the good guys. Sometimes it seems to me that I flew only with bumpkins, but I know that is far from the truth. What can I say about most of the ferry pilots who undertook the most demanding flying in the world, week after week? The ones who were so calm, so professional, and who routinely made it look easy.

Bob Iba was a pro. He started ferrying airplanes when it was still a real adventure. He got his wings as a naval aviator just prior to World War II. I wasn't even a gleam in my mother's eye. God was still an aviation cadet. Bob helped start ferry flying after the war. His war, that is.

I had flown with him from England to New Jersey in '78. For him, it was trip number 317 across the Atlantic. He had completed hundreds more to the Caribbean and South America. His log book showed more hours of ferrying across the ocean than anyone else, ever.

But even ferry pilots must fade away into faint memories. On that trip in 1978, Bob was ill and really in no condition to fly.

My fellow ferry pilots came in a variety of sizes and shapes. They fit no image in particular. Bob Iba resembled nothing quite so much as a Butterball turkey. He was sixtyish. His days and nights of ferrying would soon end. He was a real pilot and a hell of a nice guy. I never went anywhere in Europe or South America where someone wasn't asking about him. Bob attracted friends like flowers find bees.

I flew only that one trip with him. I wish I had known him longer. Bob Iba was killed in an airplane crash in Colombia in February 1979, in unexplained circumstances.

One day in March 1979, after I had landed and de-tanked my conveyance on my 110th ferry trip, (another Piper Cherokee delivery to the distributor in Kassel, Germany), I got a call from Rosemary Iba. She was trying to keep the business together after Bob's death. She had a plane sitting in London ready to be flown to the U.S. Was I interested?

Of course I was, especially as I could make three times the money for less than twice the work. I made my way to London. But as usual, Rosemary had told me only part of the story.

If Bob Iba was a prince who looked like a butterball, Rosemary was a butterball who acted like the Wicked Witch of the West. Where Bob was nice, she was hard as a rock. I met a few strange people in the ferry business, but only one who was outright nasty.

I arrived in London and checked into my hotel of choice, the Penta. All that Rosemary had given me was a name and a phone number. I called the number. It was another hotel. I left a message for a Mr. Dewey Glover. He called me back, and we arranged to meet for a drink and to discuss his airplane.

Dewey Glover looked like a character right out of *Dallas*, the TV soap opera. He came complete with well-worn cowboy boots and a Western hat to match. His story was at least as interesting as he was.

Dewey was an oil man, not from Dallas but from Wyoming. He had started small and made it big. He had set his son up in the airplane business. One day, about a year before, a gent from California had walked in and paid cash for a Cherokee 161. Of course, airplane dealers love customers like that.

He came back a few weeks later. Now he wanted to purchase a Cherokee 181. This guy talked young Glover into accepting just a little cash and a whole lot of paper. He took off in his new Piper Cherokee, not to be found again in those parts.

Since Dewey would end up paying for whatever loss might ensue, he took a personal interest. He traced the airplane from the U.S. to the Surrey and Kent Flying Club, operating out of Biggin Hill, on the southeastern outskirts of London. It still wore U.S. registration. Our friend from California was using it to train students, which was highly illegal, according to the regulations of the Civil Aviation Authority in the UK.

Dewey went to the banks holding the paper, and got them to appoint him agent so he could repossess the plane. With a great stack of legal papers in hand, he flew to England. Once there, he visited a solicitor to determine how he should proceed. The British lawyer told him there wasn't a whole lot Dewey could do. Yes, it clearly belonged to the bank. But the bank was in the U.S. The aircraft was in England. Possession in this case was the frequently cited nine-tenths of the law.

Dewey Glover thinks a lot like I do. If minor technical details get in my way, I toss them out of my way.

"What would be the legal situation," he asked the lawyer, "if I snatch the airplane and get it out of England?"

"Ah, that's a different matter," he was told. "Then it's your aeroplane, to do with as you wish."

That's where I came in.

The story fascinated me. I did feel, though, that I had an obligation to point out to Dewey that the whole thing might cost him more than the plane's value. Who knew what kind of shape it might be in after a year's use?

Dewey looked at me in surprise. "Who gives a damn what the airplane's worth? I'm not doing this for money. I'm doing it because the bastard tried to steal from me."

With that kind of logic, I knew we would get along just fine.

We hatched our plot over a few pints of good English lager. Dewey had had an extra key made. We would wait until after dark. I would sneak out to the airplane, give it a good preflight check, taxi out, and leave for Shannon in Ireland. Everybody at the airport was in the know, except the Surrey and Kent Flying Club. Dewey would fly commercial to Shannon in case I ran into any legal problems. I'd get the plane tanked at the Shannon Repair Service, or SRS. Then I'd wing my way back to the U.S.

Like all good plans, it was simple. But like even good plans do sometimes, it didn't quite work as intended.

We checked out of our hotels the next day and jointly made our way to Biggin Hill at about 6 pm. Dewey had parted with a few more dollars to have a private detective case the joint — pardon me, monitor the premises. He told us that things quietened down after 6:30 or so. Any time after seven o'clock would be a good time to depart.

I checked in with the airport authority and with the tower. Once I had started the airplane, they would freeze all other traffic at the field. I was cleared an hour in advance for taxi and takeoff. All I had to do was climb in and leave.

Darkness was upon us before I made my move. I shook hands with Dewey. I told him I'd meet him in Shannon. Nonchalantly, I sauntered over to N2645Q, my quarry. I slipped the key into the door lock. Or rather, I tried to do so.

Whoever made the key had used the right pattern, but the wrong key blank. This key was made of soft brass. It was also slightly wider than the regular key. After five minutes of tugging, twisting and pulling, I managed to open the door. I also succeeded in twisting the key beyond all possible further use. I made my way back to Dewey, standing patiently beside his car.

"Dewey, we've got problems now. I twisted the key. Now it won't fit into the starter. Do you have another key?"

"Nope. I didn't think we'd need one. You got any ideas?"

"Well, every FBO I've ever been in has a board somewhere with all the keys hanging on it. How about wandering into the hangar? See how many folks are still working. If you can find that board, I'll come up with a plan for lifting the key."

Dewey was back within a few minutes. We had to accomplish something soon, before the airport closed for the night.

"There's only one mechanic in the hangar. The key board is just inside the first office. It's about two feet wide. It must have a hundred sets of keys on it. The door to the office is open."

"OK. You wander in again. Start chewing the fat with the mechanic. Keep his attention away from the office. I'll slip in just after you, lift the key and be on my way. Try to keep him talking until you hear me start up."

Right about then, the hangar door opened. A mechanic walked out, lit a cigarette and headed for the canteen. Dewey and I looked at each other.

He said, "That's the only mechanic I saw in there. The hangar should be empty now."

"Really? Let's go to Plan Bravo," I said quietly.

"What's Plan Bravo?"

"We walk in and steal the key."

"OK. Let's go." Dewey was my kind of guy.

We walked into the hangar and went to the office with the key board on the wall. Ten minutes later, we had finished checking every single key. We had every key ever made at our fingertips, except the key to N2645Q. We were stymied, again.

"He must have kept the key. He does know I'm here, trying to recover the plane."

"Shit. That does put a crimp in our plans, Dewey." I thought for a moment. "Tell you what. There isn't all that much of a difference between all Piper keys. Grab every silver key you can that says PK on the head. One of them *must* work."

We walked out to the plane carrying dozens of keys. I sat in the pilot's seat as Dewey handed them to me, one by one. None worked. Then, with one of the last keys, I felt a slight movement. A twist and a turn later, I had the magnetos switched on. But the key wasn't quite close enough to the proper key to engage the starter. We were within a silly millimeter of success.

"Dewey, have you ever propped an airplane?" I asked.

"Why sure, Bob. Back when I started flying, airplanes didn't have starters."

"Prop me. I don't have the fuel to make it to Shannon. I can get it out of here. I'll fly it to Southampton. I know some folks who can put it into a hangar for the night. I'll have the switch changed in the morning. I can meet you in Shannon tomorrow afternoon."

I switched the master switch on, primed the engine and advanced the mixture control. I'd never before started a plane by having someone pull on the prop.

I'd read all about it, though.

Dewey pulled the prop through the first time. Nothing happened. Then again. Still nothing. On the third try, the engine caught. It purred like a kitten as I let it warm up.

I switched on the radios. I gave my prearranged coded call sign to the tower. I was cleared for taxi and takeoff on any runway of my choice.

I felt exactly like a World War II fighter ace just notified of a gaggle of Luftwaffe aircraft inbound to London. (Biggin Hill was formerly an RAF station, most notably during the Battle of Britain in 1940.) I taxied to the nearest runway. Quickly, I finished my takeoff checklist. Just before departing, I opened my door and tossed all the other keys onto the grass. I took off and quickly flew the Cherokee to Southampton.

The next morning I changed the master switch. If this airplane wasn't hot, it was awfully warm. I cleared customs and immigration outbound and set off for Shannon.

I delayed filing a flight plan until I had almost cleared British airspace. When I radioed ATC to file, they notified me that I was supposed to return to Biggin Hill for an inquiry. I asked if that was a request or an order. Their reply was that since it seemed to be a civil matter, it was a request. I continued to Shannon and landed.

I had to give the first thief of this plane an E for effort. When I landed in Shannon, I was met by two Irish policemen. Much to my dismay, they greeted me by name. But to my surprise, they then informed me that they were there to guard the plane.

I made my way to the duty office to sign in. One of the Irish fellows I had been fishing with before had the duty that day. He told me that the police had been told that the airplane was stolen. They were supposed to clap me in irons. But when my friend had found out that I was flying the plane, he told them he knew me, and that if I was the pilot, this must be a legitimate trip. The police took him at his word. Instead of arresting me, they arrested the plane. That was OK with me, because now no one but me could touch it.

I showed him all the papers I had received from Dewey Glover. As best I could, I explained who was doing what to whom, and how. Since the duty officer had vouched for me, and with a name like Moriarty, how could I be an airplane thief?

Sheep thief, perhaps; airplane thief, never.

I waited until the last flight from London had come and gone before realizing that perhaps Dewey wasn't going to make it to Shannon that day.

Once I had checked into the airport hotel, I called home to let Kathie know what was happening. To my surprise, she knew at least as much as I did. Dewey had called her from London, just before he jumped on a 747 bound for New York.

I was on my own, and had to sort out the legal mumbo-jumbo.

I took the Cherokee to SRS the next morning to have the ferry tanks installed. I was sipping my morning cup of tea in the secretary's office when the phone rang. It was a solicitor from Dublin. He represented the man from whom I had confiscated the airplane.

I let him ramble on for a while about all the dire things about to happen to me. Then I unleashed my bombshell. I figured the bozo in London had creased at least a few laws. He was a far bigger thief than Dewey and me combined. If he wanted to press charges, why didn't he just hop on over to Shannon and file away?

England and Ireland have triple-strength libel laws. As in the U.S., anyone who wants to call someone a thief can do so. Unlike in the U.S., when you play your cards there, you've bet your whole bankroll.

Not unnaturally for a lawyer anywhere, this guy was bombastic and a four-flusher. I called his bet. He folded.

This airplane proved willing to go back to the U.S., but not without a problem or two. I left Ireland the next day, directly for Gander. I got exactly to 30 degrees west, the halfway point, when the fuel system malfunctioned. I *knew* I could make it back to Shannon, whereas I only *thought* I could make it to Canada. No bold pilot, I opted for safety. I flew almost fifteen hours that day, to go exactly nowhere.

A $2 valve solved my problem. After another fifteen-hour flight, I sat down safely in Gander.

We had more than our fair share of oddballs among ferry pilots. One of the strangest was departing Gander as I arrived. Woodie, also known as Clark Woodard, was taking a Cherokee to England via Iceland. I told him that he could expect a fifteen-knot tailwind if he instead went directly to Shannon.

"I don't know, Mo. That's not what the forecasters were calling for. It didn't look like it to me. If I only got a ten-knot tailwind, I'd have to land with only a three-hour reserve."

"Woodie, I'm not talking about funny little lines on a weather chart. I just *flew* it. I know it's at least fifteen knots."

"I don't want to disagree with you, but it just doesn't look right to me."

"Woodie, are you an idiot, or what? I'm not telling you what I think. I'm telling you what I know. I never hit a cloud. It doesn't get any better."

"I don't know, Bob. I'm afraid to chance it."

The rest of the trip to Lock Haven was standard winter flying. I iced up to beat the band over New Hampshire. But that happened almost every trip. After all, it was winter. Watching ice accumulate on the wings does tend to keep you awake and alert.

I found out later that Dewey Glover wasn't rolling in money. He was swimming in it. It just doesn't make sense to mess with some folks.

To the best of my knowledge, no one has tried to steal from him since.

174th TRIP: BEMBRIDGE, ENGLAND to CALDWELL, NJ

1980	from	to	nautical miles	knots	time (hours)			
					flight	day	night	inst.
Sep 29	Bembridge	Oxford	67	84	0.8	0.8		
Sep 30	Oxford	Cardiff	73	91	0.8	0.8		
	Cardiff	Shannon	213	93	2.3	2.3		
Oct 1	Shannon	Reykjavik	812	87	9.3	5.3	4.0	2.0
Oct 5	Reykjavik	Narssaq	697	85	8.2	8.2		
Oct 6	Narssaq	Goose Bay	657	88	7.5	7.5		
Oct 7	Goose Bay	Burlington	731	91	8.0	8.0		0.8
Oct 8	Burlington	Caldwell	229	76	3.0	3.0		
TOTALS		9 days	3,479	87	39.9	35.9	4.0	2.8

My 174th trip began as a standard ferry flight. Before it was over I would help the biggest screwball I ever met to become the first man to cross the Atlantic standing on top of an airplane. He went across in the wrong direction, at the wrong time of year, atop the wrong airplane, and with the wrong crew. He also did it for the wrong reason. It was a great trip.

AFTER THE QUANTUM LEAP in oil prices in 1979, from $16 a barrel to almost $40, the Mexican government was awash in petrodollars with no place to spend them, until a bright young bureaucrat came up with an idea. I think that's the reason they hire bright young bureaucrats.

It seemed that some of the peasants lived so far out in the countryside they couldn't get their crops to market. That's why they were still peasants. If only the government would step in and help them get those crops to market, they could grow more crops, sell them for big pesos, move to Puerto Vallarta and not be peasants any more. But putting in new roads was too costly and would take too much time.

Enter the young bureaucrats with their bright ideas. Why not spend a few million petro-bucks on some transport airplanes to fly the crops to market?

People working in government really do come up with these kinds of ideas. If God didn't hate them, He wouldn't have made them bureaucrats.

So the Mexican government set out to blow some money on a few transport planes. And if you wanted to waste some money in a hurry on a bird or three, the Britten-Norman Islander was the airplane for you.

Designed in 1964 by Desmond Norman and John Britten, the Islander was supposed to compete with the Piper Aztec. It sported four more seats and came $10,000 cheaper. The first airplanes were delivered in 1967 and sold like hotcakes.

Over-engineered, the Islander is slow, noisy, uncomfortable, and ugly. The heater has a nasty habit of quitting mid-ocean on winter ferry trips. The battery costs many times as much as an equivalent battery in any U.S.-designed airplane, and tends to conk out completely the first time it loses its charge. Spare parts prices are outrageous, if you can get them. The parts manual shows 25,000 parts. The airplane has only 15,000 parts in total.

Other than these minor failings, it's a great bird and a perfect way to spend petrodollars.

The factory was selling as many airplanes as it could produce, until a spoilsport number-cruncher came along. It seemed the company was losing money on every Islander it sold. The more airplanes it made, the more money was lost. Desmond and John handled the matter with a customary British Stiff Upper Lip, and went bankrupt. But only for a year.

Along came a savior (also spelled "sucker"). The Fairey group expected to pick up a nice juicy American subcontract. It had facilities in Belgium sitting idle. Why not take Britten-Norman out of receivership and use the Belgian plant to produce airplanes until the American contract came along?

They started making Islanders in Belgium. Sales soared. So did staff numbers. In fact, the expansion of the staff looked like the Goodyear blimp being filled. These extra staff didn't build airplanes, being employed instead to push papers around and send each other important memos.

The American subcontract never arrived. Even though they were pushing Islanders out the door like there was no tomorrow, no profits arrived either.

Along came another number-cruncher. "Lots of airplanes, guys, but we ain't making any money." Maintaining a stiff upper lip of their own, the Fairey group tossed in the towel and went belly up.

Another few years went by. Along came another so-called savior. Pilatus Aircraft from Switzerland took over the company and brought it out of receivership. To give Pilatus credit where due, there was a business case to be made. Over a thousand Islanders had been sold, most were still in service, and if the company did nothing but sell spare parts for the next ten years, it should have been able to turn a profit. Britten-Norman had some nice facilities on the Isle of Wight and could be bought cheap.

If only it were possible to persuade the British that profit is not a nasty word, but a necessity for survival, it would have been possible to turn the company around. By this time, Britten-Norman had facilities in Romania. The cost of producing the airplane was under control, but they never got the admin costs under control.

The Swiss tried to apply logic and common sense. They should have brought over the Swiss Guard for a while, to get the attention of the staff.

Without exception, every customer I ever met while picking up an Islander in Bembridge figured out Britten-Norman's main problem in less than five minutes. They would look at the few guys on the shop floor, working on airplanes. Then they'd look up at the heavily populated executive offices. Each would then ask me, "How can these folks make money when fifteen people are building airplanes and hundreds are shuffling paper?"

I would reply, "They never made money in the past, aren't making money now, and if they don't get rid of a lot of deadwood, won't make money in the future."

They never did.

The Islander was the perfect airplane for the Mexicans, so they placed an order for fifteen of them.

I had picked up a Piper Lance in the U.S. and delivered it to CSE Aviation in Kidlington, Oxford. I had already taken three of the Mexican Bamboo Bombers across to Caldwell, New Jersey, and the fourth was waiting for me in Bembridge.

I caught the train to Southampton and the ferry to the Isle of Wight. A fellow named Peter Wilson picked me up at the station and took me to the factory. My Bamboo Bomber was ready to go. I installed the communications radio, signed for the aircraft, and took off for Kidlington.

CSE owned the airport there, and taught more students than any other company in Europe. There was a mess of petrodollars sloshing around Africa and the Middle East at the time. CSE was playing its part in recycling them by teaching those from their former colonies in the Middle East to take off and crash well enough to pass a flight check, so they could go home and crash airplanes, thus recycling more petrodollars.

Entering the landing pattern at Kidlington was chaotic. There would be a dozen students wandering around the field, all of them lost. They couldn't keep track of anyone else in the pattern. None of them understood English. To enter the pattern at Kidlington and land without having a mid-air was to achieve a miracle. Flying the pattern at CSE made ocean flying in a single-engine aircraft look like child's play.

I landed safely and taxied over to the hangar for tanking. CSE had tanked a few Islanders for me and were getting pretty good at it. They told me that my bird would be ready at the crack of dawn. That meant if I showed up about noon, it would almost be ready.

I got a ride into Woodstock and found a room. That night I went over to a pub called The Spud and had dinner. As usual, it was packed. I polished off more English lager than I should have and went to bed.

I went out to CSE the next day at noon, and sure enough my airplane was almost ready. I paid for the tanking and took off soon after. Every time I brought an Islander in, they tanked it in exactly the same way. Every time, they charged me a different price.

I cleared customs in Cardiff. The winds to Shannon were stiff, but after landing there I had plenty of time to get a good meal and a good night's sleep. As usual, I stopped in at the weather office to get an idea of what the winds would be like going to Iceland.

In those days, and perhaps still, the forecasters at Shannon sat around and drew circles and loops on weather charts. They hadn't a clue what they meant. A SWAG estimate from them of the velocity and direction of the winds was exactly that: a silly, wild-ass guess.

A ferry pilot no better at reading the winds than the Irish forecasters would soon be a dead ferry pilot. The Canadian forecasters in Gander remained the sole practitioners in the whole world worth their salt. The Irish and Icelandic weather-guessers were terrible.

The winds were awful. I had at least forty knots on the nose. No icing, but lots of clouds. I needed the instrument time like I needed a hole in the head. It had been solid IFR for the three previous trips as well.

When I checked into the hotel, the clerk told me that Paul Vandor from Jonas Aircraft had been trying to reach me. I was to call him urgently. Jonas was the U.S. distributor of Islanders, so this could only be bad news. I prayed that nothing had happened to Kathie or the baby. I booked a call to Paul immediately.

"Good afternoon. This is Jonas Aircraft."

"Hi, honey. This is Bob Moriarty, calling from Shannon. Will you connect me to Paul?"

He came on the line. "Hey, Bobby! How you doing?"

"What's up, Paul? Is Kathie OK?"

"As far as I know, she is. I need you to do something for us, Bob."

"Sure, Paul. What do you want?"

"That Wagner fellow that called you a year ago and wanted you to fly him across the Atlantic. He's in Reykjavik now. His Islander is broken and it sounds as if his pilots aren't too much on the ball. Get your ass up there tonight and do what you can for them. You call me as soon as you get there. I'm counting on you, Bobby."

"Fuck you, Vandor. I just got to England yesterday with a single. I got in twenty minutes ago, from Cardiff. It's five-thirty in the afternoon and there is no way I can get to Reykjavik before they close the airport. I'm bucking forty-knot headwinds.

"If his bird is busted today, it's going to be busted tomorrow. I'm going to get some chow and sip a few cool ones and hit the sack. I'll be there tomorrow afternoon. I'll call you as soon as I know what's going on."

I couldn't stand Vandor. He didn't have the brains to pour champagne out of a boot. He was a flunky but acted as if he owned Jonas Aircraft.

I had problems with my radios the next morning and didn't leave Shannon until noon. I got into Reykjavik in the evening after beating myself to death against headwinds for nine hours. If the winds didn't change direction soon, the turkey on top of his airplane was going to be stuck in Iceland for a lot longer than he planned. With strong westerlies common at this time of year, why would someone try to go westbound? He could have gone from Canada non-stop to Ireland instead.

The winds in Reykjavik were blowing forty knots on the ground. I put all the control locks on the control surfaces and secured the yoke with the seat belt. Not to do so would almost certainly result in damage to the aircraft. At this same airport, two DC-3s had been left unattended six months before. The winds came up and took the rudders right out of their fittings. They were still sitting there, waiting to be fixed.

I checked into the Loftlieder Hotel at the airport. I had another message to call Vandor right away, and a message to see Jaromir Wagner as soon as possible. I went to see Wagner first.

He was in the middle of taping an interview in German for a film crew. I still remembered my college German and could keep up with him. It sounded as if he had big problems. I thought I heard him say that it had taken his two-man crew forty-five minutes to find the airport. I assumed I had missed a verb or a tense, because it was damned near impossible to miss Reykjavik airport.

The interviewer, Michael Battenberg, came up and introduced himself to me when he was through. In German, he then introduced me to Wagner, and explained to Wagner that I was the fellow that Vandor had promised would solve all his problems. Battenberg didn't realize at the time that I understood German.

He next introduced me to the cameraman. Then, almost as an afterthought, he remembered to introduce me to the two German pilots.

I asked which of them was the captain of the aircraft. One of them said, "I guess I am." That took me by surprise. I had never heard anyone say that he *guessed* he was in charge of an airplane.

I mustn't name either pilot. My first impression was that they looked like Mutt and Jeff. The one who guessed he was the captain was tall and skinny. The other was short and scruffy. Mutt and Jeff they were then, and would remain. Between them they didn't look as if they could fly their way out of a wet paper bag. I thought even less of them as time went on.

"How much fuel are you carrying?" I asked.

"I don't know," Mutt replied.

"How much fuel are you burning an hour, with him standing on top of the airplane?"

"I don't know."

"How fast will the plane go?"

At last I had asked a question he could answer. "When we came in from the Faroes, we made it in three hours."

That told me nothing. I didn't know how far away the Faroe Islands were, and in any case, that would give me only ground speed, not true airspeed. That's what I was trying to drag out of him. Getting straight answers was like pulling teeth.

"What's your true airspeed?" I asked more directly.

"True airspeed? Is that what you read off the little dial or is that how fast you go over the ground?" It was neither, but I was beginning to form an opinion of this guy's qualifications.

"What is the problem with your airplane?" I kept trying to squeeze facts out of him. Jeff stood there with his index finger up his nose.

"Something went wrong with those little pipe things out on the wing. The mechanic wants to fix them but I think we can fly without them OK."

If what was broken was what I thought was broken, they would be OK until they reached about a hundred knots. Then they would cease to be OK, as they would all be dead in the crash that would result from the ailerons coming off.

"Did you happen to leave off the control locks after you came in?"

"Yes. How did you know? We were so tired from flying that three-hour trip. I was going to put them on the next day but I must have forgotten. Do you think that maybe that's why the little pipe things are broken?"

"Might have something to do with it." My face was turning red. I've seen some rotten pilots. These two took the cake.

I couldn't believe what I was hearing. This guy was a menace to women and little children. He must have gotten his license under false pretenses.

"By the way, how many hours do you have?"

He positively puffed up. "I have almost five hundred hours. Soon I will become night qualified and get my instrument rating."

For Christ's sake! My personal view is that no one should be allowed to fly without at least a thousand hours' experience in the air.

Wagner looked like a man watching a tennis match. I don't think he was able to follow much of what we were talking about. Every once in a while, Michael would translate. Michael told me that Wagner didn't really speak English.

"Jaromir, let me ask you a couple of questions," I said. "Why the hell do you want to cross the ocean on top of that airplane?"

"For the challenge."

Seems like a great reason to risk life and limb to me.

"It's going to get pretty cold up there. Can you take the temperature?"

"No problem."

That was pretty close to the extent of his vocabulary. I figured that if he had big enough balls to do a dumb stunt like this for as flaky a reason as "the challenge," I owed it to him to help him all I could.

Battenberg had a far better idea of what was going on than the pilots had. All the time that Mutt was talking to me, Jeff was standing there staring into space. I didn't even want to know how many hours Jeff had.

Battenberg and I went down to the bar for a drink. I needed one.

He and his cameraman had flown up in an escort bird to take pictures. The escort ship had dropped them off and returned to Germany. If possible, the film crew wanted to catch a ride with me.

Michael told me that originally, a Lufthansa pilot was to fly Wagner. The airline got wind of his plans and sat on him. They were not interested in any headlines reading, "Lufthansa pilot killed in Greenland while flying airplane with turkey on top." I understood completely.

Sigi, the local mechanic, came in as we were talking. Seeing me, he came over and sat down. Sure enough, Mutt and Jeff had left the control locks off their Islander. The mass balance arms for the ailerons were both broken. Sigi had ordered new ones from Britten-Norman and they would arrive soon. He wasn't much impressed with the pilots either.

On a ferry trip, if the plane went down, the pilot got to see it up close and early. This fact impressed itself on ferry pilots. Whenever an airplane had a mechanical fault, the pilot breathed heavily down the necks of the mechanics until everyone was certain it was fixed.

But neither of these pilots had the slightest interest in what was happening to their aircraft. This trip was getting more interesting by the moment.

I returned to my room and called Jonas Aircraft in New York.

"Good afternoon. Jonas Aircraft."

"Hi, honey. This is Bob Moriarty, in Iceland. Will you connect me to Mister Muller?" This was getting serious enough that I didn't want to speak with the minions. I wanted to talk to the big gun.

A heavy accent came over the line. It could only be Alex Muller.

"Gut afternoonk, Bobert. How ark you?"

"I'm fine, Alex. Listen, this Wagner trip is a complete gaggle. They don't have any charts or survival gear. They don't know what a survival radio is. The pilots don't have a thousand hours between them. They are the biggest yoyos I have ever seen. They shouldn't be in the U.S. around Thanksgiving, or they'll be eaten. Wagner is doing this 'for the challenge.' If you want me to help them, I will. If I help them at all, I am committed to going all the way with them. These pilots will have to be spoon-fed or they'll kill Wagner."

"Bobert, you yust do de best you can. Kip your expenses, and ve vill make it op to you. Yust get Vagner ofer saftly."

"OK, Alex. I'll keep you posted."

"Sank you, Bobert."

Now it was time for me to do the best job I could. I started the next morning by taking a look at Wagner's plane.

An American mechanic was working on one of the DC-3s. He had been there for three weeks and was just about finished. He had his girlfriend with him. That's the only way to travel.

He came over to look at the Islander. "How y'all doing? I'm Tom Danaher. An' this here is mah girlfrien', Barrel Fisher."

All sorts of people were turning up in Iceland. What the hell kind of name was Barrel? A barrel fisher sounded like some kind of giant bird.

"Hi. I'm Bob Moriarty. I'm ferrying the Bamboo Bomber and I'm looking over Wagner's bird to see if he has enough fuel."

"You'll have to pardon Tom," said his girlfriend. "He comes from Texas and has a hard time pronouncing English. I'm Beryl Fisher. As in the precious stone."

"Barrel and I are working on that DC-3. If y'all need some help, give us a shout."

It was a short conversation. But Tom Danaher and I would have our adventures in the future.

Wagner's plane had only two fifty-five-gallon drums in the cabin for spare fuel, which wouldn't be enough. I had left some fuel tanks here on previous trips; it was time to reclaim them. I stole the fittings I needed from Sigi and went to work refitting Wagner's ferry system. Mutt finally wandered down to look at his airplane.

"How about handing me a flashlight?" I asked.

"I don't have one in the airplane," Mutt replied.

I stared at him with daggers in my eyes. He was oblivious. This was like someone bringing out a plate of doggy-doo at a cocktail party. It just isn't done in proper company. A real pilot would rather take off without maps than without having a flashlight handy.

"Would you be so kind as to stroll over to my aircraft and, pretty please, bring me my flashlight?" There was no use being subtle with this dumbass.

He ambled back with no flashlight in hand. "Which one do you want?"

It would cost me $300 to repair the damage I then did, gritting my teeth.

"Could you bring me my Rudolph the Red-Nosed Reindeer flashlight? You'll recognize it right away. Rudolph's nose flashes when you switch it on."

Mutt left to search for it.

"Sigi, can you loan me a flashlight for a little while?" I asked.

"Sure. Here." Sigi was rolling on the floor with tears running down his face. He hadn't met any pilots like these two before, either.

Every few minutes, Mutt would come back and tell me he couldn't find the Rudolph flashlight. I would suggest he look in another part of the airplane. He looked for that flashlight for two hours. He never did catch on. Humor isn't the long suit of Germans.

I finished tanking Wagner's plane. Sigi told me he'd have the parts to fix it in two days. That must have been some kind of record for Britten-Norman. But we were going to break all kinds of records on this trip.

I avoided Mutt and Jeff as much as I could. I spent a lot of time talking to Tom and Barrel, and with Sveinn Bjornsson, the airport's operations manager. He and I were old buddies. Girlie magazines weren't worth much up there, but a bottle or three of vodka worked miracles.

The ugliest woman in Iceland is still stunning. And they are friendly. Taking skin magazines there is a waste. Why look at the milk when the cows are free? Or something like that. But Iceland had a hell of a drinking problem. It's the only place I've ever been where drunks came up and cadged drinks from you, all the time. If they bugged you, you just motioned for the bouncer to come over, and he would bounce them — really bounce them. I guess it didn't hurt, with all that booze in you.

Some outfit in Paris had been through and had left a poster with Sveinn. It seems they planned to hold a race from Paris to New York to Paris the next summer. I told him immediately that I was going to enter it and had every intention of winning.

Ferry pilots worked their fannies off and never got any glory. It was time for one of us to get a little credit. I wrote down the name and address of the race organization. I would send off for an application form as soon as I finished this trip.

Danaher had finished work on one DC-3 and was now working on the second. He was not only a mechanic, but a pilot too. He and Beryl were going to fly the first one to England and return for the second. I had a lot of respect for his mechanical abilities, but I had to hand it to Beryl. She would stand next to him and pass tools as he worked. It was cold and horribly windy. He had to be suffering. That's part of the game, if you're going to fix airplanes in Iceland. Beryl could have been inside, keeping her tootsies warm. But every time Tom went to work, she was right next to him. That's true love.

Kathie and I were getting along like two bucks in a rut. She acted as if she was doing me a big favor picking me up from the airport after I'd spent fifteen hours hand-flying one of these Bamboo Bombers. And things got worse with every trip. She really wanted to be married to someone like dear old dad, working in an office eight hours a day. I should have been warned early on in the relationship when she stroked my chest and told me she loved my chest hair. It was just like her dad's chest hair, she said.

The winds on the westbound route were terrible. Even if Wagner's plane was in flying condition, we weren't going anywhere anytime soon. For five days we had 30–50 knots of wind right on the nose. I figured his bird couldn't do more than ninety knots with him perched on top. I wouldn't leave in anything more than a ten-knot headwind.

I got some charts of Greenland for Mutt and Jeff, and put an HF radio in their plane. It didn't work. But what the hell, we were obeying the letter of the law. Just because you carry one doesn't mean it will work. And had it been in working order, I would have had to teach them how to turn it on.

Sigi received the parts he needed and finished Wagner's airplane. It looked as if the winds might shift to the east, so we made plans to leave the next morning. Tom and Beryl invited me over to their apartment for a farewell dinner. We stayed up late, telling lies, and I slept on the couch.

The next morning I wandered over to the weather office for a brief. The winds had indeed shifted around and we now had a tailwind of 5–10 knots. That was great news, because I still didn't know what to expect in the way of performance from Wagner's bird.

Alex Muller had told me that their insurance wouldn't cover non-pilots in a Jonas bird. I would take Jeff in my airplane. He certainly wasn't of much value in Wagner's plane. There were two extra seats in Wagner's plane, so I put Battenberg and his cameraman with Mutt. Hell, someone in that airplane ought to know what was going on. It sure wasn't going to be Mutt. I elected Battenberg.

Wagner contacted the powers that be in Reykjavik and let them know he was leaving. Several hundred people gathered in the bitter cold to watch his departure. He suited up in his three layers of clothing. He climbed on top of the Islander and got into his harness.

I took off so I could get some pictures of his takeoff. Mutt lined up in position and called for takeoff clearance. He started his takeoff roll, got airborne, and headed westbound over the Atlantic for Greenland. As he passed through one thousand feet he started screaming in German over the radio. I was unable to keep up with it.

Jeff started yelling at him. "Go back! Go back! Tell Jaromir to jump off the airplane! You're going to crash!" All in German. I didn't understand every word, but obviously something interesting was happening.

Mutt and Jeff were cool heads in an emergency; I could see that right away. I asked Jeff what the problem was. He told me that Mutt almost lost an engine. I asked him which engine. He didn't know. Was he still having problems with it? No. OK, guys. We will continue on to Greenland.

I told Mutt that he probably had a little water in his fuel. It wasn't uncommon in used Islanders. He now said that he wanted to turn back.

"Did you drain the water out of your fuel tanks this morning?" I asked.

"Of course." He was incensed that I would question his aviation skills. After all, he was a pilot, just like me. He had a piece of paper telling him so.

"How much water did you get out of the wings?"

"About a gallon or two out of the left wing. None out of the right wing."

I gritted my teeth again. More damage done. I wondered if Jonas would pick up my dentist's bill. At this rate, it was going to be big bucks. That much water in any fuel tank means you have a bad seal and could easily lose an engine on takeoff. Engines run a lot better on avgas than on water.

I asked Jeff what the German word for asshole was. He thought I was kidding.

"You had water in the fuel. Don't worry about it. The worst that can happen is that your left engine will sputter and spit for a while. Stay on your heading for Greenland."

He still didn't want to go. I ordered him to. He was a German, and they understand orders. He rolled out on a heading for Narssaq.

Wagner had told everybody that he would go across standing up in his harness. But as soon as we were out of sight of land he lay down on top of the airplane. I asked Jeff about it. It seems that he had discovered a spot of dead air on the top of the Islander. Where he was lying, there was no wind.

We pressed on, and saw the distant mountains of Greenland just when we should. We were doing about ninety knots to stay with Wagner. The engine on his bird smoothed out and Mutt wasn't unhappy any more.

As we came up on the coast of Greenland I pointed out to Mutt just where he was on his chart. There was no reason for us to stay with him from this point. I advanced the power and went ahead to Narssaq. Only an idiot could get lost from here. We were only fifty miles from landing. I called Narssaq for instructions and landing conditions. The weather was clear to the moon. I landed twenty minutes later.

Sure enough, Mutt got lost.

We had left Reykjavik at about eight o'clock that morning. I landed in Narssaq a few minutes after four. There was a crowd of people waiting to see Wagner arrive. He should have been about ten minutes behind us. I waited by my plane for longer than that, and then realized that Mutt had probably screwed up again. I rushed to the operations shack.

They were in radio contact with him. He was over the coast of Greenland, headed westbound. I told him that Greenland was an island. Once he left land, he wouldn't hit land again. This was news to him. He turned back to the east. He had managed to miss Narssaq completely.

Greenland is misnamed. It isn't green anywhere, at any time. It is a mass of mountains, fjords, and glaciers. It might be possible to become lost over the ice cap, but it was impossible anywhere else, if equipped with a VFR chart and the ability to determine the direction in which north lay.

Thinking about it now, I'll bet Mutt didn't have a clue which way was north. Whatever made me think he could follow a map in the most distinctive terrain in the world?

He finally fixed his position and read it to us in latitude and longitude. Miracle of miracles, he was thirty miles to the southwest. Then he said his estimated landing time was 22:30 GMT. I just about croaked. It was now 16:30, local and GMT. How could he take six hours to fly thirty miles?

By this time there was nothing I would put past this guy. He continued to amaze me at every step. He confirmed his position and his landing time. He landed twenty minutes later.

I went up to the plane to see if Jaromir was OK. He unfastened his harness and jumped to the ground. I half-expected to see his legs snap at the knees, but all the big pieces stayed together. He had a little frostbite on his chin from the temperature of minus twenty-five Celsius at ten thousand feet. He said he felt fine and started taking off his suit.

I went up to talk to Mutt. I looked in the airplane to see what time his clock said. It showed 12:30 but didn't seem to be running. I tried winding it.

Once wound, it seemed to work just fine. I reset the time. Then I turned to Mutt, who was looking over my shoulder with great interest.

"How come the clock wasn't running?" I asked.

"I didn't think it worked. What did you do to make it work?"

"I wound it. Did you ever try that?"

"No," Mutt replied with a vapid look.

"What time does your watch show?"

"Twenty-two thirty-five. Why?"

I pointed. "Do you see that big round thing over there?"

"Sure."

"That's called the sun. Have you ever seen the sun in the sky at ten thirty-five at night in Germany? In October?"

"No, I cannot say that I have."

"Well, the next time you're back in Germany and you see it there at that time of night, check your goddam watch, because it ain't working right."

"My watch works perfectly. I've had it for fifteen years and it has always worked perfectly."

"It's ten to five in the afternoon, according to every other watch on this island." I was sick of this jerk.

Wagner talked to the crowd for a while, then put jogging clothes on and went for a run. He was a real sucker for punishment.

I sat down to talk with Battenberg and his cameraman. It turned out that the cameraman had kept telling Mutt that he was going in the wrong direction. He didn't want to listen. Honest to God, he wanted to continue west even when they passed the west coast of Greenland. The cameraman finally gave him a heading to take, or else. He looked like a bruiser, so Mutt, thinking discretion the better part of valor, took up the heading. The cameraman had also written down the latitude and longitude, for Mutt to read to us.

I think, from the way the cameraman put it to me, that he had told Mutt to take up a heading of 040 degrees or be fed the airplane in big chunks. Or the equivalent in German.

I told Battenberg that I had serious reservations about them continuing with the flight. Even when spoon-fed, Mutt was plumb dangerous. It was one thing for Wagner to risk life and limb, I said, but they should consider staying in Greenland until they could hitch another ride westbound.

Battenberg had two years invested in this film, and the idea of dropping it in Greenland tore him up. But the idea of dropping into the Atlantic didn't appeal to him either. We finally decided that Mutt and Jeff would ride together. Nothing could possibly be worse than Mutt flying solo. I would take the cameraman and film in my Bamboo Bomber. Michael would ride shotgun with Mutt and Jeff.

The cameraman turned to me. "But I'm not a pilot. I thought only pilots could ride in the Jonas airplane."

I told him, "If you can read a map of Greenland and find Narssaq by yourself, you're ten times the pilot either of them will ever be. You're a pilot for the duration of the trip. Just keep your mouth shut when we get to New York. If we get to New York."

We were up early the next morning. The forecaster was giving us a ten-knot tailwind. The briefers in Narssaq had their act together. If they said ten knots, it probably would be. We gathered our troops and prepared to leave.

Mutt continued to dazzle me. He hadn't even stuck around the day before to watch his plane being refueled. He left it to me.

Wagner put his suit on and got snapped into his harness. Mutt and Jeff were still grab-assing. Wagner had to yell at them to get in the airplane and get going before he burned up.

It is strange to think of it, but the only problem Wagner had with the temperature was being too hot. He had three layers on. It wasn't the cold getting into his suit that created a problem. It was its inability to let his body heat out. He was literally too well insulated. The frostbite he had suffered the day before was caused by a loose-fitting face mask. Minus twenty-five Celsius didn't bother him in the slightest. He came close to overheating while waiting for Mutt and Jeff to decide they were ready.

Again, I took off first. I had drained the water from their plane myself. There was a lot of it in the left wing. I told Mutt to expect some roughness from that engine. He took off but experienced no problems this time.

I wasn't about to let Mutt alone again. He was too damned dangerous if he had to do any thinking. I stayed two hundred yards off his left wing for seven hours, all the way to Goose Bay. I even had to tell him when to switch tanks; keeping track of his fuel burn and flying at the same time was way beyond his capabilities. I made sure when we left Greenland that he wasn't chewing gum.

The weather that day was perfect. Again, the sky was clear to the moon.

As soon as we hit the coast of Labrador we established communication with Goose Bay. They were talking to a helicopter and were vectoring him to our position. I first saw him some five miles south of us. I talked the pilot over to where we were. He had a photographer from New York aboard. The photo bird flew alongside Wagner right to touchdown. I came around and landed after they were safely on the ground.

Wagner was already off the airplane and out of his suit before I shut down. After so many days of waiting, he was evidently happy to be putting some water behind him.

The Canadian customs folks came and grabbed us and hustled us in to clear formalities. Again, it seemed that the whole town was there to see this strange sight. Once finished with customs, Jaromir spent the next hour signing autographs and having his picture taken with little kids. To them, this was a big deal. But in Goose Bay, almost anything is a big deal.

While he was doing his thing, I fueled both airplanes and went over to check the forecast for the next day. The weather god was definitely on Jaromir's side. We would again have good weather and a following breeze. At no other time did I ever see three consecutive days of good weather and easterly winds on this route. It must have been his clean and healthy way of life.

When we checked into the hotel, I had a call waiting for me from the Canadian Department of Transportation (DOT), the equivalent of the FAA. Any news could only be bad news. I returned the call immediately. Luckily for me, the inspector was an old friend of mine.

"Bob, what's going on with this guy?"

I told him.

"If I come up there and inspect his airplane, am I going to find anything I shouldn't?"

"Look," I said, "don't come up. The airplane has approval from the German FAA, but you don't really want to make a close inspection. This guy has managed to get from Frankfurt to Goose Bay more or less safely. The eyes of the world are on him right now, and if you stop him from continuing you're only going to embarrass the DOT and Canada. We have good weather between here and Burlington and I think I can get him down OK. Another twenty-four hours and I'll have him out of your hair."

"Moriarty, goddamn it. If it was anyone but you escorting them, I'd stop them so fast their heads would spin. But it could get embarrassing. Please get them out of Canada in one piece. If that guy wants to crash, will you please do it on your side of the border. We won't check anything for twenty-four hours.

If you are not out of the country by then, I personally am going over that airplane with a fine-toothed comb."

He was my kind of bureaucrat.

The whole crew was sitting in the bar, drinking beer. I toasted Jaromir.

"To the second man to cross the Atlantic on top of an airplane."

Everybody drank except Wagner. He just sat there looking stunned. He spoke to Battenberg in German. I didn't catch what he was saying.

"Jaromir wants to know what you mean. He thought he was the first to cross on top of an airplane."

"He was. He was the first, and he will be the last."

Big grin from Jaromir.

I called Jonas and let Alex Muller know we had made it safely to Goose Bay. We would be in Burlington, Vermont the next day. Alex told me that Vandor would meet us there and escort Jaromir to New York.

The only thing we needed to make this party complete was Paul Vandor. Perhaps he could get together with Mutt and Jeff and trade flying tips.

The photographer who had been in the helicopter latched on to me like a leech. My ability to speak English and German must have appealed to him. He was my first experience with the news media. I wasn't impressed by his behavior but have since found it to be typical.

The news media seems to believe the entire world exists only for its benefit. The media will do anything for a story except tell the truth. I have seen stories published on things I had experienced or of which I had firsthand knowledge. Rarely did the story even resemble the facts.

"You have to get me to Wagner. I need more shots. See if I can get some pictures of him in the shower. I can make him a star. I need more shots."

I wasn't real sure how having his picture in *Blue Boy* was going to help Jaromir's career, but I thought I would pass it by him.

"Tell that creep to get fucked. He's not taking pictures of me in the shower. I've spent an hour with him, posing for his goddamned pictures. He has enough pictures of me. Bob, you have to learn that those bastards from the news media always want more, no matter how much you give them. I could spend the next ten years posing for him, and he would still want 'just one more picture.' The media doesn't give a shit about accuracy. All they want is a story or more pictures. Tell him to go fuck himself."

All this was in German, of course. His English was limited to, "For the challenge."

The photographer was crushed. If only he had a few more pictures of Wagner, everything would be perfect. I offered to let him take some pictures of me. That didn't seem to appeal to him.

Mutt and Jeff had so impressed me with their flying skills that I told Battenberg and his cameraman to continue on to Burlington on a commercial carrier. I wanted to minimize casualties. They agreed. They would fly the local airline to Montreal and charter a plane to Burlington. They seemed relieved that they wouldn't have to fly with Mutt and Jeff again.

We went through the routine of suiting up Wagner the next morning. Again, Mutt and Jeff sat around on their butts until Wagner yelled at them to get into the airplane. I supposed that if I was as bad as they were, I wouldn't want to get in an airplane with me either.

I kept trying to figure a way I could cause them to crash without harming Wagner. But I couldn't think of anything. Even if I were caught in the act, the most they could charge me with would be mercy killing.

Mutt managed to get the plane airborne, pointed towards Burlington, and somehow landed. For him that was great, and all in one day.

Burlington was overrun with tourists watching the leaves change color. There wasn't a room available for fifty miles, literally. We even tried to get the news team that met us to pull some strings, but we couldn't find anything. Someone finally said, with a laugh, that there were rooms in Lake Placid. Any port in a storm. I rented a Cessna 172 and off we went for Lake Placid, New York. Wagner kept trying to climb out onto a wing but we managed to restrain him.

We checked into a hotel and went down for dinner. Paul Vandor and another Alex from Jonas Aircraft, Alex Pag, showed up in time for after-dinner drinks. The plan was that Alex would fly Wagner from Burlington. The plane would fly down the Hudson, around the Statue of Liberty, and then land in Caldwell, New Jersey.

Wagner didn't know Alex from the man in the moon. He didn't care that Jonas was the distributor of Islanders in the U.S. He asked me to fly him because he was comfortable with me. I told him that I would check with Alex Pag, and if he would take my Bamboo Bomber, I would fly Wagner.

Everybody was happy with this, except Vandor. As we got up from the table, he announced that Alex would fly Wagner to New York. Jaromir looked at me. I looked at Jaromir. Jaromir thought something had been lost in the translation. So did I, even though we were speaking English. We had just spent two hours talking over who would fly what. With one slash, Vandor had completely rearranged the flight plan.

"Alex Muller wants Pag to fly Wagner to New York and that's the way it's going to be."

I called Muller at home. He had said no such thing. If Wagner wanted me to fly him, that was just fine with Jonas Aircraft. Alex Pag was content to fly my airplane to New Jersey and I would fly Jaromir on the final leg.

Our original plan called for us to leave Burlington at 10 am. Battenberg and his guy didn't appear, so we waited. An hour later, we still hadn't heard from them. Vandor was becoming anxious. He announced — he was always announcing things — that if Battenberg and crew didn't show up in the next thirty minutes, he would leave without them.

"Vandor, why don't you put that airplane someplace where the sun don't shine? This show is Wagner's. I'm flying him where he wants, when he wants to go. If you have such a hot date, why don't you leave? I think we can find New York without you."

I liked Vandor almost, but not quite, as much as I liked Mutt and Jeff.

Battenberg and crew finally came barreling down the road in a rented car. They had a tale of woe about their adventure since leaving Goose Bay but we didn't have time to hear it. Wagner suited up and off we went for the Big Apple, with me at the controls of his plane and Vandor flying the Jonas demo aircraft. Alex Pag flew my Bamboo Bomber down to New York by himself.

I never figured out what Vandor was doing flying with us. There was nothing to be gained by it. He had been trying to run the show ever since he had arrived the night before. Neither Wagner nor I were going to change our plans based on anything he said. I think he just wanted to get some publicity for Jonas.

Vandor had the cameraman in his airplane. Michael Battenberg flew in a front seat with me. We put Mutt and Jeff in the back of the plane, behind the fuel tanks. For once they were where they belonged, in the back of the bus, as far away from the controls as possible.

I had been warned that Vandor was a rotten pilot. I had told him on the ground that I didn't want him flying near us. The weather was beautiful and there was no need for close formation. I told him to stay off our wing and keep us in sight.

Wagner had tried to jury-rig a microphone into his helmet so he could communicate with the pilot, but it didn't work. He had put a rear view mirror on the front windscreen so the pilot could see him. The only communication was through hand signals. Or so we thought.

We heard banging. I scanned the instruments but nothing seemed amiss. The banging intensified. I looked up at Wagner in the mirror. He was hammering on the top of the airplane with hands and feet. His eyes were as big as saucers. Just a few feet above him was another Islander. I dropped the airplane down fifty feet and reduced power so it would pass us.

"Paul, do you have us in sight?"

"Sure, Bobby. You're out at my left," Vandor responded.

If that was true, then another babyshit-green Islander had just come out of nowhere, trying to decapitate Jaromir. There couldn't be two Islanders in the whole world quite that repulsive color.

Needless to say, Paul had designed the paint scheme.

He was now a hundred yards in front of us. "Look out again, Paul. I don't think you really have us in sight."

"Yea. I must have lost sight of you for a minute. Do you have me in sight?"

"I'm fairly certain, Paul, that you can't see us." Unless you have x-ray eyes in the seat of your pants. "We are below and behind you. You're an idiot. You just came whizzing across the top of us and almost chopped Wagner into little pieces. Keep your distance. Move out to our three o'clock position."

All the stories about Paul's flying abilities were true. It is always the responsibility of the wingman to keep the lead aircraft in sight. If the wingman ever loses sight of the flight lead, it is the wingman's responsibility to take action to ensure he doesn't come anywhere near the leader. It is considered bad form to have a mid-air with your leader.

The real Chinese fire drill started as we passed south of Albany, NY. We picked up our first camera helicopter. We were on a VFR flight plan but were in communication with Air Traffic Control, as we needed clearance to fly down the Hudson past Manhattan. We could hear ATC vectoring another aircraft to our position. It was a helicopter with a photographer on board. He assumed a formation position off our left wing. He started moving in closer. Closer and closer. His rotor blades actually overlapped our left wing. This yoyo was still coming in closer! It got to the point where I was having problems holding my heading due to the downwash from his blades. The pilot never bothered talking to me or discussing what he was going to do. Finally he talked to me and that really scared me.

I wasn't hearing him over the radio. I could hear him over the noise of both aircraft without him using the radio at all. That sucker was in my lap and wanted to come still closer. I think the photographer wanted to get some great shots of Wagner's head being chopped off by the rotor blades. We weren't seconds from disaster. We were microseconds away.

I got the pilot of the photo bird on the radio. I told him what I thought of his flying ability. I told him what I thought of his antecedents, of his bachelor father's antecedents, and of his bachelor grandfather's antecedents. We discussed some sexual activities in which I imagined his mother had been involved. I may have made a comment or two about his sister's pet snake and how really close they were.

Then I asked him politely to move his aircraft out to the left, about two hundred miles. He moved about three feet. The photographer made up for it by leaning out so he could get some really close shots. If he wanted to practice his freefall technique, *sans* parachute, it was OK with me. I thought photographers carried telephoto lenses for shots like this, but this guy evidently had never heard of them. Wagner told me later that he wouldn't let his dentist get quite that close.

I had made a test flight with Wagner's plane in Iceland. It was a sick, tired, worn-out bird. I don't think it would have exceeded one hundred knots if you had pushed it over a cliff. With Wagner on top, in the wind flow, it had the flight characteristics of a pregnant pig. Trying to maintain flying speed and heading was nearly impossible with a photo-helicopter overlapping our wing.

But by the time we got down to the Tappan Zee Bridge (the old one, since replaced), the helicopters had marshaled *en masse*. It looked like the battle for the A Shau Valley in Vietnam in '69. We learned later that there were only twelve of them trying to take pictures, all at the same time. It seemed to me that the sky was full of helicopters making slashing runs on my airplane. There were a mere dozen.

Some of these guys made the earlier pilot look like a gent. Nobody bothered talking to me. They didn't bother to talk to each other. It was just one giant game of chicken, with my aircraft at the focus. I wanted out. In any other fixed-wing airplane I could have outrun them. I would have paid big bucks right then for an M-60 machine gun. Hell, I could have taken these guys out with a BB gun.

I was shot at many times in Vietnam. I've been in many a tight spot that I wasn't real sure I would escape. But that trip down the Hudson was easily the hairiest flight I ever made. Those dingbats from the news media would do anything to get a picture, even if it was just a shot of us going down in flames.

As we went downriver towards the Statue of Liberty, Michael pointed out the Goodyear blimp to me. It was in the New York area for some work. It was the first time I had ever seen it in flight. A pretty sight, but it was about five miles from us and hard to make out any detail. We continued to dart and weave among the swarm of attack cameramen.

We circled the statue and headed back to Caldwell to land. The attacking mob rushed off so they could record the conclusion of Wagner's epic feat.

I was more than a little apprehensive about my landing. I had never made a landing with Jaromir standing on top and wasn't sure how the airplane would handle. If I were to blow this landing, it would be in front of God and the whole world.

I circled the field and made a long straight final, so I could feel the characteristics of the plane. It seemed to fly just like a real airplane. I reduced power. Down we came. Squeak, squeak, squeak. Not bad, if I say so myself. Another nice landing. We taxied in and shut down amidst a swarm of snarling, screaming news people.

I'd gained enough experience of the media to know I didn't need them. Mutt and Jeff had been miffed at Wagner in Burlington, when he told them that he didn't want them flying him to New Jersey. After all, they were pilots and had managed to find the airplane every day. I took them aside in Burlington. I told them that as soon as we landed in Caldwell, I'd jump out of the airplane. They could have all the glory to themselves.

I got out in time to watch Vandor land, if you could call it a landing. One advantage of the Islander is that it will take off and land on a dime, and return nine cents change. Paul attempted to impress the media with his skills. I heard his tires impact heavily on the runway. I had never before seen anyone land an Islander with its brakes locked. But the press was real impressed.

Throughout the trip, Wagner had been telling the media that its sole purpose was the glory. *For the challenge.* He was a broke car mechanic who had big *cojones* and some wild ideas. He figured he would get so much great publicity from this stunt that Hollywood would shower him with money to do further stunts.

He hadn't put up any of his own money for the plane or expenses. He had his buddy do that. Jaromir convinced this buddy to hock his bar in Germany and put the equivalent of $250,000 into this project. Jaromir would repay him out of the proceeds from Hollywood and from the book he would write about the trip.

He made only one slight miscalculation.

Wagner didn't speak enough English to ask the way to the bathroom. Now the eyes of the world were upon him as he was asked to explain his great feat. He tried answering in German. Nobody wanted explanations in German. Bless his heart, Alex Muller tried to translate but was barely understandable himself. Finally, Honey Rothschild from Jonas took over the translation. She spoke perfect English and German.

The media wasn't interested in hearing translations. They wanted the man himself. But he didn't speak English, and nobody was going to tape some guy speaking German for broadcast on American TV. Even if he had just flown across the Atlantic on top of a rather worn Islander.

Wagner was blown out of the water at that moment, but didn't realize it for weeks.

About this time a "girlfriend" rushed up. She planted a big wet slippery kiss on Jaromir. It was evident she knew him quite well.

I started thinking. Jaromir was married and had never been in the U.S. before. Where did he make friends with this gal?

She wore a knit dress that you could practically see through. I looked more closely. You *could* see through it, and she didn't seem to have any underwear on. There was nothing between her and the dress.

I went up to Battenberg. "Where did he come up with the bimbo?"

"I don't know. He doesn't know any women over here. Must be another groupie."

The pay wasn't great but the fringe benefits were wonderful.

Art Ward and his crew at C&W Electronics, who did all of the radio installations for Jonas, had laid out a party spread. We had all the free booze and beer the media could drink. Food, too, for those few interested.

The media grew bored of trying to figure out how to interview someone who spoke no English, and drifted away. The rest of us got drunk and told lies about what a great trip it had been. I wanted to go home and be with Kathie and our new rug rat, Sean. I suspected that this stunt wasn't going to pay off quite as well as Jaromir supposed.

He spent the next couple of weeks traveling around the country, trying to capitalize on his fame. He appeared on a couple of morning talk shows and on another show called *That's Incredible*, but the media soon lost interest.

Hell, if *That's Incredible* thought his stunt was amazing, they should have tried putting Mutt, Jeff, and Vandor in an airplane together. Seeing the three of them arguing about how to start an engine or wind up a clock would have been the most amazing thing I had ever seen. Imagine watching them take off.

I did get to see myself on TV, landing in Caldwell at the start of the *That's Incredible* clip. It went squeak, squeak, squeak. Nice landing, if I say so myself.

Jaromir showed up a few weeks later with his tail between his legs. No one was interested in putting out any money, for stunts or for his book. His fifteen minutes of fame came and went.

Battenberg went back to Germany to put the film together. It went nowhere either.

The airplane was sold at a big loss. Wagner's now ex-buddy went bankrupt. The last I heard, Wagner was back in Germany, fixing cars. He stiffed me out of a $750 deposit on a Porsche.

Time magazine reported a week later, "The frigid feat ended in a small New Jersey airfield, after a ritual circling of the Statue of Liberty and a near collision with the Goodyear blimp."

At least they didn't call it the Goodrich blimp.

193rd–196th TRIPS: JOHNSON, KS to JOHNSON, KS

1981	from	to	nautical miles	knots	time (hours)			
					flight	day	night	inst.
May 25	Johnson	Fort Worth	361	181	2.0	2.0		
May 26	Fort Worth	Lakeland	844	160	5.3	5.3		
Jun 1	Lakeland	Perkasie	826	127	6.5	6.5		
Jun 4	Perkasie	Bridgeport	102	102	1.0	1.0		
	Bridgeport	Gander	916	229	4.0	4.0		
	Gander	Paris	2,184	168	13.0	7.0	6.0	2.5
Jun 8	Paris	Shannon	473	135	3.5	3.5		
	Shannon	Gander	1,727	157	11.0	11.0		
	Gander	Bridgeport	916	139	6.3	4.3	2.0	
Jun 10	Bridgeport	Halifax	471	214	2.2		2.2	
	Halifax	Paris	2,640	183	14.4	8.4	6.0	
Jun 15	Paris	Shannon	473	121	3.9	3.9		
Jun 16	Shannon	Reykjavik	813	138	5.9	5.9		
	Reykjavik	Goose Bay	1,337	149	9.0	6.0	3.0	2.5
Jun 17	Goose Bay	Burlington	731	140	5.2	5.2		2.5
	Burlington	Memphis	955	174	5.5	1.7	3.8	
Jun 18	Memphis	Wichita Falls	424	101	4.2		4.2	
	Wichita Falls	Johnson	271	151	1.8		1.8	
Jun 19	Johnson	Santa Rosa	995	142	7.0	7.0		
Jun 20	Santa Rosa	Santa Rosa	205	158	1.3	1.3		
Jun 21	Santa Rosa	Johnson	995	166	6.0	6.0		
TOTALS		27 days	18,659	157	119.0	90.0	29.0	7.5

In Iceland in October 1980, while trying to shepherd Jaromir Wagner across the Atlantic, I saw a poster advertising "The First Transatlantic Air Race, Paris to New York to Paris." It wasn't the first transatlantic air race and wasn't really to New York, but who would wish to nitpick? If it was going to be an air race over the water, I was going to be in it (the race, not the water). And win.

It was called the Air Transat race.

Many months of hard work later, I was winging my way to victory after snatching Lindbergh's New York to Paris record away from my main competitor. But if he couldn't win through skill, he would try to win through treachery; if not through treachery, he would go whine to the press.

IN 1978, 1979, and 1980, U.S. aircraft manufacturers were selling aircraft as fast as they could make them. Aircraft went from being an expense to being an investment with a real return. We saw constant escalation in the prices of new aircraft in the States, but the dollar was dropping at a faster rate overseas. The oil price panic of 1979 and 1980 was just now showing up when you fueled your plane.

I had paid as little as sixty-five cents a gallon for avgas in 1976, but was now paying as much as $6 a gallon. I majored in economics in college. It didn't take me long to realize that six-dollar gas would soon put a severe crimp in aircraft sales.

Ferry companies were hiring pilots as fast as they could train them. Due to this influx, we were each flying fewer and fewer trips. The companies weren't raising their prices nearly as fast as the price of fuel was going up. The ferry pilots were caught in the middle, flying fewer trips and making less money on each trip. It was time to try to capitalize on my growing reputation.

Being around Jaromir Wagner had taught me that having your picture in the paper isn't enough to put cash in your pocket. This was the first transatlantic race in fifteen years. Surely the aviation press would jump on something this big?

I was still ferrying regularly but this race was my big opportunity. I waited for the rules to arrive in the mail. The package finally arrived.

I learned later, and repeatedly, that the French don't do a very good job of writing or explaining race rules. And even though Paris is considered a fashion capital of the world, they can't design a flight jacket that doesn't look like it was ripped off a drunk in a dark alley.

They do a great job of designing posters, though. I opened up the official race regulations packet and pulled out this really nifty poster, with an oil painting of a 1930s French biplane with New York City in the background. Any race with such a neat official poster couldn't be all that bad.

The poster was great, but it was all downhill from there.

The general layout of the race was straightforward. It was from Paris to New York to Paris. It was being held in conjunction with the giant Paris Air Show. It would start on June 7 and end on June 14, 1981. Single-engine aircraft would compete against other singles, and twins would compete against twins. Each captain was required to have five hundred hours of flying time and be instrument qualified. Each co-pilot had to have at least two hundred hours. There was a pure speed competition, with no holds barred, and a handicap competition based on the seventy-five percent power speed at optimum altitude. A competitor could enter both. No rule prevented it, although seemingly no one else thought of it.

The minimum prize for first place in either pure speed or handicap was 50,000 French francs. I pulled out my calculator — wow, that was almost $10,000, minimum. And imagine how much higher that might go when sponsors started jumping on the bandwagon. With all the press this race could generate, first prize might end up being big bucks.

I couldn't find any mention of cash payments for second and third places, but those guys could fend for themselves. The entry form did state that detailed rules would follow. It didn't say when.

It doesn't take much to win an air race. All you have to do is to find the fastest plane you can, figure out who will end up in second place, and whip his ass. Everybody else would be thinking about how to beat dozens of other people. I just want to whip the runner-up. Having spent five or six thousand hours flying the course would help, too.

My first decision had to be whether or not to fly a twin. I figured there might be some big money folks in the race, and they would all be flying twins. Skill can't beat unlimited dollars, so I quickly decided that I should fly a single. Besides, most media attention would be focused on the single-engine competition. I have never seen the press bother to take the time to understand any handicap formula.

Once that decision was made, I set out to find the fastest plane I could; to identify the single-engine aircraft that would give me the best chance to win both the speed and handicap competitions.

I was willing to consider Mooney, Beech, and Cessna aircraft. Piper had no singles with any real speed. The Mooneys turned out not to have the range I needed, since I had to carry a co-pilot instead of extra fuel tanks. I'd never been happy with Cessna's quality, in any of its products. They had the speed and range I needed but I wanted a plane that was certain to finish the course. I had always liked Beech aircraft and soon decided I needed a single-engine Beech.

I got on the phone to everyone I knew who could advise me on which model to fly. I talked to Larry Ball, who wrote *Those Incomparable Bonanzas*, a book examining just about every aspect of the Beech Bonanza line. He said I must talk to Mike Smith of Mike Smith Aero in Johnson, Kansas. Mike offered a speed conversion for the Bonanza that really made it scoot.

I was a little leery about claims from aircraft modifiers. My experience with people claiming to improve performance was that their typical improvement was to hang a bigger engine out front. Anybody can do that. Usually, the factory is the first to try it. They claim performance improvement. More engine means more fuel burned. A lot more engine means much higher fuel burn in exchange for only a little more speed.

Many of the performance enhancers could have doubled as snake oil salesmen on the side. Their product turned out to be a mystery gel that you rubbed on the inside of your left elbow just before you took off. It would reduce the takeoff roll by "at least five hundred feet," or double your money back. If you could ever find the guy again.

I called Mike. He sounded like a Midwest plowboy. Yes, he offered a speed conversion on the Bonanza. He had tried putting a 350 horsepower engine out front but it was not reliable and burned too much fuel.

His specialty was drag reduction. He concentrated more on increased fuel mileage than on just speed improvement. He claimed that with his full speed conversion, a V-35 Bonanza would go as fast on ten gallons an hour as an unmodified aircraft burning twenty-five percent more fuel.

That all sounded nice, but I wanted to know how fast it would go. Mike started hemming and hawing a little here. I started to smell snake oil. It turned out that he was guaranteeing a speed of 230 miles an hour out of a stock airplane.

I had the book handy. I looked up the top speed on the V-35: it was 204 mph. If his figures were correct, his modification was the way to go.

I asked him why he was hemming and hawing. He told me that a few of the aircraft that came in for work were pretty clean to start with. Those planes didn't see the full speed improvement. In those cases he couldn't charge them the full price. He had been burned a couple of times on his guarantee, so he wasn't claiming that he could make every plane go quite as fast.

I realized that if his claims were true, I could make his plane a winner. I asked how much it would cost to buy a good used V-35 and have him do his conversion on it. We decided that $75,000 would buy a plane equipped the way I needed it for the race.

That was a nice round $75,000 more than I had available to spend. Mike told me that it shouldn't be too hard to find someone prepared to put up the money. Companies regularly spent a lot more than that for car racing.

I made a list of all the people I knew who were in a position to spring for that kind of cash for an air race. I called them one by one. That didn't take too long, as it was a very short list. It turned out that no one I knew had the slightest interest in putting any money into such a venture.

Getting a plane was put on hold. I still had seven months before the race. Plenty of time.

My second problem was the selection of a co-pilot. I wasn't fond of co-pilots under any circumstances but the rules stipulated two pilots. I couldn't think why. There was only one airplane. We would be flying only forty hours in 2½ days. What the hell would I need a spare pilot for? I wasn't about to share the flight planning with anyone, and the quickest way of getting your arm broken is to touch the yoke of an airplane I'm flying.

My thoughts went back to the Texan I had met in Iceland while on the Wagner trip. I called Tom Danaher.

"Tom. This is Bob Moriarty. We met in October. How are you doing?"

"Well, if it isn't Robert! I was just thinking of you. What are you up to?"

"Do you remember that Twin Comanche that flew through Iceland while we were up there? They had a poster in the window, of a race from Paris to New York. I sent off for the rules and I just got them in the mail. I think that race could be won. I've got a ton of flying time over the North Atlantic. If I can put together the right team and get the right airplane, I don't think anyone could beat me. I was wondering if you would like to fly in it with me."

"What kind of airplane do you have for the race?"

"That's my biggest problem right now. I don't have one. I looked at the specs on the Mooney and the P210 but they just don't have the range I want.

I think the plane to beat would be a 1964 or later non-turbo V-35. It's not going to be a high-altitude race because you have to go across both ways.

"I talked to this guy in Kansas, Mike Smith, who does a speed conversion on the V-35. He says he can get 230 mph at ten thousand feet and thirteen gallons an hour. He has a company plane but doesn't want to lend it for the race. He says we can get a plane fully equipped and modified for $75,000. I don't have any money and don't know anyone who does. Do you know anyone down there who needs a fast single? I hear you guys are rolling in money right now."

"There's lots of money down here but everyone wants twins. I have a 1962 Bonanza but the '64s and later have the 285 horsepower engine and they are faster. I'm kind of skeptical about someone getting an honest 230 miles an hour out of the V-35. That's a whole lot faster than a stock airplane. I'd be happy to fly with you but I don't have any money to put into the trip.

"I'll make you a deal, though. You find an airplane. I'll get someone here to put up the expense money. One thing I want you to do, though. I still have the fuel tank that I used in 1954 to cross with. When you come up with a plane, I want us to use that fuel tank because it means a lot to me."

Tom had crossed the Atlantic in 1954 in a Bonanza. He was the first person since Wrong Way Corrigan to go across in a single-engine aircraft.

You could tell by looking at Tom that he had no money. He wore ratty old shirts and jeans that he probably bought at Sears, on sale. He was the tightest person I ever met. When he pulled change out of his pocket, the coins were still pre-1964 silver. He didn't buy anything that he didn't need.

Little did I know then that he was absurdly wealthy but very cheap. He had all his money in municipal bonds, to avoid taxes. He figured that the best way to prevent the government stealing your money was to loan it to them. I've often pondered that logic. He could have bought a racing Bonanza every month if he'd felt like it.

The race organizers held the first planning meeting in Paris on December 15, 1980. On December 13, I was stuck in Iceland with a broken Bamboo Bomber. It looked like I would be unable to attend.

A French crew flying a Fairchild F-27 came through. I told them my tale of woe. They were bound for Paris, and invited me to hop aboard. That trip was a tale in itself. We stopped in Glasgow, Scotland for fuel and lunch. The three crewmen polished off a bottle of wine with lunch. Back in the plane, they all drank Jack Daniel's all the way to Paris. I've been known to have a drink or two on occasion. But I had never seen anyone drink like these French guys. It seemed like drinking was part of the checklist.

Judging from the crowd that showed up for the briefing, there was plenty of interest in this air race. There were only about eight Americans present, but the price of flying commercial to and from Paris was a little steep.

To date, about twenty-five crews had paid the entry fee. The fee for a single was 5,000 francs, or about $1,000. I paid the fee for Tom and me.

Typical of the French, the entire meeting was conducted in French. It didn't matter that the international language of aviation is English, or that to participate in the race, you had to speak English. Throughout the world, Air Traffic Control is carried out in English. If you fly internationally, you must speak English.

All those not fluent in French were given headphones to listen to a simultaneous translation. I moved over to sit next to some of the Americans.

I don't know if this is true of all varieties of racing, but I met some of the most interesting people I've ever met during air races. The daughter-in-law of Igor Sikorsky, Sigrid Sikorsky, would fly a Piper Lance. Jack Cink had flown as co-pilot with Steve Oster, who had set the fastest time ever around the world in a piston engine aircraft.

Jack and Steve would be competing in an Aerostar. They would become good friends of mine, and we would compete several times in the future. We sat together in the meeting during the day and went dining and drinking together that evening. We had a great time knocking the French and their organization, or rather, their absence of organization.

I had arrived expecting to be handed a set of race rules. It was not to be. A few minor details had still to be worked out. Complete details would be provided at some point in the future.

The meeting consisted of briefings from experts about techniques of transatlantic flying, but all from the point of view of heavy jet operators. We were even briefed by a Concorde captain on the extreme magnetic deviation over areas of northern Canada and Greenland. He confused magnetic deviation, which is a function of compass location, with magnetic variation. All the Americans were splitting a gut. None of the French pilots could figure out what we thought was so funny.

Flying Concorde had nothing in common with flying a piston engine aircraft. The planning meeting was a wasted opportunity. We wanted to know what the rules were, so we could plan our technique.

I continued to ferry airplanes and to search for a sponsor. I tried all the major aircraft manufacturers and suppliers, with no luck. I was greatly surprised at the lack of interest in the U.S. at the prospect of such a race. Because the French were sponsoring it, they were concentrating their PR effort in Europe. I told them numerous times that they should direct more of their efforts toward the U.S. If they didn't get American sponsors and crews interested, the likelihood of any future races would be slight.

They ignored me. It was a French race and was going to be run the French way, screwed up to the max.

I knew that Mike Smith had an airplane available. As I was having no luck finding someone willing to buy an airplane, I tried to convince him that he should rent his airplane to Tom and me. No luck. He did realize that if we won, we would garner some great publicity for his company. But Mike was personally afraid of ocean flying. He didn't want to lose his demonstration aircraft.

The organizers held their first and only U.S. planning meeting in New York in late March, 1981. I have to admit that the French held all their meetings at first-class venues. They did not hesitate to spend money, when they felt like it.

This was the only chance to meet the American participants who had been unable to make it to Paris. Jack DeVoe, who owned a commuter airline in Florida, would participate in an Aerostar. He claimed to have made thirty-four ocean ferry trips. I had been ferrying for six years at that time and knew everyone in the business, or thought I did, and had never heard of him. It turned out that he had in fact made a good number of ocean crossings, carrying a white powder from Colombia to Florida. There are all kinds of ways to make a living. He made a hell of a lot more money ferrying his planes than I did.

I did meet one fellow who might have the solution to our airplane problem. Gerald Dietrick owned the rights to produce the Windecker Eagle, a single-engine aircraft similar in performance to the Bonanza. It had been developed by a Texas dentist. Its main claim to fame was its all-fiberglass construction. It was a beautifully built, clean airplane.

Only five Eagles were built before Dr. Windecker ran out of money. Dietrick loved to tell how he bought the bankrupt company and airplanes, literally on the courthouse steps. That pissed me off because Windecker did all of the work, but only Dietrick stood to make any money from the airplane.

He was trying to convince some local town government to put up funds to construct an airplane. He really wanted to win the race.

The wisdom of opting for a single-engine aircraft now became apparent. Jack DeVoe would fly an Aerostar. He had unlimited bucks. Steve Oster would fly an Aerostar. He had money and a great co-pilot. Russ Hancock from Colemill conversions would fly a Colemill Panther. Colemill conversions did to the Piper Navajo what Mike Smith did to the Bonanza. With Colemill's resources behind him, Russ would be a tough competitor.

All the big money guys were flying twins. Tom and I weren't in their category. I saw no problem beating any of the Europeans. My only competition would be Gerald Dietrick.

I got the impression, from the Paris and New York meetings, that most of the entrants had entered just to participate, not to win. Only a few crews were out to win. Those pilots belched smoke and fire every time they opened their mouths.

We were still waiting for the rules. DeVoe, Oster, Hancock and I wanted firm, fixed, understandable rules.

The organizers had not expected any participants to compete in both the speed and handicap races. The rules differed. For speed, the clock started when the wheels left the ground in Paris, and stopped when the wheels touched down in Paris, coming back from New York. Competitors could take any route and land at any airport. For the handicap, the clock also started when the wheels left the ground in Paris, but stopped when the aircraft was on the ground at any of the designated fueling airports. It didn't start again until the aircraft left the ground at the designated airport. Wanting to win the speed portion didn't mean we had to give up the handicap portion.

We pushed and pushed for a final definition of the rules. They would be given to us, some day, in the future.

That New York meeting sometimes became heated. The Americans had not entered merely to get an ugly flight jacket. Our expenses would be twice as high as those of the Europeans because we had to cross the ocean to get to the starting line, and cross it again to return home after it was over. Every rule change to date seemed to favor the French entrants. No one would give us any firm rules.

General aviation in the U.S. was far more advanced than anywhere else in the world. We were out to prove it.

The organizers hemmed and hawed and equivocated. The European participants seemed to accept the fact that the race was being run for the benefit of its organizers.

"These unruly Americans seem to think they should have some say in how the race is to be run. Quite uncivilized."

During the cocktail party after the meeting, I had the chance to talk with Dietrick. He was quite proud of the Eagle. It would mean a lot for him to win the race, for the future of his plane. He mentioned the possibility of entering two planes. My ears perked up. I asked if he had anyone to fly the second Eagle. He didn't. I took him over to a corner of the room so we wouldn't be overheard.

"Gerald, I'll make you a deal. I'm still sucking wind trying to find a sponsor for a Bonanza. I've got the money to pay expenses. If you'll give me or rent me your other bird, I'll give the speed portion to you. Everybody in Europe knows I'm going for speed. They are all going for the handicap portion. The handicap race would be a piece of cake for me to win. Your Eagle could take the speed side of the race without me competing. I'll wax them in the handicap. You'll get four times as much press by winning both as you would if you just win the speed race. I really want the speed race, but I'll let you win it if you make that airplane available to me."

"Bob, you got a deal. I wasn't going to even try for the handicap race. I'll rent you the second plane. But you have to give me the speed race."

I said OK. Tom Danaher and I had our airplane.

Dietrick made the biggest mistake of his life right then. He made a deal with me but later wormed out of it. I suppose he thought that by lying to me he could keep me out of the race. That was a mistake. But then, he wasn't all that bright anyway.

I'm a funny sort. I've been lied to and cheated and screwed many times. I'm a sucker. But I like people and trust them. I don't hold human nature against anyone. But if you make a deal with me, you better stick to it. I've got a memory like an elephant.

I called Tom to give him the good news. He was happy about us getting an airplane but he'd really wanted to compete in a Bonanza. He had lined up two oil men who were willing to contribute $5,000 each. The whole thing was going to cost about $15,000. I was selling survival suits and HF radios to some of the other racers. I'd make up whatever the difference was.

I had several discussions with Dietrick. Our deal was still on. While telling everyone we were going strictly for speed, I was secretly planning how to win the handicap race. I prepared flight plans for every possible route. I spent more time planning for this race than for any fifty ferry flights I ever made. I had badly wanted to win the speed category, but flying in the race was a whole lot better than sitting in Pennsylvania reading about it. We had a plane, even if it wasn't a Bonanza.

There was a final planning meeting in Paris in late April. Conveniently, I was on my way to Geneva in a Piper Warrior, so it was easy for me to stop over in Paris. There were now over one hundred entries for the race.

Again, it was held in a first-class hotel. No expense was spared by the organizers. We were still waiting for firm rules. By now, the Europeans and even the French pilots were tired of the race committee's excuses.

One rule change that clearly favored the French, but was bizarre by any standard, concerned over gross weight condition.

When ferrying aircraft, we could obtain permission from the FAA to fly at 25–30 percent over the normal gross weight. This allowed us to carry the fuel necessary to cross an ocean. In an Eagle or a Bonanza we could fly nonstop from Bridgeport, Connecticut to Paris. But westbound, due to the prevailing winds, it would be necessary to make one fuel stop.

But French aeronautical regulations did not permit flight in an over gross condition. The pilots of French-registered aircraft naturally felt that the pilots of U.S.-registered aircraft thereby gained an unfair advantage. The French race committee naturally agreed with the French pilots.

They compromised. U.S.-registered aircraft were limited to fifteen percent over gross. This would make one stop necessary eastbound and perhaps two stops westbound, depending on the winds. The race committee also gave permission to the French-registered aircraft to do the same thing, in violation of French air regulations. That was a very typical French decision.

Sigrid Sikorsky, Steve Oster and Jack Cink all attended the meeting. Dietrick didn't. We sat together again. We were still waiting for written rules to be issued. Those of us who had attended all the meetings knew clearly the general gist of the rules.

The speed race was from Paris to New York, with a mandatory layover of twenty-four hours but no longer, then back to Paris. Any airport could be used for fueling, but if a landing was made anywhere other than at one of the ten designated airports, the time spent on the ground would count against the plane in the handicap race.

For the handicap race, time in the air was all that counted, but the racer must fuel at a designated airport or lose time on the ground. Credit would be given for the actual air miles between designated airports.

A French private pilot had had the idea for the race. He and his group had done all the work to date. He had been running the management in a first-class manner and spending money at a first-class rate. But he made one slight mistake. He had neglected to recruit any sponsors and had now run out of money. The French Aero Club had taken over, and was now managing the race and its empty bank account.

One major change was made by the committee between the New York meeting and this meeting. There was now no prize money at all. The promised minimum prize wasn't a minimum any more, or a maximum for that matter. The French Aero Club handled this matter the French way, first of all by not telling the competitors, and then by figuring out a way to steal it from them.

I have to give credit to the French Aero Club personnel. They stood up in front of two hundred pilots who had alone financed the race, and who were going to lay out a collective $2 or $3 million to participate, in the hopes of collecting only $10,000 and a fancy medal. They had the balls to stand there and talk about the prizes the winners stood to collect. There wasn't a dime in the kitty. If we pilots had known what was going on, we would have taken the whole race committee out and strung them up from the nearest lamp posts.

By the time I got back to the United States, the start of the race was less than one month away. It was time to pick up the Windecker Eagle.

I called Dietrick to fill him in on the meeting in Paris. We talked about all the flip-flops in rule changes. I told him that I needed to pick up the bird I was to fly so I could have it tanked. I needed to fly it for two or three weeks to get a feel for its capabilities.

"Bob, I've decided not to enter the second airplane. I thought about it, and if I win the speed race, it doesn't make any difference about the handicap race."

"Are you kidding me? We made a deal. You promised me that airplane. You know I don't have the time to come up with another airplane now. You're screwing me and I don't much like that."

"Tough shit, Bob. That's the way the ball bounces."

I was screwed now. I didn't have a plane. Even if someone were to drop a million dollars on the table, I didn't have the time to make the necessary modifications. Dietrick wanted to win. If he had to lie or cheat to win, he was willing to do so. With one stroke, he put Tom and me out of the race.

Or so he thought. I'm not a quitter.

In the back of my mind I knew there was still one airplane that was modified and ready to race — Mike Smith's demonstrator. I called him.

"Mike. This is Bob Moriarty. I told you that we had a deal with Dietrick for an airplane. I just talked to him and he stiffed us. He knows I don't have time now to prepare an airplane. But if you would rent your demo to us, we could still compete. You're my last hope now. If we can't use your bird, Dietrick will walk away with the race. You make your living making speed modifications on Bonanzas. What better advertisement for your business than first place in this race?

"I've attended every meeting. I've looked over the rest of the pack. Dietrick is the only guy who has ever been over the North Atlantic before, and he has crossed only two or three times. We have no competition in this race. If you let us have your plane, I'm telling you we have a seventy-five percent chance of first place in the speed category, and should place third in the handicap race."

"Well, Bob, I don't know," he began. "You know how I feel about letting my demo go over the water. I'd love to see one of my modified planes win, but I'm afraid of losing it. N111MS has been my personal plane for years now. Even if the insurance covered the price of replacing it, that plane means a lot to me.

"Tell you what. You talk to my secretary and give her some background on Tom and yourself that we could use in a press release. My inclination is to tell you right up front that I don't think I want to let you use the bird. I have too much to lose. But let me sleep on it. Call me back in a few days."

Mike transferred me to his secretary. "Mr. Moriarty, Mike wants me to write down your background and that of Tom Danaher," she said.

"OK. I'll start with Tom. He's about fifty-five years old. He started flying in the Marine Corps in 1944. He flew night fighters, and was the last Marine to shoot down a Jap in World War II. He shot down three in two weeks. If the war had lasted another week, he probably would have been an ace. He flew across the Atlantic in 1954, from Canada to Ireland. He was the first person since Wrong Way Corrigan in 1940 to fly a single-engine aircraft across the Atlantic. He got a ton of press about that trip. He has about twenty-five thousand hours in light airplanes. Just recently he flew a replica World War One biplane in the movie *Death Hunt*, with Charles Bronson and Lee Marvin. He is one of the greatest mechanics I have ever seen and is one hell of a pilot. He does an acrobatic routine for air shows in a standard Baron.

"I'm thirty-four. I'm married with one child and another on the way. I learned to fly in the Marine Corps. I spent two years flying in Vietnam. I flew 834 missions and 1,150 hours in combat. I've been ferrying airplanes for six years and have ferried nearly two hundred planes all over the world. I've flown about seventy-five different kinds of airplane. My total flight time is about nine thousand hours. Last October I was responsible for the success of Jaromir Wagner's flight across the Atlantic, standing on top of an Islander."

Our fate was now in the hands of God. I had devoted months of work to this race and given it my best shot. It looked as if we were blown out of the water before it ever started. I was pretty depressed.

Mike called me two hours later.

"Bob, you guys have an airplane. I'm not going to rent it to you. You can have it for free. But I want an agreement between the three of us. You get the airplane for free. You provide insurance for it, for $75,000. If you win, I get one-third of any prizes awarded.

"There's one more thing: I have a race called the CAFÉ 250 to run out in California on the twentieth of June. That's important. I want you to promise to get the plane back to me as soon as your race is over."

Talk about snatching victory from the jaws of defeat. Two minutes before, I had been in a state of depression, possibly terminal. Now we had the fastest single in the world, for free. I had no idea why Mike Smith had changed his mind so fast, but I wasn't going to look a gift horse in the mouth.

I called Tom and gave him the good news. He was elated. He really wanted to use his 1954 ferry tank again. The race was on.

I picked up the plane in Johnson, Kansas on May 25. We were short of time but had finished all our planning. Now we had to fly it and see what it would really do. I flew to Fort Worth, Texas and spent the night with my stepmother.

Stepmothers have a remarkable ability to take the wind out of your sails. Who was I to imagine I could beat some of the best pilots in the world in a race? The fact that I had more time over the North Atlantic *before* the race than all the other pilots combined would have *after* the race meant nothing to her. I was the youngest fighter pilot in the world when I was twenty. I set a record for the number of combat missions in Vietnam. No matter; I was still a snotty-nosed ten-year-old as far as she was concerned.

I can hear her now. "Write a book? You can't write a book. You can't even spell."

The reputation of some stepmothers is well deserved. But she was right about my spelling.

I had my first chance to test the speed of N111MS on the leg from Fort Worth to Lakeland. I looked at the airspeed indicator. It wasn't showing any advertised 230 miles per hour. Mike had sold us a bill of goods. No question, this plane was a lot faster than a stock Bonanza, but it sure didn't go 230. I think that would have to be a very light aircraft right on the deck at full power but not in regular cruise at altitude.

Now we had a fairly big problem. If Dietrick's claims about the speed of the Eagle were true, he had about a 15 mph advantage over us. What to do? If our plane wasn't fast enough, I might have to dazzle him with fancy footwork.

By this time, it was years since I had flown an airplane for Phil Waldman of Globe Aero. But Globe had the widest experience in the ferry business in tanking airplanes. I called him and asked for a quote for tanking the Bonanza. To my surprise, his price was very reasonable. He could have shafted me, but instead he gave me a good price. I explained that I needed it done in a hurry. No problem. When I pulled in, his mechanics stopped what they were doing and started on N111MS.

Tom's tank wouldn't fit. It was from a different model Bonanza. Within a few hours, Phil's guys had fabricated two new tanks for me.

The airplane would now carry the permitted fifteen percent over gross weight. But the V-35 has a problem with weight and balance. Advertised as a six-passenger plane by Beech, it is out of center of gravity unless the rearmost two passengers are tiny. If we were to carry enough fuel, we would have to carry fifty pounds of ballast in the engine compartment.

I rushed out to the nearest gun store and bought two twenty-five-pound bags of lead shotgun pellets. They fit perfectly.

Phil had another tank made that would fit under the pilot's legs. Sitting in the plane was a real bitch. It was a tight fit, and uncomfortable as hell. But who cares, when fame and glory were but days away? When the tanking was complete, I paid Globe Aero and set out for Perkasie, Pennsylvania.

Tom Danaher was taking an Air Tractor agricultural spray plane to Egypt. He would travel directly to Paris from Cairo. Before he left, he asked me to take with me to Paris one of the oil men who was putting up our expense money. That would be Tom Sanders, who proved to be a wonderful co-pilot during our record setting flight.

I explained that, if possible, I was going to try to beat Lindbergh's record time for New York to Paris. Others had surpassed his time but in the eyes of the world it would always be Lindbergh's record. It would turn my journey to the starting line of the air race into a competitive event in itself. If the oil man was willing to tolerate sixteen hours or so of discomfort, it was fine with me.

Probably the most important part of any competition is psychology. When your opponent believes that they can't win, that belief becomes self-fulfilling. No race is ever won in the air. Races are won on the ground, through preparation and the adroit use of psychology.

Dietrick believed that, after denying us the use of his second Eagle, we would be unable to secure another airplane. That was his second mistake, but not his last. We had a plane, even if it might be fifteen miles per hour slower than his.

Dietrick held Lindbergh's record from New York to Paris. He had set it two or three years before. His performance was nothing exciting, though.

I made the decision. If the winds were good enough, we could beat his record by a substantial margin, and Tom Sanders and I would file for the record with the National Aeronautics Association (NAA) in Washington. No one else in the group competing for the single-engine speed prize could come close to beating either Dietrick or me. If I could beat Dietrick, I had the prize money in my hand.

I picked up Tom Sanders in Bridgeport, Connecticut on June 4. Even though the record was billed as being between New York and Paris, it was really between Bridgeport and Paris. The rules for city to city records specify that the distance flown must be from city center to city center, plus or minus one half of one percent. The NAA's record coordinator, Milt Brown, assured me that Bridgeport was sufficient. But I wanted to make sure. We took off and climbed to eleven thousand feet. We flew back to the VOR at LaGuardia airport to officially start our record-breaking flight.

Our flight plan included a refueling stop in Gander. I had arranged a fueling crew at each of the stops we might make. Jim Patterson was in charge of my crew at Gander. This would be a great way to test their efficiency. We stopped, fueled, and were on our way in just twelve minutes. Not great, but damned good.

For late spring transoceanic flying, the winds were darn good. The weather-guessers were calling for 25–30 knots right on the tail. We should break Dietrick's record by forty-five minutes or so. That ought to annoy him.

We were flying nonstop from Gander to Paris. Hours passed, uneventfully. Then, three hours short of Ireland, the engine started misfiring. We were in deep, serious trouble. So long, record attempt. We might now have a problem just reaching land.

We were still at eleven thousand feet. We flew into clouds and started picking up ice — not enough ice to justify descending to a warmer altitude, but enough to slow the airplane by ten miles per hour. I felt engine roughness. Then it smoothed out; then roughness again. I looked at Tom. From the look on his face, he felt it too. I told him to put on his survival suit, just as a precaution.

When flying over water with a passenger, whoever it might be, my flight brief was always concise and easy to understand. It was as follows. "I don't give a damn whose name is on the bill of sale of this plane. If I'm going to fly it over water, *I'm* the owner and boss. If something goes wrong, you do exactly what I say, when I say it. Don't touch anything."

Tom donned his suit. The engine got rougher. I turned the plane slightly left for Ireland, the nearest point of land. No record for us on this trip.

"Mayday! Mayday! Mayday! This is N111MS transmitting on 121.5. We have a rough-running engine. Does anyone hear N111MS on 121.5?"

"Aah, 111MS. This is TWA 401 receiving you on 121.5. We will relay for you to Shannon. What is the nature of your emergency, and your position?"

"N111MS is fifty-one north and twenty-five west at 0535 Zulu. We're on an instrument flight plan to Paris, from Gander. We have a rough running engine and are proceeding from present position direct Shannon."

"Sounds serious, 111MS. How many engines do you have?"

"Well, counting the one that's running rough, we have an even one."

I continued to play with levers and switches to try to cure the problem. It was still running, and that was good news. Tom Sanders sat there as cool as a cucumber.

The problem seemed to have started at about the time we started picking up ice. I made the decision to descend to a lower altitude so we could burn off the ice. About that time we also got an "unsafe gear" light (meaning the landing gear). That was almost certainly related to icing.

I always hated to give up altitude. If the engine quit completely at eleven thousand feet, we could glide for about fifteen minutes. At the warmer altitudes below, our glide time would be considerably shortened. While in a glide you can do neat things like communicate your position, get your survival suit on, and get your survival kit ready to throw out the door. And pray.

I dropped the landing gear, to melt any ice that might have caused the gear warning. After a few minutes at the warmer temperatures, the engine smoothed out. I supposed the roughness was caused by a piece of lint clogging one of our six fuel injectors. If that was indeed the problem, we could easily have burned up a piston.

Another hour of smooth running led me to believe we might still make it.

I asked Tom if he was willing to shoot for Paris. If we landed in Shannon for repairs, that would be the end of our record attempt. He said the decision was mine but that he was game to give it a try, even though we had a lot more water to fly over. This was not the attitude of your average rich guy. I canceled our mayday and we picked up a heading for Paris.

Tom Sanders and I landed in Paris four hours later. We smashed Dietrick's record by two hours, even though we lost a lot of time with the mayday and detour towards Shannon. I appreciated Tom putting up a fair bit of the money we needed to run the race, and he was cool in an emergency. Anyone who knows me understands I'm not a giant fan of co-pilots, but Tom Sanders was a good sport.

Tom Danaher was waiting for us. I told him about the problem we had had with the engine. He asked if I had any tools on board.

Every ferry pilot carries a bag of basic tools. I had mine in a small bank bag. I didn't have anything fancy, just some screwdrivers, pliers, and a wrench or two. Nothing really suitable for major surgery on an aircraft engine. But I didn't really appreciate then just how good a mechanic Tom Danaher was. Generally, those in aviation who are pilots make lousy mechanics and those who are mechanics tend to be poor pilots. Tom was one of the two best pilots I ever knew, and he could probably have made an airplane out of some barbed wire and chewing gum.

He spread the contents of my tool bag out on the tarmac. He shook his head as if he were slightly disappointed. Then he walked over to a trash barrel outside the nearest hangar. He fished around in it. I was reminded of "Barrel Fisher" but said nothing.

On the subject of Beryl Fisher: she had accompanied him on the trip to Cairo in the ag plane. I was amazed what she would do for him. It was a single-seater. She sat next to him for the fifty hours of flying from Texas to Cairo. Must have been true love.

Tom straightened up, turned to me, and grinned as if he had found the Hope Diamond. He held up a worn hacksaw blade.

The end of the working day was approaching. It was a Friday, and the race was to start on Sunday morning. Even though we were in the middle of the Paris Air Show, no French mechanic works on the weekend, at any price, ever. Any repairs to be made to our beast would have to be made by Tom, with what could only be termed primitive equipment.

He took this old hacksaw blade into the hangar. He talked one of the French mechanics into sticking around for a few minutes, while he used a grinding machine. He ground down both ends of the blade. He tended to whistle while he worked.

I wished that I knew what he knew. We were in deep shit. If the plane wasn't fixed soon we wouldn't be in the race. Tom said he had it under control, and that I should wander over to the race headquarters and make myself comfortable. He would fix the engine.

I went over to the race headquarters. Dietrick was there. He was livid. Not only had I found an airplane to race with, I had just smashed his record.

I made no mention of our problems with the plane.

Mike Smith had tested a much larger, 350 horsepower engine in N111MS, but had been unhappy with its reliability and had reverted to a normal 285 horsepower engine. But while he had the larger engine on board, he took the plane up to twenty-five thousand feet and flew a purported three hundred miles an hour. He had "300 mph Bonanza" plastered all over both sides of the airplane.

The race committee was in a panic about what to do with my heavily modified Bonanza. I assured them that I had an unmodified, stock engine. It really couldn't do 300 mph. I wasn't about to tell anyone how much less than 300 mph the plane would fly; it was a lot less.

Tom finished work on it and said it was now fixed. We went out to dinner with some of the French pilots we'd met during the meetings. I continued to tell everyone I could that the plane really wouldn't do 300 mph.

I wasn't lying.

At last the race committee had published the final and definitive set of rules for the race. Nothing had changed from what had been agreed to during the meetings in Paris and New York. But we finally had the rules in written form. No one could complain they didn't understand the rules.

Or could they?

The first aircraft was scheduled to take off Sunday morning. With typical French logic, the slowest aircraft were scheduled to take off first. I suppose the objective was to have us all land in Gander and try to refuel at the same time. Since Tom and I had one of the fastest singles, our takeoff time came late in the race. By now many crews had dropped out and only about sixty-eight aircraft would participate, evenly split between singles and twins. I still couldn't see any surprises. Gerald Dietrick was our only competition.

I told Tom that we should delay our departure until the last minute. I didn't want a refueling conflict with a slower plane. Any time spent on the ground would count against us. Neither did I see any wind advantage in going early, so we should wait. We would have the advantage of knowing how fast the other aircraft actually were. We would know what time we had to beat.

People think the prime racing strategy should be to go balls-out and fly as fast as you can. This is wrong. All you are trying to do is to beat the other pilots. If they were all to crash for some reason and we had the race to ourselves, I would fly like an eighty-year-old lady. I'm not interested in how fast an airplane will fly before it falls apart. I'm only interested in winning.

We launched first thing Monday morning, with only one plane behind us. It was faster than us, but not scheduled for takeoff until thirty minutes after us. We'd be in Shannon and fueled before they landed.

Without warning, the goddamned French then pulled another rule change. They were forever doing that. We had been told that takeoff times were fixed. No one could take off early. It was possible to delay takeoff, but not to leave early. But since the Aerostar behind us was the only airplane left, the race committee made an exception. *They* could leave early.

Ten minutes after we took off, we heard the Aerostar come up. Now we were in a race to Shannon. Whoever got there second would lose time, waiting for the other airplane to finish fueling.

Naturally we arrived second. I was furious. Why spend months planning a race? The French would keep on changing the rules until the last minute.

We were instructed by Shannon tower to taxi over near the tower for refueling. We could see the Aerostar on the taxiway, being refueled. Not only were they getting fuel first, they were saving five minutes of taxi time by being fueled right next to the runway.

The Aerostar finished fueling and went on its way. We were still waiting. Minutes ticked by. The fuel truck still hadn't shown up. I was fit to be tied. It finally arrived and we fueled.

Another race crew had arrived at Shannon early Monday morning. Supposedly to show their appreciation to the refuelers, they gave each of them a bottle of booze. That was actually a clever idea. The refuelers were all as drunk as skunks. I had to do the financial calculations for them so we could leave. They were too drunk to work a calculator.

I didn't bother giving the fueling crew any more booze. For one thing it wouldn't have done any good, as there were no aircraft behind us. And it would have been a waste of booze. They were already hammered.

Our first stop had cost us forty minutes on the ground. It should have taken less than half that. At this rate, an eighty-year-old would beat *us*.

We then fought strong headwinds all the way across the Atlantic. I was so keyed up for the race that I hadn't slept for forty-eight hours. As we leveled off, I told Tom to keep an eye on all the big pieces of the plane. I slept all the way to Gander.

I mentioned that I had arranged to have people help us refuel in all the places that I knew we must stop. We had lost a lot of time in Shannon. We couldn't afford any more forty-minute fuel stops.

After eleven hours we landed in Gander. Jim Patterson had the fuel crew organized. Tom Sanders and I had had a good turnaround four days before; Tom Danaher and I had a *great* turnaround. From the time our wheels touched the ground until we were back in the air, only nine minutes elapsed. The Shell Oil people didn't do anything to slow down our competitors, but I'd been through Gander over a hundred times and I was their friend. If they could help me win, they would do so.

No one in the race had a faster turnaround at any stop. We were coming back on track.

From Gander to Bridgeport there were strong headwinds at every altitude. When flying a leg that long, it was usually possible to change routing to minimize the headwinds. Often a change of altitude would help. Not today.

We climbed back to eleven thousand feet. We had a steady thirty knots against us all the way to Bridgeport. After six long hours we landed, at exactly 8 pm. Twenty-four hours later we would leave.

The plane now held two records. Dietrick had made a faster time from Paris to Bridgeport but didn't bother filing for a record. Tom Danaher and I did. Tom Sanders and I had New York to Paris in 17 hours and 41 minutes, and Tom Danaher and I did Paris to New York in 21 hours and 37 minutes.

Could Tom Danaher and I beat 17:41 on the return leg to Paris?

When I started ferrying, I lived in Stamford, Connecticut. I had told a friend of mine there about the race and asked if we could stay with her.

Tom and I put N111MS to bed. I was disappointed in the speeds we were getting, but she had a strong heart. My friend picked us up. We drove to Stamford to spend the night. One beer later, Tom and I crashed.

We woke refreshed the next morning. I was all for getting out to the airport to check on the race but Tom wouldn't hear of it. Tom ate a good breakfast first thing every morning. He wasn't about to change his schedule for such a minor thing as an air race.

Two hours later, after eating, we went to Bridgeport airport. I flatter myself that I have accomplished a lot of things in life, but budging Tom Danaher from one of his preordained rituals wasn't among them. For example, his lunch every single day consisted of a tuna sandwich on white bread followed by exactly three Oreo cookies.

Dietrick had landed in Paris by this time. I was pleased to see that his time to Paris was an unspectacular nineteen hours. With the time Tom and I had lost in Shannon, we were twenty-eight minutes behind him at Bridgeport.

I was never as concerned about the westbound leg as I was about the eastbound. Pressure pattern flying was my forte. We were behind, but hardly out of the race. I called my buddies at the Gander weather office.

"This is Bob Moriarty, calling from Bridgeport. Can I speak to one of the over-water weather-guessers?"

"This is Norman speaking. What can I do for you?"

"Hi, Norman. I need to order up some good tailwinds. What's the best route today, Bridgeport to Paris?"

"All of the other aircraft have been going Gander to Shannon or Gander to Paris. But there's a strong low pressure system to the east of Gander. The winds in the first three zones are headwinds. If you could fly along forty-six north latitude, I could give you a forty-knot tailwind all the way to Paris."

Forty knots. Hell's bells. If we had that kind of a push, we could clean Dietrick's clock and never raise our landing gear.

"I'll take it. How about working up the winds along forty-six north? Give me the terminal forecasts for Sydney, Halifax, Gander, Jersey and Paris. I'll give you a call in about four hours."

A forty-knot push was always welcome, even in the winter, when high winds were more common. During the summer, forty knots was unheard of. Nice timing on our part. Somebody upstairs was looking out for us.

When Tom Danaher ferried an aircraft, he lived with it. I found him standing by the bird, tinkering. Nothing was wrong; he had pulled the plugs and injectors just to make certain they were clean. He was thrilled to hear about the winds.

He wasn't using my makeshift bag of tools this time. Someone had parked a step van right in front of our plane. It seems Tom ran into a friend of his at the Sikorsky plant. Any tools Tom needed would be provided.

I called Gander again four hours later. The winds were just as favorable as when I first talked to them. The weather was nothing special in Canada but beautiful in Paris. Halifax looked to be the best fuel stop. It was close enough to Paris that we should have plenty of fuel if the winds were as forecast.

Bridgeport had a tower but no approach control. If another aircraft happened to be inbound on an instrument flight plan, we could have been delayed, so we would leave VFR and pick up our instrument flight plan over Boston. We filed our flight plan: Boston to Halifax and Halifax to Paris.

Since Halifax was not one of the designated airports in the handicap race, we would lose credit for whatever time we spent on the ground there. I called Shell Oil in Halifax to notify them of our expected arrival time. I told them it was important that we refuel and clear customs as quickly as possible.

We were taking a big chance by going into Halifax. If we wasted much time there with fueling or customs it would cost us the race.

Our stipulated takeoff time at Bridgeport was 20:00 local time exactly. I went up to the control tower to talk to them. I told them we were in second place in the speed race. I wanted permission for takeoff at 19:59 and I wanted time checks at 19:59:30 and at 20:00. The regulations stated we must be on the ground no less than 24 hours, but they didn't say that you couldn't be in your takeoff roll during the last few moments.

At 20:00:00 I pulled back on the yoke and we were airborne for Paris.

We got into Halifax just after a front had passed through. The weather in Gander was down to two hundred feet overcast and a half-mile visibility. Had we gone there, we could easily have been among a stack of airplanes waiting for an instrument approach. The weather in Halifax was VFR and we wasted no time in landing.

The Shell fuel guys were ready, and refueled us in a few minutes. We had to wait only a few minutes more for customs and then we were on our way. I figured on a twenty-minute stop, but we were in and out in seventeen. Not nearly as good as Gander had been, but a lot better than Shannon.

We were equipped with nothing in the way of sophisticated navigation radios. Many of the other racers had LORAN C or Omega. Those were both state-of-the-art (meaning expensive) aircraft navigation radios. We didn't have the money. Bear in mind, this was long before you could buy a box of Wheaties and get a free GPS device. Knowing where your aircraft is at any particular moment doesn't make it any faster. You only really need to know where you are as you prepare to land.

Our first landfall would be the island of Jersey, thirty miles to the west of France. By the time we picked up the first navigation signals, we were right on track and very close to our time estimate, filed some twenty-four hours earlier.

We landed in Paris 16 hours and 52 minutes after leaving Bridgeport. It was another new record. Our flight plan was for 16:55, including our stop in Halifax, and we had saved three minutes there. The wind forecast given us by Gander had been accurate to within one-half of one knot. That sort of margin of error was wholly unacceptable to me during normal navigation, but I could bring it up with the forecasters later. Our time from Bridgeport to Paris was two hours faster than Dietrick's. We had waxed him by an hour and a half.

Or so we thought.

As we taxied in, Tom noticed a dozen wilting red roses atop the Eagle. I said that Dietrick must have declared himself the winner.

A lovely Frenchwoman from the race organization greeted us at the plane with a bottle of champagne each. She wore a worried look. She confirmed that Dietrick had announced his victory as soon as he landed in Paris.

I said, "That's ridiculous. We hadn't even left Bridgeport. He may have been leading but he hadn't won. Why didn't he wait until we finished? What was his time from Bridgeport to Paris?"

"'is time from Bridgepore to Paree was two hours less fast than the time of you. Now 'e is saying you cheat because you did not file the flight plan from Bridgepore," she continued.

Who was this guy? First he screws me out of a promised airplane. Now he's declaring victory before we even land?

Dietrick and his co-pilot were in the bar, looking glum. "What's this bullshit about your declaring victory before we even landed?" I demanded.

"You guys didn't file a flight plan out of Bridgeport and you're going to be disqualified," he replied, in a petulant manner.

"What does that have to do with your declaring victory yesterday? You want to see our flight plan? What do these look like?"

I handed copies of our flight plans to him. He turned purple, and I think a little green.

"You cheated. You landed in Halifax."

"Gerry, did you ever bother to read the rules?"

I turned to the French pilot who was the original organizer of the race. "For the speed competition, was there any question, ever, that we were free to land at any airport *en route*?" I asked.

He rolled his eyes. "You may land for fuel wherever you wish. But of course, you lose time for 'andicap."

"Here, Dietrick. Since you had no time before the race to read the rules, take my copy. If you look on page forty-six you will see that it states, 'The speed race is a race from Paris to New York to Paris. A stop may be made at *any* airport for fueling.' Isn't that clear enough for you?"

"Where did you get this?" he blustered.

"In the mail, two weeks ago, like everybody else. If you want another copy, go over to race headquarters. They have stacks of them."

"Moriarty, I'm thinking of protesting you anyway. We beat everyone that flew the same course as us. It's not fair that you took advantage of the winds to beat us. We beat everyone else."

"Get fucked. The rules say nothing about having to follow in your footsteps. They say the race was from Paris to New York to Paris, period. If you're such a poor loser that you have to protest because you didn't read the rules, be prepared to shell out another thousand dollars. Or didn't you read that, either?"

"For what? Anyone can protest another racer. There isn't any fee."

I turned to the original organizer again. "My understanding is that it costs five thousand francs to enter a protest. Is that true?"

"But of course, that is very clear in the rules. But why would someone be so foolish to protest your landing in Canada? Anyone who attended the meetings would know the rules. Why waste five thousand francs when the issue is so clear?"

"Dietrick, why don't you go back and read the rules at your leisure? That way, you'll be prepared for the next race, two years from now," I said.

For some people, a race is a lot like air-to-air combat. Being second just isn't good enough. As in combat, lying and cheating and stealing are all considered fair. Sure, Dietrick tried screwing me on the airplane. I might have done the same thing to him, given the chance.

But there comes a time after you've been whipped when you concede that the other guy won. Unlike air-to-air combat, there will always be another race. If you're the better pilot, really better, you'll have another shot at him.

Dietrick was such a poor loser that he took all the fun out of the victory for Tom and me.

Of all the aircraft in the speed race, single or twin, we were the last to land. Aircraft in the handicap category continued to arrive for the next three days. We were in first place in speed, and so far, in second place in single-engine handicap.

Boyd Monroe and Russ Hancock demolished the pack in the multi-engine race. They finished in first place in both speed and handicap.

I called Mike Smith to tell him the good news. He had shown a lot of faith in us and now it had paid off. He was thrilled about our victory. Newspapers from all over the world were calling him for information.

The next day the head organizer called me into his office. It seemed that Dietrick hadn't given up yet.

"Dietrick is complaining that you landed in Halifax and that you didn't file a flight plan out of Bridgeport. What do you have to say for yourself?"

"Has he filed an official protest?"

"No, not yet."

"Look, you guys wrote the rules. All I can do is interpret them. There is a procedure for filing a protest. If Dietrick thinks I broke the rules, let him file a protest. I wish that asshole would either put up or shut up."

"Bob, don't you think there is some way we can settle this without Dietrick filing a protest? That might make the committee look bad."

By now the waffling attitude of the race committee had me pretty mad.

"I'm sorry about that, but what the committee looks like isn't real high on my priority list. What do you expect me to do? Give the race to him because he didn't bother attending meetings or reading the rules? I beat him in accordance with your published rules. If you want to listen to his whining, let him shell out a thousand bucks to get his protest thrown out."

Noon on June 14 marked the end of the race. As of that morning, Dietrick hadn't filed a protest. The results were to be announced early in the afternoon. The pilots placed from first to third in each of the four competitions were scheduled to do a fly-by of the Paris Air Show.

Tom noticed that the race committee had given us an incorrect reference speed for the handicap race. The 1968 and later model Bonanzas were shown as being 4 mph slower in the flight manual. This would drop us to third place in the handicap contest, but Tom and I both thought we should notify the race committee. We did, and were moved from second place to third in handicap. We had done our best. We were both proud of our performance.

Dietrick decided he had better things to do back in the U.S. He left before the results were formally announced. I don't mind saying that I was glad to see him leave. He had taken second place and made it seem like last. At least he was out of our hair, I thought.

The race committee announced the winners in the afternoon. They were careful, very careful, to tell us that these were preliminary results.

The head organizer came up to me to tell me that the last thing Dietrick did before he left was to protest our landing in Halifax. He assured me that there was no question that Tom and I had won. It would be a matter of "only a few months" before the results were confirmed.

An award ceremony was held outside the race headquarters. We were given our medals but the money prizes wouldn't be handed out until September, at a formal dinner.

As "preliminary" winners of the single-engine speed contest, Tom and I were given the honor of leading the fly-by at the Paris Air Show. At least we were going to get some respect from somebody.

We went out to our airplane to start up. Once in the cockpit, I set the brakes to start the engine. Or rather, I tried to. One brake was completely flat. I tried pumping it up but nothing happened.

Tom got out to see what the problem was. He looked the brake over carefully. No hydraulic fluid showed around the lines or brake pad, so it hadn't leaked out. He opened up the engine cowling to check for fluid. It had been full when we left Bridgeport. Now it was empty. Someone had gone to all the trouble of draining our brake fluid and made sure you could see any leak or spilled fluid. Gee, I wondered, who would pull something like that?

Meanwhile, the rest of the winners were preparing to taxi out for takeoff. We were parked a mile from the nearest hangar. No one near us had any spare brake fluid. Tom didn't hesitate. He reached into the back of the plane, pulled out an empty Coke can, and pissed into it. This was obviously some mechanic's magic, unfamiliar to me. Carefully he poured the contents into the brake fluid container and drained the brake lines. Off we went.

I had to ask him, "Why is that going to work?"

"Well, Bob," he drawled, "you can always use water for brake fluid. It's fine unless your brakes get hot and boil off the water. It's only a short flight."

Dietrick not only tried to take the fun out of our win; he also drained our brake fluid in an attempt to prevent our leading the fly-by. It was a good thing he had already left for the U.S.

His aircraft company needed publicity in order for him to raise the money to get into production. He could have had millions of dollars of free press with first and second places in the First Transatlantic Air Race, but he got cute. That was both greedy and stupid on his part. The company never went anywhere after that, and eventually died a death.

And since forty years have now passed since that race, I can whisper a little secret. The Windecker Eagle was a better plane than the V-35, and it would have been a piece of cake to win both the speed and handicap classes.

When you devote months of work and preparation to something like an air race, you become keyed up. We did the best job we could in planning for the race. We did the best job we could flying it. Now it was over, a slight depression set in. Dietrick took the fun out of winning. Tom and I collected our medals and headed for home.

Tom's intuitive feel for airplanes showed itself again in Shannon. We still had strong westerlies, so would fly home via Iceland. We stopped in Shannon for fuel. I had mentioned to Tom that my mechanical problems always seemed to show up at 4:30 on a Friday afternoon, because it was then too late in the day to get whatever it was fixed until Monday morning.

After I raised the landing gear handle, the landing gear refused to come up. Tom reached around to turn the gear up with the emergency handle. After a few cranks, he stopped. He felt that something was binding. If he continued to crank the gear up, he would break something.

Naturally, the mechanics at Shannon Repair Service didn't want to look at the airplane until the following morning. It was too late in the afternoon for them to work, even though it was a Monday. We would now be hard pressed to get the airplane back to Mike Smith for his west coast race. We decided to put the bird to bed. We would take a look at it the next day.

At breakfast the next morning, Tom announced, "I know what the problem is."

He had spent the entire night thinking about the landing gear system. He figured that something had dropped under my seat and was now binding the linkage. He even went so far as to say, "It's something soft, like a paperback."

Back at the airport, we looked under my seat. My trip logbook was caught in the gear mechanism. We pulled it out. The gear worked just fine after that.

The race on the west coast was on June 20. We had a lot of flying to do to give Mike his plane in time for him to put it back in shape. We flew to Reykjavik, refueled, and then on to Goose Bay, where we spent the night. We launched early the next day. We cleared customs in Burlington, fueled in Memphis, and landed at Tom's strip at night in Wichita Falls, Texas.

Tom's field was paved but unlit. I had made only one previous landing in my life on an unlit strip at night. That runway, in Windhoek, had been twelve thousand feet long. Tom's 2,500 feet was going to be mighty short.

But we had a full moon and the landing was straightforward. I dropped Tom off and continued on to Johnson, Kansas. I landed there at 6 am. Mike put his guys to work installing the seats and carpet. We left for Santa Rosa, for the first CAFE 250 air race. I hadn't planned to take part — that was Mike's deal — but he needed a co-pilot and asked me to race with him. I agreed.

Every air race is an effort by someone to prove something. I had competed in the Air Transat to gain some glory for ferry pilots. Dietrick was going to show the superiority of the Windecker but showed what a loser he was. Munroe and Hancock proved overwhelmingly the speed of the Panther in the twin contest. We brought home victory to Mike Smith, but now he wanted to show that his plane was as efficient as it was fast.

We received no publicity for it, but of the sixty-eight airplanes that flew in the transatlantic race, only four *twins* were faster than Mike's single. Tom and I came in fifth overall, and used less fuel than anyone else.

Pilots are forever comparing airplanes and telling lies about how fast their airplane flies. Here is how the CAFE 250 came about. A California dentist, Brian Seeley, flew back from the Midwest one day in the company of two pilots in home-built planes. They decided to have a race. Brian flew his specially prepared Mooney. He beat them over the course in speed.

But when they landed for fuel, the pilots of the home-builts complained that the race wasn't really fair to them. They hadn't flown as fast, but they had used only a fraction of the fuel that he had used.

Brian devised a formula that incorporated speed, fuel burn, and aircraft carrying capability. He convinced his local EAA chapter #124 to sponsor a competition that would attempt to measure aircraft efficiency fairly, using his formula. The first CAFE 250 competition was then held.

On our way to California, Mike admitted that N111MS wasn't flying as fast as he claimed it would before the race. He insisted that something was wrong; it really should have been faster than it was flying. I smelled snake oil but didn't comment. Mike was in the business of selling aircraft modifications. We knew the airplane was fast and efficient. If we made a good showing in the contest, it should boost sales.

The same thought was in the mind of Roy LoPresti of Mooney Aircraft. Roy was the genius behind the cleanup of the Mooney. He took an already clean bird and managed to wring an additional 20 mph out of it. He was so confident of its efficiency that he squeezed a couple of thousand dollars out of the Mooney coffers for prize money. The official name of the race was The Mooney Efficiency Race.

Guess who thought he had the race wrapped up?

The organizers did something I never saw in any French-sponsored race. They wrote the rules down beforehand. They were unambiguous. "Here's what you do and when you do it. If you don't, we're going to bounce you." No months of waiting for "official" results, either. The race ran Saturday morning and the results would be made known at the Saturday night dinner.

I looked over the rules on the flight out. It looked to me that we had more than a fair chance to win. The Mooney was close to the Bonanza in speed. Certainly it would use less fuel. But we were a six-passenger plane while the Mooney took only four. Unless Roy flew fifty percent faster than us, or used only two-thirds of the fuel we did, we should beat him.

Roy LoPresti was one hell of a pilot (he died in 2002), but nobody has ever spent as much time as I have squeezing fuel out of empty tanks.

It ought to be an interesting race, I thought.

The rules stated that all aircraft were to arrive Friday night, June 19. They would be weighed and impounded overnight. There would be a weigh-in of crews and passengers on Saturday morning.

We landed, waited only a few minutes to be weighed, and parked the airplane for the night. I was staying with friends but Mike wanted to stay in a motel. We bought a couple of fifty-pound bags of salt to use as ballast. We were ready for the big race.

Mike picked me up early the next morning and I asked if I could see his flight plan. He hadn't prepared it yet. I grumbled to myself, but pulled out my dividers and ruler. I sure wasn't setting off on any race without a plan. If Mike wasn't going to do it, I would.

We arrived at the airport. Mike had to stand in line to have his license and log book checked. He came over to me a few minutes later.

"Bob, are you still a flight instructor?"

"Hell, no. I gave that up years ago."

"We need to do some fast thinking. The rules say that you have to prove you have a current biannual flight review. I brought my logbook but the biannual is in my other log. I'm not legal for the race."

"Oh, great. Let me have your logbook. Thanks. Do you have any idea of what the instructor puts in the log when he gives you the check?"

"I'm not real sure."

"Here. That looks real official. Remember that flight you and I made two months ago to Wichita? I've given you a biannual on the flight."

"Looks good to me. Let's hope they don't check to see if you are a current instructor."

"Don't worry about it. I didn't use my name anyway," I answered.

We took off on the race. I did all the planning and Mike did all the flying. It went smoothly, and we knew we would be among the top three.

The race was advertised as a 250-mile triangle but was really only 205 miles. That distance gave a great advantage to smaller aircraft. In subsequent years the course would be lengthened to a more suitable 400 miles.

There was no comparison between the organizers of this race and those of the Air Transat. There were no rule changes, no modifications at the last minute. They caught one racer flying in what they considered to be an unsafe manner. A short meeting took place over in a corner of the hangar. Bang — he was out of the race. They didn't mess around.

It was organized by guys who favored home-built aircraft. They wrote the rules, so naturally, the rules favored small planes. The rules were real-world, with the exception of credit for weight carried. Speed was measured in miles per hour, and fuel burn in miles per gallon. Weight, however, was credited with only the square root of actual weight carried. Someone in an LBF carrying one hundred pounds was thus given a 10 in the formula. We carried over one thousand pounds so were given only a 33 for the formula.

There was no question but that an LBF would win first prize overall, but how would we compare to LoPresti and the rest of the production aircraft?

We got the answer that night at the awards dinner. The awards were made in Academy Awards style. Amid the sound of tearing envelopes, we heard the gnashing of teeth.

"In the production category, the winner of third place is . . ."

Wasn't us. We still had a shot at first. If only they'd announce Roy as second, we'd be in first place. More gnashing of teeth.

"In the production category, the winner of second place is Roy LoPresti, of Mooney Aircraft."

I turned to Mike and gave him a thumbs-up. Unless we had really screwed up, we had it.

"In the production category, the winner of first place is Mike Smith, of Mike Smith Aero."

We did it. We not only took first place among production aircraft, we beat most of the home-builts. We were ninth overall. LoPresti, our nearest production model competitor, placed sixteenth.

The things Mike Smith did well, he did great. But he hated public speaking. He murmured a few words and sat down.

What an incredible two weeks for him. First, his plane takes Lindbergh's record. It then places first in the longest air race ever, the Air Transat. Now, first place here. We were ecstatic.

We left early the next day for Kansas. On the way back I asked Mike what had made him decide to give us the airplane. One minute he was dead set against letting Tom and me use it, and the next minute he gave it to us with no strings.

He explained that he had tried to join the service during the Vietnam war but had flunked his physical due to a punctured eardrum. He felt he owed something to those of us who had fought. Letting us use the airplane was his way of thanking us.

He said, "I knew that anyone who could fly over eight hundred missions in Vietnam would have no problem winning a little old six-thousand-mile air race."

This was the only time since my return from Vietnam, over ten years before, that anyone did anything to say "Thanks" in my vicinity. I was quite moved. Mike Smith was and is a prince.

We flew on to Texas to participate in a celebration dinner for everyone involved in the race. I didn't even log flight time for the leg; after all, I was just a passenger. Tom was throwing the dinner to thank the oil men who had made our participation possible.

He was quite the hero of Wichita Falls. All the local TV stations sent reporters. I laughed, because all their stories started with, "Tom Danaher, local pilot, wins transatlantic air race . . . accompanied by Bob Moriarty . . ." As in dead weight, I supposed.

While having dinner at the local oil men's club, I told the story of an incident while we were in Paris. Typically, the French were holding a side competition for the best-dressed pilot. One of the French women who had signed up for the race, but who was eventually unable to compete, still wanted to participate in this contest. She was assured by the organizers that even though she had not flown in the race, that shouldn't stop her from entering this associated competition.

She came to me and asked if her boyfriend could take pictures of her with N111MS as backdrop. She assured me that if she won, she would split the prize money with me. I was all for it. We headed for the plane, which was parked out in the south forty of Le Bourget, a hundred yards from the nearest spectators. She hopped out of the car, took off her dress and put on a fur-lined flight suit for the photos.

I made the comment that "She must have needed the money badly, 'cause she sure wasn't wearing much under that dress."

Kathie turned to me. "I can't believe you looked!"

Tom Sanders' wife, Carolyn, gurgled on some asparagus.

Kathie said, "See, Bob? Now you've made Carolyn choke."

But Carolyn said, "I was laughing because it was so funny. I can't believe you said 'I can't believe you looked,' Kathie. The day Tom stops looking I'm going to shoot him, to put him out of his misery."

Mike Smith sold a lot of modification kits as a result of our twin victories. He deserved to.

Tom Danaher remains the tightest guy I ever knew. In later years he would ferry an ag plane now and then, do a lot more flying in movies, and continue to eat a tuna fish sandwich for lunch, with three Oreo cookies for dessert; not two and not four.

Many months would pass before the Transat race committee announced the final standings.

Dietrick was out $1,000.

We won.

212th TRIP: WICHITA FALLS, TX to UPPSALA, SWEDEN

1982	from	to	nautical miles	knots	time (hours)			
					flight	day	night	inst.
May 12	Wichita Falls	Wichita Falls	0	0	3.0	3.0		
	Wichita Falls	Buffalo	1,066	117	9.1	8.1	1.0	2.5
May 13	Buffalo	Sept-Îles	683	108	6.3	6.3		
May 14	Sept-Îles	Reykjavik	1,615	115	14.0	8.5	5.5	3.5
May 16	Reykjavik	Uppsala	1,150	109	10.5	10.5		3.5
TOTALS		4 days	4,564	105	43.9	35.9	6.5	9.5

Over the years I found two ways of running a trip. There's the professional approach. When landing in New Jersey with a turkey strapped on the roof, you must look like a pro. The world is watching. When examining the innards of the Eiffel Tower through your windscreen, you must maintain a calm, collected, cool attitude. You're on camera. Every twitch is being recorded for posterity. If you've got the name, you've got to act the part.

On the other hand, the only rules in the official ferry pilots' manual specified survival first, aircraft delivery a distant second. Any professional pilot worth his salt would have blanched at the aircraft that ferry pilots flew. When a ferry pilot crawled out of his hole after another fifteen-hour flight, downwind goats keeled over, women and children screamed, grown men cried.

Professional pilots flew airplanes. Ferry pilots wore them. It was important to know when to be which one.

TOM DANAHER MAY NOT HAVE BEEN the best pilot in the world. There was a fellow I flew with in the Marines, an old World War II ace named Marion Carl, who maybe, just maybe, could have edged Tom out.

But Tom was good; much better than me. He was a fine professional pilot. I tried my best to cure him of this, because at times, professionalism got in the way of delivering planes. As a matter of fact, sometimes it could get in the way of surviving.

This trip did much to bring him around to my way of thinking. It tended to make a Christian of him, too.

For me, AD 1982 was one of those years that come along only once in a lifetime, if you're lucky; a year when you wish you had stayed in bed.

My marriage with Kathie had started its slide into hell with the birth of our first child in February, 1979. Kathie had fixed ideas of what a father should be. They had been handed down to her by her dad, much as Moses received his stone tablets.

Under "acceptable occupations," I was allowed to do anything I wanted, as long as it was 9 to 5. That did tend to eliminate ferry flying. As far as I was concerned, the only thing that should be carved in stone was a headstone.

I also didn't need a rule book to figure out how to love little people. Sean and I took to each other like bears take to honey. But that didn't impress Kathie.

By the time of the birth of our second child, Christopher, in July of 1981, I had pretty much been relegated to the status of roommate. My birthday had been dropped from her calendar. Her wedding ring didn't quite fit right, she said, so it came off. There was nothing I did that was not criticized. Finally, in an act of mercy, she walked out in January of '82. For a tenth anniversary present, she filed for divorce and then told me about it six weeks later. I became an ex-husband and an ex-father at the same time.

My kids never really figured out what happened to their dad. But then, neither did I. Losing them opened a good-sized gap where my heart used to be. I wished I'd stayed in bed.

Once the divorce was in progress, Kathie became surprisingly easy to get along with. All she wanted in the way of child support was the U.S. dollar equivalent of Brazil's external debt. Once the checks started arriving, by 9 am sharp, each and every Monday, she considered upgrading me from ex-father to Disneyland-daddy.

But life, no matter how lonely, no matter how dismal, rolls along. Ferry flying did not satisfy the 9 to 5 rule, and never would. But it did pay the bills.

Tom Danaher had a most interesting attitude toward work. He didn't like it. He also didn't do it, much. Over the years he had squirreled away more than a few million acorns. With a million or so acorns stashed in a nearby tree, any squirrel can do as he pleases. It pleased Tom to ferry a few airplanes a year. When he wasn't off in Kenya or Spain, flying in another movie, it also pleased him to do all the test flying for Leland Snow in Olney, Texas.

Over the years, I ran into almost everybody who was anybody in general aviation. To my surprise, there were perhaps no more than five real airplane designers in the whole world. Leland Snow and Roy LoPresti were accepted as being the best. Leland was to airplanes as Browning was to weapons or Tiffany to jewelry.

Leland was a little kinky, possibly due to his matriculation at Texas A&M University. He built by far the best ag or spray planes in the world. He thought of them as trucks with wings. He even called his planes "ag trucks." He named the company Air Tractor. A lot of folks in aviation didn't know of him because of his preoccupation with spray planes. But his were the best-made planes in the world.

He had a mind like a steel trap. When asked any technical question about any aircraft made, he'd refer it to his four-function electronic Bowmar brain. Within seconds he had an answer correct to the seventh decimal place. He had a wife of beauty and brains in equally generous quantities. He had two talented and stunning daughters. Other than that, he was OK.

I had been keeping Tom informed of the progress (or lack thereof) of the awards ceremony for the Air Transat race. Originally scheduled for September, 1981, the French rescheduled it each and every month. It took them until December, six months after the race, to announce us as winners. Now it seemed the prizes would be awarded in Paris on May 14, 1982.

Tom had a pair of Snow's AT-400 ag trucks scheduled to go to the Sudan. It looked as if we could run them over to Africa and then swing up to Paris to collect our accolades. I flew down to Wichita Falls, Texas, to help him finish the ferry installation.

Planes to be ferried never seemed amenable to human schedules. I arrived in Texas in late April and waited. And waited. The planes were ready to go, but payment wasn't yet in hand. No airplane manufacturer ever let a plane go until the money sat in his bank. To occupy my time, I moved a couple of Snow's piston-powered winged trucks from Olney to Arkansas. It wasn't much, but it beat working for a living.

D-Day or $-Day finally arrived, but with one variation. Instead of delivering our turbine-powered beasts to the Sudan, we were to take them to a small airfield near Uppsala, Sweden. The company buying them operated in the Sudan under government contract, and was based in Sweden. That was fine with me. I was unsure about the statute of limitations for skullduggery in the Sudan. I wasn't all that sure I wanted to find out.

We were delayed and delayed until there was no possibility of Tom and me being in Paris on May 14. I was terribly disappointed. Due to the amazing degree of ineptitude shown by the French organizers, we hadn't garnered much recognition for our feats. It would have been great to have at least met with the other contestants. Tom couldn't have cared less.

We made our first stab at leaving early in the morning of May 12. We promptly ran into a line of thunderstorms that looked like a scene out of Dante's *Inferno*. Springtime Texas-style breeds nasty thunderbumpers with not a few embedded cumulonimbus. We made it at low altitude almost to the Arkansas border before running short on courage. Gingerly we retraced our path back to Tom's strip just outside Wichita Falls.

Flying formation with Tom took me back to my days as a fighter pilot. Tom was a World War II vintage ex-Marine fighter pilot. He was very professional. I knew what to expect of him. Our flight was a far cry from those I had flown with most other ferry pilots. I was far more willing to take on nasty weather because I knew I could depend on his good sense.

When we landed, he jumped indoors to check the weather forecast on the boob tube. The line that had resisted our penetration so strongly was moving rapidly east. If we were to run north, then east, we should be able to outflank it. I'm not much on the boob tube, but it sure is nice to actually look at the systems.

We strapped on our chargers and once more went forth to do battle with the dragon. Nine brutal hours later we landed in Buffalo, New York. On the way north we ran into a few residual clouds from the squall line. I got to practice a couple of hours of instrument formation flying. It wasn't any more enjoyable than I had remembered.

I mentioned that Tom was a man of firm and fixed regularity. He liked to sleep in, eat a leisurely breakfast, and finish flying in time for a hot dinner. Ferry flying and that kind of flying don't have a whole lot in common.

We left Buffalo at about 11 am. If it had been up to me, I would have pressed on to Goose Bay. Our critical leg lay between Goose Bay and Reykjavik, and I do all my planning around the critical leg. But Tom led and ran the show. We stopped in Sept-Îles, three hundred miles short of Goose Bay. We ate a hot dinner, but I know the $30 taxi fare grated on Tom's soul.

Every silver lining has its thunderstorm attached.

Sept-Îles, on the north bank of the St. Lawrence River, was the first stop where we filled all of our ferry tanks. All ag planes being ferried carry fuel in the chemical hopper. We carried more than four hundred gallons in our hoppers.

Our AT-400s were powered by a 650-horsepower turboprop engine that guzzled forty gallons of jet fuel per hour. With that sort of consumption, we needed all the fuel we could carry. Tom had installed another forty-gallon tank in each aircraft, in the belly under the pilot's seat. Via an electric pump, fuel was transferred into the hopper and then directly to the engine.

We filled every tank to the brim. We departed Sept-Îles for Reykjavik at about 11 am. As the ocean came closer, my natural ferry pilot instincts tended to take over the control of my plane.

I repeat that Tom was a superb pilot and a professional pilot. But he had yet to become a ferry pilot. He hadn't been imprisoned yet. To the best of my knowledge, he hadn't even been scared silly yet. He still put comfort first and delivery second.

But God didn't intend for ferry pilots to be comfortable. If He did, all Cherokee 181s would be factory equipped with a full set of radios, autopilot, and an HF that worked.

As we passed Goose Bay, I reminded Tom to get into the habit of using his most inaccessible fuel first. He wanted to burn his wing fuel first, then his hopper fuel. I told him I had heard of pilots running into rain. The rainwater settled into the bottom of the tank and then froze solid, so the rest of the hopper fuel became unusable.

At 2000 GMT I told Tom that he could walk up to the podium first.

"What are you talking about?" he responded.

"The awards ceremony has just started in Paris. You and I have to go up to collect first prize. How about a little more bubbly first?"

"OK, I'll drink to that."

Eight months of planning, five days of backbreaking flying, and eleven months of waiting for the honor of the awards ceremony. And I'm sitting in an unheated, marginally instrumented spray plane on my way to Iceland. Flying on the wing of another pilot, in and out of the clouds. If it weren't for the lousy $20 an hour, I'd give it up.

For this I lost my kids?

We were halfway across the Barents Sea to Greenland when Tom made a comment about how smoothly his plane flew once he got his tail streamlined. I glanced back at my tail to see how close I was to being in trim. To my utter surprise, I was some two inches out of trim. We had identical planes, identical fuel loads, and only twenty pounds difference in pilot weight. I wrinkled my brow for a few minutes.

"Tom, we've got a hell of a difference in trim. What order have you been burning your tanks?"

"I went to my wings first. I'm on my hopper now. Pretty soon, I'm going to switch to my belly tank."

Here, readers need to know a little about airplanes and how they fly. Aircraft move in three dimensions. To go up you have a flight control called an elevator, for obvious reasons. To turn, you must bank the aircraft. To do so you use items called ailerons, for less obvious reasons. And to align the aircraft with the wind you have a rudder, as on a boat. It is always necessary to take the forces out of the control surfaces for efficient flight, so you have tiny things called trim tabs that do exactly the same thing as the three primary control surfaces. A clean aircraft in trim will continue to fly straight and level without any stick or rudder inputs, and will fly faster.

"Tom, I don't need to teach you how to fly. But if you don't start using your most inaccessible fuel first you're gonna get in a world of hurt. You lose your electrical system now and you're gonna have to figure out how to drink that belly fuel. *Use your most inaccessible fuel first.*"

The Trim God must have been snooping. A little while later, Tom turned on his belly tank pump. At least, he flipped the switch. Nothing happened. The pump had run fine over land. It even worked when we were still in range of Goose Bay. Now we were in the middle of nowhere, it didn't work. If he crashed — when he crashed — he would have run out of joy juice while sitting on forty gallons of prime 1982 vintage jet fuel.

We spent an hour exploring our options. In the worst case, he could declare an emergency. Narssaq in Greenland lay some two hundred miles north of our track. The landing fee would be humungous, but I couldn't think of a better way to teach Tom good ferrying habits. Or, with a following breeze and a lot of luck, maybe Iceland was in range.

I didn't make decisions for other pilots in flight, ever. If Tom wanted to try for Iceland, I'd go along with it. I had no doubt what my choice would have been. Greenland was damned expensive, but it was close. Any ferry pilot who made airplane decisions based on financial considerations would soon become mackerel bait.

Tom opted for safety. He banked to the left and headed for Narssaq. I continued on alone to Iceland.

Greenland has developed the neatest stunt since the Brooklyn Bridge was sold the first time. Any pilot arriving outside normal working hours gets to buy a good-sized chunk of the runway. It doesn't matter what currency you pay in, the landing fee has zeroes to the right of the most significant digit and to the left of the decimal point. To be fair, they allowed you to take your piece of runway with you, if you wished. Funny thing, but nobody's taken that option yet.

I landed in Reykjavik late at night. No question about it, it's nice to start flying after several lazy hours on the ground, having breakfast. Professional, even. But I always thought I needed the rest more *after* the flying.

I dragged my now depleted body into the nearby Loftlieder Hotel. I had every intention of crashing for the next eight hours or so. But as I lay with my head resting on the pillow, I realized that Tom would be even more bushed. He was over twenty years older than me, and far less used to twelve-hour flying days.

I stumbled back into my clothes. They were standing up in the corner waiting for me. I went out to the ramp to wait for him. No matter how tired I was, he would be in worse shape. I waited and waited. No Tom.

After about four hours, I watched as the Icelandic government Queen Air taxied out and took off. Bewildered, I wandered over to Air Traffic Control. I asked about the status of SE-IMI, the call sign for Tom's plane.

I could tell that the controllers were familiar with his registration. They all looked at each other. None of them looked me in the face.

Finally, one of them cleared his throat. "Yes. We just heard from our Queen Air. He flew two hundred miles south. He could just barely reach SE-IMI on the radio. Somehow your friend missed Iceland by three hundred miles or so. He radioed that he would try to make it to Shannon."

I knew instantly that that was the end for Tom. We didn't even have a wind forecast for his route. Whatever failure it was that had caused him to miss Iceland by such a wide margin had led him to his death.

In shock, I made my way back to my room. I didn't want to call Leland Snow. Tom was not just his chief test pilot, he was Snow's friend. I didn't get to sleep for a long time.

I lost a lot of friends in the Marine Corps. Everyone knows we lost thousands of pilots in Vietnam. Few people realize how often military pilots are killed in ordinary flight operations in the U.S. When I went into ferrying, I started hearing about friends of mine being killed ferrying airplanes. Tom may have stood to make $5,000 on this trip. It seemed a low price to pay for the life of one of the world's top pilots.

Sveinn Bjornsson, Reykjavik's operations manager, woke me the next day with a phone call. I hadn't had a chance to check in when I arrived. He asked my destination and intended time of departure, so he could set up a weather brief for me.

"Sveinn, I really don't know. I've got to call Leland Snow and tell him what happened to Tom. I don't know what he will want me to do. I may be here a few days."

"Don't worry about it, Bob. I got a call from Tom this morning. He said for you to meet him in Sweden tomorrow afternoon."

That took me off guard. This morning? But Tom was dead. What was he doing calling Sveinn? From where?

"What do you mean? When did you talk to Tom?"

"About two hours ago. He'd just gotten into Shannon. He had some problems with his ADF. He was too tired to wait up to talk with you."

"That son of a bitch. I thought he was dead. I've been trying to figure out what to tell Leland. I'll kill him the next time I can get my hands on him. Does he have any idea what he's put me through?"

I left the next day for Uppsala. I had a straight shot for the Norwegian coast, then over to Sweden. I read a book and proceeded east. Halfway to Norway I looked down and saw land, to my surprise. The maps didn't show any landfall prior to the European land mass. But I had done lots of ferrying by this point, and I knew land when I saw it.

I rotated my VOR from channel to channel until my indicator showed a strong signal. Then I checked my chart to determine the station I had locked onto. Strange; either someone had moved Scotland two hundred miles north, or I was two hundred miles south of track. I tapped my wet compass with a finger. It rolled over and died.

By now I could use VORs for navigation. I called ATC and asked permission to fly from my present position direct to Norway. It was granted. I didn't tell them exactly what my present position was.

I arrived three hours after Tom. I told him what happened in Iceland. But what I wanted to know was what had happened to him.

"Well, Bob, it took me about two hours to refuel in Greenland. Fuel was so cheap, I figured I should load up. I took off for Iceland about midnight. I sort of homed in on the national radio station on frequency 217. It worked OK for a while. Then all of a sudden it started showing thirty degrees to the right. I figured my compass wasn't working so I kept on trucking toward the ADF.

"About 5 am I should have been receiving Keflavik on the VOR. I wasn't picking up a cotton-pickin' thing. I turned up the ADF to make sure I was on the right station. Realized the folks were speaking in French. Realized right away they don't speak French in Iceland. I pressed on. Finally found Ireland about the time I was fixing to run out of gas."

What Tom and I didn't know at that time was that Iceland radio went off the air at 1 am. He had indeed homed on Iceland. For one hour, right up until it went off the air. Then a French radio station came on. So Tom homed in on France for the next ten hours or so.

We removed our equipment from our airplanes the next day. We were only forty miles north of Stockholm. We caught a train and spent the night there.

Tom just hated parting with money. He tended to pick hotels solely on appearance: the seedier, the better. He figured they would be cheaper. We spent an hour wandering around outside the railway station, looking for the cheapest, saddest place he could find. He didn't enjoy paying cab fares, either. Besides, we needed the exercise, or something like that.

He found a suitable place. Since it was still springtime, it was hardly packed.

Tom went into his poor routine. To understand it, you have to picture him. He waited until J C Penney's had a sale before he bought clothes. He always wore a t-shirt under his polyester Penney's special shirt. The t-shirt always had the center cut out of it, for comfort. Tom looked like he was on his last dime. Actually he was still on his first dime.

We learned that this hotel had two rates: about $30 a day with a bath, perhaps $27.50 without.

"Golly, that's a lot of money to spend on a room. Do you really want a room with a shower, Bob? It's all up to you."

I felt like a nerd. I hadn't had a decent night's sleep in a week. I smelled like something the cat had brought in. And now Tom was grouching about $2.50 for a bath. It was all part of the act.

"Gee, Tom. It would be nice to have a bath. Sure you can afford it?"

He turned back to the desk clerk. "You folks don't look all that full. Couldn't you give us a room with a shower for the lower price?"

The clerk looked us over. We sure did look poor. He went for it. It was no wonder Tom still had his first dime.

We caught a flight to London the next day. I had to get back to the U.S. to make a speech. Tom was going to wait around in England to see if he could scratch up a ferry flight home. He gave me a ride out to Heathrow airport so I could catch my flight.

"Well, Bob. How much do you figure I owe you for the trip?"

"Tom, we agreed on two thousand dollars to go to Khartoum. That would have taken about sixty hours' flying. Since it took us forty-five hours to Sweden, I think fifteen hundred would be fair."

"I'm sorry you said that, Bob. I was thinking of giving you fifteen hundred. But you got greedy. I'll pay you a thousand dollars."

My nostrils flared. I wasn't a giant fan of someone wanting to renegotiate a trip after it was complete. I knew then that this was my second ferry trip for Tom Danaher.

My first and my last.

He was a great pilot but he was cheap.

POST-216th TRIP: WASHINGTON, D.C. to KITTY HAWK, NC

I SET MY FIRST official world record in 1981. It was a record I was particularly proud of — speed between New York and Paris. The first guy to hold it was a young sprout by the name of Charles Lindbergh, back in 1927.

I met many folks in aviation after that. I spent a lot of time studying the aviation record book. Steve Oster was the only other pilot I ever met who knew the record book as well as I did. He, too, had noticed a gaping hole in the book that almost any pilot could fill.

One day in late '82 I was talking to Colonel Milt Brown from the NAA. The NAA handled prospective U.S. attempts at world records. Casually, Milt mentioned the upcoming eightieth anniversary of the Wright brothers' flight. Did I know anyone who might be interested in setting any records? I did. All I needed was an excuse and an airplane.

I found breaking records to be not unlike ferry flying. The average guy is quite capable of flying on the edge, then turning around and doing the dumbest, the most dangerous stunt possible. But, sure as God made little green apples, She didn't give all good pilots good sense.

I did just about enough flying in 1983 to stay current. Plans for a second Paris to New York to Paris race sat on a shelf, gathering dust. A Frenchman I knew named Richard Fenwic was talking about an air race to Africa, but that was months in the future.

I heard rumors of a company called Air America doing conversion work to Cessnas, similar to what Colemill did to the Navajo. I liked the Cessna 210, its top-of-the-line single. It had one defect: the engine wasn't worth a damn. The 210 needed more horses than any Continental engine could safely deliver. Air America had in progress a project to install a 350-horsepower turbocharged Lycoming engine. That airframe bolted to that engine should be a fire-breathing winner.

A year before, I had set up some amphibian records for a business partner. All he had to do was pay for the fuel, fly the course, and collect his records. He never even thanked me. Then he screwed me in the business, too. This time, I decided, if I was going to do all the work, I wanted to share the credit.

I called Ric Lujes from Air America to inquire about the status of his 210 project. I learned to my dismay that it was months from fruition. But he did have a Cessna 414 with the big Lycos hanging on each side. The airplane flew like a scalded ape climbing a tree.

We agreed to meet in Washington, D.C. on the morning of December 17, 1983. I'd handle the legwork, Ric would hand out the money, and we'd split the records.

I was funny about records. I liked setting them. I didn't much care who took the credit. Every record I ever set, I shared it with whoever I flew with.

I received the 414 specs from Ric and immediately went to the record book. At a minimum, we could break two speed records over a closed course altitude in level flight, and as many city to city records as Air America could afford.

I called Milt Brown to arrange the record attempts. If we could run the closed course records out of Dulles International airport, he could easily supply timekeepers. Then we would try for the altitude record *en route* from Washington to Kitty Hawk, North Carolina, where Orville Wright had made the world's first powered flights. If other pilots had only known how easy the NAA made record-setting, far more of them would have attempted aviation records. As usual, Colonel Brown did everything for us but fuel the plane.

I flew up to Washington on the evening of December 16 with a friend of mine from Miami, Trigg Adams, and his son Sean. I couldn't share my love of aviation with my own kids when they were only an hour's drive away. By now I had moved to Miami. I had become an ex-father. Trigg thought it worth sharing with his son.

Ric showed up the next morning. He even brought along a TV crew to record our attempts from the ground. Trigg would fly with us, to record them from the air. With his usual efficiency, Milt Brown had done the real work. He now called the tower at Dulles. They allowed us to tie up one of the twin runways for the thirty minutes necessary to complete our runs.

The timekeepers took up their positions along the runway. Milt had measured a three-kilometer course right on the runway. The best conditions for any speed records include a hot day at a high altitude airport, but that was a bit much to hope for in Maryland in December.

We ran the course back and forth, four times, mere feet above the runway. Our efforts were hardly earthshaking but were record-breaking. Then we ran the 15-kilometer course twice.

Due to our delayed start, we were running behind schedule. We were supposed to arrive in Kitty Hawk by 11 am.

To make up for lost time, Ric and I combined the altitude record attempt with the Washington to Kitty Hawk speed record attempt. We needed 33,500 feet to beat Steve Oster's record. Without specially prepared magnetos, our engines started cutting out as we passed 34,000 feet before running out of steam.

The city to city record, Washington to Kitty Hawk, was easy to set. There was no record. All we had to do was to complete the journey, and we'd have our fourth record of the day. We touched down only a little late.

For some reason, the adrenalin rush that results from going to the edge of the flight envelope seems to breed a sense of infallibility. I often saw this in Vietnam. A pilot would fly a mission to hell and back. Then he would kill himself while showing off. The fighter outfit I flew with in Vietnam lost more pilots in the year after completing its Vietnam tour than we lost in combat.

I flew in the rear of the Queen Air escort on the trip back to Washington, D.C. Trigg flew as co-pilot, video camera in hand. Ric was flying the record-breaking Cessna 414. Just for kicks, he did a barrel roll around our plane. Neither Ric nor the pilot in the Queen Air was ex-military. Neither had any idea of how to do formation aerobatics. Neither had a lick of sense.

Trigg switched on his camera as Ric started his second barrel roll about our craft. Then he lost sight of us. I realized, seconds ahead of anyone else, that we were flirting with disaster. I didn't know if our pilot realized how close we were to our final flight.

Trigg finally picked up on what was happening. In the most terror-filled voice I've ever heard, he screamed, "Pull up! Pull up! Dammit, pull up!"

Ric missed us by a few silly millimeters. An extra coat or two of paint on either aircraft might have changed the course of our flight, or ended it. Ric never even saw us as he passed over us.

It turned out later that Air America was a front for some king-sized dopers. Ric Lujcs and crew had been smuggling drugs for years. When the *federales* clamped the handcuffs shut on him, he blew the whistle on his whole crew. For this bravery in the face of adversity, he walked away scot-free, even though he was the organizer and ringleader. Everyone working for him went to jail. Around such heroes American justice revolves.

He returned to the business he knew best — drug-smuggling. He and Air America were caught a second time. This time he couldn't chirp his way to freedom. Lujes wasn't much, either as a man or a smuggler.

He wasn't much of a formation aerobatics pilot, either.

1984	from	to	nautical miles	knots	time (hours)			
					flight	day	night	inst.
Mar 10	Wash., D.C.	Paris	3,331	173	19.2	6.2	13.0	
Mar 15	Paris	Faro	839	168	5.0	5.0		3.0
Mar 16	Faro	Paris	839	140	6.0	6.0		
Mar 31	Paris	Moisselles	10	12	0.8	0.8		
	Moisselles	Shannon	458	131	3.5	3.5		
Apr 1	Shannon	Gander	1,727	144	12.0	12.0		6.0
	Gander	Bangor	561	224	2.5	2.5		
Apr 2	Bangor	St Louis	1,108	221	5.0		5.0	2.5
Apr 3	St Louis	Johnson	554	185	3.0	3.0		1.0
TOTALS		24 days	9,427	165	57.0	39.0	18.0	12.5

"For want of a nail the shoe was lost.
For want of a shoe the horse was lost . . ."

Sometimes in life it's the little things that make the difference. For example, a smoked ham was sufficient to persuade a professional cameraman to fly under the Eiffel Tower with me. It takes big cojones to hurl 3,500 pounds of airplane at a structure of that size. The previous guy who tried it had to be scraped off the side. But it takes even bigger cojones to ride in a plane, sitting on a garment bag, with no seat belt, taking video pictures all the way.

All it took to persuade him was the sight of a $27 ham.

RICHARD FENWIC had finished in a dismal fourth place in an Aerostar in the 1981 Paris to New York race. He contacted me a few months later to ask for help in setting an around the world speed record in a turboprop airplane.

Since no one had attempted the feat in a turboprop, all we had to do was to complete our route and the record would be ours. I would be responsible for the airplane and technical matters. He would get someone to sponsor us.

Fenwic talked a lot but never came through with the promised sponsor. He always had a great reason why he couldn't deliver. We put the record attempt on hold.

I flew a Twin Comanche in the Dulles 400, an east coast knock-off of the CAFE 250, in October of 1982. He came along with me. I didn't know how good a pilot he might be. I flew the plane and he navigated, or tried to. I hoped his piloting skills were better than his basic map reading, because he couldn't navigate for diddlysquat.

I spent so much time planning how to beat Steve Oster that I let a dentist from Arizona sneak past me and win first place in the twin competition. It was the only time ever that I would not place first in my category.

Fenwic called me again in the fall of 1983. Would I be interested in flying with him in the first Paris to Libreville race, to be held in March of 1984? Of course, I would have to be his co-pilot because he would do all the important things, such as finding the elusive sponsor. My responsibilities would be limited to securing the airplane and doing all the planning.

I was all for it. I told him to send me a copy of the regulations.

They arrived a few days later. The race was from Paris to Libreville, the capital of Gabon. We had to make two overnight stops in Africa and had to fly only 1,500 miles a day. The heart stopper was the prize for first place. It was an airplane worth $60,000. We weren't flying for a paltry $10,000 this time. This was the big time, with some real money.

Instead of being a pure speed race, like the Paris race in 1981, each aircraft would be given a handicap based on horsepower, wing area, and sixty-five percent speed at best altitude.

I sat down with my computer and came up with reference speeds for all the airplanes that might be competitive. A few minutes' work showed me that this would be a single-engine race. That meant it would be damn difficult for contestants to spend their way to victory.

The next question to consider was whether the prevailing winds would favor a high-altitude turbocharged aircraft or a normally aspirated low-altitude aircraft. I was lucky; at that time I lived in Miami, near the National Hurricane Tracking Center. If out of idle curiosity you should happen to wonder what the prevailing winds are, somewhere in the world, you want to live near the Center. They have rooms full of books filled with such esoteric information. Two days of research gave me all the available knowledge of prevailing winds over Africa in March, at high and low levels.

I called Fenwic in Paris. "Dickie, I've got some good news and some bad news. Which do you want first?"

"Give me the bad news first."

"I've put the handicap formula in a computer. I've run every plane I could think of through the program. No twin stands a chance. The airplane with the biggest advantage over its reference speed is the Piper Malibu. We don't have a chance in hell of getting our hands on one, unless you can find someone to buy one. Piper have a six-month waiting list."

"Jesus, Bob, that's grim. What good news could you possibly have?"

"Winning this race is going to be easier than falling off a bar stool. If the race committee has a lick of sense, they'll cancel it right now and send us the prize. Anyone who puts a tankful of gas in their airplane to try to beat us is just wasting money. We're going to clean their clocks."

"You've completely lost me now. If we can't get our hands on the plane with the largest advantage, what's going to stop someone else from getting their hands on one and cleaning our clock?"

"Dickie, every turbocharged plane I've run through the computer comes up with a big advantage over its reference speed. The Malibu has the greatest advantage. No non-turbo plane even matches its handicap. But computers don't win races. Anyone could come up with the same computer program I did. It will look to them too like you have to go with a turbo and fly at high altitudes. But what if the prevailing winds are always headwinds at high altitude? Might just be that the prevailing winds favor the low altitude airplanes in a big way."

"We better find out what the prevailing winds are in March. To tell you the truth, I don't know of anywhere in Paris I can get that information."

"I'm one step ahead of you, Dickie. I went down to the Hurricane Tracking Center here. The winds over southern Europe and north Africa at eighteen thousand feet and above are always eighty knots and higher, from the west. Anybody flying in a turbo is going to eat a fifty-knot headwind the whole trip."

I continued: "The plane to beat in this race would be Mike Smith's Bonanza. When the guys in the turbos get a gander at the first winds forecast, they are going to run to the nearest window and jump out. This is a low-altitude race. I don't give a damn what the computer says."

"OK, I like your thinking. Give Mike a call and see if he'll let us use his airplane. I've got two or three people lined up here as sponsors. I'll have no problem getting a sponsor this time. I can raise a hundred thousand here, no problem at all. We'll split the prize money, you and me."

"I can get the plane, but we must have a sponsor. If you really want to win this race, we have to have money. I'm broke. I want you to understand that I don't have a dime to put into this. And I can't afford to fly this thing for free. Get one of those guys nailed down."

I called Mike Smith. "Mike, I need N111MS again. Fenwic has come up with this race from Paris to Libreville. First prize is a French-built plane worth sixty thousand bucks. It's a handicap race. The numbers seem to favor turbocharged birds but I checked with the weather folks over at the Hurricane Tracking Center. The winds on the route are always strong westerlies at high altitude at that time of year. It will be easier to win than stealing candy from a baby. How about letting us use your plane?"

"It's yours, Bob. You can have it for free. You know, I told you last year that she wasn't flying as fast as she should. I just did a top overhaul. The chrome was worn off the rings. She really scoots now. You're going to be pleasantly surprised. When do you need it and how long do you want it for?"

"That's really great of you, Mike, but Fenwic is going to fly as captain and probably hog all the glory. You know how he is about that kind of thing. Figure out what you think it's worth to rent it to him, and charge him. Don't give him the airplane as a favor to me."

"Glad you told me that, Bob. Tell him that he can have it for ten thousand. Of course, I expect him to insure it and pay for any maintenance. When do you need it?"

"The race starts March fifteenth. I need to pick it up the first week of March and will have it back to you at the end of March."

Months passed. Dickie still hadn't found a sponsor, but he had some new and wonderful excuses.

Patrick Fourticq had flown to victory in the single-engine handicap competition of the 1981 Paris race. For this new race, he ran all the possible planes through his computer. He came up with the same numbers I did, but he didn't think about the winds. He got a liquor company in Scotland to put up $125,000 to sponsor him. He rented a Piper Malibu and had a whole heap of money left over to put in his pocket.

The money was out there. If only Fenwic could find a sponsor like that for us. We could *buy* a plane and still have a lot left over. But the excuses kept coming.

Psychology always played a big part when I planned a race. Fourticq stole one of my tricks. On his way across the Atlantic to Paris for the 1984 race, he smashed my three-year-old New York to Paris record. But comparing his Malibu to N111MS was like comparing apples and oranges. He was pressurized and turbocharged.

So I flew nonstop from Washington, D.C. to Paris. He might be faster than us but he sure didn't have our range. On one of the legs across Africa, and unlike us, he would have to make a fuel stop. I wanted him thinking about the time he must then make up. I didn't want him to start thinking about prevailing winds. I wanted that to be a last-minute surprise.

I arrived in Paris three or four days before the race. This was a French race, and so the rule changes continued until the last minute. The first set of rules specified a fairly direct route from Paris to Gabon. But nobody had bothered to check if that was OK with the countries to be overflown.

Somebody is always at war in Africa. They have a War of the Week on the continent. Each country is on a list, and when their week comes up, they declare war on somebody else. Or hold a revolution. That's considered fair, under the rules.

It was Algeria's week. Algeria wasn't interested in a bunch of little planes flying past while they organized their War of the Week. So the route was changed to Paris to Senegal to Gabon. Senegal is on the west coast of Africa. Our low-altitude airplane had a slight advantage under the first set of rules, but we gained an incredible advantage with this revised route.

The night after I arrived in Paris, I went out to dinner with a reporter who had covered the 1981 race. He and I went over to eat at the house of a friend of his. There I met a lovely French woman named France K—. She decided there and then that she was going to take me home and that we would do fun things together. She did. We did.

Fenwic still hadn't found a sponsor. But he had found a passenger for us. Dead weight — just what we needed! He was a French TV star, I was told.

Dickie's rationale was that by having him on board, it would be easier for us to land a sponsor. He could gain us a lot of coverage during the race. But Dickie still hadn't found us a sponsor.

He let me know about this guy on the morning of the race.

"Fenwic, what good will some TV star do us now? You don't have a sponsor. We have room for him, but he's just ballast. Are we in an air race or an old ladies' social? I like the guy, but all he's going to do is slow us down."

"I promised him that he could go. He can give me some really great coverage. If you don't want him to go, you tell him."

"Great, make me the bad guy. We just can't afford to take him. We're too heavy now. If we take him and someone wants to challenge our weight, we're going to get bounced right out of the race. You haven't found a sponsor. If we don't win first place, I'll be going home without a penny in my pocket. I told you I couldn't afford to fly for free."

"Don't worry about rules in a French-run race. The rules are never written in stone."

Sometimes they aren't written at all. Like the heels of a hooker, they are flexible, very flexible.

We had our pilots' briefing at noon. The organizers passed out the weather briefing. Fourticq could read a wind chart as well as I could. Not only did he have headwinds the entire route, we actually had a tailwind at low altitude over most of it. If he stayed high to get the fastest true airspeed out of his machine, he would get his lunch eaten. If he came down low to take advantage of the tailwinds, he would lose all the advantage of the turbocharger and we would still eat his lunch.

He turned pale. I smiled. The Wind God was on our side for sure. He looked for a window to jump out of but we were on the ground floor. He wasn't even bruised.

The race started officially at 5 pm. The fastest airplanes took off first.

We took off on schedule. We'd make our first fueling stop in Marrakech, Morocco, and then fly on to Dakar, Senegal. We took the TV star. He was a nice guy, and we had so much advantage over Fourticq that actually I wasn't too concerned about the speed we might lose.

Our routing was from Paris direct to the northwestern corner of Spain, over Portugal, and direct to Marrakech. We wanted a good fast turnaround in Morocco, so Fenwic sent a friend of his down on a commercial flight to pass out some bribe money. In Africa, a little lubrication always makes the wheels turn more smoothly.

We were at twelve thousand feet over Portugal. Mike had indeed fixed the problem with the engine. We had a true airspeed of 190 knots. The bird really was scooting.

The winds were horrendous even at that altitude. We didn't dare go lower, due to the mountains. Fourticq was at twenty-two thousand feet, where there was sixty-knot headwind. We were getting hurt but he was getting murdered. We would pick up so much time on this first leg that he'd never be able to make it up.

Then the engine started running rough. It sounded a lot like it did when Tom Sanders and I flew the same airplane to Paris in 1981. But this time I didn't have Tom Danaher around with his little bag of magic tricks.

I told Fenwic to change seats with me so I could play with the engine. I enriched the mixture and put the fuel boost pump on. If there was a piece of lint in one of the fuel injectors, extra fuel pressure might clear it.

No luck. The engine continued to sicken. I thought that it might be an icing problem. N111MS never liked to fly in ice. But we couldn't descend until we had passed to the south of Portugal.

We finally passed the coastline. I dropped the nose and went down to four thousand feet. We burned off all the ice and the engine seemed to run smoother. We'd have the injectors cleaned in Senegal.

I glanced at the oil pressure gauge, and then with growing horror at the oil temperature gauge. We had zero oil pressure, while the temperature was headed off the gauge. We had had minor engine problems before but were now up a creek without the proverbial paddle. We were fifty miles south of land and the engine was ready to quit, real soon. I turned back for Portugal.

"Mayday! Mayday! Mayday" I transmitted on 121.5. "This is N111MS. We are presently five-zero miles south of Faro on the one-eight-five degree radial. We have zero oil pressure and are preparing to ditch. I will attempt to return to Portugal for landing. Requesting assistance from any aircraft.

"Fenwic, get your ass in the back. Both of you, get those survival suits on in a hurry. I don't think we're going to make it back before the engine quits. Get ready to ditch," I ordered.

As chance would have it, the only aircraft to hear our call was that of Richard Fourticq. He came back on 121.5 and told me there was an airport at Faro, and that he'd had them turn on their lights.

At four thousand feet we might glide for eight miles. We were a long, long way from that airport and the engine could quit at any moment.

Time flies when you're having fun but it sure drags when you don't have any oil pressure. We were traveling at almost three miles a minute but it seemed to take forever to regain sight of land. Naturally, we had only two survival suits on board. They had both been filled by this time. I did the only thing I could think of. "Fenwic, how about getting me a pack of cigarettes out of the grocery bag?"

Fenwic and our passenger both laughed. I don't know why; I was being serious. I might be dead in a few minutes. This was no time to be worrying about lung cancer.

I stayed at four thousand feet until we had the runway under us. If the engine quit, I could still glide to a safe landing. I pulled the power back and made my approach. Made a perfect squeak, squeak, squeak landing. I did make nice landings. We taxied in and I shut the engine down.

Anywhere in the U.S., we would have had a dozen fire trucks surrounding us. In Faro, Portugal, we had none. They had no fire trucks. Or air-sea rescue. Had we gone down at sea, we'd have had to float until they sent out a boat, if they could be bothered.

We cleared customs and immigration formalities and went back out to the airplane. I had the fuel guy add engine oil until we were full. The oil capacity of the engine was twelve quarts. He put in twelve quarts. That brought us up to full. We had no oil when we landed. *Nada.* That's Spanish for "not a drop of oil in the *engineo.*"

"Dickie, the race is over for us. I don't see any oil leak, but it sure went somewhere. I'm sure the oil problem is related to the engine roughness, but you couldn't get me to fly this beast over water right now for all the tea in China. Let's go and get some sleep. We'll find someone to fix it tomorrow."

We'd just seen a $60,000 first prize disappear. There could never be another race which would be as easy to win as this race should have been. If the damn plane had just kept flying for another twenty hours, we'd have had the money in our hands.

It would not be inaccurate to describe my mood as glum. Very fucking glum. Bye-bye food, and rent. Bye-bye, seeing my kids.

The TV reporter had to return to Paris. He was supposed to be covering the race, and the horse on his chariot just died. I told him that his best plan would be to fly back commercial. Yes, I understood the terrible risks, but he would have to take his chances with an airline.

We found out in the morning that the only light aircraft mechanic in Portugal had died in 1961. If we wanted the plane fixed in Portugal, we would have to fly in our own mechanic.

Fenwic had been so convinced of our impending victory that he hadn't bothered to find a sponsor. He had financed the trip out of his own pocket, knowing we would win, and planning to take his expenses out of the prize money. Now the purse strings were closing in a hurry.

He said, "Let's just fly the plane to Paris. If I have to fly a mechanic down here, it's going to cost me a lot of money. I don't want to put any more of my money in the plane."

"We damn near didn't make it back to land last night. I can't say that I'm very interested in flying back across the mountains to France."

We still didn't have a clue where the oil had gone. I checked the engine compartment, looking for the source of a leak. The engine looked just fine. The dipstick still showed the twelve quarts we'd added the night before. I told him that we would make a test flight. If the bird seemed OK, I'd fly it to Paris. But only during the daytime and along the coast.

We fired up the engine. All the gauge readings were normal. We took off and climbed out. Gauges were still normal. Flew all the way back to Paris. Gauges still perfectly normal. The engine burned more oil than usual but ran just fine.

At Paris–Le Bourget airport I always based my airplane at Transair, the Beechcraft dealer. We nosed into their hangar and I told the sad story of our flight to the head mechanic. He nodded and sighed sympathetically a few times. He mentioned that $60,000 was almost half a million francs.

A couple of mechanics rolled their toolboxes over to the airplane and started removing panels. The head mechanic kept murmuring, "It's terrible, terrible." He wasn't talking about the plane, he was talking about the half-million francs. I knew how he felt.

Thirty minutes later, the diagnosis was complete. We had one clogged fuel injector. That caused a super-lean, super-hot mixture. That burned a piston. That broke part of a valve. That jammed the piston rings. That caused all of our oil to be pumped out the exhaust.

The mechanic spelled it out for me. "M'sieu, eet eez very simple. Thees leetle piece of lint 'as done ze engine for you. Of course, eet eez eazee to feex. We must change ze cylinder and ze piston. Zis will cost only twenty or sirty souzand fronk. Zat eez nussing to someone 'oo can lose one 'alf-million in only one night."

Fenwic was thrilled with the news. Meanwhile, back in the race, Fourticq walked away with first place. Now he had a plane worth an additional $60,000 to split with his co-pilot.

Never one to be caught off-guard by a little adversity, Fenwic began to cast around for someone to blame. He tried laying it on me first. "It's all your fault, Moriarty. You were pushing the airplane too hard."

I reminded him that he had been flying it.

There was a moment's silence. Undaunted, he switched to another target. "Then it's all Mike Smith's problem. Mike shouldn't have let us have the plane in this condition."

"Look, Fenwic. Let me tell you a little something about airplanes. Every once in a while they break. It's not anybody's fault, they just break. Believe me, Mike would have loved for us to win this race. He wouldn't let the airplane go over water if it wasn't working right. If you want to assign blame, you might accept a little responsibility for not finding a sponsor. If we'd had the hundred and twenty-five thousand dollars that Fourticq managed to raise, I'd have installed a brand new engine. But that's all spilt milk now. We have to fix it and get it back to Mike. Air races are like women; wait around for a few minutes and another one will come along."

We got the plane fixed. I was anxious to get back to the U.S. This race had been a complete waste of time. But Fenwic came up with the idea of setting some new city to city records while he had the plane available, and I agreed to stay for a few more days.

I moved in with France K. She owned a dress shop just off the Champs-Élysées. We stayed up partying every night, slept until noon, and then got her to her shop to open up by 3 pm.

Ferry flying did have its advantages at times. She had a very dirty mind. I like that in a woman.

We were leaving a restaurant one evening. She wanted to go to the "loo," she said, "to remove some of my undergarments." Very sexy. On the way to the car, she told me to put a hand on her shoulder. No, not on the outside, on the inside. Under her full-length black sable coat, she wore nothing. We made a mad dash for her apartment and made love on the coat.

Every afternoon I would crawl back to Dickie's apartment for a rest.

We went out for dinner one night with Fenwic and his girlfriend, Maureen. He was growing more depressed about the race as time passed. He had to do something to regain his honor. He started counting how much the city to city records were going to cost him; it was a bundle. The purse strings snapped shut again. After drinking about two bottles of wine more than we should have, he came up with a brilliant idea, from his viewpoint at least.

"What we must do is fly under the Eiffel Tower. I don't think anyone has done it before. You file the flight plan and get the airplane out of the country after it is done. The French authorities won't do anything to you because you are an American. I'll fly with you but we must not let anyone know I was with you until much later. The authorities might take my license away."

"Let me think about this. Are you saying that the two of us fly under the tower together? And I take all the heat from the authorities? And after the uproar has died down, you'll say you were doing the flying?"

"But of course," he responded.

"You have to be kidding. If you want to do the flying, why don't you take the credit along with the heat? How come it's OK for me to lose my license, but not you?"

"But Bob, the French won't be able to get their hands on you. What can they do? Just stay out of the country for a few years."

"I'll think about it. But you seem to be out of your mind." He was insane. The idea did intrigue me, though.

The next day, after the wine wore off, I walked to the Eiffel Tower. I staggered past it every afternoon, returning to Dickie's apartment from France's dress shop. But I'd never before assessed it from an aeronautical point of view.

I asked a guide about the dimensions of the arch. I was told that it was 280 feet across and 189 feet high.

Maybe nobody had ever flown through it, but that wasn't because it was too small. Hell, a Boeing 747 could go through.

I walked up and down, inspecting the tower from every angle. I shot rolls of film. I spent hours studying every possible approach. Not only would it be easy to do, it would be a piece of cake.

We had dinner again with Fenwic and Maureen. France K. thought I was out of my mind to even consider such a stunt.

The last time anyone had attempted the feat was in 1926. A Frenchman, Leon Collot, was blinded by the sun during his attempt and crashed and died. I told France that he hadn't planned it properly. He approached from the northwest, flew over the Trocadero and then had to dive steeply to line himself up with the arch.

If I were to do it, I would approach from the opposite direction, over the École Militaire. I would have twenty or thirty seconds to stabilize the airplane. She still thought I was crazy to listen to Fenwic.

Fenwic really wanted to fly in the plane. But he was adamant about not taking any risk. If he had to take any of the grief from the authorities, he wouldn't go.

I asked him why he wanted to do it in the first place. Anyone could claim to have flown under the tower. If all the people who claimed to have done it during World War II really had done it, it would have been busier than LaGuardia airport during the Thanksgiving holiday. But of all the people who claimed to have done so, none had any pictures or documentation.

I wouldn't get the full picture for about another year. Fenwic had intended to sit on the ground, let me fly through, let me get in trouble. Then later, much later, he would claim that it was he who had done it. Not bad, even for a Frenchman.

The technical details of the flight were easy. I had landed on aircraft carriers during flight training in the service. This target was so much easier than landing on a carrier, it was ridiculous.

But I wasn't greatly interested in a little more glory. It's fun, but it doesn't pay the bills.

Richard Fenwic was a very important man in Paris. If there was any doubt in your mind, you had only to ask him. He was very important, and he was the first to tell you so. He was a personal friend of everyone and could get anything done. If you lived in France but didn't know him, that meant you were a nobody, because he knew everyone and could do anything.

But I'd been hearing his stories for years. Nothing ever materialized from his many connections. Now he was going to peddle the rights to our story and photographs for *biggo buckso*. That's Spanish for *mucho dinero*.

I was broke. I had needed the money from the Libreville race much more than Richard Fenwic or Mike Smith did. What should have been sixty hours of flight time in N111MS was worth $10,000 to Mike, but sixty hours of my flight time turned out to be worth a big fat zero. Fenwic hadn't come up with a sponsor for the race and I was fixing to head home with lint in my pockets.

I laid down the law to him. *No tickee, no laundry.* If he didn't cough up some money by the end of the week, I was heading home. I didn't give a damn if I flew through the Eiffel Tower or not. I already had a stack of records piled in a corner of my house and they weren't earning me a dime. I wasn't doing any more flying for free.

If I'd had a lick of sense, I would have turned the PR effort over to France K. She felt no need to talk about it all the time, but she really was connected. She could have sold my story in one day, and for a lot more than Dickie would ever come up with. She really did know everybody.

The days passed. Dickie couldn't do anything because he was just too busy. But tomorrow he would get right on it. *Mañana*, always *mañana*. He couldn't get himself organized.

On Wednesday I told him I'd had enough. I was leaving on Saturday morning. If I had some cash in my hand I would fly under the Eiffel Tower before I left. If he didn't come up with some money, I wouldn't do it.

I must finally have gotten his attention. He spent Thursday and Friday scurrying around trying to sell the story.

He called me Friday afternoon. "I've done it, Bob. The Sygma photo agency will pay me forty thousand francs, that's about five thousand dollars, for the exclusive right to take photos of you flying through the tower. We have to meet with them tonight."

"Hang on just a minute. I'm not interested in how much you are getting paid. You ain't going. How much am I getting paid for this stunt? What are you trying to pull now?"

"But Bob, I spent almost thirty thousand dollars on the race and I have nothing to show for it. I'll split the money with you, sixty-forty. You get two thousand dollars. That way, I recover some of my race expenses. Sygma will also pay us forty per cent of anything they make over one hundred thousand francs on the photos. When this hits the newspapers, I'll push the photos with all my contacts. We could really make a bundle out of this."

Any port in a storm. While $2,000 wasn't much for one month of my life, it was better than going home with nothing.

The folks at Sygma were nervous. I wondered what they knew that I didn't. I wasn't so naïve as to think that Sygma was really paying me to fly under the Eiffel Tower. They might make some money selling shots of a successful flight, but they would prefer shots of me splattered all over the base of the tower. Those would be worth a bundle.

But that hole was a lot bigger than they realized. I could have made it through with the autopilot flying the plane.

They wanted a cameraman inside the plane. They planned to have six photographers taking stills from the ground but also wanted live coverage. Lots of people photograph the Eiffel Tower; not many stand around with a video camera waiting for someone to come along and fly through it. That would require some explaining.

They couldn't order the cameraman to fly with me. After all, they didn't really think I could do it. But think of the value of live action footage of the flight from inside the plane. You could be the first at the scene of the accident. The cameraman was somewhat nervous.

Our plan was to have Dickie drive me out to Le Bourget the next morning. The cameraman would meet me there. I'd file a VFR flight plan for Shannon. Once released by Paris control, I'd fly around to the west of Paris. When I had the École Militaire lined up with the Eiffel Tower, I'd come in at rooftop level, dive down over the gardens, line up with the arch and do it.

Fenwic would be under the tower with a handheld aircraft radio. He would make sure there were no cables in the way or any other nasty surprises. When he knew I was making my run, he'd tell the photographers to get ready. It would be a piece of cake.

I would then fly to the north of Paris, to a small uncontrolled grass strip. I'd drop off the cameraman and depart for Shannon. And stay out of France for a few years.

Like all of Dickie's plans, it went awry. He was late in getting me to Le Bourget. I should have known he would be. We arrived just as the video cameraman was about to give up and leave. He was really nervous now. We were about to do the deed but he didn't know me from the man in the moon.

He looked around the airplane, took some pictures, and calmed down. In moments, he went from jittery to completely calm.

We had time to kill, waiting for Fenwic to get into position. The Sygma video photographer followed me around, taking short video clips all the while. For the first time in years, I gave an aircraft a complete preflight. At the inquest, at least they couldn't accuse me of neglecting to do that.

The time came for our departure. I told the cameraman that I knew what I was doing. If he had any problem or became scared, I would call off the mission. I had the $2,000 in my pocket. I didn't really care if we did it or not. I had been paid.

He was all set. The co-pilot's seat had been removed because of the ferry tanks. He had to sit on my garment bag, with no seat belt. He didn't care. When flying under the Eiffel Tower, complying with minor regulations such as wearing a seat belt doesn't mean much.

It was a beautiful spring morning. Paris, like most large European cities, is often bathed in fog and mist. But today the sky was clear to the moon. We had great visibility. As I passed out of Paris control, I wondered just how soon they would realize this wasn't a normal Saturday morning jaunt. How soon before the Mirages would arrive to shoot me down?

I understand that when Christ was on the way to His crucifixion, He was asked how he felt. He said that frankly, He wasn't all that eager to go through with it. It was quite an honor, though. He would just have to make the most of it. I knew how He felt.

I flew the plan just the way we had discussed it the night before. My communications with Fenwic were perfect. As I dropped down to rooftop level, I realized I had made one slight miscalculation. From rooftop level, I couldn't see the École Militaire. I had planned all along to use it as my aiming point. Now, all of a sudden, I couldn't see it. But it was impossible to miss the Eiffel Tower or the Champ de Mars, the long public park that separated the tower and the École Militaire. I just worked the problem out backward.

I finally came up on the school. This was really the only hairy part of the flight. I had to come over the building as low as possible, for my letdown to street level. The building bristled with radio antennas. I couldn't see them now but I knew they were there. If I went too low I would hit one. If I stayed too high, I would have to dive for the arch.

I called it perfectly. I didn't wrap up the airplane in antennas, but got right down to street level.

At this point I started having some serious reservations about the flight. I looked at the Eiffel Tower, lined up not a half-mile from me. It looked a lot smaller than it had yesterday. My enormous airplane would never go through that little arch. I thought it over for a few seconds. The arch grew larger, and larger, and larger.

Then I was through. I pulled the nose up slightly so as to miss the Trocadero.

I said I would do it and I had done it. It wasn't quite as easy as I had thought but it sure wasn't hard. If Dickie would now get off his fanny and sell those pictures, maybe I could salvage this trip yet.

He had planned an elaborate getaway for me, so I would miss all the radar sites. But a couple of thousand people had just seen me fly through the Eiffel Tower. The French police aren't a whole lot more efficient than their American counterparts, but there was only one black Bonanza near Paris and I was in it. It wouldn't take long for the word to get out.

That word might be: shoot on sight. It was high time to get out of Dodge.

I headed directly for the grass strip. Fenwic told me that it was uncontrolled. It was, but the airport operator did have a radio and pilots were supposed to make contact with him.

I entered the landing pattern from the wrong side. The operator was screaming at me in French during the whole approach and landing. It was a good thing I didn't understand or I might have taken umbrage at his remarks. I opened the door and tossed out the cameraman.

"Tell that fellow that I'd love to stop and chat, but I've just remembered that I have a hot date in Limerick. So long."

I split for Shannon.

I listened on the emergency channel, 121.5, but nobody seemed very interested in my flight. I didn't talk to anyone until I passed out of French airspace over the island of Jersey.

I landed at Shannon. No one took any special interest in me or the plane. I was unsure how long that state of affairs might last.

The next day I left for Gander. I had heard nothing about my flight being mentioned on the radio or in the newspapers. I concentrated on putting as much water between me and France as I could. I delivered the airplane back to Mike Smith in Johnson, Kansas two days later.

"Mike, I couldn't discuss it with you before I did it, but I flew your plane through the Eiffel Tower on my way out of Paris. I knew you wouldn't approve but it needed doing and I did it. Fenwic set up a bunch of guys to take pictures and we should have some really great shots."

"I know. He called me from Paris to tell me about it. By the way, the FAA wants you to give them a call."

That didn't take long. Now I was in the soup.

My twin brother was an attorney in Houston. Discretion being the better part of valor, I thought I should call him first.

"You did what? No wonder the FAA wants to talk to you. I don't really think they can do anything but you better call them. I don't think they have any jurisdiction over flights in Paris. But let me warn you about one thing. Don't lie to them. If you don't want to answer a question, don't answer, but don't lie to them."

I called the man from the FAA. All he wanted to know was whether I had been the pilot of N111MS three days earlier on a flight from Paris to Shannon, Ireland. And could I comment on a report of a flight of a plane through the Eiffel Tower?

Yes, to the first question. No, to the second question. I certainly didn't want to make any comment on such a flight. Imagine someone actually flying under the Eiffel Tower!

Is the news we see censored? It's a good question, and not one that I can answer in the case of the U.S. But in France, you bet your bippy it is.

I made my flight on a sparkling Saturday morning in spring, at about 11:15 am. Thousands of Parisians and tourists were around the Eiffel Tower. Two minutes after my flight through its arch, everyone for blocks around would have known about it.

There wasn't one word about it in any French newspaper the next day, or the next, or the next. Ten days later, one French news magazine defied the government ban and broke news of the flight.

I learned, many moons later, that the video cameraman had decided to back out of the flight while waiting for Fenwic and me. He changed his mind due to my love of French dried ham. Since I was going to fly under the Eiffel Tower, I figured that a charge of smuggling a French ham into the U.S. would not add greatly to the long list of charges against me. I had gone out the night before the flight and bought a ham. I had put it in the airplane, on top of the ferry system.

When the cameraman saw it, he rationalized: if I planned on getting the ham back to the U.S., evidently I fully intended to get myself back home. From that moment on, he had complete confidence in my flying abilities. That was why he had so suddenly calmed down.

It was a great ham.

We made one serious mistake during our planning. To this day, I'm amazed that no one made the simple suggestion that would have made the flight so much more newsworthy.

I made the flight on March 31.

I should have waited until the next day.

People would have argued for years about whether or not it had taken place.

222nd TRIP: LAKELAND, FL to SHANNON, IRELAND

1985	from	to	nautical miles	knots	time (hours)			
					flight	day	night	inst.
Jan 14	Lakeland	Perkasie	826	127	6.5	5.0	1.5	
	Perkasie	Hartford	137	91	1.5		1.5	
Jan 15	Hartford	Bangor	251	96	2.6	2.6		
	Bangor	Stephenville	478	81	5.9	2.9	3.0	4.5
Jan 16	Stephenville	Gander	159	106	1.5	1.5		
Jan 19	Gander	Lajes	1,404	143	9.8	6.8	3.0	
Jan 20	Lajes	Shannon	1,128	134	8.4	5.9	2.5	3.0
TOTALS		6 days	4,383	121	36.2	24.7	11.5	7.5

Many times we think from our vantage point that we're big wheels. From another point of view, it's evident that all we are doing is traveling in circles.

I had started ferrying in 1975, for Phil Waldman. Now, more than two hundred trips later, I was back in the fold, more experienced, older, a little wiser. And making perhaps half as much money as I did when I started.

Sometimes we go round and round in life to get exactly nowhere. I was sans wife, sans kids, sans happiness.

It's easy to become complacent, even when flying on the edge of the envelope becomes commonplace. I took another winter ferry trip, got iced up, almost crashed, fought through horrible weather in a plane I had no business flying, landed softly, then almost got run over by the crash truck.

It's a tough job, but somebody's got to do it.

Why me, though?

THE GENERAL AVIATION BUSINESS in the U.S., and in the world, died in the mid-1980s. From all-time record sales in 1979, unit volume had dropped ninety percent by 1985. More airplanes had been sold in 1940.

Needless to say, the ferry business perished. Phil Waldman still had five pilots more or less employed, mostly less. They all still hated flying LBFs.

He called me one day in November, 1984. He had a pair of Cherokees bound for Australia. Did I know anyone who could take one?

"Phil, I know only one pilot crazy enough to take a Cherokee to Australia, and that's me. What's the contract?"

"Fifteen hundred."

These planes had lacked willing pilots when the contracts paid three times as much. But my larder was bare. I took one, then the other.

The following January, Phil called with another trip. Was I willing to take a Maule to Shannon for $1,000? I had really made it into the big time. This trip would pay almost half of what it was worth ten years before. But the rent was due. I flew to Lakeland to pick up the plane.

The M-6 Maule was a little tiny taildragger with a good-sized engine. Designed especially for short field operations, the factory still sold one now and again. I had never delivered one. I'd never even flown one before.

I performed my preflight, pre-ferry check, just as I had done so many times before. I kicked the tires. I counted the wings.

I left Lakeland for Perkasie, Pennsylvania around noon. Before leaving I had called Kathie, to see if I could at least see the kids. She agreed.

The field in Perkasie had changed a lot in the three years since my last trip through. So had my life. The airport had improved.

I called Kathie to ask her to pick me up. She did.

I really don't know how other men handle being ex-fathers. Maybe it took more practice than I'd had. I wasn't very good at it. After having spent next to no time together in three years, my two sons and I were losing touch. I looked at them for an hour or so, then left.

Kathie and I talked about the situation between us. I kept on thinking it could not get any worse, and then somehow, in some way, it always did. Kathie made a lot of promises that night. They all turned out to be empty. But then, they always did. In here mind, ex-husband and ex-father was the same thing. All she wanted was money from the Moriarty money tree that all she had to do was shake.

My takeoff from Perkasie was rough; real rough. I was leaving a lot more than just a runway behind. It's hard to fly a plane with tears in your eyes.

I walked into Bangor the next afternoon for a weather brief. It was like homecoming. There too, I hadn't flown through in three years.

Modern technology had made its inroads in the weather briefs. My upper level winds were all computer generated. I insisted on looking over the weather charts. The computer winds showed a twenty-knot tailwind to Gander. Sure didn't look like it on the map. But I had a two-hour reserve, so I wasn't much worried.

I should have listened to my instincts.

I took off on what I expected to be a 4½-hour trip. A piece of cake. At no time during the flight would I be more than eighty miles from land. I couldn't possibly get into trouble.

By the time I reached the Gulf of St. Lawrence, I suspected the computer program might have suffered from bugs. The 150-mile leg that should have taken just over an hour took an hour and three-quarters. My next leg should have been eighty minutes long; it took almost forever.

Northeastern Canada's best January weather is plumb nasty. I had passed the Magdalen Islands, smack dab in the middle of the gulf, an hour or so before. I ran into a solid deck of clouds. As the time slowly passed, I started picking up ice. I flew on toward St. John's.

At any point on a ferry flight, I always knew where my nearest safe harbor lay. I reserved a portion of my brain for keeping track of the nearest airport. At this point, on this flight, I believed Stephenville in Newfoundland to be within a few miles.

The conditions were ideal for icing and disaster. The temperature at my altitude of nine thousand feet was minus ten degrees Celsius. On the ground it was minus three. I couldn't go up and I damn sure didn't want to go down.

Sometimes in life we flat run out of options. The ice built up to the point at which its sheer weight started to bring me down. My airspeed fell to the point that I was just mushing through the air.

I had learned over the years that when you *think* you've got a problem, *you've got a problem.* Let everybody know. Perhaps someone can help.

"Mayday! Mayday! Mayday! This is N7449C. My aircraft has picked up severe airframe icing. I estimate my position to be ten miles southwest Stephenville. I'm unable to maintain nine thousand feet. Requesting immediate clearance to five thousand. Presently passing seven thousand feet descending," I yelled into the radio.

A response came at one. Great word, mayday.

"Hello, N49C. This is Gander Center. You are cleared for descent to five thousand. Maintain five thousand. The minimum safe altitude in your area is three thousand, six hundred. We show your position to be twenty nautical miles on the two-five-zero degree radial St. John's. What are your intentions?"

Intentions? First, to try to survive.

"Center, this is 49C. I'm going to be unable Gander. I will divert to Stephenville. Say Stephenville terminal, please."

"49C, Gander. Stephenville reports eight hundred overcast. Half-mile visibility in blowing snow. Winds are zero-nine-zero degrees at eight-zero knots."

Eighty knots. Holy cow! No wonder I scarcely outpaced a speedy snail. But I was only twenty miles from the airport. Even with eighty knots on the nose, I could make it in half an hour or so. But when I got close to the surface I would be beaten to death by the turbulence.

My plane had the flight characteristics of a brick. I reached five thousand feet but couldn't hold it, even with full power. Finally, my fall ceased at two thousand, five hundred. I was below the mountaintops, but had no choice.

In any emergency, our perception of the passage of time changes. On this flight it seemed to have come to a complete halt. I had noted the time when I contacted Gander. Twenty minutes later, I called for a position update. To my horror, I was only five miles closer to St. John's. The headwinds were in excess of one hundred knots. My speed over the ground was fifteen knots.

I requested radar vectors from Gander directly to Stephenville. Gander came back with a clearance to the VOR some six miles from the airport. They continued to insist that I climb to three thousand, six hundred feet to clear the mountains. But I wasn't down low because I wanted to be. I couldn't climb a foot. It took full power just to stay airborne.

With airplanes, problems come in clumps. I was short on fuel, carrying enough ice for Princess Di's coming-out party, and bucking a hundred knots on the nose.

Then it got worse. I got vertigo. All my instruments indicated one flight altitude. My body told me they were lying. Twenty years of flying had hammered into me the need to believe my instruments. My body kept telling me they lied. As marginally as my bird was lumbering through the air, I knew that if I lost it, I would come spiraling out of the clouds in just a few seconds.

Gander and I argued for some time about my clearance. They wanted me to go six miles from the airport — twenty-five minutes' flying under present conditions — to start my approach.

I told them firmly that they were out of their ever-lovin' minds. I wanted to be pointed directly at the end of the runway. If I couldn't find the airport, well then, I was up a creek without a paddle.

They wanted me to fly by the book. But the book didn't apply to the conditions in which I found myself trapped.

I was two miles from the airport. I nosed my plane over and started my descent. I expected severe turbulence at the lower altitude. If I didn't carry a little extra airspeed, I would run into real trouble trying the maneuver. I was already too damn close to the edge of the envelope. One slight gust could shove me beyond it entirely, into the area where airplanes no longer fly.

I dropped to eight hundred feet and still couldn't see the ground. Gingerly I inched my way down to seven hundred, then six. I caught sight of the city just below me. Now all I had to do was find the airport. Then my problems would really start.

Gander Center was in uproar. My behavior was wholly irregular. But I'm not the kind of pilot who confuses the regulation book with the Good Book. I'd seen too many pilots killed because they had listened to controllers sitting in their warm cocoon, sipping hot coffee.

I found the airport, finally. At last I had something going for me. The wind blew with the strength of Hercules, but it came from the east, right down the tubes of Runway 09.

I fell from the sky onto a gentle blanket of snow covering the runway. My total ground roll didn't exceed three hundred feet. My legs shook as I held the brakes. I wasn't in any condition to taxi the aircraft in. I shut my engine down to wait for a tow truck.

I never discovered why it was that airport tower personnel were so eager to launch the crash crew. But they were. I've fought my way through the hinges of Hades several times, only to find a smiling crash crew upon arrival. After all, the fun and games were over. After I had come to a safe stop and shut down, there was the crash truck barreling down the runway, straight towards me.

I found out later that the winds varied between sixty and eighty knots as I landed directly into them. But my sixty-knot headwind was a sixty-knot tailwind for the crash truck. Wisely, the driver started braking about 1,500 feet from my plane. My gentle blanket of snow turned into his ice rink.

As I watched in horror, the truck started turning in circles. As if drawn to me by a piece of string, it came closer and closer. It grew bigger and bigger. It was beyond the control of human hands. All I could think about was the irony of being crushed to death by a crash truck. Especially after all the work I had done to make it onto the runway.

The truck made a broadside slide to the plane. It came to a stop only a few feet in front of my propeller. If my engine had still turned, I would have hit the truck's door when the driver opened it.

It took five of us another two hours to put my iron butterfly to bed. I was exhausted, tired, freezing cold. Somehow, after what I went through, the very air smelled fresher.

The Canadians sent me a citation for not carrying an approach plate for Stephenville. I kept it. I saved all of them. I've got a stack of them in a long-forgotten corner in some closet.

A few days later I completed the delivery to Shannon. The crew at Shannon had wondered if I was still alive and flying. I was, but barely.

227th and 228th TRIPS: MORRISTOWN, NJ to TULSA, OK

1985	from	to	nautical distance	knots	time (hours) flight	day	night	inst.
Jun 15	Morristown	Montreal	271	100	2.8	2.8		
Jun 17	Montreal	Frobisher Bay	1081	208	6.1	6.1		
Jun 19	Frobisher Bay	Godthåb (Nuuk)	427	164	2.6	2.6		
Jun 20	Godthåb	Reykjavik	726	177	4.1	4.1		1.5
Jun 22	Reykjavik	Aberdeen	793	162	4.9	4.9		1.5
Jun 23	Aberdeen	Pontoise	494	198	2.5	2.5		2.0
	Pontoise	Le Bourget	23	77	0.3	0.3		
Jun 25	Le Bourget	London	189	185	1.0			
	London	Le Bourget	189	189	1.0		2.3	
Jun 26	Le Bourget	London	189	189	1.0			
	London	Le Bourget	189	245	.77		2.1	
Jun 29	Le Bourget	Gander	2200	131	16.8	14.0	2.8	6.5
Jun 30	Gander	Bangor	560	181	4.0	4.0		1.5
	Bangor	Caldwell, NJ	337	169	2.0	2.0		
July 1	Caldwell	Tulsa	1040	274	3.8	3.8		
TOTALS		16 days	8,708	164	53.2	47.9	7.2	13.0

Everything that has a beginning has an end. It works that way with air races, airplanes, operas, pilots, and books. But as they say, the opera ain't over 'til the fat lady sings. I always loved the part of an air race when I started to hear a slight trill. Months of blood, sweat, toil and tears finally start to come together.

Air racing is like baking a cake. The ingredients consist of aluminum, money (lots of money), sweat, inspiration, skill, hope, psychology, tears, and a dash of luck. Every pilot believes his way of cooking is the only way. This is hardly unnatural, since air racing is the equivalent of a bakeoff.

In every race I've ever been in, ninety percent of the pilots are there merely to participate. It's always easy to figure out who the serious cooks are. When racing a field of pilots, no matter how many, it's hardly necessary to

*compete against every other pilot. Victory requires only the determination of
who will finish second. If you can just beat him, the rest will follow.*

*In my years of travels, I've met and talked to lots of folks. Every once in a
while, somebody says something I wish I had come up with. I file it mentally
and then wait for the perfect time to regurgitate it, just as if I came up with it
myself.*

*One line I wish was mine, but isn't, and which I never quite had the
opportunity to use, had to do with George Washington.*

*Good ol' George is regarded as the father of this country. It is said that
he was first in war, first in peace, and first in the hearts of his countrymen. But
often we forget that George Washington married Martha Custis, a widow.*

Even George wasn't first in everything.

WHEN I ARRIVED back at Johnson, Kansas in April 1984 after my flight
through the Eiffel Tower, Mike Smith flew me down to Tulsa, Oklahoma. He
had a customer. J. Richard Blissit was the head of an interior design firm. He
wanted Mike to do his amazing cleanup job on a Bonanza.

Mike suffered from the same malaise as me — an overwhelming urge to
compete. While his company cleanup of Bonanzas was going great guns, he
had invested every penny of profit into research. So while he still loved air
racing, he didn't have the funds to build the ultimate racing machine.

The V-tail Bonanza had proven itself in a dozen or so races to be the
fastest, most efficient racing machine in terms of speed, fuel economy, or
payload.

In hours of conversations over the years, Mike and I had talked about
what we would include or discard in a plane, if we had unlimited bucks.

His company aircraft, N111MS, was about everything a race pilot would
want in a non-turbocharged aircraft. Together, we winged our way to victory in
the 1981 Paris to New York to Paris race, cut Lindbergh's New York to Paris
record in half, set half a dozen other speed records, and even flew through
the Eiffel Tower. He and I waxed the field in the first CAFE 250 race in
California. After that, Mike placed first or second in all of the other CAFE
races. N111MS was ugly as sin, but flew like a scalded ape.

In any handicap race, a normally aspirated engine (that is, not
turbocharged) should win, unless the race is run west to east over a
considerable distance.

My study of the prevailing wind conditions had played a large part in my selection of N111MS back in 1984 for the Paris to Gabon race. That race appeared at first blush to favor turbocharged aircraft. Several hours of research at the Hurricane Tracking Center in Miami, however, convinced me that by staying low, we could have an unbeatable advantage. And we were winning, up to the point some sixty miles south of the Portuguese coast when we ran out of oil.

I would concentrate completely on a race, right up until we reached the starting line. Then I would start thinking about the next race.

Frogs have been big on racing, at least since Mark Twain wrote a story about Calaveras County. Now a Frenchman named Laffargue had organized a race or rally from New York to Paris. It was billed as the first New York to Paris air race. It was hardly the first, and it wasn't from New York to Paris.

Laffargue was close enough to La Frog to be remembered easily. Since Canada didn't have the same fraud laws as the U.S., it was a better base for a company running an air race.

In any case, La Frog or Laffargue had been advertising a transatlantic race to be run in June, 1985. Since the course was west to east, clearly a turbocharged steed was needed.

Mike Smith had flown me down to Tulsa. He had to meet with his new prospective customer.

"Bob, I don't want to tell you about his airplane. But if you want to set some more records, he might have just what you need."

We met Richard Blissit in the airport cafe at Riverside airport in Tulsa. As he described what he wanted done to his turbocharged V-35, N777RB, my eyes grew bigger and bigger.

Blissit had purchased a clean used V-35 with a worn-out engine. He wanted Mike to do a total speed conversion on the plane, and then install a factory remanufactured engine. Once that was complete, he planned an all-new radio package, a new interior, and a new custom paint job. For a total investment of $125,000, Blissit would get an as-new airplane in every detail. Except that for $125,000, the factory would sell you a new V-35 TC some twenty knots slower. His plane would have every modification Mike Smith and I had ever considered when specifying our dream racing machine.

This discussion between Smith and Blissit went on for over an hour. I felt like a kid back in second grade who needed to do number one real, real bad. I just had to raise my hand.

"Richard, I've done a little racing and have set some records. Mike and I have talked about creating the ultimate turbocharged V-35. There are a lot of records just waiting to be broken. We could put your aircraft in the record book permanently."

All journeys start with that first small step. J. Richard Blissit, N777RB and I would cover a lot of ground, and some water, over the next year or so.

Back in 1982 I had made a list of possible record attempts for a V-35. I had listed twenty-three records that could be set or broken. Since no single aircraft had ever set more than four or five, twenty-three would be a nice, neat, round number.

Work progressed on N777RB. It was slow and expensive. Like most construction projects conceived by man, it cost more than expected, and took longer.

But in January 1985, like a phoenix, Richard's Bonanza emerged from the flames. Bear in mind that Mike Smith and I were primarily concerned with speed and power.

Mike's company airplane, N111MS, was sleek and fast, but so ugly that only a mother could love her.

Some wag had suggested within Mike's hearing that the only reason the Lockheed SR 71 Blackbird had been painted black was because the color added three knots to its top speed. He promptly ran to the hardware store to purchase multiple cans of *el cheapo* black spray paint. The next day, N111MS rolled out sporting basic black. I could not discern the slightest improvement in speed. But God, it was ugly. It was a very fast plane but it looked like it fell out of an ugly tree and hit every branch on the way down.

Blissit sent me a picture of N777RB. Not for nothing was he the head of an interior design firm. His plane gleamed. It was sleek, smooth, fast. And beautiful. Now all we needed was a good race to prove her bloodlines.

Laffargue's New York to Paris race was scheduled for mid-June. As the date grew closer, the prize money promised grew smaller. But a Frenchman was organizing the race. That was the way it worked.

Airplane owners are often like new car buyers. They tend to suffer a kind of buyer's remorse. They love their airplane, but would rather look at it than use it. I'm like Mike Smith. I love planes for what they can do, not for what they look like. Blissit wanted to fly in the race, but didn't want to fly in the race. I just wanted to win. I had about as much need for another race victory as I had for an extra set of toenails, but the money would come in handy.

In 1984 the Jesus factor, the unforeseeable, fickle finger of fate, had robbed me of an airplane worth $60,000. I had let Dickie Fenwic make far too many silly decisions. It wasn't going to happen twice. J. Richard Blissit might not take part but I would be flying his airplane, if I had to steal the damned thing.

I think the tide turned in his mind after he read an article in *Private Pilot* magazine. A pair of west coast pilots, Art Hefferman and Chuck Geiger, had purchased Judy Wagner's pet E-33 Bonanza after her untimely death. Judy was a superb pilot who took N775JW to numerous victories. Its new owners figured all that was necessary to win an air race was a superfast airplane. They were quoted as saying, "We'll race any Bonanza. Any time. Any place."

So will I. But I'll *beat* any Bonanza. Or, for that matter, any other airplane with any other pilot. I just can't stand coming in second.

The article inflamed Blissit. Any doubts, any question of his participation, evaporated. He now thirsted for blood. He wasn't about to admit the existence of a superior Bonanza.

I was in it for the money. My ex-wife sounded like a screech owl, except with a call of, "More! More!" Her whole world revolved around me handing her more and more money. Ferry flying had dribbled to a near halt. I made just about enough money to starve.

N777RB, newly christened *The Spirit of Tulsa*, enjoyed her coming-out party on May 3, 1985. Blissit told me it was to be a fundraising event. It turned out to be more of a public pat on the back for his good taste.

I'm a pretty basic guy. I suppose I like people admiring me about as much as the average bear. But flying across the ocean becomes tiresome after about ten thousand hours. My log book overflowed with detailed entries of poorly-paid trips. I needed to make some money. Admiring yourself on TV is a pleasure that fades rapidly. The thrill of depositing checks with lots of zeroes on them is long remembered.

Why, in the 1984 race, the victors each deposited $50,000 (from their sponsors) before the race started.

Unfortunately, beggars can't be choosers. The debut of *The Spirit of Tulsa* came and went without a peep from J. Richard about needing money to run the race. I found myself again, as so often in the past, flying on another free, glorified ego trip.

But every cloud has a little silver lining. I met a long-legged filly at the party, named Diane T—. She made it clear that she found me not unattractive.

I must digress for a moment. I had married the most wonderful woman in the world in 1972. We had a great marriage right up to the point when we had children. I was then supposed to metamorphose into the mirror image of Kathie's father. I guess I tried, but I was never a 9 to 5 man. I haven't lived my life by other people's rules. Once Kathie had decided that I must be like her father, or else (about three minutes after Sean was born), my life turned into a living hell. I couldn't or wouldn't do anything right, in her view.

By the time our second son was born, Kathie had pulled the plug on our marriage. Every time I left on a trip, she moved in with her parents. When I came home, so would she.

In early 1982, after returning from another trip across the North Atlantic in an unheated Islander, I committed the ultimate *faux pas*. I spilled a bowl of popcorn on the rug. After two hours of screaming, Kathie stormed out. For all practical purposes, I would never again be a part of my kids' lives.

My troubles were hardly over. After ten years' marriage, Kathie was convinced of her right to live in a style to which she wished to become accustomed. Upon learning that no alimony was possible under Pennsylvania law, she tacked. All she wanted was the first $25,000 I made each year.

With one hand she continued to chop me off at the knees. With the other she grasped for more and more money. I was to hand her the riches of Kubla Khan. In return, she would send pictures of our kids occasionally.

By 1985 I was a shaken, beaten, battered shell of what I used to be. I was so tense, so stressed over my boys, I literally couldn't speak. Diane was like the first breath of spring warmth. I wasn't much, but I was all I had. She treated me as if I really was a warm, desirable human being.

She earned her keep as a stockbroker. I had toyed at broking a year or so earlier. I was doing great, right up to the point when I lost the ability to speak. I've known lots of brokers, but damned few who put their clients' interests ahead of their own. Diane was a superb broker with a lot of very happy clients. She reaped the rewards, one of which was her own thirty-foot sloop.

We went sailing one glorious late spring day. I was actually far more interested in finding out what was within her bathing suit than in sailing. Seems she felt the same way about my trunks. We returned to the dock post haste and then went below to satisfy our mutual curiosity.

I needed a lot of healing. Diane didn't win any prize in me, but she will always have a place in that part of my heart reserved for the special people I have known.

I left Tulsa for Miami in far better shape than I'd arrived. I may even have had a spring in my step. I know I smiled more than I had in years.

The day of the race drew closer. I took yet another Britten-Norman Islander from England to Australia. I kept in frequent contact with Richard. He was like a momma cat worrying about her kittens. He was worried about my not returning to the U.S. in time for the race. Upon arrival in Sydney, I was given a message to call Phil Waldman. He shot me to Singapore to bring back a DEA poppy-field-spraying Thrush. Five days later, I arrived in Tulsa.

Diane and I spent a few days inspecting her new sheets. Once I had got the hang of it once again, it turned out to be quite a lot of fun. I completed my Thrush delivery to Georgia, and continued to Florida to meet Richard.

As in so many other areas of human endeavor, air racing operates under the Golden Rule: him what pays the bills, makes the rules. Like Fenwic before him, Richard Blissit wanted me to race with him because of my superior knowledge of ocean flying. Like Fenwic before him, he wanted to make the decisions. Both wanted my experience, but ignored my suggestions for running the race.

When I had viewed *The Spirit of Tulsa* in Oklahoma just ten days before, it had carried a throw-over single wheel. To me, that was ideal. We had only one plane. We needed only one pilot. I was content to let Richard do the flying. The flying has nothing to do with the winning of air races.

But when I saw the plane on the ramp at Melbourne, Florida I noticed a dual wheel yoke. Blissit had gone out of his way to find and install an extra wheel so we could both fly it.

Now, one big problem I discovered on my very first ferry trip was the acute lack of space. I didn't take up a whole lot of space, and that was handy. Planes rigged for ferry flight, or for transatlantic air races, are short on the commodity known as extra space. Blissit stood six feet and four inches tall with thin nylon socks on. When he was in a plane — any plane at all — it was crowded in there.

I loved the Beech throw-over wheel. On long trips I used to roll it over, out of the way. I flew the plane with just trim. With the dual yoke, we had about fifty hours of supercramped flying ahead of us. Richard was pleased with his efforts. I was not. He would notice the problem as soon as we installed the ferry tanks.

That afternoon, at his beachfront condo, he came up with his next surprise. We were required to carry survival suits. I'd found a one-size-fits-all suit that could be put on in the airplane. It was the same as the suits donned by Fenwic and our passenger when we almost went in the water south of Portugal in 1984. They cost $300 apiece. Blissit had rented two form-fitting dry suits for $50.

We went down to the beach. He carefully removed his suit from its container. Fifteen minutes later he was bobbing in the surf, safely encapsulated in it. I took pictures.

"Put yours on, Bob. Try it. They work great."

"I'll pass, thanks."

"What's the matter? Don't you think you should try it out?"

"I'm sure it works just fine. But there's no way you could ever get it on inside the airplane. And where we're going, your survival time in the water will be about six minutes."

"Really?"

"Yup. Seems to me, if we can't get them on inside the plane and if we freeze before we can get them on in the water, they are dead weight."

"Sorry 'bout that. It didn't really occur to me."

"No sweat. Everyone else in the race will make the same mistake."

They did. Fortunately, nobody had to try out their suits for real.

We flew over to Lakeland, to Globe Aero, to have our ferry tanks installed. The extra range gained precluded the need to make fuel stops during the race. It was a small but vital consideration.

When Blissit crawled into the driver's seat after we were tanked, he immediately realized why I'd wanted the throw-over wheel. His seat was now so far forward that he couldn't move his wheel. His knees were in the way.

Short of amputation, there was nothing we could do.

We switched seats. I would now do all the planning and all the flying. Of such problems air races are made.

We flew up to Morristown, New Jersey. Although the race was billed as starting in New York, we took off from Morristown. The race started there, so the two legs we flew to get there do not appear in the flight log above.

We had three days to kill. Kathie had mellowed sufficiently to permit me to take my older son, Sean, to Florida after this race. We were only a two-hour drive from her parents' home. I called to see if I could bring Sean up to stay with me until Saturday morning, when the race would start.

Sean was six years old; old enough to get a big kick out of meeting a crowd of pilots in an air race, but not so young as to be too much of a handful. Kathie was friendly and agreeable. After all that had gone before, I should have been suspicious. I made plans to pick up Sean the next afternoon.

Between early 1982 and mid-1985, he and I had spent a total of five weeks together. That was hardly what I called reasonable visitation. If Kathie had had her way, I wouldn't have seen him at all.

On my way to Pennsylvania, I was as excited as a kid in a toy store. Kathie refused to have anything to do with my life in aviation, but at least I could share a little of it with Sean. When I was six, I would have found an air race an unforgettable experience.

I arrived in Perkasie a little early. Kathie's father had taken Sean to the circus. They weren't due back for two hours. I figured it would be nice to take Kathie and our four-year-old, Christopher, out to dinner. It wasn't the first dumb thing I had ever done in my life and I suppose it won't be the last.

Kathie announced that she would drive. She handed Chris to me. I was told to entertain him. I held him and tried to talk to him. After 3½ years of ex-fatherhood, I wasn't exactly comfortable, and neither was he. He screamed all the way to the restaurant. We were off to a bang-up start.

Kathie's idea of retraining me as a parent was to let me take care of Chris during dinner. He continued to scream. I was so tense at being around her, I couldn't eat anyway. It was a wonderful meal. Poor kid, it wasn't his fault. I was as much a stranger to him as he was to me.

On the way back to her parents' house, Kathie let me know who was boss. Since she was being so generous in letting me have Sean for two days, it wouldn't be necessary and nor would it be possible for me to take Sean to Miami for two weeks after the race.

"That's the deal. Take it or leave it. If you don't like it, maybe you shouldn't even see him for the two days."

I know — I was stupid. Kathie had developed this particular game into a fine art. I would get my expectations up, and she would crush them. I suppose someone won. I've never figured out who, though. I lost, and the kids lost. I never played it again.

I crawled back to my car and drove off without seeing Sean. I still don't know which was worse: not seeing him at all, or seeing him for two days every three years. Again, I left Perkasie with tears in my eyes. I haven't been back.

Back in Morristown, Blissit made sympathetic noises. He too had been ravaged by a bitter ex-wife. He told me about all the things I could do to fight back, but I never did. I'd never in my life had my butt trounced so soundly and so often as by my ex-wife. I sure missed those kids, but I wasn't quite up to her games. I guess she had been serious about "Become a daddy or else." The "or else" part has been painful.

The race was another of the Chinese fire drills favored by French race organizers. La Frog was no more organized than the folks behind Air Transat. Its only purpose was to put as much money in his pockets as possible.

In 1981 some 115 contestants paid their dues. This time only sixty-eight signed up. Not everybody was born yesterday.

This event was a combination of a rally and a race. Only eleven crews had signed up for the race portion. We raced only between stops. I knew, I just knew, that it wasn't going to be much of a race. It wasn't.

Like in every other race, the crews were far more interesting than the organizers. Like the 1981 race, La Frog designated what we were to wear. Everyone but Blissit and I wandered around in garish blue flight suits that looked like Salvation Army rejects. La Frog sauntered about in a white flight suit. One of the press people promptly called it his "sperm suit." The nickname stuck. At least we could still make fun of the organizers.

Since this was billed as an air rally rather than an air race, we had an entirely different type of crew than in the 1981 and 1984 races. I preferred the hard-drinking, fire-breathing hell-raisers. This group was mostly older and more conservative. They drank hard, then went to bed at a sensible hour.

The air race portion looked like a three-crew race. Of course, we had Chuck Geiger and Art Hefferman in their E-33, *Mi Querida*. Steve Oster participated in his bloated but high-performance Aerostar 601P, *Miss Liberty*. As in 1981, his partner in crime was Jack Cink.

I wouldn't want to take anything away from Steve. But Jack was another Tom Danaher. A superb pilot in his own right, he knew airplane and engine repair inside out. His skills would eventually determine the winner of the speed race.

In that race, the plan had been to have twins in a separate class from the single-engine aircraft. But as we were so few in number, the race organizers lumped us all together in one class. For good measure, they then threw in a Cessna Citation jet. We mixed apples with oranges and then tossed in an egg. The mixture satisfied no one.

J. Richard Blissit proceeded to make one additional slight booboo. When he gave our handicap reference speed to the organizers, he gave them the wrong speed. With all of Mike Smith's aerodynamic improvements, we should have had an absolute advantage. As it was, we struggled throughout the race to become an also-ran.

Wisely, Richard did not mention his error until months after the race.

Since our reference speed was so high, we were third to depart on Saturday morning. I waited, hoping that Kathie would at least drive the kids up. I guess $5 worth of gas was too much to expect of her. She never showed.

The official start of the race was when we flew past the Statue of Liberty. We tipped our wings in salute. The race was on.

In about everything I've ever done, including air races, I much preferred to make all my mistakes early on. Blissit hadn't gotten around to doing any test flights at race weight. We didn't know what our best altitudes or speeds would be. I knew we could count on a healthy tailwind on two or three of the six legs. On those legs, we should walk away from the rest of the pack.

But we were in a dismal sixth place when the eleven race planes landed in Montreal. I had warned Blissit beforehand that it wouldn't be our leg. But sixth place wasn't even in the top half.

The rally portion of the race was like a Cook's tour of Europe: if it's Tuesday, this must be Greenland. La Frog and his crew had us scheduled every minute of the day. I liked racing because of the freedom, not the chains. To console myself, I mentally counted the $100 bills waiting for us in Paris.

Richard became a little nervous when he learned about our performance on the first leg. Gently but firmly I reminded him that "the opera ain't over 'til the fat lady sings." He looked at me skeptically but made no comment.

This race held together right up until the second leg.

On Monday morning we left Montreal for Frobisher Bay, in the far hinterlands of the Northwest Territories of northern Canada.

The race aircraft departed according to their relative standings, so we were sixth to depart, but bad weather caused serious delays in Air Traffic Control. The organizers had not considered the possibility of bad weather. Neither had they considered the effects of faster aircraft overtaking slower aircraft at similar altitudes. We had aircraft departing Montreal for ten hours, at every altitude. Some wouldn't arrive in Frobisher until the wee hours of the next morning. Tempers began to fray.

This hardly affected Blissit and me. We had enough fuel to fly to Frobisher nonstop. Hell, we could have loaded enough fuel to make Paris nonstop. We cruised far above the tundra, at twenty-one thousand feet. I was counting on cruising at twenty-seven thousand to gain an extra ten knots of true airspeed, but Blissit wasn't up to the rarefied atmosphere.

We still didn't have our desired tailwind, but long-distance flight was the forte of N777RB. We placed second to Steve Oster on this leg and also made up a few valuable minutes on *Mi Querida*.

I'd been across the North Atlantic nearly two hundred times. This was perhaps my twentieth trip to Frobisher. It wasn't much even in the summer. But I was a ferry pilot, and we had lots of nice upper-class and upper middle-class folks with us.

Food and shelter was costing $200 per crew per day. In Frobisher we slept in a former military barracks with co-ed shower facilities. I can still hear the cries of anguish. I walked into the shower just as a red-faced, betoweled male pilot rushed out. The pilot in the next shower along had asked to borrow his shampoo. She was out. So he figured he was in the wrong shower. So did she. I laughed.

The race turned into a circus on Tuesday. There was no positive radar control by ATC between Canada and Greenland. ATC would allow instrument departures only every thirty minutes.

Around thirty aircraft started up and taxied out to the holding point. There was no rhyme or reason to the sequence in which ATC launched them. At a rate of two per hour. Tempers flared.

The situation called for timely management by the race committee. We watched in wonder as they marched aboard the support Queen Air and departed for Greenland. All around I heard the sound of jaws hitting the ground. There were minutes of silent bewilderment. Then, as realization sank in, howls of anger.

Soon we had aircraft departing every which way. Some left and headed north, some south; some under instrument control and some not. I was laughing so hard I was crying. I had prior experience of French-run races. So far, this race was well up to (or down to) the standard I expected.

Richard Blissit wanted to know what we should do. "Richard, we're going to die soon enough. Let's not rush into it. We have a dead day, anyway. We can leave in the morning with no penalty. Let's just spend the night here. Let the others all kill themselves if they want to."

Some of the more foolish contestants continued to depart, until 10 pm. Since at least half of any race consists of meeting and talking to the other crews, we weren't unhappy to spend an evening in a relaxed atmosphere.

Perhaps it was my imagination, but those that opted not to rush off seemed to be the most professional crews.

At our leisure, Richard and I left the next day. The speed portion turned into a three-way race, as I had expected. Our very necessary tailwinds never did materialize, but we continued to nip at the heels of whoever led.

Flying across the northern route in mid-June is about as dangerous as making love, but less interesting. Probably the most difficult part was finding a comfortable position in which to sleep. But if there was a way to make an easy flight dangerous, the French would find it.

On each leg there were various tests of skill. Sometimes it was precision navigation. Or a spot landing. Once or twice, we were required to determine the exact amount of fuel used. (That was a tough job. We had a Fueltron meter aboard which read off fuel burn, accurate to one-tenth of a gallon.)

La Frog had combined a navigation problem with a spot landing for our arrival at Godthåb (now known as Nuuk), in Greenland. If he had intended to try to kill someone, he couldn't have devised anything more effective. We passed over a fix, and were then to touch down on that point on the runway four minutes later. It sounds easy enough and safe enough. But Godthåb had the shortest runway of any in the whole race.

A few crews found themselves so far behind time that they tried landing at maximum speed. Three aircraft touched down nose first. Two ran off the end of the runway and came to a stop mere feet short of a cliff edge. The third porpoised about three times and whacked both props on the runway. (That was quite a trick. I wouldn't have believed it possible if I hadn't seen it.) After blowing the nose wheel, the plane slid to an ignoble halt.

I had flown through Godthåb a few times but had never spent a night there. Since we weren't scheduled to leave until the next day, Blissit and I killed some time wandering around. He needed some extra tapes for his pocket tape recorder. We found an audio and video shop. There we struck pay dirt. He didn't get his tapes but we did discover something far more valuable.

The fellow who owned this shop had followed the race with great interest. In fact, he'd gone to the airport to record the arrival of each aircraft. He played us the tape with the three near-disasters on it in living, screaming color. I persuaded him to make a copy for me.

As the race continued, it became less like fun and more like work. It was so disorganized that crews started dropping out in Frobisher. At best, the prize money would cover expenses. The North Atlantic in June is hardly difficult or dangerous, but the organizers were determined to make it so.

On Thursday we departed for Reykjavik, Iceland. Again we placed second in the speed portion. By now, the top crews were out for blood. A few crews still strove to be top of the heap. We couldn't have cared less.

We had spent so much time at altitude that *The Spirit of Tulsa* needed oxygen. As soon as we landed, I went in search of the race organizers to see what had been done to ensure a supply of oxygen for those needing it. Not to my surprise, all prior promises to the contrary, they hadn't done a thing. We were on our own.

I returned to the aircraft. Richard had been running around trying to line up some oxygen, with no luck. He was in a bit of a panic as we were almost out. No oxygen meant no race.

My good friend Sveinn Bjornsson, the operations manager at Reykjavik airport, drove up at about that time. I explained our problem. A little later he came back with an oxygen canister. Richard was surprised at how easy I made it look. I was surprised that he was surprised. I'd known Sveinn since 1976. If anything could be accomplished in Iceland, Sveinn could organize it.

For some strange reason, Blissit wanted to spend time on the ground doing flight planning. I had worked up detailed flight logs weeks before. I wasn't even looking at a forecast twenty-four hours in advance. It was a guess at best anyhow.

One of the things no race organizer ever discusses is how much of a pain in the ass it is to sit next to someone in an airplane all day, then be around them all night. I'm a private person. I like to do all my planning well in advance of a race. Blissit wanted to eat, drink, and sleep air race. I wanted to get laid.

He went back to the room to study weather briefs and flight logs. I went to the Hollywood Disco to fall in love. We both did what we enjoyed most.

I've commented before on Icelandic women. Since they are about the most beautiful women in the world, I may as well elaborate.

Iceland, the world's first democracy, is one of the most interesting places I've ever been. It's a land easily misunderstood. First of all, it's not ice. Reykjavik in winter has a climate similar to that of Washington, D.C. In summer, with almost constant daylight, you can almost see the grass grow.

It is an island, about the size of Kentucky, with only 370,000 inhabitants at present, more than one-third of them resident in Reykjavik. Reykjavik had all the amenities found in Stockholm or Oslo. That included fine restaurants, discos, and lots of stunning blonde Viking goddesses (and gods, if one swings that way).

I think what I always enjoyed most about Icelandic women was their effect on American women. The blue-eyed blondes, all seemingly well equipped with big busts and narrow waists (some men like that, I understand) tended to take the starch out of normally confident American woman.

I sat in the Hollywood Disco listening to one such tale of woe. The American female pilot next to me felt outclassed and unloved. I hastened to reassure her that she had hardly turned into a wallflower. She invited me to prove it. I did.

I got to sleep after 5 am. I awoke after 8 am and rushed back to the hotel. Richard had already left for the airport. Seems we were supposed to have been airborne by 7:30. First things first, however.

At the airport, Blissit was fit to be tied. I did my best to calm him as I loaded our craft. Unmollified, he continued to grumble all the way to Scotland, our next stop. I guess he had a point. Still, it had been a long dry spell for me.

The North Atlantic has a nasty habit of turning flight plans into mush. I guess if good weather is an imperative, June is as good a time as any other. But European weather is far soggier than U.S. weather. They don't get our aircraft-crunching cumulonimbus. But we don't get their frequent week-long periods of extremely low ceilings. Any European pilot has far more experience with approaches to minimum conditions than his U.S. counterpart.

In the air race we needed a good tailwind and visual flight conditions. We found neither. To win, we wanted to go point to point as rapidly as possible.

After *The Spirit of Tulsa* left Reykjavik, we leveled off at twenty-three thousand feet. I promptly went to sleep. Richard pointed the airplane where it was supposed to go with the autopilot. As we neared Aberdeen, Scotland he woke me up.

Aberdeen reported a ceiling at four hundred feet. We needed to be in VFR conditions by three hundred feet above the ground, or we would have to divert to another field. We completed a ten-minute holding pattern before we could start our approach. I was as nervous as a dog shitting peach pits. Every minute of delay cost us precious points.

Richard, too, was nervous. But for other reasons.

"What's the lowest approach you've ever shot, Bob?"

"Zero, zero. Why?" (He understood that I meant zero visibility, zero ceiling.)

"Zero, zero," he mused. "How'd ya do that?"

"I just considered the alternatives. I was taking a Cherokee to England. I filed for Gatwick. When I got there, the weather was right on the deck and going down fast. I slowed my beast down, kept a little above the glide slope, and just kept coming down 'til I could see the runway directly below me. No sweat, when you consider the alternatives."

"Why didn't you shoot the missed approach?"

"Missed approach? There wasn't a field open within two hundred miles. I had no other choices. The weather was so bad that the tower had to send a fire truck out to lead me in. The driver got lost in the fog! I pulled the plane off onto the taxiway, shut down, and walked to the terminal. When you run out of options, your choices become crystal clear."

We shot the approach. I set the autopilot and watched it as the plane twisted and turned down the approach. It could do almost as good a job of flying as I could. Richard got twitchier and twitchier as we got closer to the ground. The plane was still in and out of the clouds at three hundred feet. Finally, as we passed two hundred, we broke into the clear. Blissit was straining his eyes looking for the runway.

"Richard, calm down. Watch the autopilot. I'll let it take us to fifty feet."

He squirmed in his seat. Another half-minute passed.

"Now watch. The autopilot is off. We've still got lots of time and altitude. The only trick to shooting a low approach is mental control. Don't panic. You're nervous because you've never been in these conditions before. Believe me. Every student pilot here has been through this a dozen times."

We landed and taxied in. It took two hours to finish our ground handling. The race was now a week old. It had come apart a long, long time ago. I was physically and mentally beat.

I saw my honey from the night before. I looked forward to another night of consoling her. She ignored me. In Iceland, she was a serf. In Scotland, she was a queen. It was a short but refreshing experience.

Steve Oster hadn't been subjected to the instrument hold that we had. He leapt ahead of us in the speed race. But he had big problems. One of his turbochargers had been acting up the entire race. Jack Cink performed surgery, but it looked as though the patient was terminal.

I've got to hand it to J. Richard. He was a true sportsman.

"Bob, I really want to win this race. But I don't want to win because Steve's plane broke. I'm going over to see if I can help Jack."

"Go ahead. I'll check us into the hotel."

By this time the race had begun to look like a three-ring circus. Some aircraft were still in Greenland. The rotten conditions in Scotland left aircraft all over northern Britain and Iceland. We went to a big dinner thrown by the welcoming committee in Aberdeen. Only about a quarter of the participants attended.

Spirits were low. An air race is supposed to be fun. This thing stopped being fun right after Frobisher Bay. But we were no longer involved; we were committed.

Unless Jack came up with a miracle, he and Steve were sunk. We were still a few minutes behind *Mi Querida*. I continued to reassure Richard about the opera and the fat lady singing. But we had only one leg left to run. I had to come up with something, and quick.

The race organizers didn't announce the takeoff times until 2 am. I shuddered when I saw the list. We were right in the middle of the pack. *Mi Querida* would be third to leave. If they had no landing delays but we did, we were in trouble.

We launched early the next morning. The forecast called for soggy weather all the way. The only good news was that Jack had managed to fix Steve's ailing 601P. *Miss Liberty* would compete. If we lost, at least we would lose to a good friend.

We passed over hundreds of miles of thick stratus cloud. It wasn't but a few thousand feet thick, but it was low. Trapped above it, we would certainly have to shoot an approach at Pontoise, in the suburbs of Paris. We were then sure to lose.

Ahead of us I could see an open area. We were close to the south of England.

"Richard, I think I hear the trill of a fat lady warming up. Get us an actual weather report for Paris."

He picked up the mike. "Hello, London. Hello, London. This is N777RB requesting a weather forecast for Pontoise for one hour from now."

"N777RB, this is London. Stand by."

"Blissit! I don't want a fucking forecast. We've got the forecast. I want an actual. If they don't have Pontoise, get Le Bourget or Charles de Gaulle."

"OK. Hello, London. This is N777RB requesting the Paris actual."

"N777RB, London. Paris, Charles de Gaulle is reporting fifteen hundred feet overcast. Visibility three miles. QNH 995. Winds two hundred and seventy over ten." QNH is the European way of saying altimeter setting, and we were being told that the wind was 10 knots, from the west.

"Roger, London. N777RB. Thank you."

"Blissit, the sound you hear is the overweight female singing. Pontoise was calling for an eight hundred foot ceiling in the forecast. That open area ahead of us is the English Channel. We're going down and we're going to sneak in underneath this shit. What we lose in air speed we will more than make up for by not shooting the instrument approach."

"But, Bob. What if there are mountains between the Channel and Paris? We don't have any VFR charts."

"J. Richard, my boy, that's the point. Nobody else does, either. There weren't any mountains the last time I was here, just rolling hills. No one else will think of coming down. I think we've got it licked. Call London and cancel our instrument flight plan."

We zoomed toward Pontoise. Just as I suspected, we were well clear underneath the clouds. We circled Pontoise once and landed.

Ours was the second aircraft to land there. *Mi Querida* had taken off thirty minutes before us. I knew we had them beat as they were already in sight, on their approach. Behind us.

Mi Querida landed and taxied in. Chuck Geiger and Art Hefferman wore wide grins, right up until the moment they spotted us. I smiled as I watched the look of astonishment that passed between them.

"Moriarty, how the hell did you guys get here? Weren't you supposed to take off thirty minutes behind us?"

"We did. But the weather sounded pretty good here so we came in VFR." I managed to look innocent.

Chuck looked up at the solid layer of clouds some 1,500 feet above. He knew we had snookered him but he couldn't figure out how.

We managed to nose out *Mi Querida* but couldn't quite overcome the insurmountable lead of *Miss Liberty*. Steve and Jack took first place. Blissit and I were second. Chuck and Art took third. I didn't feel any pain at losing to Steve and Jack.

The awards dinner was held in a Paris club that night. Contestants were still drifting in as the awards were being made. It was garish, as I had expected. The winners then spent months trying to get their checks from La Frog, as I had expected. Nothing ever changes in air races run by the French.

Dickie Fenwic showed up at the awards banquet. A year before, he had set a Paris to London speed record in Mike Smith's race plane. Now he wanted Blissit to let him use *The Spirit of Tulsa* to set a London to Paris record. Blissit was willing, but only on the condition that I do all the takeoffs and landings. He trusted only me to fly the plane as she should be flown.

Richard had to fly home commercial to finish a contract bid. He would return in a week to make the trip home. I had a week to kill in Paris.

Paris is hardly the worst place in the world in which to kill time. I called up France K—. She moved me, bag and baggage, into her apartment. So far I hadn't made a dime off this dumb race, but a few pretty neat women had helped my heart to heal.

Fenwic and I met a couple of days later to plan exactly how to set the records we wanted. He wanted London to Paris. I wanted something, too, seeing as how I had come up with the plane. I decided to run a round trip, Paris to London to Paris.

We were all set. Fenwic would meet me at Le Bourget at six. He'd have an official from the French Aero Club to record our flight time. First we would fly his record attempt, then mine.

As usual, he was late. I had walked the mile and a half over to the weather office to get a brief. At the surface we had a twenty-knot wind from the southwest. At eighteen thousand feet the winds increased to sixty knots, from the west. Clearly, the flight should be made as high as possible to take advantage of the strong winds.

Fenwic disagreed. "You Americans don't know a damned thing about flying in Europe. I will run the flight. I will fly at three thousand feet."

I steamed. My worst showing in any race, ever, was second.

I think I'd spotted the reason for Fenwic's anger the night before. Over at his apartment he had a king-sized blowup of N111MS passing under the Eiffel Tower, along with his signature and the date. He had taken my flight, for which I took all the heat, and had turned it into his flight. He didn't have either the balls or the skill to fly the trip. But he had the *chutzpah* to claim it. Poor Fenwic glowed bright green with jealousy.

The Paris to London record was one hour and three minutes, set some twenty years before. Fenwic beat it by four minutes. I wasn't impressed. He was using none of the potential of N777RB.

When we arrived back at Le Bourget, he and the official timekeeper from the French Aero Club walked off.

"Wait just a fucking minute, Fenwic. What's this? I thought this guy was supposed to ride a trip with me. What are you pulling now?"

"He doesn't have the time tonight. If you want to try to break the record, you must set it up yourself. I'm not doing anything for you."

I had had it with Fenwic. He had used me as a rug to wipe his feet for years. Promise after promise had turned to dust. His word didn't mean diddly. I made my mind up, then and there, to show him just how little mere Americans knew about flying in Europe.

I made arrangements with the French Aero Club official to return the following night. Perhaps I'd make a stab at Fenwic's new record as well.

I had promised France the year before to take her on an attempt at a record flight. As usual, my promise meant nothing to Fenwic. He had bumped her at the last minute in favor of one of his friends. Again, his promises had turned to ashes. I told her not to worry. She could go with me on the Paris to London to Paris attempt.

I'm hardly religious, but sometimes, the way things happen, you just have to wonder.

The three of us set out the next night. The French Aero Club official, who spoke no English, sat in the right seat. France was in back. Conditions were virtually identical to those of the night before. I would brief France on what we were doing. She would translate for our timekeeper.

We crossed London at twenty-five thousand feet, just as I had suggested to Fenwic. What can I say? We boomed, zoomed, sped toward Paris. Fenwic had made the trip in fifty-nine minutes at an average of 185 knots. We ran the course in forty-six minutes at a speed of 248 knots. I acted nonchalant but I knew it was one of my best flights, ever.

The official watched in amazement. He'd flown the same course on consecutive nights with different pilots. The plane was the same, the winds identical.

This particular pilot may have known nothing about flying in Europe but I highly suspect that I would have whipped Fenwic's donkey any time, any place, any aircraft.

The rest, as they say, is history. Richard Fenwic became president of the French Aero Club. For two years he managed to block my application for the London to Paris record. Of course, there were no politics involved.

Richard Blisset and I managed to get *The Spirit of Tulsa* home in one piece after landing in Gander with three minutes' usable fuel. We had some frozen water in the lines from the tip tanks.

He told me how he would try to get me on the Phillips Petroleum payroll, to race and set records. It took me a year to find out that he was doing a better job of blowing his own horn than sounding mine. By then, airplane sales were so slow that it wasn't worth Phillips' while to put any more advertising behind their new wonder oil. The deal fell through.

Mike Smith was racing towards victory with N111MS in yet another CAFE 400 race. His engine blew up due to some bad fuel. He was forced to land downhill, downwind, on a dirt road. He tore through a fence before coming to a stop. Damage was sustained to his pride and to the plane. A rebuild was due, anyway.

My ex managed to use the kids as weapons to beat me to death for enough years that I finally realized she would never stop. It was either go insane or give up the kids. I gave them up and haven't seen either of them in thirty years.

I remember them.

APPENDIX A: AIRCRAFT

Beech 18, military C-45

Length	35 ft 2 in (10.72 m)
Wingspan	49 ft 8 in (15.14 m)
Cruising speed	185 mph (298 km/h)

Highly variable. Twin-engine, low wing, distinctive Beech twin tail: note that tail plane does not extend through fins. Seen with rounded (early) and squared-off (late models) wing tips.

The durable Beech 18 was built from 1937 to 1972, with thousands made during WW II as C-45s. It was refitted in a bewildering variety of forms: with tricycle gear to replace the semi-retractable tail-dragging gear; in a stretched version; in long-nosed models; with turboprop engines; with conventional rather than double-fin tails; and in one bizarre case, with a t-tail. The final production 18s were sold to Japan Airlines.

Beechcraft Bonanza 35, 33

Length	26 ft 5 in (8.05 m)
Wingspan	33 ft 6 in (10.21 m)
Cruising speed	190 mph (306 km/h)

Anything with a V-tail is a Bonanza 35. Built from 1947 to date, more than 10,000 are flying in North America. A variety of engines were installed, including turbocharging. Of all-metal construction since its inception.

Beech Queen Air, U-8, U-21 Seminole

Length	35 ft 6 in (10.82 m)
Wingspan	45 ft 10 in (13.98 m)
Cruising speed	230 mph (370 km/h)

Midsized low-wing twins. Matching 7° dihedrals in wing and tail; strongly swept tail fin. Earliest models (B65) had a vertical tail fin. Beginning with the Queen Air 65 in 1958, a long series of successful small twins with various engines.

Britten-Norman Islander, Trislander

Length   35 ft 8 in (10.87 m)
Wingspan   49 ft 0 in (14.94 m)
Cruising speed   150 mph (241 km/h)

A plane of odd geometry. Fuselage rectangular in cross-section; Hershey-bar wing and tail; curved wing tips are auxiliary fuel tanks. Double wheels on lumpy non-retractable landing gear.

Designed for fuel-efficient, low-speed, low-density commuter routes. More than 1,000 Islanders have been delivered worldwide since 1967. The earlier versions had a short nose. The last version, the Trislander, has a longer fuselage, a T-tail, and a third engine mounted high on the tail fin. A low-technology airplane, it has been manufactured under license in Romania and assembled from supplied parts in the Philippines. Seats up to 18 passengers and a single pilot. No aisle; entry through doors directly to seats.

Cessna 401, 402, Utiliner, Businessliner

Length   36 ft 1 in (11.00 m)
Wingspan   39 ft 10 in (12.15 m)
Cruising speed   200 mph (322 km/h)

A low-wing twin with that Cessna look: straight leading edge to wing; no fairing in the wing at all; slight dihedral in the wing, none in the tail. All 402Bs have tip tanks.

Carrying a crew of one or two and 6–9 passengers, Utiliners and Businessliners serve feeder airlines and corporations. They aren't pressurized or particularly fast. As their names indicate, they are intended to be economical rather than exotic.

Cessna 411, 414 and 421A, 421B Golden Eagle

Length   33 ft 9 in (10.29 m)
Wingspan   39 ft 11 in (12.17 m)
Cruising speed   226 mph (364 km/h)

A series of similar twins. Tip tanks, long noses, no ventral fin; strong dorsal fin fairing to highly swept tail fin. All have the typical Cessna wing, straight leading edge, slight taper of trailing edge beginning at engine nacelles. Dihedral in the wing, none in the tail plane. The 414 is a less expensive, lower-powered version of the 421.

Cessna Ag Truck, Ag Wagon, Ag Pickup, Ag Husky

Length   25 ft 3 in (7.70 m)
Wingspan   40 ft 4 in (12.30 m)
Cruising speed   100 mph (161 km/h)

Wing is braced by a single, streamlined strut that is faired into the wing; unbraced tail plane; single spring-steel struts to front wheels; very short (9°) dihedral that begins after the wing leaves the fuselage horizontally.

Developed in 1965, the Cessna Ag series has a variety of engines, load-carrying capacities, and variations in windows. Many early models before 1969 lacked the rear and top cockpit windows. A few models beginning in 1971 had high-lift drooped wing tips. All models (and other Cessna singles) have the conical camber wing tips.

Fokker, Fairchild Hiller, F27, Mk 500

Length   82 ft 2 in (25.04 m)
Wingspan   95 ft 2 in (29.01 m)

Cruising speed   298 mph (479 km/h)

The largest of the high-wing airliners; heavy tail fairing parallels slight upsweep of the lower fuselage; very pointy-nosed, with prominent, long engine nacelles.

U.S. production by Fairchild ceased in 1966, but continued to be built in the Netherlands. The Mk 500 was by far the most common model, plus a few of the original F27s (length 77 ft 4 in) and a variant, the FH227 (length 83 ft 8 in). Although not numerous, the Fokker F27 was always highly visible as a feeder airliner into major airports.

Helio Courier, U-10

Length   31 ft 0 in (9.45 m)
Wingspan   39 ft 0 in (11.89 m)
Cruising speed   150 mph (241 km/h)

Not common. Unbraced high, constant-chord (width) wing; usually a tail-dragger; a very few with fixed tricycle gear. On tail-draggers, the forward gear is on extremely long struts and is set well forward of the wing. Very tall, upright tail fin.

Manufactured from 1955 to 1978, about half of the small production went to the USAF as the U-10, a common liaison, cargo, and anti-insurgency plane in the Vietnam War. The only airplane completely designed by Harvard and MIT faculty members. Full-length leading-edge slotted flaps and massive slotted trailing-edge flaps give it a bizarre short takeoff and landing capability. Seats up to six. Whatever the gear or engine type, the tail and wing configurations are consistent.

Lockheed C-130 Hercules

Length   97 ft 10 in (29.78 m)
Wingspan   132 ft 7 in (40.41 m)
Cruising speed   340 mph (547 km/h)

Common, nationwide. Combined upswept fuselage with conventional tail, radar dome nose, and classic Lockheed wing; straight leading edge at right angles to fuselage; four turboprop engines. C-130s have been used by all four U.S. services, in modes from gunships to weather observation and search and rescue, as well as transports.

Maule Rocket, Strato-Rocket, Lunar Rocket

Length	22 ft 0 in (6.71 m)
Wingspan	29 ft 8 in (9.04 m)
Cruising speed	156 mph (251 km/h)

Not common. A chunky four-seater, V-braced, high-wing tail-dragger. The V-bracing is simple, without return or supplementary braces. Odd little close-out (drag-reducing) fairings behind the wheels, like Mercury's winged heels. An unusually large tail fin for such a short aircraft. All models have distinctly drooping wing tips. Engine nacelles vary with the variety of engines supplied. Wings are short and wide compared to other constant-chord types.

Went into production in 1963. Later models had powerful engines and outstanding short-field landing ability: 400-foot (122 m) takeoff and landing rolls. The variance between maximum speed of 170 mph (273 km/h) and landing speed with flaps of 40 mph (65 km/h) is as great as you will find in a civilian aircraft.

Morane-Saulnier MS.760 Paris Jet

Length	32 ft 0 in (9.75 m)
Wingspan	36 ft 5 in (11.13 m)
Cruising speed	488 mph (785 km/h)

In North America, seen only in Canada. Small jet with a very slim rear fuselage; T-tail; large canopy covers side by side; two-man cockpit; quite small air intakes forward of wing root. A somewhat variable Canadian trainer, first flown in 1960 and adopted by the RCAF in 1964 after being invented and used as a primary training jet in France.

Piper PA 60 Aerostar, Ted Smith Aerostar

Length   34 ft 10 in (10.62 m)
Wingspan   36 ft 8 in (11.18 m)
Cruising speed   231 mph (372 km/h)

Not common, unique design. A mid-wing twin; slight dihedral in wing, none in tail; leading edge of wing at right angle to fuselage, trailing edge tapers sharply to tip; tail plane strongly swept; bulbous-nosed; wraparound windshield, with two small windows above cockpit; fairing to tail fin is cut off abruptly.

Ted Smith, a California designer, tried to build Aerostars from 1967 to 1978 in competition with the big three American builders. Although it's an attractive design and simple to construct, after several reorganizations, his company ended up as the Santa Maria division of Piper. Typical of the Ted Smith touch, the three swept tail surfaces (fin and planes) and the three tail control surfaces are interchangeable.

Piper PA 28RT Arrow IV

Length   27 ft 0 in (8.23 m)
Wingspan   35 ft 5 in (10.80 m)
Cruising speed   165 mph (265 km/h)

Not especially common. Tapered wings, T-tail, fully retractable gear. Conventional and turbocharged models.

Piper PA 23 Aztec

Length   31 ft 3 in (9.52 m)
Wingspan   37 ft 3 in (11.35 m)
Cruising speed   204 mph (328 km/h)

Conventional tail, low-wing twin; swept angular tail fin; three side windows; noses varied in length from medium (Aztec B, C) to long (Aztec D and later models). Seen from overhead, the wing has complicated geometry: basically a Hershey-bar shape, but with added rounded wing tips and fairings from the fuselage to the leading edge of the wing at the engine nacelle, and from the outboard side of the engine nacelle into the wing's leading edge. The Aztec F had an angular outline to the wing tips, as though one had simply taken the old rounded shape and snipped it two or three times with a pair of shears. The Aztec is a six-passenger twin available with turbocharged engines.

Piper PA 28 Cherokee Warrior, Warrior II

Length	24 ft 2 in (7.37 m)
Wingspan	32ft 0in (9.75 m)
Cruising speed	162 mph (261 km/h)

Common. Fixed tricycle gear; always with wheel pants; note streamlining on main gear wheel, compared to nose; dihedral in wing, none in tail; three side windows. Wing is of complicated geometry: leaves fuselage with fairing to leading edge; short equal-span section; leading and trailing edges taper to tip at unequal angles. Tail plane a pure Hershey bar rectangle.

Flown since 1974, and the first Piper to abandon the trademark constant-chord (width) wing plans. Sold under various names with slight differences, including engine horsepower: Cherokee Warrior, renamed Warrior II (160 hp), Dakota (235 hp), and Archer II (180 hp). All versions seat four, including the pilot.

Piper PA 28-180R Cherokee Arrow, Arrow II, Arrow III

Length	24 ft 2 in (7.37 m)
Wingspan	32ft 0in (9.75 m)
Cruising speed	162 mph (261 km/h)

Less common than the non-retractable Cherokee series. Identical to the fixed-gear Cherokees.

Wing is of complicated geometry: leaves fuselage with fairing to leading edge; short equal-span section; leading and trailing edges taper to tip at unequal angles. Tail plane is pure Hershey bar rectangle. All versions seat four, including the pilot.

Piper PA 30, PA 39, Twin Comanche

Length	25 ft 2 in (7.67 m)
Wingspan	36 ft 9 in (11.22 m)
Cruising speed	186 mph (299 km/h)

A small low-wing twin. Manufactured with and without tip tanks; engine nacelles stop well short of trailing edge. Though it has the characteristic Piper fairing from fuselage to engine nacelles, it gives the wing the illusion of leaning forward. Dihedral in wing, none in tail plane. Comes with two or (more commonly) three side windows, including the pilot's.

A successful and popular series that first flew in 1962. All seat four persons, including the pilot. Various models with turbocharged engines, counter rotating propellers, and internal layouts. Models with tip tanks somewhat resemble the Cessna 310, but 310 nacelles extend beyond trailing edge, 310 wing has no fairing between fuselage and nacelles, and 310 has two windows on each side, including the pilot's.

Piper PA 32 Cherokee Six, PA 32R-300 Lance, PA 32RT-300 Lance II

Length	27 ft 9 in (8.45 m)
Wingspan	32 ft 9 in (9.95 m)
Cruising speed	158 mph (254 km/h)

A common, large, fixed-gear airplane. Typical early Piper wing: a Hershey bar rectangle with fairing to leading edge. A retractable Cherokee Six with Hershey-bar wings is a Lance, of which a few models had T-tails. Carries six, including the pilot. For many years (1964–79) it was Piper's largest single-engine model, and the largest fixed-gear single in private aviation. When equipped with an optional 300 hp engine, it is suitable for use on skis or floats. Last produced in 1979.

Piper PA 31 Navajo, Chieftain, PA 31-325 Navajo CR

Length	32 ft 7 in (9.93 m)
Wingspan	40 ft 8 in (12.40 m)
Cruising speed	244 mph (393 km/h)

A family of low-wing twins, with flattened engine nacelles housing opposed six-cylinder engines. All have the characteristic Piper wing: a distinct leading edge fairing from fuselage to engine nacelle, both edges tapering from nacelle to wing tip; dihedral in wing, none in tail plane. Engine nacelles on the PA 31-325 Navajo extend beyond trailing edge of the wings. Nacelles on PA 31 Navajo stop well short of the trailing edge. Navajos carry six passengers.

Piper PA 34 Seneca

Length	28 ft 6 in (8.69 m)
Wingspan	38 ft 11 in (11.85 m)
Cruising speed	187 mph (301 km/h)

A common sight. Small low-wing twin, equal-chord (width) Hershey-bar wing and tail plane; swept tail fin. The tail assembly appears stuck on as an afterthought; the fin and tail planes protrude well aft of the end of the fuselage proper.

A popular five-seat or six-seat (including pilot) business and private aircraft. It essentially takes the single-engine Cherokee Six and substitutes two turbocharged engines. The test prototype was a Cherokee that retained the nose engine. It was flown, in fact, as a tri-motor; one of the last, and briefest, pulling tri-motor flights in the history of aviation.

North American Rockwell Commander 111, 112, 114

Length	25 ft 0 in (7.62 m)
Wingspan	32 ft 11 in (10.04 m)
Cruising speed	157 mph (253 km/h)

Not common. Best field mark for this low-winged single is the tail plane, mounted midway up the tail fin. Overhead, the wing's leading edge is straight, at right angles to leading edge; strong (7°) dihedral in wing, none in tail plane. A wide, chubby look to the cabin area.

First produced in 1971, it's a high-performance four-seat single. The unusual tail design caused some difficulty at first, including loss of a prototype, and the requirement to redesign the rear fuselage and tail assembly. The interior cabin space is unusually wide for a four-passenger single, and gives the aircraft its look of being bulky forward and over the wing.

Rockwell (Fuji) Commander 700

Length	39 ft 5 in (12.00 m)
Wingspan	42 ft 5 in (12.93 m)
Cruising speed	252 mph (405 km/h)

A low-winged twin; upswept and level tail plane mounted part-way up fin; slim wings with dihedral; opposed-cylinder engines carried in flattened nacelles well forward of the wing; air scoops under nacelles for turbochargers.

A joint design of Fuji in Japan and Rockwell International in the U.S., it was first flown in 1975. Seats 4–6 in a pressurized cabin, and has a crew of two. Its practical range is over 800 miles (1,300 km). One of the few light twins built that used National Advisory Committee on Aeronautics (NACA) wing designs, though the slim and symmetrically tapering wings were constructed entirely in Japan.

Snow Air Tractor

Length	27 ft 0 in (8.23 m)
Wingspan	45 ft 1 in (13.75 m)
Cruising speed	130 mph (209 km/h)

Typical low-wing agricultural plane. Unbraced wing, fixed gear; single spring-steel strut carries each wheel; wing of equal chord (depth) with straight squared-off wing tips; pair of light braces on the underside only of the tail plane.

Manufactured in various models since 1972. The plane is equipped with radial engines (model 301) or turboprop engines (models 302, 400). Designed by Leland Snow, who also designed the Snow S2 ag planes, which became the Rockwell Thrush, and the Ayres Thrush. Not manufactured as a two-seater.

Windecker Eagle

Length	26 ft 6 in (8.7 m)
Wingspan	32 ft 0 in (9.75 m)
Cruising speed	204 mph (328 km/h)

A composite construction, low-wing, retractable gear, light single aircraft designed to compete with the Beech Bonanza V-35. It first flew in 1969. A Chinese company bought the type certificate and planned to put the aircraft back into production.

APPENDIX B: GLOSSARY

ADF   automatic direction-finding (radio)

ARINC   Owned by Collins Aerospace. Handles all over water
             communications once aircraft are beyond UHF or VHF range.

ATC   Air Traffic Control

Avgas   aviation gasoline

BOQ   bachelor office quarters

CG   center of gravity

DME   Distance Measuring Equipment

DOT   Department of Transportation

EAA   Experimental Aircraft Association

EGT   exhaust gas temperature

ELT   Emergency Locator Transmitter

FAA   Federal Aviation Administration

FAI   Fédération Aéronautique Internationale

FBO   fixed base operator

FNG   ferry new guy

GMT   Greenwich Mean Time

HF   high frequency (radio)

IFR   Instrument Flight Rules

ILS   Instrument Landing System

INS   Inertial Navigation Systems

ITC   Intertropical Convergence Zone

ITCZ   (as ITC)

ITZ   (as ITC)

LBF   little bitty fucker

MSL	Mean Sea Level
NAA	National Aeronautics Association
NCO	noncommissioned officer
Notam	Notice to Airmen
OPEC	Organization of the Petroleum Exporting Countries
PR	public Relations
RPM	revolutions per minute
SAR	Sea-Air Rescue
SRS	Shannon Repair Service
SWAG	stupid wild-ass guess
T&A	tits and ass
VFR	Visual Flight Rules
VHF	Very High Frequency
VOR	Very high-frequency Omnidirectional Range

Made in the USA
Monee, IL
15 December 2022

5b4cf273-9dd3-4fd1-ad79-995f579574c3R01